MYSTICAL LANGUAGES OF UNSAYING

MYSTICAL LANGUAGES OF UNSAYING

. . .

Michael A. Sells

The University of
Chicago Press
• • •
CHICAGO AND LONDON

The University of Chicago Press, Chicago 60637
The University of Chicago Press, Ltd., London
© 1994 by The University of Chicago
All rights reserved. Published 1994
Printed in the United States of America

16 15 14 13 12 11 10 09 08 07   3 4 5 6 7

ISBN-10: 0-226-74787-5 (paper)
ISBN-13: 978-0-226-74787-3 (paper)

Library of Congress Cataloging-in-Publication Data

Sells, Michael Anthony.
    Mystical languages of unsaying / Michael A. Sells.
        p.   cm.
    Includes bibliographical references.
    1. Mysticism—History—Middle Ages, 600–1500.   2. Rhetoric—
Religious aspects.   I. Title.
B728.S45   1994
291.4′22—dc20   93-23488

♾ The paper used in this publication meets the minimum requirements
of the American National Standard for Information Sciences—
Permanence of Paper for Printed Library Materials, ANSI Z39.48-1992.

. . .

Ce sont ceulx qui n'ont en terre ne honte ne honnour ne crainte pour chose que adviengne. Telles gens, dit Amour, sont segurs, et si sont leurs portes ouvertes, et si ne les peut nul grever.

"They have no shame, no honor, no fear for what is to come. They are secure, says Love. Their doors are open. No one can harm them."

The Mirror of the Simple Souls
Marguerite Porete
(d. June 1, 1310, Place de la Grève, Paris)

CONTENTS

• • •

ACKNOWLEDGMENTS ix

NOTE TO THE READER x

Introduction/Unsaying 1

1 Awakening without Awakener: Apophasis in Plotinus 14

2 The Nothingness of God in John the Scot Eriugena 34

3 Ibn ʿArabi's Polished Mirror: Identity Shift and Meaning Event 63

4 Ibn ʿArabi's Garden among the Flames: The Heart Receptive of Every Form 90

5 Apophasis of Desire and the Burning of Marguerite Porete 116

6 Meister Eckhart: Birth and Self-Birth 146

7 Porete and Eckhart: The Apophasis of Gender 180

EPILOGUE 206

NOTES 219

SELECTED BIBLIOGRAPHY 305

ACKNOWLEDGMENTS

. . .

With gratitude

To Janet, Ariela, and Maya

To good friends from the University of Chicago, the Stanford University Departments of Religion, Classics, and Comparative Literature, and Haverford College, especially my colleagues and students, past and current, in the Haverford Department of Religion, from Cairo, and from Medenine, Foum Tatahouine, and Jerba in Tunisia.

To those who have read and commented on earlier versions of this work: Jennifer Almquist, Ellen Babinsky, Anna Blau, David Carpenter, Carin Companick, David Dawson, Don Duclow, Antony Dugdale, Erica Gelser, Mark Gould, Regan Heiserman, Emil Homerin, Aryeh Kosman, Richard Luman, Danielle MacBeth, John McCudden, Kevin McCullough, Anne McGuire, Ann Matter, James Morris, Saskia Murk-Jansen, Willemien Otten, Elizabeth Penland, Judy Saltzman, John Seybold, Susan Shapiro, Ruth Tonner, Jacqueline Veal, Chris Wilkins, and Michael Zwettler.

To Fredric Schlatter, S.J., and friends from Gonzaga University.

With special gratitude to Bernard and Pat McGinn.

To the Harvard Theological Review, History of Religions, and Studia Islamica for permission to publish sections of chapters 1, 3, and 4, to the Whiting and Mellon Foundations for their support, to the International Society for Neoplatonic Studies, the Muhyiddin Ibn ʿArabi Society, the Eriugena Society, and the Eckhart Society for their efforts to support the study of these literatures.

To the Haverford College community for its humanity and integrity.

For the people of Bosnia.

NOTE TO THE READER

. . .

This book is addressed to an interdisciplinary audience. It presents an argument concerning the nature of mystical languages of unsaying, and offers seven readings of key texts in translation.

The readings are based upon analysis of the texts in the original languages. I have included the original language versions of the texts in the endnotes.

I have chosen not to add an index. The critical vocabulary in English is outlined in the Introduction, and reviewed more fully in the Epilogue. The critical vocabulary in the various languages (Greek, Latin, Arabic, French, and Middle High German) is chapter specific; the reader can turn to a particular chapter and find the key terms in italics, defined in context, with extended discussions in the notes on issues of translation and definition.

Introduction: Unsaying

> Were it the case that a fly had reason and could rationally seek out the eternal abyss of divine being, from which it came forth, we say that God, insofar as he is God, could not fulfill or satisfy the fly. Therefore pray God that we may be free of God.[1]

We do not find these words from Meister Eckhart's famous sermon on poverty in most editions and translations of Eckhart's writings. The modern editor of Eckhart's German works selectively interpolated inverted commas into the text in order to distinguish between God and "God": *got mit allem daz er 'got' ist* (God, insofar as he is "God"). The interpolation of a graphic distinction between *got* and *'got'*—in this instance and in several others throughout the sermon—has been accepted by the majority of Eckhart's modern translators. One translator has extended the selective interpolation of inverted commas to the final prayer—"Let us pray to God that we may be free of 'God'." The translator explained that Eckhart was making the commonplace scholastic distinction between God as he is in himself (God) and God as he is in creatures ("God").[2]

Such interpolations and the widespread acceptance they have received are indicative of a pervasive modern dis-ease with the kind of mystical language composed by Eckhart. Without editorial and hermeneutical alteration, the actual words of Eckhart's prayer to God to be free of God are inconsistent with modern and postmodern constructions of the monotheistic tradition and the medieval mind.

Unsaying and the Dilemma of Transcendence

Eckhart's prayer to God to be free of God invites us to reconsider the conventions, the logic, and the paradoxes of the distinctive mode of discourse it embodies. That mode of discourse begins with the *aporia*—the unresolvable dilemma—of transcendence.[3] The transcendent must be beyond names, ineffable. In order to claim that the transcendent is beyond names, however, I must give it a name, "the transcendent." Any statement of ineffability, "X is beyond names," generates the aporia that the subject of the statement must be named (as X) in order for us to affirm that it is beyond names.

At least three responses to the primary dilemma of transcendence are conceivable. The first response is silence.[4] The second response is to distinguish between ways in which the transcendent is beyond names and ways in which it is not. In the medieval context, the most common appeal is to a distinction between two kinds of naming; between God-as-he-is-in-himself and God-as-he-is-in-creatures, for example, or the incommunicable deity as it is in itself, and the deity as it is in our mind. Such distinctions underly the interpolation into Eckhart's prayer of a graphic distinction between God and 'God'.[5] The third response begins with the refusal to solve the dilemma posed by the attempt to refer to the transcendent through a distinction between two kinds of name. The dilemma is accepted as a genuine *aporia*, that is, as unresolvable; but this acceptance, instead of leading to silence, leads to a new mode of discourse.

This discourse has been called negative theology. It is negative in the sense that it denies that the transcendent can be named or given attributes. The formal denial that the transcendent can be named must in some sense be valid, otherwise ineffability would not become an issue. Insofar as it is valid, however, the formal statement of ineffability turns back upon itself, and undoes itself. To say "X is beyond names," if true, entails that it cannot then be called by the name "X." In turn, the statement "it cannot then be called X" becomes suspect, since the "it," as a pronoun, substitutes for a name, but the transcendent is beyond all names. As I attempt to state the aporia of transcendence, I am caught in a linguistic regress. Each statement I make—positive or "negative"—reveals itself as in need of correction. The correcting statement must then itself be corrected, ad infinitum. The authentic subject of discourse slips continually back beyond each effort to name it or even to deny its nameability. The regress is harnessed and becomes the guiding semantic force, the *dynamis*, of a new kind of language.

Apophasis is the common Greek designation for this language. Apophasis can mean "negation," but its etymology suggests a meaning that more precisely characterizes the discourse in question: *apo phasis* (un-saying or speaking-away). The term *apophasis* is commonly paired with *kataphasis* (affirmation, saying, speaking-with). Every act of unsaying demands or presupposes a previous saying.[6] Apophasis can reach a point of intensity such that no single proposition concerning the transcendent can stand on its own. Any saying (even a negative saying) demands a correcting proposition, an unsaying. But that correcting proposition which unsays the previous proposition is in itself a "saying" that must be "unsaid" in turn. It is in the tension between the two propositions that the discourse becomes meaningful. That tension is momentary. It must be continually re-earned by ever new linguistic acts of unsaying.

From this perspective, all discourse on the transcendent contains both saying and unsaying. Apophasis is a relative term. A purely apophatic language would be an abstract and mechanical turning back on each reference as it is posed. On the other hand, some of what has been called *apophasis* is apophatic theory as opposed to apophatic discourse. Apophatic theory affirms the ultimate ineffability of the transcendent; but as opposed to apophatic discourse, it affirms ineffability without turning back upon the naming used in its own affirmation of ineffability. This study will reserve the term *apophasis* for those writings in which unnameability is not only asserted but performed. In those writings, the effort to affirm transcendence leads to a continuing series of retractions, a propositionally unstable and dynamic discourse in which no single statement can rest on its own as true or false, or even as meaningful. In such discourse, a rigorous adherence to the initial logical impasse of ineffability exerts a force that transforms normal logical and semantic structures.

Performative intensity is a function of the frequency and seriousness with which the language turns back upon its own propositions. At the low end of the scale would be an assertion of ineffability, followed by a full chapter or treatise that freely employs names and predications of the transcendent, and then at the end reminds the reader that the transcendent is beyond all names and predications. At the high end of the scale of performative intensity are passages, such as those discussed here, in which the mystical discourse turns back relentlessly upon its own propositions and generates distinctive paradoxes that include within themselves a large number of radical transformations, particularly in the area of temporal and spatial relationships.

The position taken here is that the paradoxes, aporias, and coincidences of opposites within apophatic discourse are not merely apparent contradictions. Real contradictions occur when language engages the ineffable transcendent, but these contradictions are not illogical.

For the apophatic writer, the logical rule of non-contradiction functions for object entities. When the subject of discourse is a non-object and no-thing, it is not irrational that such a logic be superseded. Of course, apophasis is not the only discourse that cannot directly name its subject. Poetry, drama—almost any form of art—risks being trivialized when its meaning is defined and paraphrased discursively. Anyone who has attempted to explain discursively the humor of a joke knows how the humor disappears when removed from its performance. Apophatic texts have suffered in a particularly acute manner from the urge to paraphrase the meaning in non-apophatic language or to fill in the open referent—to say what the text really meant to say, but didn't.

HISTORICAL AND GEOGRAPHICAL PARAMETERS

Apophasis can be defined either historically or formally. A historical approach would limit "apophasis" to those writers who employed the term in their own writings, and to writers with a clearly demonstrable historical connection to such writings. It would trace the development of a particular tradition, with attention to the identification of verifiable patterns of influence.[7] The formal approach would apply the term "apophasis" to any text that fit its formal definition. Apophasis could then embrace a large number of Eastern texts, such as the Taoist *Tao Te Ching*, which begins with the statement "The *tao* that can be spoken is not the *tao*."[8] It could include the Mahāyāna Buddhist *Vimalakirti Sutra* which asserts that "all constructs are empty," and then playfully turns that statement back upon itself with the assertions that "the construct that all constructs are empty is empty," and "the construct that the construct that all constructs are empty is empty is empty."[9] It could also include more recent writings that engage explicitly the dilemma of saying the unsayable.[10] To broaden the inquiry to include all discourses responding to a formal definition of apophasis would be a massive enterprise. Yet apophasis as a distinct mode of discourse is not easily treated in terms of the development of a single tradition or the tracing of textual influences. Apophasis appears in traditions, and may be the result of developments within particular schools of thought, but it does not typically form into schools.[11]

This book examines five mystical writers from separate religious traditions, but who share the cultural heritage of the West defined as the legacy of the encounter of Semitic prophetic traditions with the Graeco-Roman cultural world. These traditions shared both a highly developed Ptolemaic symbolic cosmology and a central assertion of one, transcendent principle of reality. Rather than focusing upon the textual "borrowings" of one tradition from another, it seems more profitable to see these traditions as competing within a partially shared intellectual and symbolic world, defining themselves in conversation with one another and against one another.

An overview of Western apophasis would begin with Plotinus (d. 270 C.E.). Though elements of apophasis existed earlier,[12] it was Plotinus who wove these elements and his own original philosophical and mystical insights into a discourse of sustained apophatic intensity. After centuries of Neoplatonic writings (some more apophatic than others), a mysterious writer of the sixth century C.E. who wrote under the name of Dionysius, the companion of Saint Paul, placed apophatic discourse centrally within the Christian tradition. It was Dionysius who wrote most specifically of the twin elements of kataphasis (saying) and apophasis (unsaying) in "mystical theology" (a term Dionysius coined), with the apophatic element being the "higher" or more accurate.

One of the ninth-century Latin translators of Dionysius, John Scotus Eriugena (or simply John the Scot) went on under the influence of Dionysius to write his own masterwork, *Periphyseon*. Though the Latin Christian tradition contains earlier efforts at apophasis,[13] John the Scot's *Periphyseon* (On Nature) stands out as the first major Latin work of apophatic discourse. Another medieval Christian text heavily influenced by Dionysius was the anonymously authored *Cloud of Unknowing* which would have wide circulation in European vernaculars. By the ninth century C.E., Jewish and Islamic traditions were developing their own sophisticated varieties of apophatic discourse.

The 150-year period from the mid-twelfth to the beginning of the fourteenth century constitutes the flowering of apophatic mysticism. Almost simultaneously, the apophatic masterpieces of the Islamic, Jewish, and Christian traditions appeared, which would include, among others, the writings of Ibn ʿArabi (d. 1240), Rumi (d. 1273), Abraham Abulafia (d. ca. 1291), Moses de León (d. 1305), the twelfth- and thirteenth-century Beguine mystics culminating with Hadewijch (fl. 1240) and Marguerite Porete (d. 1310), and Meister Eckhart (d. ca. 1327).[14]

Apophasis lived on after this period in the post-exilic Kabbalah of Isaac Luria, in the Spanish mystics, in Jacob Boehme, and widely throughout the Islamic tradition.[15] Yet it never again held as central a place in mystical language. The question of apophasis in our own cultural world becomes particularly intriguing in view of the burgeoning of contemporary languages of the unsayable.[16]

Performative apophasis results from a particular intuition into the dilemma of transcendence and a particular response to it. A performative apophatic writer, such as Plotinus, Ibn ʿArabi, Moses de Leon, or Meister Eckhart, may found a tradition, but later members of that tradition may, in systematizing or regularizing the thought of their founder, write in a more formal, less performatively intense mode of discourse. Apophatic discourse is not without links to certain schools of thought, but school traditions are neither a necessary nor a sufficient cause for the emergence of the mystical language of unsaying (as a mode of discourse rather than an exposition of doctrine) as it is depicted in this study.

In the following seven chapters I offer "readings" of classical apophatic texts from five writers. The writings have in common both a saying and an unsaying of the premise of transcendence within the Western monotheistic traditions. These readings do not attempt a comprehensive portrait of theological systems. They selectively engage the most intensely apophatic aspects of each writer's work. The readings might be called "intersections." The primary mode of analysis is literary and synchronic. The goal is to establish the implicit logic and conventions of apophasis as a mode of discourse. Within the framework of that synchronic analysis, the readings will allow the apophatic writings to echo and respond to one another in a variety of historical, theological, and cultural contexts directly related to the rhetorical and literary questions at the center of the analysis.[17]

Mysticism and Unsaying

Classical Western apophasis shares three key features: (1) the metaphor of overflowing or "emanation" which is often in creative tension with the language of intentional, demiurgic creation; (2) dis-ontological discursive effort to avoid reifying the transcendent as an "entity" or "being" or "thing"; (3) a distinctive dialectic of transcendence and immanence in which the utterly transcendent is revealed as the utterly immanent.

Apophatic writers use a number of metaphors of "flowing out" or "flowing over": a spring overflowing and pouring forth water; rays emanating from the sun; heat emanating from fire. In nonapophatic uses of the emanation metaphor, a defined and stable hierarchy is constructed, from the source of emanation through descending levels of distance to the final, furthest level. In apophatic discourse, the overflow devolves into a series of logical and semantic dilemmas. The dualisms upon which the language of "flowing out" is based, such as the distinction between the vessel that receives the flow and the content it receives, are ultimately fused into paradoxes (the vessel is the content) as the apophasis unravels its initial premise about the source of emanation.

That initial premise is that the source of emanation is not a supreme being, not a being or entity at all. In the words of Eriugena, it is nothing, or no-thing.[18] Again, a distinction can be drawn between asserting that the subject of discourse is not an entity, and pushing the discursive consequences of that assertion to the extreme. In the very act of asserting the nothingness (no-thingness) of the subject of discourse, apophasis cannot help but posit it as a "thing" or "being," a being it must then unsay, while positing yet more entities that must be unsaid in turn. The result is an open-ended dynamic that strains against its own reifications and ontologies—a language of *disontology*.[19] Ironically, the form of mystical union found in apophatic discourse has been traditionally named "substantial union," despite the fact that it is the apophatic union that occurs most emphatically *in nihilo* rather than in substance or being.

Thus the hierarchical levels of being that are posited are unsaid from within. At the heart of that unsaying is a radical dialectic of transcendence and immanence. That which is utterly "beyond" is revealed or reveals itself as most intimately "within": within the "just act," however humble (Eckhart), within the basic acts of perception (Ibn ʿArabi), within the act of interpreting *torah* or fulfilling the *mitzvot* (Moses de Leon), or within the act of love (Marguerite Porete). When the transcendent realizes itself as the immanent, the subject of the act is neither divine nor human, neither self nor other. Conventional logical and semantic structures—the distinction between reflexive and nonreflexive action, the distinction between perfect and imperfect tense, the univocal antecedent of a pronoun—are broken down.

This moment in which the boundaries between divine and human, self and other, melt away is commonly called mystical union. Mysticism is often associated with the extraordinary. In apophatic mystical texts, there is indeed a sense of the extraordinary, but the extraordinary, the transcendent, the unimaginable, reveals itself as the common. For Eckhart, any act of justice, however humble it may appear, is nothing other than the one birth of the son of God that always has occurred and always is occurring. In the *Zohar*, the carrying out of a *mitzvah*, however humble it may appear, is nothing less than the healing of the world, the healing of the relationship between the world and the deity, and the healing of the deity itself.[20] In Ibn ʿArabi, the relinquishment of the reified "God" of one's belief to accept the perpetually changing image of reality is nothing other than the eternal self-manifestation of the transcendent in each new moment. Eckhart is most explicit in countering the notion of mysticism as something extraordinary and removed from everyday reality. In a distinctive version of the dialectic of transcendence and immanence, he states that the most noble, the most extraordinary of all events (the birth of the divine son in the soul), is the most common (any act of justice, insofar as it is just).

A key component of mysticism in apophatic writings is the location of "mystery." Mystery is neither a set of abstruse doctrines to be taken on faith nor a secret prize for the initiated. Mystery is a referential openness onto the depths of a particular tradition, and into conversation with other traditions. The referential openness is fleeting. As Plotinus said, as soon as one thinks one has it, one has lost it. It is glimpsed only in the interstices of the text, in the tension between the saying and the unsaying. Yet as elusive as it is, it is in principle accessible to all. The decision to write takes the discourse out of the immediate control of its author and opens it to readers beyond any particular group or school.

At this point, the question poses itself: what is this "it" that is glimpsed in the interstices of the text? It is not even an "it" since a pronoun implies a previous name as its antecedent. (The commentator on apophatic language finds himself struggling with the same dilemmas that haunt the original texts.) The refusal by apophatic writers to define the subject of discourse is neither a mystification nor the result of inability to use language clearly. The readings offered here will demonstrate that it is only upon a foundation of conventional logic and semantics that the apophatic text, at the critical moment, can perform (rather than assert) a referential openness—by fusing the various antecedents of the pronoun, or the perfect and imperfect tenses, or by transforming the spatial and temporal structures of language at the level of article, pronoun, and preposition.

We return to the dilemma of transcendence. Plotinus spoke of the transcendent as "beyond-being" (*epekeina ontos, epekeina ousias*). Pseudo-Dionysius placed the term "hyper" (beyond, above) in front of all predicates of the deity. Of course, as a name, the names (beyond being and hyperessential) fail, because in the view of apophatic mystics all names reify. Just as the expression "X is beyond all names" turns back upon itself, so the expressions "beyond-being" and "hyperessential," insofar as they are true, lead to their own undoing. Apophasis moves toward the transreferential. It cannot dispense with reference, but through the constant turning back upon its own referential delimitations, it seeks a momentary liberation from such delimitations. In terms of a spatial metaphor, to the linear referential motion apophasis adds a circular turning back (*epistrophē*). The combination yields a semiotic spiral motion ever deeper into the pre-referential ground (or groundlessness) of the discourse.

How are we to approach critically a discourse that claims to speak from the point where subject and object, self and other, are one? Simply put, does one have to be a mystic to understand the transreferential language of mystical unsaying? Many apophatic writers suggest that the reader cannot understand what is being said unless she becomes it. Is not such a discourse then limited to its function within the particular community (Beguine, Dominican, Sufi) of the author, to those sharing the same liturgical and meditational practices, to those cultivating the same states of consciousness? This question becomes particularly acute given the modern tendency to view mysticism in terms of personal experience.

This study makes no presuppositions concerning mystical experience on the part of the writer or the reader. The goal is to identify the distinctive semantic event within the language of unsaying, what I will be calling the "meaning event." To clarify what is meant by "meaning event," it may help to contrast it with the well-known distinction between meaning (as sense and reference) and event (as predication).[21] Meaning event indicates that moment when the meaning has become identical or fused with the act of predication. In metaphysical terms, essence is identical with existence, but such identity is not only asserted, it is performed. The readings below will attempt to identify the semantic location of this performance, and the manner in which the identities of meaning and event, reference and predication, essence and existence, are fused. The meaning event is the semantic analogue to the experience of mystical union. It does not describe or refer to mystical union but effects a semantic union that re-creates or imitates the mystical union. That semantic re-creation can be read as a meaning event in various contexts. No doubt its significance will be different for the practicing mystic of a particular tradition than for readers who do not practice or confess a particular tradition. The mystical writers discussed below claim a moment of "realization"—a moment in which, again, the sense and reference are fused into identity with event. In contrast to the realization as an instance of mystical union which entails a complete psychological, epistemological, and ontological transformation, the meaning event is a semantic occurrence. It can occur to readers within and without a particular religious community (though its significance may be different for the two groups of readers).

The concept of meaning event is used in this study in contrast to the modern concept of experience. As defined by many, experience presupposes (1) a grammatical object of experience; (2) mediation; (3) constructedness.[22] Rather than attempting to redefine the concept of experience, I use the term "event" in a manner that does not carry such presuppositions. The readings of apophatic language of mystical union that follow focus upon how such language displaces the grammatical object, affirms a moment of immediacy, and affirms a moment of ontological pre-construction—as in the paradoxical refrain that in mystical union the soul reverts "to where it was before it was." The meaning event is transreferential. Rather than pointing to an object, apophatic language attempts to evoke in the reader an event that is—in its movement beyond structures of self and other, subject and object—structurally analogous to the event of mystical union. Although evocative language has been criticized as a protective strategy (and can be used as such in certain cases) the goal here is to understand the apophatic displacement of the grammatical object as a key moment in a distinctive literary mode with its own rules, conventions, and fields of meaning, and to develop a critical vocabulary for better understanding that literary mode.

Classical Apophasis and the Present

This introduction began with a discussion of the editorial alterations by which Eckhart's prayer to God to be free of God was changed to a prayer to God to be free of 'God'. The tendency to transform apophatic discourse into another set of discursive categories is not limited to direct editing and commentary on apophatic writings. It is inscribed in much modern God-language. The conventional practice of capitalizing pronouns and nouns thought to be referential of the divine is a case in point. At the critical center of apophatic discourse—the moment of mystical union—apophasis is "performed" through a fusing of divine and human referents. This capitalization convention (in English and the Romance languages) presumes a pronoun must refer either to the divine or the nondivine. Translation based upon such a convention must choose between the uppercase (divine) and lowercase (nondivine), thus undoing the reference fusion that is a distinctive semantic feature of unsaying. An alternative is to use slash marks to indicate moments of such fusion (Him/him, It/it, Her/her).[23]

A more complicated issue remains with the word "God": is the uppercase due to the status of "God" as a proper name or to its status as divinity? Unlike YHWH or Allah, "God" and its Greek and Latin predecessors, *deus* and *theos*, do not appear explicitly as divine self-naming within a sacred text. Nor were they always considered proper names within the Christian theological tradition.[24] Modern God-language is now so embedded in postmedieval constructions of deity that whatever choice one makes (God or god), language falls on one side or the other of these complex, intertwined issues in a way that medieval language (without the uppercase / lowercase dichotomy) could avoid. I have adhered to the modern convention of translating *deus*, *theos*, *dieu*, and *got* as "God," with reservations. From an apophatic perspective, the uppercase offers a temptation for "easy reference," a phenomenon viewed by apophatic writers with the same concern that "cheap grace" has been viewed by twentieth century theologians. It also aligns itself too easily with the modern hypertrophy of the word "God" through which the richness and differences of medieval languages of deity have been reduced to a single name. Part of the modern misunderstanding of classical apophasis is due to the projection back upon late antique and medieval writers of a mononomic, generic God divorced from particular traditions and language.[25] If the apophatic intuition of unnameability has validity, then a reconsideration of apophatic writing is particularly needed in view of the modern domination and deification of the generic name.

The domination of the generic name entails a domination of the "what." Much discussion of mystical union and comparative mysticism has been based upon substantialist language of whatness or quiddity. Do adherents of differing traditions "worship the same God," "believe the same thing," or "experience the same thing"— i.e., is *what* someone from tradition X experiences or believes the same or different from that experienced or believed by someone from tradition Y. The question of whatness shades into the question of conditioning: is "what" the mystic experiences conditioned or unconditioned?

The nonsubstantialist understanding of the transcendent common to apophatic mystics does not fit the premises of such questions. In the words of Plotinus, there is no thus or not-thus. In the words of Eriugena, the transcendent is nothing, i.e., no-thing, beyond all entity and quiddity. The apophatic language of disontology, in continually moving toward a removal of the "what" (a removal that is never achieved, always in progress), suggests a different mode of comparison, one less likely to reduce the particularities of differing traditions to a "what," to a homogeneous set of doctrines, propositions, or descriptions of experience.[26]

The "negative theology" of Plotinus, Pseudo-Dionysius, and Eckhart has been accused of posing a "being" beyond being, a kind of metabeing, which is just another form of entity, a God beyond God, a hidden God.[27] This charge is founded upon the common assumption that apophatic mystical union is a union "with God."[28] The following seven readings will examine how in apophatic mystical union reference to the transcendent is undone, and how that undoing is reflected within language by a disorienting—at certain key points—of standard rules of reference and antecedence. In Eckhart, mystical union occurs when the human soul gives up attachments and images, and when the deity gives up its properties and persons. At this point the deity and the soul revert to the state of nothingness, out of which and in which the mystical union occurs. Eckhart uses the same word, *eigenschaft*, for both the attachments of the soul and the properties of the deity. *There is no union "with God"*; rather the union occurs within and beyond the deity.[29] Eckhart writes of the deity as having to give up its own "properties" in order to be born in the soul in mystical union. He writes of a religion based upon *eigenschaft* as a religion of traders and sellers. It may be that the modern "God" is in some instances a form of property, allowing an easy purchase on the meaning of religious traditions, a purchase that can be used to stake out positions and mark off boundaries.

The discovery of hidden Gods within Eckhart's writings tells us little about apophatic discourse. At any point in apophatic discourse one can find an entified deity—pantheistic, transcendentalist, theist, atheist, or nihilist—depending upon the particular proposition chosen. The abstraction of single propositions and the judgment of them as heretical or orthodox was the procedure used at Eckhart's inquisition, a procedure, Eckhart argued, that misconceived the way his discourse generated meaning.[30] The modern procedure (used by both defenders and critics of apophatic mystics) of rephrasing apophasis into single-proposition assertions about a substantialist deity is not all that different. Apophasis is a discourse in which any single proposition is acknowledged as falsifying, as reifying. It is a discourse of double propositions, in which meaning is generated through the tension between the saying and the unsaying.[31]

Classical apophasis has been viewed as religious and as antireligious; as theistic, pantheistic, and atheistic; as pious and libertine; as orthodox and heretical. At its most intense, apophatic language has as a subject neither divine nor human, neither self nor other. It can be read as a relentless critique of religious traditions or as a realization of the deeper wisdom within such traditions. It can be read as grounded in the intimate specificities of particular traditions or as opening onto intercultural and inter-religious conversation. These possibilities may not be mutually exclusive.

CHAPTER ONE

Awakening without Awakener: Apophasis in Plotinus

According to the biography written by Porphyry, Plotinus (d. 270 C.E.) was born in a village in lower Egypt and came to Alexandria where he acquired a passion for philosophy.[1] After much searching and discouragement, he finally found the teacher he was seeking in a certain Ammonius Saccas. After eleven years with Ammonius, he decided to travel to Persia and India to study firsthand the philosophy of the East. Transportation was difficult, so he hitched on with the military expedition of the emperor Gordian III—serving as camp philosopher, as it were. Gordian's troops mutinied in Mesopotamia and the emperor was killed. Plotinus escaped to Antioch and from there, in the reign of Philip the Arab, he made his way to Rome where he settled at the age of forty—an ironic terminus for a journey to the East.

Nothing is known of the teaching of Ammonius, who compelled his students (one of whom may have been the great Christian exegete and theologian Origen) to vow that they would never divulge it. For some time, Plotinus conducted his school in Rome in a similar fashion. The teaching was exclusively oral, and students were forbidden to publish any of it. Notebooks began circulating, however, and Plotinus was finally persuaded to put his teachings in writing. Porphyry, Plotinus's student, biographer, and editor, tells us that Plotinus would write a treatise in a single sitting, in a kind of white heat of inspiration, refusing to move until it was finished, and then refusing to go back over it for revision and editing. Porphyry grouped the treatises into six groups of nine, thus the name *Enneads* (the groups of nines). He did his best to correct the spelling and grammar and sent a copy to Longinus, who replied—to Porphyry's evident annoyance—that this was truly the work of the "philosopher of the age" but was in such a garbled and poorly edited condition that he couldn't understand it.[2]

The *Enneads* are commonly presented as comprising a philosophical and cosmological system of causality based upon a hierarchical series of "hypostases": "the one" (*to hen*), mind (*nous*), and soul (*psychē*). The one emanates into nous and nous in turn overflows and emanates into psyche. Finally, psyche emanates out into the material world. The philosophical and mystical goal is for the individual soul to turn away from the material world back to the world soul, to rise back from the soul to nous, until it reunites with the source of emanation, "the one." A more apophatic reading of the *Enneads* will focus upon those moments in which such fixed hierarchies and directionalities are displaced or transformed. Reference to the one—as an objective source of emanation—devolves into an infinite regress in which every referent recedes beyond the name that would designate it. Language becomes indefinite and open-ended. No closure is reached. Each saying demands a further unsaying.

Such a self-critical and agonistic position may seem surprising in view of the piety of later Platonism, with its serene affirmations of a world of fullness and perfection beyond the realm of the senses. The view that the first principle of Plotinian thought represents a "static felicity" is deeply ingrained.[3] Writers on later apophatic mystics such as Eriugena, Eckhart, and Ibn 'Arabi commonly defend the later mystics by distancing the thought of such mystics from the allegedly static perfection of the Neoplatonic one.[4] The premise of this chapter is that any "static felicity" or "superessential presence" of an entity called "the one" is undone within the *Enneads*, and that it is undone precisely in those passages where the expressions of Neoplatonic faith are most intense.

Regress from Reference

> "The beyond-being" does not refer to a some-thing since it does not posit any-thing, nor does it "speak its name" [Plat. *Parm.* 132 a 3]. It merely indicates that it is "not that." No attempt is made to circumscribe it. It would be absurd to circumscribe that immense nature. To wish to do so is to cut oneself off from its slightest trace.[5]

For Plotinus, "being" implies form and therefore a delimited entity (*hōrismenon* 5.5.6.1–11).[6] The unlimited must be "the beyond being" (*epekeina ontos, epekeina ousias* cf. Plato, *Rep.* 509b). However, it is not only being that implies delimitation. The very act of naming delimits. A name's referent is, by the act of naming, marked off in some manner from those things which it is not. It is a *tode ti*, a some-thing, a delimited entity. If denomination and reference are necessarily acts of delimitation, how is it possible to refer to the unlimited (*aoriston*)? Names such as "the one" or "the beyond being" cannot refer to the unlimited since, insofar as they refer, they delimit. Plotinus referred to this *aporia* as an "agony" or "birth pang" (*odis*) of signification: "We find ourselves in an *aporia*, in agony over how to speak. We speak about the unsayable (*ou rhētou*); wishing to signify it as best we can, we name it" (5.5.6.23–25).

In exploring Plotinus's most intensely apophatic passages, we will be caught in a similar aporia. The statement made above that the unlimited is beyond all names—including the name "the one"—falls into its own critique; "the unlimited" is itself a name. Because a pronoun implies a previous name as an antecedent, we cannot even call it "it," but again the very form of reference that is being called into question is needed to call itself into question. Like the rigorous apophatic writer, the commentator who would be faithful to the apophatic aspect of the text is caught in a referential regress.

A critical exploration of apophasis faces two dangers. It should not merely reduplicate the apophatic moves of the original. Yet it also needs to avoid translating the apophasis into nonapophatic language. It is the second danger that has caused the most damage in modern studies of apophatic mystical writings. Critical methods based upon nonapophatic premises have tended to fill in the open referent. The openness of referent—in both the Plotinian original and in this study of it—will manifest itself as an ambiguity of pronominal antecedent; the "it" that is being discussed may be impossible to define or may take more than one antecedent. In these cases, it is critically necessary to preserve such ambiguities in order to render a faithful account of Plotinian discourse. The goal here is not to define the referent, but to examine as precisely as possible the way in which Plotinian discourse achieves the referential openness, and the significance of that openness in the generation of meaning within the text.[7]

Not only the apophatic writer but anyone who attempts to discuss that writer's work without betraying it must enter with the reader into an engagement with the dilemmas of delimitation. Plotinus frequently acknowledges that the terms used in reference to the unlimited are formally incorrect and should not be taken referentially. I begin with a similar apology; in many cases the terms used (the one, the infinite, the unlimited) and the propositions in which they occur are acknowledged as self-deconstructing. A second apophatic convention is the apophatic marker. Plotinus often uses the term *hoion* (as it were) to indicate that a name or predicate should not be taken at face value. Though we have a wider variety of apophatic markers (quotation marks, brackets), to place an apophatic marker after every problematic reference would dilute the impact of the marker and result in an unreadable text. Just as readers of poetry agree to accept certain features (syntactical ambiguity, referential multivalence) that would be problematic in discursive prose, so apophasis is based upon a kind of apophatic pact between the text and the reader. The reader is asked to bracket the apophatically self-deconstructing propositions, to recognize their aporetic nature with the expectation that their meaningfulness will be retrieved in a nonreferential or transreferential mode of discourse.

As an example, Plotinus suggests the Pythagorean use of the term Apollo as a "symbol" of the "not many." This is not a negation, but something more complex, an open, never ending process of apophasis (speaking away).

> The name "the one" is merely a denial of multiplicity. The Pythagoreans signified it symbolically [*symbolicōs*] among one another through the term Apollo [*a-pollōn:* not-many], by apophasis of the many. If *the one* is to be taken as a positing [*thēsis*], name [*onoma*], and referent [*dēloumenon*], we would express ourselves more clearly if we did not speak its name at all. We speak it so that we can begin our search with that which signifies the most simple, ending with the apophasis of even that.[8]

Apophasis does not merely substitute a negative term (the not-many) for a positive term (the one). The term Apollo is used to signify the not-many, but it is followed by "the apophasis of even that." As in the example above, "we can't even call it 'it'," the negation must in turn be unsaid. The infinite regress within the initial aporia finds itself at the center of what Plotinus terms symbolic language.

Immediately after the discussion of Apollo as a partially adequate symbol for the unsayable, Plotinus contrasts the direct reference he associates with saying—with speaking, naming, and calling—with seeing (*idein, blepein*). This seeing, however, is not the seeing of a form (*eidos*).[9] Elsewhere Plotinus uses the term *theōria* to indicate this special kind of seeing (*theasthai*), which is a seeing that turns inward, an in-sight.[10] *Theōria* for Plotinus is not "theory" nor is it a spatialized, organizational gaze.[11] Rather it is the insight that points beyond the limitations inherent within the referential discourse, and by doing so leads the Plotinian discourse of saying and unsaying. It is the insight into what lies just beyond the reference that guides the transformation from the referential to the transreferential through an unending process of apophasis—the withdrawal of a delimitation, the withdrawal of the delimitation posited in making the first withdrawal, ad infinitum. The mind, conditioned by the language and logic of entities,[12] moves inexorably toward delimitation, a tendency that must be continually transformed by new acts of apophasis as long as the contemplative gaze remains. The dynamic of symbolic engagement tends to revert to static reference, to being paraphrased as a symbol "of some-thing," the reversion of the symbol into a name. Plotinian language seeks to avoid reversion through the continued "apophasis of even that."

Plotinus also uses the term *aphairesis* (abstraction) to name the discursive practice of removing linguistic dualism. Earlier Greek writers had established a model of abstraction based upon the movement from a three-dimensional space, to a two-dimensional plane, to a one-dimensional line, and finally to a point. The point has no dimension and can be grasped only by successive abstractions.[13] Plotinian understanding of apophasis as a process of abstraction is vividly demonstrated in Plotinus's famous example of the glowing mass in the center of a hollow sphere. Light is wholly present over every spot on the sphere. Then:

> If someone should take out the corporeal mass, but preserve the power of the light, would you then speak of where the light was? Or would it not be everywhere, distributed in and over the entire sphere? No longer can you say through *dianoia* where it was first located, and no longer can you say whence and how it came. You will be brought into perplexity and wonderment.[14]

The hand of the author reaches back into the image to pull out the glowing mass, a kind of *manus ex machina*, as it were. This is apophatic abstraction: to reach into a reference and withdraw the delimited referent, to reach into the notion of contemplating something and withdraw the "some-thing." What appears to happen "ex machina" is not really artificial, however. The apophatic withdrawal is governed by the inner logic of the aporia. In the above example, the entire image was not withdrawn, only the central mass. An analogous situation holds for propositions. Apophasis does not negate the first proposition, it withdraws from it a delimiting element. The original regress that turns back away from saying anything is transformed into a movement turning deeper into the prereferential, or rather, trans-referential symbol. The categories of discursive reason (*dianoia*) are transformed into a open-ended process of *theōria*.

Disontology and Double-Proposition Semantics

Plotinian apophasis reaches one of its most intense points in the final section of *Ennead* 6:7 and throughout *Ennead* 6:8. These treatises argue that the primal emanation or "overflow" occurs neither out of will nor out of necessity. Plotinus rejects the notion that his first principle overflowed out of an act of will. "Will" would imply some kind of need or lack. What would "the unlimited" will to be, will to have, or will to do, if it is already perfected and complete? On the other hand, Plotinus rejects the notion that the one overflowed out of the necessity of its own nature. From the perspective of Neoplatonic piety, the notion that "the one" would be compelled by anything, even its own nature, is viewed with horror.

Yet within this effort to preserve the one from any implication of need is an apophatic dialectic that turns the Plotinian language back upon itself and back upon its own affirmations of fullness and perfection. Against the implication that the unlimited would be compelled by its own nature, Plotinus formulates the counter claim that "it is as it willed itself to be." This statement may satisfy the imperative to keep the unlimited beyond all compulsion, but the resulting proposition deconstructs itself. It also generates one of the more intense passages of apophasis in the classical tradition.

In the following passage, Plotinus begins by disallowing all forms of referential delimitation and predication. He then turns to the notion of the unlimited "willing itself to be." As that proposition deconstructs from within, two phrases occur that will be key to the apophatic dialectic: "the power of absolute ontological self-mastery" and "the being that it wills itself to be, it projects out into beings":

> Then there can be no "thus." It would be a delimitation and a some-thing. One who sees, knows that it is possible to assert neither a thus nor a not-thus. How can you say that it is a being among beings, something to which a thus can be applied? It is other than all things that are "thus." But seeing the unlimited (*aoriston*) you will say that all things are below it, affirming that it is none of them, but, if you will, a power of absolute ontological self-mastery. It is that which it wills to be; or rather, the being that it wills to be it projects out into beings, while it remains greater

> than all its will, all will being below it. So neither did it will to be a thus, so that it would have to conform (to its thus), nor did another make it so.[15]

Critique of predication (the "thus") is tied into a critique of ontology.[16] Both ontology (the placement of the unlimited within the category of being) and referential delimitation, as represented by the predications thus and not-thus, are set aside. The unlimited must be free of all categories, including the category of being. The argument can be diagrammed as follows: (A) Because it is free, no other makes it what it is. It is what it wills itself to be. (B) But it cannot even be said to be limited to what it wills itself to be. (C) We should say that it projects the being, the quiddity, the "what" that it wills itself to be, out into the realm of beings. It always remains beyond its own being and its own willing. This series of apophatic withdrawals is an explication of the dense expression *dynamin pasan hautēs ontōs kyrian*, "power of absolute ontological self-mastery." The "projection" of being outside of itself is the prime Plotinian symbol. Later, even the notion that "it projects" will be transformed, since the subject of such a predication implies an actor or being, but "being" is precisely what is being projected out.

Disontology, mythically represented by this "projection," is the ongoing discursive attempt to gain a momentary liberation from the delimitations of predication and reference as represented by thus and not thus. To say that "it is X" is to delimit it, to mark it off from the "not-X." It is also to mark it off even from the X it is said to be; if it were not in some sense delimited from "X" the statement "it is X" would be a mere tautology. To say that "it is here" is, therefore, to mark it off not only from "there," but also from "here." If the statement "it is here" is not to be a tautology, there must be something in its "hereness" from which it is distinguished. A similar case of double delimitation would occur for the "not thus." We cannot even say "it is" since this would imply a category (beingness) from which it would be marked off and delimited—or again, the statement "it is" would be redundant. The urgency of Plotinus's concern with such delimitations and the seriousness with which his apophatic discourse attempts to counter them might be translated into modern terms as implying the belief that language—in its most material and most minute aspects—determines consciousness in a manner both subtle and profound.

When Plotinus writes that "it is neither X nor not X," he violates the logical rule of the excluded middle. When he writes that "it is both X and not X," he violates the law of noncontradiction. I argue that these statements are paradoxical in a very strong sense. They are not rhetorical paradoxes or "seeming contradictions" that can be used for effect and then be resolved by further explanation. Real contradictions arise when the delimited, referential function of language encounters a rigorously apophatic notion of the unlimited. Such contradictions are not illogical, however. The rules of non-contradiction and excluded middle apply specifically to delimited language reference. The coming together of opposites (*coincidentia oppositorum*) results logically from any reference to the unlimited. Conversely, it can be interpreted as the means by which language is transformed from the referential to *theōria*. The coincidence of opposites is a form of dialectical logic that plays against and upon the linear logic of delimited reference.

The dialectic of immanence and transcendence is the primary example of such dialectical logic. "It is beyond all things" is a statement that delimits. If it is beyond all things, then there is a conceptual 'space' (all things) from which it is excluded, and another conceptual 'space' (the beyond all things) in which it is confined. Apophasis denies that the problem can be solved by the assertion that terms like "beyond" and "within" should not be taken spatially; the power of language over thought is resistant to such assertions. Such affirmations of transcendence are a subtle form of delimitation. They are particularly dangerous because in the very act of asserting transcendence they delimit and and reify what they assert to be transcendent.

The act of unsaying such a false affirmation of transcendence often leads to an affirmation of immanence: "it is within all things." Each of these propositions (it is within all things—it is beyond all things) taken alone places the unlimited in a conceptual space ("beyond" or "within"), thus delimiting the unlimited. Each proposition taken alone is self-contradictory, analytically incoherent. Meaning is generated between the two propositions: it is within all things—it is beyond all things. In effect, the smallest semantic unit is not the sentence or proposition, but the double sentence or dual proposition. It is to this new semantic of the double proposition that apophatic dialectical logic applies. This double semantics is the enactment within discourse of the Plotinian notion of *theōria*. Plotinian *theōria* was symbolized by the glowing mass within the sphere; the contemplation was valid only when the first image was altered by the removal of the glowing mass.

The human mind, conditioned by language, has an ingrained tendency to treat the sentence as the semantic unit. Although Plotinus does not discuss his own discourse explicitly, it is apparent from the way he structures the apophatic propositions that he is attempting to counter the tendency to give independent propositional status to the last sentence. Plotinus connects the various sets of dual propositions so that the last sentence of the first dual proposition forms the first sentence of the second dual proposition. For example, after stating some version of the dual proposition "It is within all things—it is beyond all things," Plotinus resists any validation of the second sentence. To take the sentence on its own would be to reify a "something" contained in all things as in a place. A new proposition suggests a stronger assertion of immanence: it is not "in" all things but "is" all things, or is the very "place" of all things. If the movement through the dual propositions came to a halt, the mind would be trapped in the false signification of the last single proposition.

Ironically enough, apophatic writers are accused of pantheism, the denial of the transcendent. They begin with the premise that one-proposition affirmations of transcendence are incomplete. When they are taken as complete, they mislead. The attempt to find a meaningful formulation of transcendence leads ineluctably to the discovery of radical immanence. The charge of pantheism is often countered by saying that we shouldn't take seriously the more extreme statements of immanence. But as has been shown above, dialectical logic is a logic of extremes: the "absolutely transcendent" is meaningful only if it is simultaneously the "absolutely immanent." Outside of a dialectic of transcendence and immanence, the transcendence is just another being, however great, among beings.[17]

Dialectical logic as defined here appears in Plato's *Parmenides* where the hypothesis of "the one" results in a plethora of *coincidentia oppositorum*.[18] We now turn to specific passages in which Plotinus lends to this schematized logic a dynamic principle, making it come alive.

Subject-Predicate Fusion

For Plotinus, discursive reason reflects alienated consciousness. It must "run after" the object of its contemplation through activity. It is caught in dualisms of subject-object, cause-effect, origin-goal. The overcoming of these dualisms occurs in *nous*.[19] Plotinian nous is commonly translated as "intellect" but such a translation gives a cold or "intellectualist" connotation to a term that for Plotinus signified both impersonal truth and the most personal and intimate mode of contemplation. The complex embedding of Plotinian discussions of nous within the Platonist and Aristotelian traditions of late antiquity tends to further remove it from our immediate access.[20] Here, I will be able to discuss only that side of nous directly relevant to Plotinian apophasis, the inward side of nous, the relationship of nous to the one, nous as *theōria*. Nous as *theōria* involves several acts of union. In schematic forms these acts of union include:

1. The union of subject, predicate, and object. Nous is thought thinking itself, or it is the union of being (*ousia*) and act (*energeia*).

2. The union of all activities in one act. In nous, to think something is to make it, rather than to consider a preexistent separate object, and both acts are identical with willing, loving, and living.

3. The union of the divine and human. Insofar as the human psyche achieves *theōria* it is by that fact united with nous. Nous is considered by Plotinus to be divine. Nous is an event. From the human perspective we might consider it the event of union with the divine.

4. The union of all three unions in nous. The three occur simultaneously and imply one another.

The statement "thought thinking itself" still contains dualisms. Although subject, predicate, and object are said to be identical, they are linguistically differentiated and thus delimited. The most radical unity resides beyond even this self-reflexive union. Nous can be realized only when the contemplative gaze is focused not on nous but on the one. For nous to be nous it must look beyond itself.

If nous is thought thinking or contemplating itself, what does it mean to say that nous contemplates the one? Two problems arise here. First, the one cannot be an object of contemplation, because that would make it a delimited entity, marked off logically from the subject that contemplates it. Second, if nous is self-contemplation, then to say that it contemplates the one is to say that it is the one. Similar problems arise when we try to refer to the activity of the one. To say "the one wills" creates several delimitations marking off the one as subject from the activity in which it engages, marking off the activity of willing from other activities. To say that the one is "self-willing" does not solve the problem since it is nous that is defined as self-reflective act. In a key passage, Plotinus takes up this problem by suggesting that the one can only be intimated when languages arrives "Where there is not 'two as one,' but one—either because there is act only, or because there is no act at all" (6.8.12.35–37).

As opposed to the noetic identity of being and act, or subject and predicate, the identity here can be called *fusion identity*. Again, such a notion can only be expressed in a dual proposition. The first step posits a predication ("the one wills") and the second step reaches into the glowing sphere, as it were, in order to withdraw the glowing mass, this time in the form of either the subject or the predicate. We are asked to think of an act so total that the subject has been utterly fused into the act: a willing without willer. Or alternatively, we are asked to think of a pure subject, a subject that does not act, but serves as the bottomless ground or depth out of which the divine willing and divine consciousness (as nous) wells up or emanates. Because referentially conditioned thought gravitates toward the subject-predicate, being-act dichotomy, a willing-without-willer or willer-without-willing can only be glimpsed momentarily in the interstices of the dual proposition. Apophasis must keep the mind from settling into the delimitation by creating ever new dual propositions. This being-without-act or act-without-being attempts a momentary transcendence of predication. The following passage begins with an apophatic apology, then shifts into the most intensely apophatic language. The goal is to "say" a union of act and being, an act so intense that the subject of the act and the act itself are one. The particular act in question is that of will, so that the willer and the willing are said to be the same. The crucial moments are signaled by the use of the apophatic marker (*hoion*, as it were):

> But given that we must incorrectly employ predications for the sake of the inquiry, then let it be said once again that they are not being spoken correctly, since a duality must never be posited, not even for the sake of obtaining a notion [*epinoia*]. We use these names now for the sake of persuasion and in doing so we depart from strict accuracy. If we give it activities, and imply that its activities are through its will, for it would not act will-lessly—the acts must *be* as it were its being, its will and its being will *be the same*. If this is so, as it willed to be, it is.[21]

The statement that the being of X and the will of X are the same contains a tension between the fusion identity evoked, and the noetic, linguistic identity which is the most that any one-step proposition taken by itself can actually say (a tension I have highlighted through italics). Through *theōria*, Plotinus implies, the mind glimpses an identity of fusion beyond referential closure before it settles into normal habits of reference. In other passages, the author attempts to prolong such a glimpse by an apophatic withdrawal of the subject from the proposition, by speaking of an "awakening without awakener," for example. In the extended passage given below, it (the one-nous) is said to cause itself, to be its own very act of self-causing, to be its act of contemplating itself. This turning inward, this motion towards itself, is an acting out of the "power of absolute ontological self-mastery" that was encountered in the passage from 6.8.9 cited above. The disontology consists of a continual fusing of the subject-predicate dualism, and a continual displacing of the tendency for the one to revert to simply an opposite of duality and thus be reified within a dualistic relation. The apophatic marker *hoion* appears with such frequency that to translate it each time as "as it were" would be cumbersome. I simply mark it with the sign: ( ). Despite Plotinus's intense use of the marker, this passage and others like it have been read as if there were an entity engaging in activities.[22]

> He is everywhere and nowhere . . . if nowhere, nowhere has he happened to be, and if everywhere, then just as he is, he is everywhere so that he is the everywhere and the everyway. . . . If then he exists in view of holding fast toward himself and gazing ( ) toward himself, and the being ( ) is for him that very gazing toward himself, he would then make him(self) ( ), and then he is not as he happened to be but as he wished to be. . . . The being that he is is that very act toward himself. . . . If then his act did not come to be, but always was, an awakening ( ) without awakener as other ( ), an eternal awakening and a supra-intellection, then as he waked to be he is: awakening beyond being, and nous, and rational life ( ), though he is these ( ), act beyond nous and understanding and life, which are from him and from no other. By himself, in himself, and from himself is his being. Not therefore as he happened to be, but as he wished to be, he is.[23]

Predications imply that a subject engages in an activity, that there is a "remainder" within the subject that is not that activity itself. Plotinus evokes an act without subject to overcome such remainders. He evokes an act so utterly complete and instantaneous that the subject is fused into the act to the point of no longer existing. At this point one is not aware of acting; indeed the one has completely merged into the act. In terms like "awakening without awakener," the fusion of normal grammatical polarities reaches a culmination of semantic intensity.

Split, Fused, and Shifting Reference

The one is nous, yet is beyond nous. Or the one-nous is the being it makes itself to be and then, in disontology, is said to project outside of itself. This disontology is reflected in language by a splitting of normal reference, and by a subversion of normal distinctions between reflexive and nonreflexive. When Plotinus writes in the above passage that "he would then make himself" or in another passage that "Logic leads us to the discovery that it made itself," the reflexive pronoun is subverted by the infinite regress embedded within the notion of self-causality.

This is the critical moment. The infinite regress that constituted the original aporia returns as the interior principle of mystical dialectic, splitting apart normal reference structures from within:

> And if someone should say: "What! doesn't it follow that he would have had to come into being before coming into being? For if he makes himself, then insofar as he is made, he is not yet in being, but from the perspective of the act of making he is before the self as made, which he is said to be?!" To whom it must be replied that he cannot be taken as made, but only as maker. The act of making himself must be freed from all else.[24]

The dual proposition now takes on a new form. The one makes/wills/thinks itself to be (self-causality)—the one cannot be taken as the object, it transcends the self it makes itself to be (self-transcendence). I use parentheses to translate the fusing of reference: It is as it makes it(self) to be. From the point of view of the pronoun, the reference is split, referring back to two different possible antecedents. From the perspective of the antecedents which are semantically fused at such a moment, the reference can be fused. Viewed in another way, instead of a synchronic splitting or fusing, there is oscillation and continual shifting of referents. Split, fused, and shifting reference occurs not only in the object (it makes it[self]) but throughout the proposition, in the subject and predicate. What is it that makes itself? It must be nous since nous is defined as reflexive act. But then it would have had to make itself in order to exist in order to make itself. Nous as self-making devolves in infinite regress. On the other hand, if we say that the one makes itself, then we must withdraw not only the "itself," but also the division between maker and making by posing a making without a maker or a maker without a making. Insofar as "it makes," it cannot be the one because the one cannot be referred to in a subject-predicate delimitation. Nous both is and is not the one. The double dialectic of self-causality and self-transcendence brings to life the underlying apophatic logic. This analysis accounts for the disagreement among editors in many cases over whether the antecedent of the pronoun is nous or the one.[25] As in other examples of mystical apophasis, Plotinian discourse achieves a temporary fusion of two possible referents or antecedents. At the moment of reference fusion, the basic grammatical distinction between the reflexive/nonreflexive, self/other division is undone.²⁶ The fusion of reference is performed at the grammatical level by a perfect coincidence of possible antecedents (nous and the one) of the pronoun. Yet this moment of reference is fleeting and the fused referent continually slips beyond the proposition.

Below, Plotinus writes of the beyond-being projecting being outside itself. As indicated in reference to the "power of absolute ontological self-mastery," the predication "it projects" cannot stand. To the extent it is projecting outside of itself its being, it has no being that it might be thought of as "a being" that projects. The proposition turns in upon itself in apophasis, transforming itself on ever deeper levels of disontology into a transreferential *theōria*.

> So we should intuit the beyond-being spoken as a riddle by the ancients. Not only did he beget being, but he is subject neither to being nor to him-self, nor is his being a principle of himself, but he, being the principle of being, did not make being for himself, but having made it, he projected it outside himself—he who is in no need of beingness, who made it. Thus he did not make in accordance with his being.²⁷

Self-making refers then to nous (noetic self-reflexivity) and to the one (fusion identity) at the same time. The propositions "it is as it willed/made/thought it(self) to be" not only split the reference, but the infinite regress implied in them continues to split the reference as long as the gaze (*theōria*) is maintained. The split reference of self-causality, the "projection" of being outside the self, the process of disontology, the breakdown of the self/other dichotomy are all aspects of emanation (literally "outflowing," though the term also refers to overflowing). Emanation is reified when presented nonapophatically as if there were some place or thing from which things "flow out." In Plotinus there is always that second step, the reaching in to pull out the glowing mass.

Emanation: The Overflow of Meaning

One of the most powerful emanation passages within the classical apophatic tradition is the extremely short *Ennead* 5.2. The treatise opens, already in mid-stream of apophasis, with a series of tentative referential forays. The opening statement sets the tone: "The one is all things but no thing." This claim is followed immediately by its own unsaying; it "is not all things, but is all things in 'that' way." Suddenly the classic question of "the one and the many" is posed: from absolute oneness, how can there appear many? This question is followed by a statement of great apophatic intensity: "because there is nothing in it, all things are from it." The projection of being outside of itself, disontology, is then evoked: in order for "being" to be, the source of being cannot be being. There follows a dialectic of "nothing and all" that will recur in all the apophatic writings explored in this study: "Seeking nothing, having nothing, needing nothing, it overflowed." It is emptiness, having nothing, that overflows into being. At this point the classic apophatic motif of "turning back" (*epistrophē*) is depicted. But what is it that turns back toward its source? It could be nous that turns back and by doing so becomes "being." Or perhaps "being" itself turns back and by doing so becomes thought (nous). However, since being and nous are one for Plotinus, in some sense nous must turn back to its source in order to become nous. Plotinus uses as a partial symbol of the unsayable one the demonstrative adjective "that," which highlights its own lack of a proper referent. The passage ends with the reference to "the pouring forth of a vast power":

> The one is all things but no thing. The principle of all things is not all things, but is all things in "that" way. For there all things run within, as it were. Or they are not, but will be. How then from the absolute one, in which no multiplicity appears nor any duality whatsoever, [can there be a many]? Rather, *it is because there is nothing in it that all things are from it*. In order that being be, that must not be being, but rather being's begetter. This is, as it were, the primal genesis. Perfect, seeking nothing, having nothing, needing nothing, it overflowed, as it were, and its overflowing made its other. This begotten turned back toward it(self) and was filled and became the contemplator of it(self) and became nous. Its standing before it made being, and the contemplation toward it made it nous. When it stands before it, so that it sees, at one time it is engendered as nous and being. Thus, since it is, as it were, *that*, it brings about likenesses—pouring forth a vast power, and that is its image.[28]

This passage contains coiled within it the entire mystical dialectic. Through the unravelling of the dilemmas within it, the inner semantics of Plotinian apophasis are revealed. The primal act of generation (*prōtē gennēsis*) is called an overflowing. The overflowing produced an "other," which turned back (*epestraphē*), was filled, and became a contemplator and nous. However, if the one produced the other by overflowing, and if that other is what flows from it, then to state that the other is filled by the same perpetual overflowing is to fuse together the vessel-content dualism on which the metaphor is based, or to first pose the dualism and then withdraw one element. This is the dilemma that the vessel is the content.

A similar dilemma is intimated by the meanings of the English term "emanation": the act of flowing out or of causing to flow out, or that which flows out. What flows out is identical to the act of flowing out, the result of the process is the process. In regard to the one and nous, it [fused reference] is the motion of procession and return (or turning back), the motion of which it is at other times called the result.

Another dilemma is the fact that what flows out cannot really "be" until it "turns back." In apophatic writings of other mystics, this dilemma can take the form of the dilemma of procession and return: that the procession cannot be said to have occurred until the return. Here nous is said to proceed, but it only becomes itself, nous, when it turns back. However if it wasn't yet nous, how can it be said that nous proceeded or turned back?

The dilemma of "turning back" in Plotinus is not resolved but further deepened by the complex relationship of being to nous. Being and nous are both identical and correlative (one can only be understood in relation to the other).[29] What is of interest for this study is not only Plotinus's assertion of correlative identity, but the way in which he engages the topic. The last four sentences of Plotinus's depiction of emanation in the above passage offer conflicting accounts of the priority of being to nous or nous to being. Deductively, there seem to be two possible paradigms of emanation if one accepts the Neopythagorean principle, accepted by Plotinus, that "from the one can come only one." Either it is "being" that flows out and becomes nous when it turns back toward its source; or it is nous that flows out and becomes being when it turns back toward its source. In the *Enneads*, both paradigms can occur.[30] In our passage above, the two paradigms continually push against one another. In the semantics of the double paradigm, no single, static paradigm is meaningful: "A then B" leads ineluctably to "B then A."

A final factor in the apophatic implosion of this passage is the fused or split reference that occurs with the object of nous's "turning back" and contemplation. When it (nous/being) turns back in contemplation, the object toward which it turns back could be either itself or the one; it is not clear whether the Greek pronoun is reflexive or nonreflexive at this point. Nous turns back toward the one, but it also turns back toward itself. This dual object of contemplation is often reflected in Plotinus's text by a fused reference: it turns back toward it(self). The textual difficulties that occur in determining whether the antecedent for the pronoun is nou*s* or the one can be read as a result of this fused reference in which the distinction between self and other, between reflexive and non-reflexive act, is breaking down. Split or fused reference involves a double gaze. Nous looks toward its source/self. Plotinus accepted Aristotle's nous as thought thinking itself, but criticized making it the ultimate principle.[31] Nous becomes itself by gazing beyond itself. The enigma of the double gaze relates to the problem of predication. If it is reified as a principle, as subject of predication, then the thought-thinking-itself freezes into a static concept. In the simultaneous contemplation of source/self, contemplative mind is led by the aporia into reenacting the very unions mentioned above as being part of nous: union of subject and predicate, or of all acts in one act. The unlimited, like a magnet, keeps nous in a state of constant activity.

One could go on explicating the dilemmas of emanation. Later Neoplatonists did so systematically.[32] What concerns us here is the aporetic function these dilemmas represent. The aporia keeps the mind in incessant activity, never allowing it a fixed referent. The mind is led from one facet of the aporia to another. Earlier on in this study, we encountered Plotinus's image of the sphere illumined by a glowing inner mass. After depicting the image of the sphere, Plotinus then removed the glowing mass from its center. This act of apophatic abstraction is performed continually in the Plotinian texts on emanation. The logical regress within the aporia continually turns back upon the previous propositions and—to use Plotinus's metaphor—pulls out the glowing mass. The glowing mass in this case is the "being" of the source of emanation. The aporia governs a discourse that combines the metaphor of emanation with an inner dialectic that transforms the dualistic structures upon which the emanation is based, forming a metaphoric dialectic. Insofar as the "projection of being outside of itself" is a myth of origination, the transformation of the dualistic structures upon which the myth is based forms a mythic dialectic.

Emanation is commonly treated as a metaphor in the service of causal explanation.[33] The "genesis" Plotinus writes of here would be nothing more than the one's engendering of nous, and the subsequent positing of lower realms. The inner apophatic logic, however, subverts the dualisms and delimitations upon which such narrative, explanatory language is based. Explanatory language is transformed into a language of *theōria*. Until now I have refrained from translating *theōria* as contemplation since contemplation is most often seen as contemplation of some thing, and reification of "some thing" is precisely what Plotinian apophasis seeks to avoid. Nous is contemplation, but the "object" of its contemplation is constantly being pulled away through apophatic abstraction (*aphairesis*).

The transformation of a minute quantity of matter into energy, through nuclear fusion or fission, releases an unimaginably great energy. Such analogies may only be suggestive. However, when apophatic language is able to fuse—in however a fleeting or partial manner—the subject or "being" into pure act, it generates a semantic intensity that overflows standard linguistic structures and limits. This is the semantic equivalent of the "pouring forth of a vast power" which occurs with the Plotinian *epistrophē*, the turning back to the self/source.

Ingress into Symbol

Plotinus called his apophasis a "symbolic" use of language. Plotinian apophasis is not, however, a form of prereferential signification. Apophasis uses language and language reference. It "proceeds" out into delimited language reference, only to "return" back toward a referential openness. Both steps are necessary to generate meaning. The first or "kataphatic" step sets the context, the cultural-linguistic context of a given tradition, in this case the philosophical tradition of late antiquity. The apophatic turn is a continually repeated effort to turn back upon the referential reification by withdrawing the glowing mass of reified entity.

The second stage can take on meaning only within its context. Taken out of context, the nothingness of referential openness can never be discursively distinguished from "mere nothingness." From the standpoint of the apophatic moment, the question "does it exist or not" cannot be answered. On what grounds could one affirm or deny the existence of "what" is beyond the delimitations of quiddity and predication, of "whatness," of "it exists" or "it does not exist?" When the apophatic turn is viewed out of context it can sound nihilistic. However, to attempt to preclude such a misreading by filling in the open reference with a "something" is to betray the discourse. Apophasis demands a moment of nothingness. After speaking of absolute unity as that which is most powerful (*dynatōtaton*) in an animal, a soul, or in the all, Plotinus writes of "the one":

> But should we grasp the one of authentic beings, their principle, wellspring, and *dynamis*—will we then lose faith and consider it nothing? It is certainly nothing of the things of which it is the origin, being such, as it were, that

> nothing can be attributed to it, neither being, nor beings, nor life. It is beyond those. If then by withdrawing being you should grasp it, you will be brought into wonder [*thauma*].[34]

After contemplating the world view of his tradition, the mystic then withdraws being from the source. At this moment the soul "fears that there be nothing" (6.9.3.6). Apophasis demands a moment of receptivity free from the security of referential delimitation. At this point Plotinus writes of not losing faith. This faith is not a faith in anything, but a willingness to let go of being. Such a letting go results in wonderment (*thauma*). The wonder here is not the wonder produced by the miracle worker and thaumaturge. It is the semantic reflection of emanation, and an overflow of meaning. That overflow constitutes an event. It is fleeting. It cannot be held or possessed. At the moment of most intense apophasis, meaning is neither "the thing one intends to convey by language" nor "the thing that is conveyed by language."[35] It is not a thing, a content, a "what." This meaning event is empty in itself, but its overflow ramifies through the kataphatic meanings expressed within the discourse. (To paraphrase Plotinus: it is because there is nothing in it that all things are from it.) On the semantic level, the *dynamis* of absolute ontological self-mastery is the meaning event that comes about through apophasis.

My reading has focused upon linguistic elements, such as subject-predicate dualisms. The objection might arise that Plotinus does not usually use grammatical terminology. It is true that he speaks ontologically, of the "other" proceeding from the one and then realizing itself as it turns back toward it(self). Yet, there are clues throughout that these passages are to be read symbolically as disontology. When Plotinus speaks of an awakening without an "awakener as an other," in the context of act-without-being, his discourse reflects upon its own generation of meaning. What proceeds is the subject-predicate dualism that is language reference. That reference cannot be what it is until it returns to itself (we can't speak of the proceeding until the result, the subject-predicate, allows us to say "it proceeds"). But the language reference is not *fully* itself until it turns back towards its source in intuition (gazing inward)—insight into the pre-predication, the un-delimited—and undoes itself as reference. These two turns occur simultaneously in the split or fused reference. The original aporia that turns upon itself, back away from any reference, is transformed into a turning back ever more deeply into what Plotinus called the symbolic. Ironically, the most intensely apophatic language within the *Enneads* occurs at precisely those moments in the text when the effort to refer to the transcendent is strongest, such as those passages on "ontological self-mastery." It is at those moments, when on the rhetorical level the Neoplatonic piety is at its most confident and serene, that the referential aspect of discourse unravels itself most dramatically. At this point, ontological self-mastery becomes disontology, being's projection of being outside itself.

The vast philosophical movement of Neoplatonism systematized and expanded upon the Plotinian world of emanation. The essential Plotinian aporias were played out historically in subsequent discussions. The paradox of self-causality, for example, led to two radically different positions. In the works of Iamblichus, a new principle, the ineffable, was posed as beyond the one and the dualisms set forth by self-reflective activity. In the works of Porphyry, the self-reflective activity of the one/nous was expanded and refined into differing phases, and the one was identified with nous in its phase of intellect before it finds an object of intellection.[36] Similar dynamics were to be recreated in post-Zoharic Kabbalah centuries later, with some schools claiming that the *ayn sof* (unlimited) could be identified with the highest of the sefirot, and others holding that it was utterly beyond them.[37] In chapter 6, I will trace the emergence of an almost identical double paradigm in the writings of Meister Eckhart. The above discussion suggests that these developments are inherent in the double-proposition semantics of apophasis and within the apophatic treatment of emanation.

My reading has emphasized the dialectic of transcendence and immanence in Plotinian writing and those moments when the articulated structures of hypostases seem to collapse into one another as (in Plotinian terms) the psyche rises to nous and finally encounters the source of emanation. These particular passages are apophatically intense, that is, they turn back upon their own propositions in a particularly relentless manner. Such passages are balanced by other Plotinian texts, not discussed here, where the hierarchy and structure appear more stable. In addition, the dramatic apophatic dialectic of transcendence and immanence found in selected passages of the *Enneads* is contextually located within a late antique worldview that stressed the mediations and levels that exist between the world and the transcendent. A profound change in the "location" of the meaning event of apophatic discourse would be effected within the Abrahamic religious traditions. For a new stage in this process, we turn to the writings of John the Scot Eriugena.

CHAPTER TWO

The Nothingness of God in John the Scot Eriugena

In 827 c.e., the Byzantine emperor Michael the Stammerer sent a gift to the Frankish king Louis the Pious. His gift was a copy of the Greek writings attributed to an Athenian companion of St. Paul, Dionysius the Areopagite.[1]

Still a mystery is the actual identity of the author of the works that circulated for centuries under the name of Dionysius. He is now thought to have lived in the sixth century c.e., perhaps in Syria, and to have written under the influence of the Athenian Neoplatonist Proclus (d. 485). The legitimacy of the Greek writings attributed to Dionysius had been attacked and championed throughout the sixth century. The commentaries of the influential Byzantine theologian Maximus the Confessor (d. 662) marked a major step toward establishing those writings within the Christian canon.[2]

When the Greek texts arrived at the court of Louis, Hilduin, the royal chaplain of St. Denis, was asked to translate them into Latin. Hilduin announced that the Areopagite disciple of Paul (who had already been conflated with Dionysius, the first bishop of Athens) was no other than St. Denis, the bishop and martyr of Paris.[3] Hilduin's conflation of the three revered figures conferred an authority upon the Dionysian texts that was to remain unassailable throughout the medieval period.

The translation by Hilduin proved to be unsatisfactory. Charles the Bald, the successor to Louis the Pious, commissioned the Irish scholar John the Scot Eriugena (810–77) to prepare another version.[4] Eriugena translated all the major surviving texts attributed to Dionysius, and later translated works by Maximus the Confessor and Gregory of Nyssa (d. 394) as well. Under the influence of the Greek texts he translated, Eriugena went on to compose his own masterwork, *Periphyseon* (On the Divine Nature), a work that incorporates key Dionysian themes and modes of discourse into a new philosophical and theological context.[5]

IRISHMAN AND AREOPAGITE

Although the *Periphyseon* could be approached from a number of perspectives, this chapter will focus on how Eriugena created an apophatic discourse in the context of his exploration of a nonsubstantialist view of deity. The Dionysian texts most important for this aspect of Eriugena's writing are the *Divine Names* and the *Mystical Theology*.[6] In both treatises, Dionysius demonstrates his understanding of theology as a continual interplay between the kataphatic and apophatic modes of discourse, neither of which can function authentically without the other. The kataphatic statement affirms the divine names, such as goodness, being, wisdom, and life. The apophatic statement asserts that the deity must be considered beyond-goodness, beyond-being, beyond-wisdom, beyond-life. In the *Divine Names*, where Dionysius is most concerned with the emanation of the deity out into the world, he stresses the kataphatic mode. In the *Mystical Theology*, he stresses the apophatic mode in discussing the return to a deity beyond all attribution and beyond all knowledge.

Although the kataphatic and apophatic modes of discourse function interdependently, Dionysian theology privileges the apophatic mode as approaching closer to the truth. In the context of his exploration of the unknowability of deity, Dionysius invented the expression "mystical theology." *Agnosia* (an unknowing that goes beyond rather than falling short of kataphatic affirmations) was at the center of his mystical theology.[7] This *agnosia* begins with the contemplation (*theōria*) of the "place" of the deity beyond all gaze or contemplation. One is then freed from what is seen and what sees and plunges into the "truly mysterious darkness of unknowing" (*ton gnophon tēs agnosias ton ontōs mystikon*). The Dionysian expression "darkness" or "cloud of unknowing" was to ground the medieval meditation on apophatic theology, including the works of Eriugena, the anonymous author of *The Cloud of Unknowing*, aspects of Beguine spirituality, and the works of Eckhart. The Dionysian darkness of unknowing is an encounter with that which is beyond all attributes, including the attribute of "being."[8] It is the subjective correlate to the nonsubstantialist deity beyond being. It is encountered when the self-other polarity is transcended, when "one is neither oneself nor another." Thus, while keeping much of the apophatic dialectic of Plotinus and

Proclus, Dionysius reversed the sense imagery, placing darkness above light, non-seeing above seeing. Ultimately of course, the transcendent is beyond all attributes and polar oppositions:

> There is no speaking of it, nor name nor knowledge of it. Darkness and light, error and truth—it is none of these. It is beyond assertion and denial. We make assertions and denials of what is next to it, but never of it, for it is both beyond every assertion, being the perfect and unique cause of all things, and by virtue of its preeminently simple and absolute nature, free of every limitation, beyond every limitation; it is also beyond every denial.

In Dionysius and Gregory of Nyssa, Eriugena found an alternative to the substantialist view of deity propounded in the Church councils, which had consistently applied the term *ousia* (substance, being) to the nature(s) of Christ and to the trinity,[9] and which through the writings of Augustine had become central to the Western Christian tradition. Within the *Periphyseon*, Eriugena integrated into his own apophatic discourse both Dionysius' affirmation that the deity was "beyond-being" and Gregory's suggestion that the "nothing" in the doctrine of "creation from nothing" (*creatio ex nihilo*) was the divine nothingness out of which all being proceeds.[10]

The *Periphyseon* begins with a division of nature into two categories: all things that are (i.e., that can be grasped by the mind) and all things that are not (i.e., that transcend the mind's grasp). This first division of nature establishes the interrelation of ontology and epistemology. To be is to be able to be grasped by the mind. That which transcends the mind must necessarily transcend being.

A second division of nature includes four categories: (1) that which is uncreated and creates (the deity as creator god); (2) that which is created and creates (the eternal ideas or "primordial causes" within the divine word); (3) that which is created and does not create (the world); and (4) that which is not created and does not create.[11] The first and last categories are identified with deity, the first as creator deity, the last as that which transcends all predications and dualities, including the duality between creator and created. The entire schema is based upon an emanation pattern of procession and return, the emanation out from the deity with creation and the eventual return of all things back to and beyond their primal source.

The ontological movement of all things from their primordial unity out into the multiplicity of the world and back to their source is mirrored in the operation of reason itself. Reason consists of division (*divisiori, diairetikē*) by which the one is divided into its constituent parts, and resolution (*resolutiva, analytikē*) "which unravels the composite into simple parts through separation."[12] Thus ontology and intelligibility can be said to "completely presuppose and condition each other."[13] Indeed, reason's movement back toward unity through resolution is, in a strong sense, nothing other than the ontological and cosmic return.

Of *Periphyseon*'s five books, Book 1 takes up the first category of nature (that which is uncreated and creates), Book 2 the second category (that which is created and creates, the primordial causes), Book 3 the third category (that which is created and does not create, i.e. the temporal and spatial world), and Books 4–5 the final category, the return of all things to their primal source beyond all predication and dualism, including the duality of creator and created.

Eriugena's masterwork takes the literary form of a dialogue between an experienced philosopher or *nutritor* and an *alumnus* (an adept or novice) who is of rather ambiguous status as either the student or junior colleague of the nutritor. At key points in their discussion, the nutritor refers to his major souce of authority, Dionysius the Areopagite. While Book 3 was originally supposed to be a discussion of the temporal and spatial world, it includes a remarkable opening section on the question of creation from nothing (*creatio ex nihilo*). This section (chaps. 5–23) comes at the end of a summary of points that had been made about the second category (the primordial causes) in Book 2. Only at the end of this long excursus does the discussion move on to the third category, the spatiotemporal world of creation, with a discussion of the first five days of creation (chaps. 24–40).

The self-contained essay on *creatio de nihilo* within Book 3 can be read as a commentary on key Dionysian paradoxes of the self-causing deity: (1) as "beyond being" but also as "the being of all things"; (2) as that which "overflows all things"; (3) as that which "makes all things and is made in all things"; and (4) as that which "limits all things, yet is their boundless infinitude." Yet Eriugena's evocation of these Dionysian formulas goes beyond appeal to authority and explicative commentary. The Dionysian paradoxes are placed within a highly original dynamic of emanation that draws out their apophatic and nonsubstantialist premises to the most radical expression.

The emanation pattern of procession and return enables Eriugena to develop his own nonsubstantialist view of deity. Eriugena uses the emanation metaphor to destabilize various structures embedded within the text. The hierarchical conception of a chain of being (implicit in the second, fourfold division of nature) becomes subject to an apophatic dynamic which challenges the hierarchy's spatial and temporal categories. As in Plotinus and Dionysius, the graded levels of being (semantically dependent upon such spatial and temporal distinctions) ultimately return back into a primal unity. As in Plotinus and Dionysius, there is also a tension between the emphasis upon a graded succession of processions and an immediate relationship of each being with the source of being. Eriugena, however, does away with the elaborately graded series of hypostases and hierarchies found in the writings of his predecessors.[14] He places the tension more directly, or at least more insistently, within the emanation paradigm itself as a tension between procession and return as simultaneous movements.

The Eriugenean discourse not only challenges the hierarchy of being, but also the hierarchy of mastery between the teacher and student. Although personal descriptions are not offered, the nutritor and alumnus show a subtle, sometimes ironic understanding of the tension between their hierarchically structured roles and the radically unrestricted dynamics of learning. The nutritor rejects the causal, temporal, and spatial reifications posed by a substantialist deity that creates *ex nihilo*. But in the face of deferential and relentless questioning from the alumnus, the nutritor tries to back away from the implications of his position. By the end of Book 3, the nutritor returns to the former view and fiercely defends even its most radical implications. In effect, the nutritor and alumnus become two equal voices pushing one another toward a conclusion that neither seems willing or able to conceive alone.[15]

Participation, Emanation, Ontological Shadow

In Book 3, the nutritor pursues his critique of the substantialist deity during a dialogue with the alumnus on the concept of participation. The doctrine of participation posits a chain of being with various levels, from the source of all being, to the primordial causes (which are both created and creative), to the temporal and spatial world which constitutes the effects of the primordial causes. The beings of a given level proceed from the level above their own. In addition, insofar as they truly exist, they exist within their source.

When questioned about the concept of participation, the nutritor appeals to the etymology of the original Greek terms as a way of easily (*facillime*) understanding the Latin *participatio*.

> [N]ote that participation is denoted by the Greeks in a more meaningful, expressive, and easily understandable manner. In their language *metoxe* and *methousia* signify

> "participation": *metoxe* as if it were *metaexousa*, that is "having after" or "having second," *metousia* as *meta-ousia*, that is "after-essence" or "second essence." From this it is most easy to understand that participation is nothing other than the derivation from a superior essence of a second essence, and the distribution from that which first has being [*esse*] to the second that it may be. This we can argue through examples from nature.[16]

The words "to the second [essence] *that it may be* [emphasis added]" (*secundae ut sit*) already contain within themselves the interior unravelling of the very model of participation that the nutritor is attempting to establish. The grammatical logic implies that the second essence must already in some sense "be" in order to receive the distribution of being that will allow it to "be" in the first place. The second essence is posited as a being that must pre-exist its own being in order to be in order to receive its being. Eriugena's language does not distinguish between essence and existence in a manner that allows us to solve the dilemma by simply conceiving of essences subsequently given existence.

The being that preexists its own being haunts the passage as an ontological shadow. The dilemma will be recognized by the alumnus, and what begins as an intimation will expand to challenge the intelligibility of the language and tradition of both nutritor and alumnus. The facility with which the nutritor begins his exposition of participation will turn, under sharp questioning from the alumnus, to an argument that hovers at the edge of collapse, and to a general critique of spatial, temporal, and causal signification within the language of creation.

The nutritor goes on to explain the doctrine of participation through the use of an emanation metaphor.

> A river first flows entire from its source. The water which first wells up in the source extends along all channels and is poured forth continuously. In this way the divine *bonitas*, essence, life, wisdom and whatever is in the source of all things, flow out first into the primordial causes and make them be. They then run through the primordial causes into their effects in an ineffable way through the orders of the universe that are appropriate to them, flowing forth through the higher to the lower; to return back again to their source through the most secret channels [*poros*] of nature by a most hidden course.[17]

This flow through the levels of being has two phases: it first wells up (*surgit*) within the source and then flows from the source (*ex fonte* . . .

manat). The words that are used for "flow out" (*ex manare*) form the Latin root of "emanation." After welling up within the source, the good (*bonitas*),[18] essence, life, and wisdom, and everything "which is in the source of all things" then "flow out first into the primordial causes" and "make them be" (*eas esse faciunt*).

There is an inescapable dilemma in the nutritor's image of a river gushing from its source and pouring down into the various levels of being. How can "being" flow into the primordial causes and "make them to be?" They would first already have to "be" in order to act as vessels receiving the flow of being. The language of emanation (the flowing out of being) carries within itself, even more deeply than the language of participation, the ontological shadow; the object of the phrase "make them to be" implies a being that must preexist its own being in order to be the object of the activity that posits its being. Another aporia can be found in the emanation metaphor with the preposition "into." The spatial paradigm invoked by the phrase "[of the flowing] into the primordial causes" (*in primordiales causas*) is being used to express causal or existential meaning.

It would be easy to dismiss such a concern with the minutiae of grammar and with what might seem an unduly literal reading of a preposition. For the nutritor, however, such a summary dismissal has serious consequences. The delimitations of language become invisible and consequently much more powerful and destructive. At issue is the dependence of thought upon language. To claim that such language should not be taken spatially is to ignore the power of language. The spatial element in a preposition cannot be willed away as if it were not fundamental to the word. As the dialogue proceeds, the nutritor will insist that to believe such spatial connotations can be willed away is to become all the more vulnerable to what he will call the "monstrous and abominable idols" hidden within such language.

Before They Are (*Priusquam Essent*)

The nutritor expands upon the overflowing, self-diffusive character of the good (*bonitas*), a concept that can be traced back chronologically to Proclus, Plotinus, and Plato. Like Dionysius, Eriugena identifies the good with the trinity. The threefold good's unexhausted diffusion "from itself in itself back to itself" is first said to be the cause of all (*omnia*), and then said to be all.[19] The following passage begins with a statement of the good's diffusions of itself. Then in several successive, parallel sentences, the grammatical subject changes from the good, to understanding (*intellectus*), to the gnostic power (*virtus gnos-*

tica), and finally to the deity (*deus*). It becomes clear that all these terms are viewed as the identical source of emanation:

> For the motion of the supreme and threefold and only true *bonitas*, which in itself is immutable, and its being multiplied while yet remaining simple, and its unexhausted diffusion from itself in itself to itself, is the cause of all; indeed is all. For if the understanding of all is all and it alone understands all, then it alone is all. Only that is the gnostic power which knows all things before they are, and does not know all things outside itself because outside it there is nothing; instead it holds all things within itself. For it encircles all and there is nothing within it, which, insofar as it truly is, is not itself,[20] for it alone truly is. The other things that are said to be are its theophanies, which also subsist in it. Therefore God is everything that truly is because he himself makes all and is made in all, as St. Dionysius the Areopagite says.[21]

Apart from having to sift through the subject nouns in order to locate possible antecedents for the final pronoun "it," the alumnus has to deal with a deeper problem. The laws of causality seem to be violated in the claim that the diffusion is *both* the cause of all things *and* at the same time the "all things" of which it is the cause.

The passage also offers some particularly rich examples of the transformation of the spatial and temporal into the causal and existential. Temporal and spatial meanings of *ambit* (encircles) and *priusquam essent* (before they are) are put under particular pressure. The meaning of "it encircles" is distorted. Encirclement is the movement of one object around another object. That second object exists before it is encircled or independently of its being encircled. In the emanation metaphor, however, the things that are encircled are the result of the encircling. In addition, the objects encircled are said to be within the gnostic power that encircles them (not within the circle traced by an exterior object). Finally, insofar as they are within the power that encircles them, they are the power that encircles them. The "all things" as objects of the verb "encircles" in its standard sense exist outside of that activity of encircling only as ontological shadows— affirmed at one level of being and negated at another.

Similar transformations occur with the phrase *priusquam essent*. The gnostic power is said to know things "before they are," i.e., in their existence within the primordial causes. This term "before" is not meant to be understood in the temporal sense. The nutritor states explicitly in a later passage (644b; SW 3:130–31) that there is no temporal priority between one level of reality and the next. The priority implied by the term *priusquam* is neither temporal nor spatial, but rather causal. The gnostic power causes all things by knowing them. Rather than knowing things that exist independently of that knowing, things exist because it knows them. To better evoke this creative knowing, the nutritor changes from a temporal to a spatial metaphor: the intellect "knows all things but not outside itself since outside it there is nothing, but it possesses all things within itself." The temporal metaphor of knowing things "before they are" is joined by the spatial metaphor of knowing things as "within it." In the metaphor of encirclement, the temporal and spatial possibilities of *priusquam* are fused and then transformed into a causal sense. *Priusquam* can govern a purpose clause (e.g., he destroyed the bridges "before" they could arrive, i.e., in order that they not arrive), but a purpose clause is usually one of anticipation or prevention. Here the clause is existentially causal. The gnostic power "befores" the objects it encircles into being, as it were.

Are these spatial and temporal metaphors not simply a tortured way of speaking of potentialities actualized in time and space? As with other apophatic writings, the point is not so much what is being said as how it is being said. The confusion of cause and effect points to a larger conflict between two paradigms of being that are posited within this passage. The first is a nonapophatic hierarchical paradigm of participation: each level of being "participates" in the higher being immediately above it. Yet when the nutritor's understanding of that participation is pushed to its logical conclusion, then all things, insofar as they truly are, are nothing other than the good, the supreme source of the diffusion. From this latter perspective, the levels of being, and the diffusion down through the levels of being, no longer exist. The second paradigm collapses the levels into one another. As the nutritor says, "It [the good or the gnostic power] alone truly is."

The phrase "insofar as" is the key link between the diffusion down through the levels of being (a diffusion that posits those levels of being even as it flows over them) and the true existence of all things in the original source. The good or the gnostic power encircles all things, and "there is nothing within it, which, insofar as [*in quantum*] it truly is, is not itself." We can formulate this principle, which I will henceforth call the *in quantum* principle, as follows: when X is in Y, insofar as X truly is, it is Y.

In linking the two paradigms, the *in quantum* principle provides a glimpse into the deeper apophatic dynamic: the movement down and out into the articulated levels of being and the movement back up to the true being of all things in the one source are the same movement. We might conceive of the procession as a telescope unfolded out into its articulations and the return as the collapsing of the layers of the telescope back in on one another. There are three stages to this simultaneous expansion and retraction:

1. The good or the gnostic power diffuses itself out into the articulated levels of beings, and in so doing "makes them to be."

2. But insofar as they truly are, all these graded beings are in their source, and insofar as they are in their source, they are their source.

3. Thus the diffusion that flows out and makes them to be is the same movement by which, when they truly are, they become identical to their source.

It is within the double motion that the spatial and temporal terms "within," "before," and "encircles" are syntagmically altered by their apophatic context, creating a series of implicit, contexted metaphors in which the good knows all things (*omnia*) into being, befores things into being, encircles them into being.[22]

Theophany

In the midst of these transformations of spatial and temporal senses of "before," "within," and "encircles," the nutritor introduces the word "theophany" (*theophania*). The word is derived from the Greek *theos* (god) and *phaino* (bring to light, make appear, come to light, appear). A theophany is an appearance or manifestation of deity. After saying that "it [the good, the gnostic power] alone truly is," the nutritor goes on to say that "the other things that are said to be are its theophanies, which also subsist in it." The nutritor sums up the theophanic conception of participation toward the end of this passage with a play upon words *in ipsa vere subsistunt*: "[They] subsist truly in it." It is as if the expression were being broken down into its components: stand (*sisto*) under (*sub*) in (*in*). This single phrase contains both the opening and closing of the telescopic levels of being. The "under" refers to the layers of articulated beings, one under the other. The "in" refers to the existence of all beings in their source. The concept of "subsistence" is revealed to be an oxymoronic standing-under-in, as if one could simultaneously be under and in something.

The subsistence of all things in their source echoes previous transformations of spatial and temporal terms: *ambit* (encircle), *priusquam essent* (before they are), *ut sit* (that it might be), and *eas esse faciunt* (make them to be). Each term moves through a variety of meanings within the procession and return: from the temporal and spatial modes; to the causal level where the encircling causes the things it encircles, for example; to the final level of identity, where the gnostic power is said to cause all things and to be the things it causes. "It is the cause of all, truly it is all" (*causa omnium, immo omnia est*). Or, as the nutritor puts it, replacing the gnostic power with *deus*: "Therefore God is everything that truly is because he himself makes all things and is made in all things."

Theophany, as embodying the complex set of temporal, spatial, and causal transformations, also expresses itself in an extended series of antinomies:

> For everything that is understood and sensed is nothing other than the apparition of the non-apparent, the manifestation of the hidden, the affirmation of the negated, the comprehension of the incomprehensible, the utterance of the unutterable, the access to the inaccessible, the intellection of the unintelligible, the body of the bodiless, the essence of the beyond-essence, the form of the formless, the measure of the immeasureable, the number of the unnumbered, the weight of the weightless, the materialization of the spiritual, the visibility of the invisible, the place of the placeless, the time of the timeless, the definition of the infinite, the circumscription of the uncircumscribed, and the other things which are both conceived and perceived by the intellect alone and cannot be retained within the recesses of memory and which escape the blade of the mind.[23]

The above theophanic antinomies are likened by the nutritor to the working of the human mind. The mind is unmanifest in itself but is capable of manifestation and communication when it takes on sensible "vehicles" (*vehicula*) through words. It is silent, yet cries out; invisible, yet apparent. The antinomies are all oblique. In each case the negative term remains at a higher level of being than the positive term. Just as the gnostic power knows all things "within" itself rather than "without," so the working of the logos entails an oblique dialectic: invisible internally (*intrinsecus*), yet seen externally (*extrinsecus*).[24] The intrinsic element is opposed to the extrinsic within the spatial metaphor, but from the perspective of the higher level of being the intrinsic element is beyond all duality of intrinsic and extrinsic. The interiority, then, has a double function. It is opposed both to exteriority and, through the contextual transformation, to the duality of interiority and exteriority. Once exposed, this oblique dialectic can be read back into the more dynamic language of emanation, e.g., into the distinction between welling up and flowing out.

The nutritor sums up this theophanic understanding by stating that "the ineffable diffusion makes all and is made in all and is all."[25] This formula, similar to the earlier formula that "it is the cause of all and is all," is now more comprehensible in view of the previous discussion of theophany and the "insofar as" principle. Yet its full significance cannot be grasped until the onto-theology of the early Church councils is replaced by a nonessentialist understanding of deity. The alumnus senses that a step has been skipped:

> The mind, as you say, makes and takes from matter created outside itself those vehicles in which it is conveyed to the senses of others. The divine good, however, outside of which there is nothing, takes the matter for its manifestation not from something, but from nothing.
>
> But when I hear or say that the divine good created all from nothing, I do not understand what is signified by that name, "nothing," whether the privation of all essence or substance or accident, or the excellence of the divine beyond-essence.[26]

Overflowing All

The alumnus has hit upon the key to the argument of Book 3. In the second half of the book, the nutritor and alumnus revisit the question raised earlier concerning that which makes and is made in all things, but now from the perspective of an interpretation of *creatio ex nihilo*. The argument is not developed sequentially. It wanders out into ever more digressive orbits in which several key themes—the nature of matter, lack of temporal priority, participation, identification, and nothingness—recur in differing patterns.

The nutritor's discussion of *creatio ex* (or *de*) *nihilo*, "creation from, or out of, nothing" is founded upon a critique of the three most common interpretations of the phrase *ex nihilo*: temporal, spatial, and material. The temporal meaning implies that the creator exists prior to this creation, and that "nothing" was there prior to its becoming the creation into which it was made. In the common analogy of the sculptor and the statue, there was a time when the statue did not exist. The spatial meaning and the material meaning are closely related. The word "from" relates a creator or maker to something outside of itself, to some kind of material or place out of which he fashions his creation. Thus an artist might fashion a sculpture from a rock, and we might be tempted to think of the creator fashioning its creation out of a blank area outside of itself. The block is both the locus and the material cause of the sculpture. The block is a thing different from the sculpture that is made "out of" it, just as it is a thing different from the sculptor, the efficient cause. Each of these three meanings of "making from" will be destabilized through the language and logic of apophasis.

The discussion of *creatio ex nihilo* begins with the tension between the temporal sense of the terms "from nothing" and the nutritor's assertion that there is no temporal priority of the eternal source or creator over the created primordial causes. Even matter is "eternally made" within the divine mind.[27] Thus there never was a time when all things did not exist in their primordial causes. But the temporal sense of "from nothing" implies that there was a time when they were not: "How can all things be eternal in the divine wisdom and yet made out of nothing in the sense that before they were made they were not?"[28]

Against this objection, the nutritor argues that the temporal sense of *ex nihilo* is in contradiction to the principle that "nothing happens accidentally to God" (*nihil deo accidit*). If the priority of creator to created were temporal, if the deity were to be unwilling to create at one point and then willing to create at another, that deity would be subject to change and accident. The priority can only be causal (*qua causa omnium*). This causal priority is then referred back to the concept of participation, the subsistence of the effect within its cause.[29]

The effort to go beyond the temporal sense of "from nothing" leads to a breakdown of the spatial sense of the preposition "in." Divine priority over the universe is solely causal, not temporal. The universe always has participated in its cause. It therefore follows—as indeed the nutritor had shown earlier—that the universe is eternal in its cause, the divine word.[30] The alumnus points out how all numbers subsist eternally in the monad, their cause, even as they proceed from it. As a prime example of effects subsisting in their reasons or causes, the nutritor cites our own human existence: "We are nothing else, insofar as we are, but those reasons of ours subsisting eternally in *deus*."[31] The statement that effects subsist *in* their causes is the first step in making explicit the alteration of the meaning of *in* from spatial to causal.

The *in quantum* or "insofar as" principle reappears here with both its importance and its seeming absurdity more apparent. In other contexts, the expression "what we are, insofar as we are," would be a pointless redundancy. Here the expression is used in connection with the concept of subsistence (that the effect subsists in its cause) to relate (and collapse) the levels of being. The "insofar as we are" presupposes an "insofar as we are not" as its counterpart. This counterpart is the same "ontological shadow" that haunted the doctrine of participation in which all things were said to "receive their being" from a higher essence. For what were they before they received their being? If we take the temporal priority out of the last question, out of the "before," then we ask: "what are they insofar as they are not?" If we define participation as subsistence in one's cause, then we ask: "what are they insofar as they are 'outside' their cause?"

After reaffirming the existence of all things in their primordial causes or reasons, the nutritor connects the eternal being-of-and-in the primordial causes with the divine word itself. The telescoped layers and levels of being are enfolded back into one another: all things are in their higher principle and insofar as they are in the higher principle, they are that higher principle.[32] The effects *sub*sist *in* the primordial causes. The primordial causes *sub*sist *in* the word. Once again the tension between under (*sub*) and in (*in*) is the linguistic hinge for the expanding and collapsing of the hierarchical levels. The word's diffusion *is the subsistence of all things*.[33] We have here a classic paradox of emanation and return: (1) The procession of the word out into all things is the subsistence of all things; but (2) the subsistence of all things is nothing other than ontological return in which each thing subsists—and thus truly "is" insofar as it is—*in its cause.*

The spatial, temporal, and material senses of *creatio ex nihilo* have been exposed and critiqued. Temporal and spatial relations, at the microlevel of the preposition, have been destabilized and reconfigured within the paradox of procession and return. Within this reconfiguration, the nutritor directly cites Dionysius' language of "transcendence" and "overflowing." The immediate context of the citation evokes a transformation and reconfiguration of meaning in the terms *trans* and *over*. By citing Dionysius' passage on overflowing, the nutritor is preparing the way for his most dramatic and far-reaching move in his reinterpretation and retrieval of the self-diffusive quality of the Neoplatonic good. The passage of Dionysius, as translated by Eriugena and cited by the nutritor, refers to the divine word as

> undiminished even as superseding [*superans, proexon*] and overflowing [*supermanans, hyperbluzon*] all things in itself in a single and incessant bounty that is overfull [*superplenam, hyperplērē,*] and cannot be diminished.[34]

Eriugena has placed this citation from Dionysius within an apophatic context that multiplies its interior shifts in meaning within the paradox of procession and return. Thus the *logos* flows into all things (the spatial metaphor is exposed), it flows them into being (the metaphor of diffusion), and it overflows them, i.e., it transcends the things it has flowed into being, or it transcends the self it has flowed into being.

One final step is needed before Eriugena can complete his exploration of the metaphor of overflowing. This final step was foreshadowed by the alumnus's question cited above: "But when I hear or say that the divine good created all from nothing, I do not understand what is signified by that name, 'nothing', whether the privation of all essence or substance or accident, or the excellence of the divine beyond-essence." All understandings of nothing as privation—be they based upon temporal, spatial, or material paradigms—have been discredited. The alternative, hinted at by the alumnus in his mention of the "beyond-being," is the nonsubstantialist understanding of deity.

Being as Beyond Being

To set the stage for this final step, the nutritor offers another version of the metaphor of diffusion. The word or wisdom is depicted as "running and extending itself into all things," an extension that is itself all things.[35] This formula occurs in a passage that completes the critique of the substantialist interpretations of *creatio ex nihilo* and paves the way for a nonsubstantialist understanding. The passage culminates in a rejection of such substantialist reifications—temporal, spatial, and material—as monsters and abominable idols (*monstra abominandaque idola*):

> Wisdom's fusion, or extension, or running, or however else the infinite multiplication of the word is denoted, is not, as it were, into what already existed *before* the word or wisdom of the father was diffused or was extended or ran, but that very effusion or extension or running precedes all and is the cause of the existence of all and is all. For who, bearing in mind the truth, would believe or conceive that God had prepared for himself places through which he might diffuse himself, he who is contained in no place since he is the common place of all and therefore, as place of places, is confined by no place; or that he had prepared for himself spaces or times through which he might extend himself or run his course, he who lacks all spaces and transcends through his eternity all times? Or who would say something even more unbelievable; I mean that spatial, temporal, or other kinds of quantitative intervals had been prepared for God himself as though by another principle

for him to then fill by the diffusion of himself or traverse in his motion or solidify by the extension of himself? For not only to say such things of the ineffable nature beyond-essence, but even to conceive or picture them in false imaginings is most ridiculous and dangerous. There is no more disgraceful death and none worse for the rational soul than to conceive of the creator of all things with such monsters and abominable idols.[36]

The nutritor has combined his critique of temporal and spatial delimitations of the divine with an explicit statement of what such delimitations entail: death of the rational spirit. By "reason" the nutritor has in mind something other than the respect for rules of logic and argumentation that is sometimes called discursive reason. Elsewhere he characterizes reason as a being-in-constant-motion, a continual movement of the mind, an infinitely deepening exploration of a reality that itself has no end.[37] Finally, in its movements of division and resolution, reason not only mirrors but enacts the procession of all things out into multiplicity and existence and the resolution back into the unity beyond being (and beyond reason itself).

At odds with this conception of the rational spirit is what may be termed the idolatry of the preposition. Locked within seemingly innocuous words like "in," "to," "into," "from," and "before" is a semantic delimitation, a circumscribing of the unlimited within spatial and temporal categories. That delimitation is all the more effective in suffocating the rational spirit when it goes unrecognized or when theologians attempt to dispel it by fiat, claiming that no spatial or temporal sense is intended.

For the nutritor, such idols of the preposition cannot be willed away or asserted away. Mere assertions, such as the assertion that the terms are not to be taken temporally or spatially, fall apart in the face of the inherent linguistic structures built around a substantialist understanding of the divine, structures that lock the referent of theological language into spatial and temporal categories, all protestations notwithstanding. Yet up to this point no alternative to the temporal, spatial, and causal interpretations of *creatio ex nihilo* has been offered. The alternative is discovered in yet another Dionysian paradox: "the being of all things is the beyond being." The nutritor makes a direct citation: "He [Dionysius] says":

> It is true that through the universal good, the divinity beyond being has brought out into being the essences of the things that are by substantiating them. For this is proper for the cause of all and the good beyond all: to call the

things that are into communion with itself as it is determined for each according to its appropriate analogy. All things, therefore, participate in the providence flowing forth from the divinity beyond-essence and beyond causation. For perhaps they would not exist except by taking upon themselves the essence and principle of all that are. Therefore all that exist participate in its being [*esse*]—*for the being of all is the beyond being, divinity* [*esse enim omnium est super esse divinitas / To gar einai pantōn estin hē hyper to einai theotēs*].[38]

This quote from Dionysius brings together the paradoxes of Eriugena's doctrine of participation and identification. Dionysius says that the good calls beings into communion with itself, but he also says that this communion or participation is their being. By the time the nutritor cites this passage, the previous discussion has made a central issue of the ontological shadow: what were the beings *before* they were called into being in order that they could be "called?" The paradox destabilizes the temporal sense of the "before." This is the stage of identification and immanence. The beings participate in the being of the good, they are that being, or rather it is their being. Then Eriugena uses Dionysius to make the final step into complete paradox: "The being of all is the beyond-being, divinity."

In chapter 1, we saw Plotinus depict a glowing mass within an illumined sphere. Then, in a second step, he asked the reader to withdraw the glowing mass, so that the source of light is everywhere and nowhere. I used this two-step illustration to represent Plotinian apophasis. In Eriugena, one of the most powerful moments of "withdrawing the burning mass" occurs here where the nutritor and alumnus withdraw being from the deity, arriving at a nonsubstantialist understanding of *creatio ex nihilo*.

Eriugena has placed in close proximity the key Dionysian metaphor of "overflowing all" and the Dionysian paradox that the being of all beings is the beyond-being, divinity. The effect of the metaphor and the paradox are heightened by the previous destabilization of the temporal, spatial, and causal implications of the *ex nihilo* and by the use of the paradox of procession and return. By placing the Dionysian formulations within such a context, Eriugena has given them a particular apophatic intensity. By intensity, I mean the ability for a single formula to contain an unusually wide set of semantic transformations. We can outline the transformations in these two formulations as follows.

Overflows All (The Emanation Formulation)
1. Transformation of the normal spatial sense of overflow (i.e., "flow over").
2. Transformation of the normal temporal implications of "overflow all things": the things in our context do not exist before they are "flowed over," but rather exist as a result of the flowing over.
3. Transformation of the sense of "overflow" from spatial and temporal to causal.
4. The stage of identification and immanence: the cause is the effect, the flowing is identified with the things it "flows into being."
5. Assertion of transcendence with a new meaning of "over" in "overflow." The one "overflows," i.e., it transcends the things it flows into being.

The Being of All Things Is the Beyond-Being, Divinity: (The Participation/Identification Formula)
1. All things assume their being from the being of *bonitas*, all things participate in the higher being. They subsist (stand *under*) *in* it.
2. Insofar as they are, they *are* in the being of the good. This expression puts pressure upon the "under" in *subsist*. Insofar as they *are*, they are *in* the good, since goodness is their cause (*in* as causal rather than spatial).
3. The phase of immanence, the identity of cause and effect: insofar as they are *in* the good they *are* the good.
4. The being of all things is beyond being (the good), divinity. The last statement affirms transcendence (through the "beyond"), and immanence (through the identity form of the sentence: being *is* beyond being).

Further on in the dialogue the nutritor recalls still another key Dionysian passage:

> [Providence, *pronoia*] proceeds into all things, is made in all, and contains all, and yet in itself it is, through its excellence, nothing in nothing through nothing, but surpasses all.[39]

The above passage continues with a characteristic Neoplatonic assertion that while it [wisdom] proceeds, it remains, and while it remains, it proceeds. Again Eriugena renews and intensifies Dionysian paradoxes by placing them within his destabilization of temporal and spatial semantics at the level of the preposition. The nutritor plays the Dionysian dialectic of transcendence and immanence upon the previously established transformations of the meaning of "in." A growing number of linguistic vectors have been applied to such prepositions throughout the dialogue. The wisdom proceeds *into* all things, and contains all things, i.e., all things are *in* it. In proceeding *into* all, it becomes all, it can be said to proceed into itself, become itself, contain itself, and transcend itself.

> The Self-Containment Paradox
> 1. Wisdom proceeds into all things: transformations from spatial sense (of being contained in all things) to a causal sense (of causing all things) to identification (as being all things).
> 2. Wisdom is made or becomes (*fit*) in all.
> 3. Wisdom contains all: transformations from spatial sense (as containing all things) to a causal sense (of being the cause of all) to identification (as being all).
> 4. Wisdom transcends all.

When wisdom proceeds into all and is in all and is all there occurs a transition from unity (before it proceeds) to a posed duality (proceeds into all things) to a reaffirmation of unity or an identification (is all things). To say all things are *in* it, are it, but are transcended by it, is to reverse that process. The two "in"s hold the immanence-transcendence dialectic within a paradoxical movement of procession and return. From the perspective of procession, the higher essence proceeds "into" (causally) the lower essence and identifies with it. From the perspective of return, the lower essence is "in" (causally) the higher essence and thus is identical with it. Thus it transcends itself insofar as it is identical with the higher essence that is its source.

Eriugena then uses another Dionysian paradox of transcendence and immanence to comment in more general terms upon the apophatic, semantic transformation of temporal and spatial categories: "It appoints all beginnings and orders, yet is above every beginning and order. It is the measure of the things that are and their durations, yet is beyond and before duration."[40]

Just as it is the measure of all things yet is beyond measure, so in another Dionysian formula "It is the limit of all things, itself unlimited either by limit or limitlessness, beyond the contradiction between them."[41] This formula is not cited directly by the nutritor at this point in his argument, but it seems to underly his language. It could be outlined in a similar manner to the other dense Dionysian formulas outlined above. The nutritor ends his tour de force of Dionysian paradoxes by returning to his central claim, that the divine word makes all things and is made in all things, and thus is both eternal and made. The conclusion, of course, is that if such a statement is true, then all things are both eternal and made.[42]

The dialogue has now been charged by the Dionysian paradoxes and the Eriugenean refraction of them through semantic transformations. When the alumnus hears in this new context the claim that all things are "both eternal and made," he cries out: "I die, struck stupefied as a dead man" (*moror ac stupefactus velut exanimis haereo*, 646c). The reference to the dead man, in addition to adding emphasis to his exclamation, also serves to recall the previously evoked "death of the rational spirit." The immediate occasion for the alumnus's sense of dying is the identification of cause and effect, so that the *same things* are said to be both eternal and made (647a-b). However, underlying that paradox is the entire range of semantic transformations that the nutritor has previously established. A further implication generates an even stronger reaction on the part of the alumnus:

> And incomparably more lofty and amazing than these things seems to me to be what you assert on the authority of St. Dionysius the Areopagite, namely, that God himself is both maker of all and is made in all; for this was unknown and unheard of—by me, by many, by nearly all. For if this is so, who will not immediately burst out, exclaiming in this voice: "God is all things and all things God?" It will be considered monstrous even by those considered learned.[43]

The alumnus has been tactful, using deferential language and couching his objection as that of an anonymous third person. But his criticism is sharp. He has now turned back upon the nutritor the same word, monstrous, that the nutritor had used earlier. A chasm separates two different paradigms, two different modes of language. On one side is the scandalized reaction of one adhering to the distinction between creator and created, a distinction perceived as the sine qua non of creation language. On the other side is the apophatic abhorrence of the traditional interpretation of *creatio ex nihilo* as the mistaking of a temporally and spatially delimited image for the unlimited.

Apparition and Nothingness

The nutritor has used the Dionysian paradoxes to intensify and dramatize the apophatic transformation of temporal and spatial categories. He is now ready to recall and to deepen the notion of theophany that he had introduced earlier in the discussion.[44] Theophany is a form of *apparition*, he asserts, comparable to the appearance in visions of long-dead prophets. Matter does not cause visibility because in itself matter is incorporeal. Rather, quantities and qualities, formless matter, shapes and colors, all incorporeal in themselves, combine to form corporeal reality.[45] This position on corporality raises questions about the status of the four basic elements (air, earth, fire, and water). Are they not made "from nothing"? What does the "from nothing" mean? The question signals the return to and completion of the *ex nihilo* inquiry.

However, at this critical moment of tension, that return is displaced. When the alumnus asks again how all things can be both made and eternal, the nutritor wavers. Perhaps he is shaken by the alumnus's persistent objections. Perhaps he shrinks from elucidating what will become one of the strongest formulations of nonsubstantialist thinking ever offered in Western Christian tradition. In answer to the alumnus's question about things "being made and being eternal at the same time," he states: "they were always; they were not always" (*semper erant semper non erant*). He explains that the first half of the antinomy refers to their virtual being in the primordial causes, the second to their procession into the temporal world. "They 'were always' as causes in the word of God, in potentiality, beyond every quality and quantity." They "were not always":

> because before they flowed out through generation into the forms and species, places and times, and all the accidents which come upon their eternal subsistence that subsists incommunicably in the word of God, they were not in generation.[46]

However, the status of the "before" in the above statement is problematic. Throughout Book 3, the perspective has been nontemporal and temporality has been the center of apophatic critique and transformation. Here the nutritor speaks of a time "before" all things flowed out into their times and spaces. From the immediate perspective, in which temporal categories are submitted to a rigorous analysis, the question poses itself: how can there be a time "before" things flowed into time?[47]

The nutritor goes on to speak of just such a procession of things *into* space and time and their resolution back into their causes, bringing into play the combination of Neoplatonic emanation and Christian sacred history that will be the subject of much of the rest of the

Periphyseon. The tension between the atemporal perspective of the *ex nihilo* section of Book 3 (chaps. 5–23) and the sacred history that follows is ultimately resolved through an apophatic interpretation of the fall of Adam: there never was a time when humankind occupied paradise, never was a time "before" the fall. The fall cannot be truly the fall until the return is completed and there is an actual dwelling in paradise. This notion combines Christian sacred history and the Plotinian paradox that the procession is the return. However, within the context of Book 3, the nutritor has strayed from his perspective.[48] The apophatic voice wavers under the persistent questioning of the alumnus. The nutritor had begun the discussion assuring the alumnus that *participation* was "most easily" understood. The alumnus then forced him to follow his apophatic position to its logical extreme. The nutritor is now in a position of vulnerability, and the humble questions of the alumnus—which are in fact the questions of later institutional opposition to apophatic mysticism—come close to overturning the authority relation of nutritor and alumnus, and to breaking the nutritor's resolve.[49]

The nutritor's earlier prediction that "participation" was most easily (*facillime*) understood now takes on its full irony. Behind the deference of the student has been a rigorous questioning that may have led the nutritor to a more radical position than he might have originally envisaged. Past scholarship has raised questions about the genuineness of the dialogue between nutritor and alumnus, if in fact the alumnus is a not a mere literary foil for the nutritor's expositions. At this key moment in the dialogue, the answer to that question becomes clear. The nutritor is thrown off balance and is searching to find a way out of his predicament. The stakes have been raised progressively to the point that any error will take on the status of a monster or an abomination. The classical interpretations of *de nihilo* have been thoroughly exposed and unraveled, but no clear alternative has been discovered. A true drama is unfolding within the technical language and academic niceties. Not the least element in that drama is the sense that at this point in the dialogue the nutritor and alumnus have become equals in the discussion, pushing it toward a conclusion it might not have reached had the nutritor merely propounded his own preconceived ideas.

The alumnus acknowledges that all things are eternal ("in the word of God") but are also made ("in time through generation in forms and species and accidents"). But then he admits he still doesn't understand how it can accord with reason that in the word of God all things are both eternal and made.

> Do you think, therefore, that I wished to teach that all things insofar as they are eternal are eternal in the only begotten word of God, but insofar as they are made are made apart from the word?[50]

Although the alumnus was perhaps too polite to say it, he might well have argued that the position from which the nutritor here recoils is in fact a very reasonable inference from his earlier distinction between all things as they are in the word of God before the procession into time and space, and all things in their concrete temporal and spatial instantiations. Throughout the preceding dialogue, the nutritor has placed the temporal paradigm (before, after) and the spatial paradigm (within, without) in rigorously parallel constructions. The intricate semantic transformations that were carried out in the critique of classical understandings of *creatio ex nihilo* intensified the parallelism between spatial and temporal paradigms. When the nutritor distinguishes all things in their eternity "in" the word from all things "after" they proceed into space and time, the previously constructed parallelism does suggest that in spatial terms the being of all things after their procession into space and time is a being outside of the word.

In order to avoid the implication from which he is recoiling, the nutritor must transform the meaning of "before," along the lines of its transformation in early discussions of emanation. But in order to do that he must now find an alternative to the meaning of "nothing" in "creation from nothing." The nutritor has saved face by attributing to the alumnus a possible implication of his own, wavering position. Now he clarifies his *in quantum* (insofar as) language by showing what it does not mean. It does not mean (as his own previous formulation had implied) that things are made insofar as they are in the sensible world, and are eternal insofar as they are in the logos. The position is now more extreme and more paradoxical: all things, insofar as they are, are *both eternal and made in the logos*. The real beginning of things is not their beginning in time, but rather within the eternal divine word which circumscribes all times. Whereas earlier the nutritor spoke of all things as being eternal "before" their being made through procession into temporal and spatial effects, now he claims that all things eternal and temporal—and eternity, time, space, and everything that is either substance or accident—are all both eternal and made "simultaneously" (*simul*) in the only begotten word of God.[51] Within their eternal beginning in the divine word is the reason (*ratio*) and occasion (*occasus*) for their procession into temporal reality. The divine word or wisdom in which all things have their beginning "is called by the Greeks *epekeina* ["beyond"] because it creates in itself and circumscribes all times, while in its entirety it is above all times, preceding, surrounding, concluding all intervals."[52]

Throughout this passage, the nutritor seems to allude to Dionysius' famous discussion of time in the *Divine Names*, and his solution is similar to the Dionysian formulation mentioned above, "It limits all things yet is their boundless infinitude." The word is said to precede, surround, and conclude all intervals of time. Again we find paradox. How can the timeless *precede* temporal intervals? As with *ambit* and *priusquam essent* in the earlier passage, the temporal sense of terms such as *praecedens* (preceding) and *concludens* (concluding) is subverted by the context. How can one precede or conclude time itself? This classic dilemma appears here not primarily as a doctrinal dispute on the eternity of the world, but rather as a continued linguistic saying and unsaying of temporal and spatial meanings. The apophatic language of emanation brings out the spatial reifications implicit in the concept of creation and by doing so begins the process of unsaying those reifications by turning them back upon one another.

Still, at this point, the assertion of an *epekeina*, of a beyond-time or beyond-space, cannot fully escape its status as mere assertion. As long as this "beyond-being" is treated ontologically, its appearance as a grammatical subject ("it" circumscribes) locks it into categories it allegedly transcends.[53] Even the act of calling it "beyond" reifies it through the spatial or temporal senses of "beyond" and through the implied deliminations within the act of naming it *epekeina*.

The nutritor goes on to make explicit what was implicit in the earlier text on participation.[54] There the understanding of all things was said not to be the understanding of preexistent objects. Instead, the understanding of them is their being itself. The equivalence of understanding and making is reflected in the union of other divine attributes:

> But if its will is its vision and its vision its will, everything that it wills is made, without any interval intervening; and if everything it wills to be made it sees to be made, and if what it wills and sees is not external to itself but within itself, and there is nothing within it which is not itself, it follows that everything that it sees and wills should be understood as coeternal with it, if its will and vision and essence are one.[55]

The alumnus is finally forced to conclude that since the divine nature is simple, and since it eternally willed, beheld, and made all things in itself, then the things it made in itself are nothing other than it (since a simple nature could contain neither foreign elements nor parts). The conclusion is remarkably similar to the Plotinian one when it was depicted as "being as it willed/made/thought (causal) himself to be," with the identification of act and essence. And just as with Plotinus's one, so Eriugena's nature transcends the self that it made itself to be.

The vision of a nonentified divinity can now burst through:

> *Alumnus:* Please explain what holy theology means by that name of "nothing."
> *Nutritor:* I would believe that by that name is signified the brilliance of the divine *bonitas*, ineffable, incomprehensible, inaccessible, and unknown to all intellects whether human or angelic—for it is beyond being and beyond nature—which while it is conceived through itself neither is nor was nor shall be, for it is understood to be in none of the things that exist because it surpasses all things, but when, by a certain ineffable descent into the things that are, it is beheld by the eyes of the mind, it alone is found to be in all things, and it is and was and shall be. Therefore so long as it is understood to be incomprehensible by reason of its transcendence it is not unreasonably called "nothing," but when it begins to appear in its theophanies, it is said to proceed, as it were, out of nothing into something, and that which is properly thought of as beyond all essence is also properly recognized in all essence, and therefore every visible and invisible creature can be called a theophany, that is, a divine apparition. For every order of nature from the highest to the lowest, that is, from the celestial essences to the furthest bodies of this visible world, the more secretly it is understood, the closer it is seen to approach the divine brilliance. Hence the inaccessible brilliance of the celestial powers is often called by theology darkness.[56]

From here the nutritor is led to cite the Psalms ("as his darkness is, so is his light") and to speak of a continuity whereby things become more manifest the further they are from this darkness beyond being: "The further down that the order of things descends, the more manifestly that order opens itself to the eyes of those contemplating it, and therefore the forms and species of sensible things receive the name 'manifest theophanies'."[57] The nothing of "creation from nothing" is now understood as the incomprehensible beyond beingness of the word, and "being" is now understood as the manifestation or comprehensibility of that nothingness. The term "comprehend" (*comprehendere*) has a concrete sense related to other spatial terms of Eriugenian apophasis such as "encircle." Eriugena combines both the concrete sense of spatial motion and the more abstract sense of comprehension (which in English as "understand" has its own hidden, spatial metaphor, "standing under") when he calls the beyond-essence "incomprehensible."

At one point in Book 3, in an apparent aside, the nutritor had stated that one can know *that* the divine is but not *what* it is. In Book 4 he will state that not even God can know what God is. And later in Book 3 he cites Dionysius' claim that one cannot say "it is this kind of thing but not that" since it is all.[58] "Nothing" is the word before it makes itself to be, before it comprehends itself into being.[59] When the circle is completed, the word comprehends itself and makes itself within the forms of its theophany, yet it also transcends that theophany. Eriugena's view of reality is one of apparitional, nested layers of being whose ground is not a supreme being but a point that recedes infinitely just beyond every approach, a point he calls "nothing." Without a final "being" to which it can point, language is placed into perpetual movement. Or conversely, we could say that the theophanic and nonsubtantialist view of deity propounded by Eriugena can be glimpsed only momentarily through the interstices of apophatic discourse. That glimpse cannot be maintained. Apophasis is continual movement. When the semantic gaze is fixed, it is confronted with linguistic idols, the temporal and spatial reifications of a supreme being.

Eriugena was not the first to interpret *creatio ex nihilo* as emanation from the nothingness of deity. Gregory of Nyssa had suggested such an interpretation long before, and it has been suggested that a ninth century Latin work by the Carolingian author Fredegisus may have been moving in that direction.[60] What is distinctive about the *ex nihilo* section of Book 3 is the apophatic tension Eriugena generates by weaving key Dionysian passages into his own language. Just as the alumnus pushes the nutritor to a conclusion more radical than the nutritor may have achieved on his own, so Eriugena brings the paradoxes of his own nutritor, Dionysius, into a new register of semantic transformation.

Is the *Periphyseon* a mystical text? If we define mystical writing as the autobiographical account of personal, subjective experience, then the answer is no. Eriugena is explicit in his devotion to dialectical reason as a method of exploring nature. Just before the dramatic, final discussion of nothingness, when the alumnus is pressing him on how all things can be both eternal and made, the nutritor exclaims that the alumnus is seeking reason in those things in which all reason fails (*rationem in his in quibus omnis ratio deficit*). The original division of nature between things that are (things that can be grasped by the mind) and things that are not (things that transcend the grasp of the mind) has tied ontology to epistemology. To consider that which is not, the divine as nothing, is to consider that which is beyond even the broad and dialectical reason of Eriugena. The Eriugenean conception of the nothingness of deity entails a vision of reality as endless, of theophany as an apparition out of a bottomless ground of being. The mystery of being, of life, and of consciousness is unfathomable. No mind, not even the mind of the deity, can fully comprehend these mysteries, or as the nutritor says at one point, not even God can know God. Reason is led, by its own reasoning, beyond itself, continually, without arriving at a final entity or conclusion. In that particular sense of allowing reason to lead beyond itself, Eriugena can be considered a mystic.

Epilogue

In addition to his nonsubstantialist understanding of deity, Eriugena took a number of other controversial positions, including an open acknowledgment of the purely symbolic and conventional nature of the masculine imaging of the divine in Christian tradition, and a stark formulation of the conundrum that if the divine knew evil, then—being all-powerful—it would necessarily be the cause of evil. Protected by the French monarchy, Eriugena escaped persecution during his own lifetime, and his influence continued long after his death, reaching a high point in the prescholastic period. Among those who echoed Eriugena's ideas were Alan of Lille, Hugh of St. Victor, Joachim of Fiore, and members of the Chartres school. A popular paraphrase of Eriugenean thought entitled the *Clavis physicae* became a major vehicle for Eriugenean influence throughout the Middle Ages. By the early thirteenth century, according to Pope Honorius III, Eriugena's *Periphyseon* was being studied assiduously in monasteries and other study centers.[61] In the same period, however, Eriugena's work was associated with the followers of the condemned heretic Amalric of Bene. The council of Paris that condemned the ideas of Amalric ordered the burning of the books then in the possession of Amalric's disciples; among those books was *Periphyseon*. In 1225, Honorius III repeated the order, in more specific terms, that all copies of the *Periphyseon*—"swarming with the worms of heretical perversity"—be burned under threat of excommunication.[62] The condemnation quelled the direct and explicit influence of the *Periphyseon* in the later thirteenth century, the very age when the apophatic traditions in Judaism, Christianity, and Islam were reaching their culmination. The destruction of a large number of the Eriugenean texts also complicates our efforts to determine more exactly the influence of Eriugena on figures such as Meister Eckhart, though Eckhart seems to have known of Eriugena's work.[63]

The condemnation of Eriugena in the thirteenth century and the partially successful repression of his writings did not prevent his name from reemerging centuries later in a most intriguing way. Although there is no mention of Eriugena's death in the early sources, by the sixteenth century the legend had grown that before his death Eriugena left France for England, where he was put in charge of a monastery and later martyred. "John the Scot Eriugena" even appears in some of the sixteenth-century lists of martyrs. According to later legend, Eriugena was killed by sharpened styluses of his own students. The twelfth-century account of William of Malmesbury emphasizes the bitterness of his death; the combination of his students' vigorous malevolence and weak hands resulting in a prolonged agony of repeated stabbings. What relevance this legend may have had to the actual death of Eriugena, to the apophatic endeavor, or to the fate of teachers is difficult to define. It is a story, however, few writers on John the Scot are able to resist telling.[64]

The effort of the medieval Church to eradicate Eriugena's name and writings was only partially successful. Perhaps more successful in obscuring Eriugena's significance is the tendency to interpret the claim that *deus nihil est* (God is nothing) as meaning simply that the deity is beyond our normal categories and perceptions. As with other apophatic writers, Eriugena can never achieve an actual linguistic reference to any nonsubstantial deity and can never bring the unlimited into the delimiting categories of language reference. Any single proposition will contain a "something" and a substantial deity: theist, monist, pantheist, or atheist, depending upon the proposition chosen. But the nothingness of the deity is not a claim used merely for rhetorical effect or shock value. It is the unsayable premise that guides the language of saying and unsaying in an attempt to liberate it, however momentarily, from the spatial and temporal idols ("monsters and abominations") that are posed even in the attempt to affirm the transcendence of the deity.

Ironically, the tradition of mystical union that has come to be called "substantial union" is based upon the very nonsubstantialist principles that are given their most dramatic articulation in Eriugena.[65] The terms "monism" and "pantheism" as applied to specific authors like Eriugena or to generalized trends of thought are replete with reference to the divine as *substance*. Common generalizations about monotheism, about the difference between Western and Eastern concepts of deity, and the divinity itself—whether viewed as existing or nonexisting—are based upon a substantialist understanding of deity. However, the nutritor's critique of substantialist understandings of "creation from nothing," leaves no doubt that to make his "nothing" into a "something" is to betray his thought. Language "overflows" with meaning as the reified and substantial deity momentarily recedes. The transcendent nothingness engenders fear and repulsion as "monstrous," but for Eriugena it offers the possibility of a moment of authenticity, a letting go of the need to possess and control being.

CHAPTER THREE

Ibn ʿArabi's Polished Mirror: Identity Shift and Meaning Event

While looking at a smudged mirror the viewer sees the glass. If the mirror is polished, a shift occurs. The glass becomes invisible, with only the viewer's image reflected. Vision has become self-vision. Sufi mystics used the polishing of the mirror as a symbol of the shift beyond the distinction between subject and object, self and other.[1]

The language of Ibn ʿArabī (d. 1240 C.E. / A.H. 638) works continually toward a "polishing of the mirror."[2] It does not attempt a semantically stable reference to mystical union. The moment of transformation from nonreflexive to reflexive constitutes a "meaning event" that is continually reenacted as Ibn ʿArabi both uses and struggles against the dualistic structure of language.

Ibn ʿArabi was born in 1165/560 in Andalusia. After he passed his early childhood in Murcia, his family moved to Seville, the flourishing capital of the Almohad state. While still an adolescent, he achieved such a reputation for learning and wisdom that the aging and famous philosopher, Ibn Rushd (Averroes) asked for an audience with him. It was in Cordoba, the former capital of the Umayyad Caliphate, that he was initiated into the Sufi way of life. He then began a life-long journey from Andalusia, across the great cities of North Africa (Fez, Tunis, Cairo), to Mecca, to Konya in Asia Minor,[3] and finally to Damascus where today his tomb is a popular shrine.[4] More than two hundred works are attributed to him, and he is commonly acknowledged as the grand master (*al-shaykh al-akbar*) of Islamic mystical thought. Yet despite a strong renewal of scholarly interest in Ibn ʿArabi, he is still relatively unknown in the West.[5]

Ibn ʿArabi brings together in textual interplay the language worlds of classical Islamic civilization: Arabic poetry, scholastic theology (*kalām*), hermetic sciences (astrology, alchemy, and magic), Islamic law, and the various modes of Sufi literature.[6] In each new context, the event symbolized by the polishing of the mirror takes on a new hue, clothes itself in new vocabulary, and functions in a slightly different manner. As in a continually turning kaleidoscope, the configuration changes before we can adequately take it in. Although the various contexts are not systematized in a linear fashion, they are integrated dynamically. A passage will play on several language worlds simultaneously through the use of terminological polyvalence, or differing themes will be developed concurrently in a fugue-like movement. No single expression is self-sufficient. Each new passage reveals something and veils something. There is always an obscurity, an undefined term, a new paradox. The reader is led from passage to passage, from one question to another. It is the moving image rather than any particular frame that is significant. The perceptual shift symbolized by the mirror serves as the bridge between what is said and how it is said. It constitutes not only the subject of Ibn ʿArabi's discourse (the mystical experience of passing from duality to nonduality) but also the meaning event, the semantic dynamic of the text.

The meaning event occurs within a dialectic between two modes of language. The problems posed by this bimodal reference are contained in the Andalusian master's conception of *al-ḥaqq*, and the effort to translate the term faithfully requires a provisional strategy in dealing with these two modes. *Al-ḥaqq* means simply "the real," "the true," or "reality." The Qur'an placed the term in apposition to Allah, and thus it became commonly identified with the deity. In some Sufi contexts it is simply identified with Allah; in other contexts it is used to express a more abstract or less personal sense, what we might call today the ultimate or the absolute. Throughout the two chapters on Ibn ʿArabi, I will translate the term as "the real"—thus preserving its etymological sense (a sense often played upon in Sufi discourse) and its distinction from the personal name of the deity, Allah.

The first mode of the real is the *dhāt* (identity),[7] the absolute unity beyond the dualistic structures of language and thought, beyond all relation. The second mode consists of the divine names (*asmā'*) or, as they were called by the scholastic theologians, the attributes (*ṣifāt*), which correspond to the kataphatic realm in which the real can be named and placed into relationship with the world. Although in Islamic tradition there are said to be 99 divine names used in the Qur'an, for Ibn ʿArabi the divine names represent the entire range of references and predications that can be applied to divine reality. The number of divine names is therefore infinite, though Ibn ʿArabi usually has in mind the standard attributes such as will, knowledge, life, perception, compassion. "Allah" is viewed as the comprehensive divine name that includes all the others within it.

Ibn ʿArabi's approach to the divine names stands out in contrast to that of the scholastic theologians (*mutakallimūn*). The unity of deity is powerfully and continually affirmed in the Qur'an. At the confessional level, the affirmation of unity (*tawḥīd*) is simply the affirmation that there is no other deity than Allah. For the scholastic theologians, *tawḥīd* poses an urgent problem in interpreting the divine names or attributes. What does it mean when Allah is called in the Qur'an "the hearer," "the seer," or "the compassionate?" Are these attributes eternal? If the answer is yes, would not such a position contradict the interior unity of the deity by posing a number of eternal powers? If the attributes are not eternal, are we to imagine that the deity is subject to change and contingency, that at one time it was not hearing and then came to be hearing? Another question arises: are the attributes identical with the essence of the deity, or are they accidents?

To affirm the attributes is to risk the charge of *tashbīh*, the depiction of the deity by likening it to the human. If the deity "sees," does not such a characterization imply a human form of perception, and perhaps even an organ of perception? Particularly controversial were Qur'anic expressions referring to the "face" or "the two hands" of Allah. For some scholastic theologians, such expressions must be subjected to figurative interpretation (*ta'wīl*); the hands of Allah are figurative as allusions to the divine power, for example. Within the proliferation of positions and the intensification of polemic, a common dilemma recurs. The figurative interpretation risks vacating (*ta'ṭīl*) the deity of its Qur'anic attributes by explaining them away, while the literal affirmation of attributes entails anthropomorphism (*tajsīd*). Some simply affirmed that the attributes were valid, that Allah does see, hear, have a face, two hands, and sits upon a throne, but in a way that does not correspond to what creatures understand by such terms; such terms are to be affirmed without explaining "how" they are to be understood (*bi lā kayfa*).[8]

For Ibn ʿArabi the controversy over the divine names is epitomized by the dispute over the *ḥadīth* (saying attributed to Muhammad) that "Allah created Adam in his *ṣūra* [image, form]." For some theologians, the notion that Allah could have an image or form is inconceivable. How could a transcendent, unbound, absolutely unified deity have an image or form? The "his" in "his image" must refer simply to Adam's image: that is, Allah created Adam in Adam's image. Such a statement might mean, for example, that Allah created Adam as a fully developed human, rather than having him develop through the various embryonic and postembryonic stages of development. Other parties maintained that the "his" refers back to Allah.[9]

Ibn ʿArabi did not attempt an objective theological solution to the question. He did not add yet another position to the proliferation of increasingly sophisticated theological perspectives. The analysis that follows will demonstrate that the issue of the divine image was one of those issues that, rather than yielding to solution through rational argument, instead reveals the limitation of such argument. The issue forms an aporia, a dilemma within the categories of conventional logic and language. Rather than trying to find a theological position that would avoid both anthropomorphizing and explaining away the distinctiveness of the expression, Ibn ʿArabi, through the metaphor of the polished mirror, will imply that the antecedent to the "his" is neither the deity in itself nor Adam. Rather, it is at the moment of mystical union, symbolized by the polished mirror, that (to use the old convention of capitalizing pronouns referring to deity) His/his image is constituted. The constitution of this image occurs within the heart of "the complete human" (*al-insān al-kāmil*).

The Complete Human: Cosmogonic Aspect

The "complete human" has two aspects, cosmogonic and mystical. The cosmogonic myth of creation that recurs throughout the writings of Ibn ʿArabi includes the following stages: (1) "Before" the creation of the universe, the real existed only in its unmanifest stage, and thus did not know itself through its names. The names, which imply a relationship with the world, were unactualized. (2) The names (nonexistent in themselves) can be actualized only through the entities of a cosmos. In order to actualize the names, the real created a cosmos. The process of creation is called by Ibn ʿArabi, the "breath of the compassionate" (*nafas al-raḥman*). In some versions of the myth, Ibn ʿArabi draws out the paradox of the nonexistent names through an elaborate etymological and cosmic joke. The seven gatekeeper names (*sadana*) approach Allah in a delegation to complain that they are "tense" or constrained by the fact that they are unactualized (in fact, nonexistent). They are relationships, but the objects of the relations they signify do not exist; they are "keys to a treasure without a treasure."[10] Allah instructs the name "the compassionate" to breath into existence the world, a breathing or inspiring that will actualize the meanings of the names and "relieve" (*naffas*) them of their tension.[11] 3) The cosmos is like an unpolished mirror. In order for the mirror to shine and for the divine names to achieve actuality, the complete human is needed.[12]

Ibn ʿArabi's myth of the "breath of the merciful" has as a subtext the Qur'anic accounts of the creation of Adam. Two accounts are particularly important. In the first, the deity announces that it will create a caliph or regent (*khalīfa*) on earth. The angels ask why Allah would create a creature that "will spill blood and corrupt the earth" while they are perfectly obedient in reciting the praises of the deity. At this point the deity asks the angels if they know "the names." When the angels answer in the negative, they are taught the names by the newly created Adam and commanded by the deity to prostrate themselves before him. All do, except Iblis, who refuses to prostrate himself before Adam and is expelled from the divine presence (2:30–33).[13] Qur'anic exegetes offered various interpretations for the names that Adam taught the angels. For Ibn ʿArabi they are the "divine names" and Adam becomes a central symbol for the dilemma of how to name the divine.[14]

In the second account, Iblis's refusal to bow before Adam is woven into a direct reference to Adam's special place in the cosmos. Adam is unique in that the Qur'an depicts him as kneaded from clay by the "two hands" of God, and because of this two-handed kneading he received the spirit (*rūḥ*) breathed into him by the deity (38:71–75):

> When your lord said to the angels,
> I am going to create a person from clay.
> When I have shaped it
> and breathed into it of my spirit,
> fall bowing before it!
> All the angels fell bowing together
> Except Iblis who acted proud
> and became a disbeliever.
> He said: O Iblis
> what has prevented you from bowing
> before what I created with my two hands?
> Are you too proud or are you too lofty?[15]

The Qur'anic account of the angels' objection to the creation of Adam, their subsequent prostration before Adam, and Iblis's punishment for refusing to prostrate himself before Adam, became an interpretive touchstone for humanist, spiritualist, and intellectualist tendencies of Islam. A major arena of contention was the medieval cosmology of concentric spheres or heavens (seven to ten of them, depending upon the particular paradigm), and the myth of the ascent through the spheres or heavens to the divine throne. In Islam the *miʿrāj* of Muhammad became the paradigm for the ascent as well as a model for later Sufi ascents of Bistami and Ibn ʿArabi. Whether the guardians of the various heavens were intellects (as with the philosophers), angels, or human prophets, whether the guardians were hostile or benevolent to the human voyager, how the voyager moved from heaven to heaven (by secret password, inner purity, or some other test) all were clues to the ultimate goal of the quest. The voyager could seek to become more angelic, more intellectual, or, in the case of Ibn ʿArabi, more deeply human.[16]

The interpretation of the Iblis-Adam rivalry by al-Hallaj (d. 922 C.E.) offers a sharp contrast to Ibn ʿArabi's humanist interpretation. In Hallaj's version, Iblis is the most intimate companion of Allah and a tragic lover. He refuses to prostrate before Adam, a creature made of mud. Iblis argues that to prostrate himself before any other than God would be idolatry and polytheism. He interprets Allah's command to prostrate himself before Adam as a "test" that is at odds with Allah's inner will. He appeals to the fact that Allah has always already predetermined that Iblis could never prostrate himself before an other-than-God, even if at God's command. He states that he is willing to endure eternal punishment out of his loyalty to his beloved, Allah, even if that punishment includes banishment from the presence of the beloved.[17] Throughout this majestic interpretation, with its central ambiguities over Iblis's sincerity, a spiritualist position is assumed; humans should strive to become as purely spiritual as the angels.

Ibn ʿArabi emphasizes, in contrast to Hallaj, the humanist perspective.[18] Despite his human limitations, Adam has a distinguished place in the cosmos. That distinguished place is signaled by the reference to his having been made with the "two hands" of deity. Iblis, by refusing to bow before what Allah has made "with his two hands" shows his ignorance—an ignorance shared by the other angels who protested against the creation of Adam—of the place and role of the complete human being. Ibn ʿArabi's discussion of Adam is a deepening series of interpretations of the two poles or "hands" out of which the human is formed.

The Complete Human: The Mystical Aspect

In the image of the polished mirror, Ibn ʿArabi brings together the cosmogonic aspect of the complete human being, represented by the myth of the "breath of the compassionate," with the "passing away" (*fanāʾ*) of the ego-self in mystical union. By Ibn ʿArabi's time, after four centuries of development, Sufism had developed a number of interrelated discursive worlds: (1) a moral psychology with a highly sophisticated analysis of human self-deception; (2) a series of stations (*maqāmāt*) along a Sufi path leading to the passing away of the ego-self (*nafs*); (3) a complex of superogatory devotions, vigils, fasts, and meditations built upon the foundation of the prescribed ritual of the *shariʿa*; (4) a developed psychology of altered consciousness, with depictions of the various states (*aḥwāl*) that come upon the Sufi during the course of asceticism, devotions, and meditation; (5) a Sufi approach to the Qur'an and the hadith (extra Qur'anic statements attributed to Muhammad or to the divine voice), with special emphasis on the prophetic experiences of Adam, Abraham, Moses, Jesus, and Muhammad, and the *miʿraj*, Muhammad's ascent through the heavens to the divine throne; and (6) an exploration of erotic love, "erotic" in the sense of a love that causes the lover to lose consciousness of self—in the words of the poets, to go mad, to perish.[19]

The foundation text for Sufi understandings of mystical union as passing away was the *ḥadīth qudsī*, (a hadith in which the speaker is Allah) of "free devotions." The "godservant" (*al-ʿabd*) who fulfills both ritually prescribed and supererogatory or free devotions draws close to the deity and incites divine love. Then, in the words of the deity:

> When I [Allah] love my servant . . . I become the hearing with which he hears, the seeing with which he sees, the hand with which he grasps, the feet with which he walks, the tongue with which he speaks.[20]

For the Sufis, the condition indicated by this hadith cannot be attained as long as the Sufi is seeing, hearing, walking, touching, and speaking for and through himself. Through a quest for a life beyond egoism, through the ritual devotions of the Islamic *sharīʿa*, and through the supererogatory or free devotions of meditation, vigils, fasting, and devotions the Sufi arrives at the taming or the "passing away" of the ego-self. When the ego-self passes away, the divine sees, hears, walks, touches, and speaks, through the human faculties. Divine names (such as "the seer," "the hearer") are no longer "predications" of an exterior deity but realizations that occur at the moment the duality between human and divine is transcended.

The last phrase, "the tongue with which he speaks," was critical to explaining certain of the ecstatic sayings (*shataḥāt*) of the early Sufis, such as Abu Yazid al-Bistami's famous saying "Glory to me" (*subḥānī!*). Bistami's defenders interpreted the saying as actually being spoken by the deity at the moment of Abu Yazid's passing away.

A clear reference to the "hadith of free devotion" and to the mystical experience of *fanāʾ* occurs at the end of a passage attributed to Bistami in which mirror imagery is used as a symbol for mystical union. Various versions of the mirror image are offered, with a final comment that "with my tongue he [Allah] speaks and I have passed away":

> For thirty years God most high was my mirror, now I am my own mirror and that which I was I am no more, for "I" and "God" represent polytheism, a denial of his unity. Since I am no more, God most high is his own mirror. Behold, now I say that God is the mirror of myself, for with my tongue he speaks and I have passed away.[21]

It is at the intersection of the cosmogonic and the mystical that the divine image appears in the polished mirror. The cosmogonic perspective is mythic; it occurs out of time, at the creation of the cosmos (of which time is an element). The mystical perspective occurs in a moment of time that Ibn ʿArabi believes must be continually reenacted. The image occurs in the polished mirror in an "eternal moment" in which the distinction between the eternal and the temporal is displaced.

To reveal to It(self) through It(self) Its Mystery

Ibn ʿArabi's most widely read work, *Fuṣūṣ al-Ḥikam* (Ring Settings of Wisdom) consists of twenty-seven chapters, each dedicated to the wisdom of a particular prophet, beginning with Adam and ending with Muhammad.[22] Each prophet represents a "facet" of the complete human being. The Adam chapter opens in a hymnic mode, with a homage to Adam as the exemplar of the complete human being, the prototypical human consciousness that serves as the polishing of the mirror of the world. The metaphor of the polished mirror will ground Ibn ʿArabi's response to the theological question of the divine names. Through that polished mirror, the divine attributes or "most beautiful names" are refracted and reflected into their individual realities. The following discussion of the polished mirror will focus upon the hymnic opening of the Adam chapter. I have divided that section into three subsections in translation, called here sections 1a, 1b, and 1c.[23]

Section 1a weaves into Ibn ʿArabi's myth of creation the following particular themes: (1) the will of the real to see the instantiations of its "most beautiful names"; (2) the distinction between knowledge through another that "acts as a mirror" and knowledge without such an outside reflection; (3) the Qur'anic account of the "shaping" of the form of Adam and the inspiriting of Adam; (4) two modes of emanation or overflowing (*fayḍ*); (5) the procession of the world out from the real and the return back to it; (6) the world as the mirror of reality;

and (7) Adam as the "instantiation of the polishing of that mirror and the spirit of that form."

The first verses of this famous passage center upon the distinction between the divine names and their instantiations (aʿyān). These instantiations or determinations—in which the divine names as purely nonexistent relations are actualized—occur in two modes: as the established (thābita), nonexistent entities within the divine mind, and as existent (mawjūda) entities within the world. The opening lines evoke the myth of the divine names and their "tension":

> when the real ( ) willed
> from the standpoint of its most beautiful names
> which are countless
> to see their instantiations

The expression "from the standpoint of" (min ḥaythu) is ambiguous here. The expression can mean that the real, in response to the tension of the divine names, willed to see their instantiations (or, in an alternate reading, willed that they [i.e. the names] see their instantiation). It can also mean, however, that the real—in respect to its names, i.e. its manifest aspect which is the only aspect about which we can speak—"willed." The latter meaning places the entire myth within the tension between the manifest aspect of deity (in which the creator depends upon its creation to be in fact a creator) and the unmanifest identity (dhāt) beyond all names and all distinctions between creator and creation.[24]

The tension between these two modes of the real is also evoked by the term in the first line signified by ( ). The term is commonly translated as "may he be glorified." Such terms abound in Islamic discourse and sound repetitive in English. They are usually taken as a sign of piety. However, in Ibn ʿArabi the term may have another purpose as well, as an apophatic marker (like the Plotinian hoion). It might be translated as "may he be glorified by the attribute now being ascribed to him but may he also be exalted beyond any attribution."

The polished-mirror imagery of passage 1a gains its effect as performative apophasis by acting out semantically the aporia evoked mythically in the story of the nonexistent divine names complaining of their tension. At the moment of the polishing of the mirror, the distinction between self and other is semantically undone by a fusing of the antecedents of the pronoun "he/it" so that it can be read either reflexively or nonreflexively. I have signaled the moment by using parentheses to translate the key phrase: "to reveal to it(self) through it(self) its mystery." The analysis that follows passage 1a will focus upon the aporia within the polishing of the mirror and how that aporia allows a temporary displacement of the reflexive/nonreflexive distinction. Passage 1a:

> when the real ( ) willed
> from the standpoint of its most beautiful names
> which are countless
> to see their instantiations
>
> or you could say
> when it willed to see its own instantiation
>
> in an encompassing entity,
> qualified with existence,
> that would contain its order entire
>
> to reveal to it(self) through it(self)
> its mystery
>
>> for the self-vision of a being through itself
>> is not like its self-vision through something outside
>> which acts as a mirror
>>
>> its self appearing to it
>> in a form
>> in a plane of reflection
>>
>> a form which could not occur
>> without the existence of such a plane
>> and the self-manifestation in it
>
> and when the real ( ) had brought into being
> the world entire
> as a shaped form
> without spirit
>
> the world was like an unpolished mirror
>
>> for divine providence never shapes a form
>> unless it receives divine spirit
>> which is called
>> the "inspiriting"
>>
>> which is the activation
>> of the potential of that shaped image
>> to receive the overflowing,
>> the eternal manifestation
>> that always was and always will be

> outside of which there is only the vessel
>
> which itself exists
> from its most holy overflowing
> for the entire order is from him
> beginning and end
> "and to him returns the order entire"
> as from him it began—
>
> what was required
> was the polishing of the mirror
> that is the world
>
> and Adam was that very polishing[25]
> of that mirror
>
> and the spirit of that form.

This passage relates how the divine names were actualized as "instantiations" through the world that serves as a mirror for them, and through the human being who serves as the polishing of that mirror. The mirror thus has a double function, reflecting back the names but also prismatically refracting them into various individuations.

The basic aporia—that the divine creation is the *cause* of a process of which the revealed creator-deity and its names are the *result*—is performed semantically through a fusion of antecedents in the phrase: to reveal to it(self) through it(self) its mystery. On first glance, the problematic phrase *wa yuẓhira bihi sirrahu ilayhi* would mean "it reveals through it its secret to it," an awkward, but literally correct translation.[26] It is awkward in English because English demands that we choose between reflexive and nonreflexive pronouns (it reveals to it, i.e. something other, or it reveals to itself). Ibn ʿArabi does not make such a distinction; the creative ambiguity between the reflexive and non-reflexive marks the perspective shift. It becomes impossible to determine whether the antecedent of the pronoun is the divine or the human.

At the narrative level (which has not yet engaged the aporia that unravels the narrative as narrative), the pronouns here are not ambiguous. The real creates the world as its mirror and thus reveals to itself through the polished mirror its mystery. Such subtle referential security is challenged, however, by the dilemma latent within the notion of the polished mirror. The mythic aspect of the dilemma is that in order to reflect, the mirror must in some sense become invisible. The mystical aspect of the dilemma is that in order for the mirror to be polished, the human (who is the polishing of the mirror) must "pass away." Because Arabic (like Plotinian Greek) can use the same pronoun for either reflexive or nonreflexive activity, an undertone can be heard in each pronoun. To bring out these undertones, it might be helpful to give a schematic analysis of the ambiguities of the question "Who reveals to whom whose mystery?" Bistami alluded to these ambiguities in an elliptical way through his enumeration of various possibilities of who was mirroring whom. Below I draw out the undertones and ambiguities of Ibn ʿArabi's phrasing in a schematic fashion.

I. Through whom is the mystery revealed?
   A. The mystery is revealed through the complete human being who acts as the polishing of the mirror.
   B. But insofar as the complete human being is the polishing of the mirror, all that is left "in the picture" so to speak, all that exists, is the real. The polishing of the mirror as symbol of *fanāʾ* is the disappearance of everything (including the mirror) but the real's self-manifestation.
   C. The mystery is revealed through the real.
   D. But the real as revealer does not preexist its own formation in the mirror, but rather is constituted by that formation and reflection. Insofar as the real pre-exists the polishing of the mirror, it is beyond the distinctions of creator and creation and of subject and predicate.
   E. What remains is the divine self-manifestation revealed in him(self), it(self). The referent of the pronoun is both the divine and the human, both the self and other.

II. To whom is the mystery revealed?
   A. The mystery is revealed to the real, in the act of self-revelation.
   B. But the real as identity (*dhāt*) is beyond all duality and thus beyond being an object (indirect object of revelation, "to whom" the revelation occurs), or a subject of predication (an entity said "to know"). To say either would be to pose it within a dualistic, delimited, and already manifest state.
   C. In another sense it is the complete human being that is the realization of the divine manifestation. The mystery is revealed to Adam, to the complete human being.
   D. But the complete human being, as the polishing of the mirror, is the passing away and disappearance of everything but the reflections within it. Adam actualizes himself as the polishing of the mirror by his own passing away.

E. This antecedent of the pronoun him/it is neither the real in itself nor Adam in himself, but both at the moment of their union. Though on the mythic level the primary antecedent is the real as deity, the interior aporia (that the deity is not deity until the creation of the cosmos and the polishing of the mirror) results in a referential "slide" toward Adam as the one who receives the revelation. This slide can operate in two directions depending upon which meaning is primary or most evident within a particular expression. But whenever the metaphor of the complete human being as the mirror occurs, or whenever the experience of *fanā'* occurs, such a slide will occur.

III. Who reveals the mystery?
A. The real reveals the mystery.
B. But insofar as it can be given a predication (it reveals) it is no longer the real in the aspect of its identity, but rather in its manifest aspect of the divine names, the totality of which are actualized in the complete human being. The real as identity continually recedes to its transcendence of such predicative delimitation.
C. The real as subject of predication is actualized within the complete human being, and thus it is the complete human being who reveals, as the polishing of the mirror, the mystery.
D. But insofar as the mirror is polished, only the reflections—the divine names—remain. As Ibn ʿArabi is fond of saying, quoting the Qur'an, "All passes away [an Arabic word based on *fanā'*] except the face of God."
E. The revealer is neither the real in itself nor Adam in himself who reveals, but the polishing of the mirror in which the complete human and the manifest deity are united.

I have used parentheses in the translation in order not to lose the perspective shift by being forced to choose between the reflexive or the nonreflexive: "it reveals to it(self) through it(self) its mystery." In a later passage I use both upper and lower case to show how in the mystical moment of *fanā'* the reference splits between the divine and human referents: "He/he gives him/Him of Himself/himself in accordance with the image in which He/he appears to Him/him."²⁷

In each case of antecedence fusion, ambiguity, or slide, the same aporia is at work: the real as creator-deity and deity with revealed names is presented as the cause of the creation of which it is also the result. Before the creation of the cosmos and the complete human being, we cannot speak of the real as creating. Such predications are part of its self-manifestation. But that self-manifestation is a result of its creation of the cosmos. Normal causality is subverted from beneath and falls into a circular or reciprocal causality (A results from B which is the result of A), an infinite regress that underlies all attempts to link causally the transcendent or unlimited to phenomenal reality through delimited reference. Similarly, the creation story presupposes a temporal framework (When the real willed . . .), but according to Ibn ʿArabi, time is part of the world that is the result of the creation;[28] the "when" of the divine will to see the instantiations of its names can be meaningful only after the instantiation of time within the created cosmos.

Ibn ʿArabi embeds the polishing of the mirror within both the Qur'anic "inspiriting" and the Neoplatonic image of emanation or overflowing. There are two phases of emanation. First, the real flows forth into the purely nonexistent established instantiations (*aʿyān ath-thābita*) which serve as the archetypes of phenomenal existents. The emanation through which the archetypes are formed is called the most holy overflowing. The second phase of emanation is the holy overflowing or creation. In the second phase the real, in its manifest aspect as creator, commands the archetypes to come into phenomenal existence, thus allowing the divine names to be actualized through their relation to existing entities.[29]

The archetypes as established instantiations of the names in the mind of the deity are nonexistent. They are intelligible in the mind of the real but exist only insofar as they flow out into the phenomenal. But phenomenal existence, like the divine self-revelation, receives form and instantiation through the complete human being. The "see" in "to see their determinations" shifts from normal dualistic vision (the seeing of a preexistent, exterior object) to creative vision, the simultaneous creation/seeing of what is self/other.[30] The meaning shifts from "seeing" in the normal sense of the term, to "realizing," the simultaneous bringing into actuality and perception of the actuality. In this realization the seer and the seen are simultaneously constituted.

This correlative constitution of seer and seen is followed by the fusion of vessel and content prominent in Plotinian emanation language:

> for divine providence never shapes a form
> unless it receives divine spirit
> which is called
> the "inspiriting"

> which is the activation
> of the potential of that shaped image
> to receive the overflowing
> the eternal manifestation
> that always was and always will be
> outside of which there is only the vessel
>
> which itself exists
> from its most holy overflowing

The paradox of Ibn ʿArabi's myth of the non-existent divine names asking for creation in order to be relieved of their tension is reflected in the double emanation. The place or vessel (*qābil*) corresponds to a *materia prima*, an intelligible matter or substratum. This prime matter or archetypal substratum is said to be nonexistent. It comes into existence only through the second emanation, the inspiriting (*nafkh fīhi*) of Adam. But that inspiriting is both the actualization of the archetypes as phenomenal existents and the passing away of the phenomenal existence through the polishing of the mirror. In the metaphor of the mirror, Adam is created insofar as the mirror is polished (Adam is defined as the polishing of the mirror), but insofar as the mirror is polished, the cosmos (defined as the mirror) passes out of the picture. In mystical terms, the names are actualized in the cosmos when the human self passes away and the names appear in the polished mirror of the human heart.

Insofar as Adam, the *insān kabīr* (great human, or macrocosm), comes to life through the divine inspiriting, he becomes the *insān kāmil* (complete human being), the mirror is polished, and the division between the real and phenomenal reality yields to the single image in the polished mirror. The two phases of emanation begin to collapse into one another; the "holy overflowing" into the "most holy" overflowing; the vessel (which exists only from the holy overflowing) into the content (the breath of the compassionate).[31]

The first section of the above passage ends with the following verses: "for the universal order [*amr*] is from him / beginning and end / 'and to him returns the entire order' / as from him it began // what was required / was the polishing of the mirror / that is the world // and Adam was the essence / of the polishing / of that mirror // and the spirit of that form." The *amr*—which can mean order in both the senses of command or ordering, or, more generally, a state or affair—is in Ibn ʿArabi related to the divine *logos*.[32] The mystery of that *logos* is that it is both first and last, beginning and end, polarities used in their strong, nondual sense: the end is the beginning, the *amr* can only proceed once it has returned. The perspective shift here is expressed in the classical Neoplatonic paradox of procession and return, that there can be no real procession until the return.

In section 1a, the perceptual shift was represented symbolically and metaphorically through the image of the polished mirror, mythically through the emanation and creation myth, and cosmologically through the double use of the term "determinations." The references to the mirror that evoked the shift were separated by philosophical and mythic "digressions" (on different kinds of knowledge, on the divine names, on the creation story, on Adam as regent and pupil of the eye) that refracted the shift into other languages, even as they increased poetic tension by delaying the realization of the shift. That realization, the actual polishing of the mirror, was not mentioned until the very end of the section.

HUMAN VS. ANGEL

Section 1b consists of an apparent digression on the angels. The angels are said to be certain powers of that *nash'* ("nature" in the sense of "formation") which is the "great human." The great human represents the entire *amr* (affair, command, cosmos) of which the complete human being is the actualization. We might think of it as Adam before the divine inspiring brings him to life. Angels represent powers of this cosmos, but each power is limited to itself, just as each human sense is limited to its own sphere of activity.[33] The eye, for example, cannot hear. The angels, regardless of the intensity of their powers, are not universal. Only human nature can achieve universality or completeness.

The validation of human nature in the face of angelic criticism is developed more fully in a later section of the Adam chapter. There, Ibn 'Arabi uses the Qur'anic story of the angels' prostration before Adam as a basis for a homily on the error of binding (*taqyīd*). The error of binding consists in the belief that the form, name, or determination in which one views the real is the only form in which the real manifests itself. The angels are said to have boasted that they praised Allah through the divine names and exalted him above them. However, because each angel is veiled from the other and represents only one power, no angel can perform a complete praise (*tasbīḥ*) and affirmation of transcendence (*taqdīs*) beyond all praises. By complaining about the creation of Adam, the angels betray their own belief that the particular name each angel knows is the only and complete name with which to praise the divine.[34]

The angelic boast is an example of the error of binding. To bind the real into a particular form is the fundamental error, and Ibn ʿArabi's critique of it becomes the basis for his critique of all forms of dogmatism. The real has an infinite number of names and manifestations. Each manifestation is valid in itself. The manifestations are in constant flux, however. The divine self-manifestations are realized in the polished mirror of human consciousness, and human consciousness is also in constant flux. Both the real and the complete human being are in a state of perpetual transformation (*taqallub*), and an individual can realize union with the divine only by realizing a state of complete, perpetual transformation. The angels (and others who fall into the error of binding) attempt to fix the deity within a particular manifestation.

For Ibn ʿArabi, the Qur'anic story of the angels' prostration reveals the centrality of the complete human being (represented by Adam) in the cosmos. This centrality exists on two axes. On the horizontal axis, the complete human contains, reflects, and refracts all of the divine names, whereas each angel, however pure or powerful, represents only one aspect of reality. On the vertical axis, the complete human encompasses all strata of reality, from the eternal to the mortal; from the divine, through the spiritual, to the rational, to the animal, to the vegetative, to the elemental.

Ibn ʿArabi is executing here a brilliant and provocative play upon the meaning of the Arabic term *kāmil*. The strongly ascetic tendency of much of early Sufism was spiritualist in character. The goal of the Sufi path was to shed one's humanity and to become as like the angels as possible. The goal was to become as "perfect" (*kāmil*) as possible. Although Ibn ʿArabi maintained the ethical seriousness of the early Sufis, he placed the Sufi life, both in its attempt to adhere as loyally as possible to the shari'a and in its own ascetic, devotional, and meditative practices, in a new context. Adam's central place in the cosmos is due to his being *kāmil*, not "perfect" in the sense of having shed human imperfections, but rather "complete" in the sense of embracing all realities. The statement takes on a dramatic edge, given the propensity of those who seek the perfection of the angels rather than the deepening of the human to read *kāmil* as "perfect" rather than "complete."[35] In another work, Ibn ʿArabi makes explicit the implication throughout his homage to the complete human that the complete human is in fact more *kāmil* than the deity because it exists on all levels, from the eternal to the mortal, from the spiritual to the elemental. The complete human is an isthmus (*barzakh*) between the creator and creation and as such encompasses both realms, while deity is confined to the divine realm and the created world confined to the world of contingency:

> The human alone has two complete relations; one whereby he enters into the divine realm and the other whereby he enters into the created. He can be described as a servant insofar as he is subject to obligation and insofar as he did not exist and then came into being, but he can be described as deity insofar as he is the *khalīfa* of Allah and in view of his form [*ṣūra*] and his formation in the best of possible constructions. He is like an isthmus between the world and God, combining in himself creatureliness and divinity; he is the dividing line between the divine and the created realm, like the line between shade and sunlight. This is his reality. He possesses absolute completion [*al-kamāl al-muṭlaq*] in the originated and in the eternal world. God is absolutely complete in the eternal realm, without share in the originated realm because he is beyond it, while the world is absolutely complete in its origination, with no share in the eternal which it falls below.[36]

In passage 1b, Ibn ʿArabi is more cryptic. He refers to the "divine aspect," that is, the universality of the divine names and the "aspect of universal nature" as a *materia prima*, prime matter as the pure receptor or vessel (*qābil*). This validation of nature, elementality, receptivity, and constant flux is another aspect of Ibn ʿArabi's tendency to place mystical humanism over against the spiritualism of other mystical thinkers. The intermediary between these two worlds he calls the "reality of reality," which he depicts elsewhere as that which is "created with the created, divine with the divine, eternal with the eternal, and temporal with the temporal."[37] The passage ends with the statement that the reality discussed here cannot be known through rational speculation (*naẓar*), but only through that "art of apprehension" that originated in the divine self-unveiling (*kashf*). At the end of this chapter, we will return to this "art of apprehension."

> the angels were certain powers of that form
> which the folk call the great human
>
> the angels were to it
> like the spiritual and perceptual powers in the human nature
>
> but each power is veiled in itself
> and sees nothing that is better than it
>
>> for they [the angels] claim kinship
>> to every high station and exalted rank before Allah
>> to divine comprehensiveness

> whether it pertain to
> the divine aspect
>
> or the aspect of
> the reality of realities
>
> or, in the nature containing all these attributes,
> to what is required by
> universal nature
>
> which encompasses the vessels of the world
> all of them, high and low
>
> and this no mind knows by rational speculation
>
> but only by that art of apprehension
> that originated in divine unveiling
>
> which reveals the origin of the forms
> that constitute the world
>
> and receive the spirits.

Although Ibn ʿArabi prefers the metaphor of the polished mirror, the implication of the complete human as an isthmus and locus of refraction suggests as well a kind of twice-doubled prism. The complete human refracts the divine unity into its various names even as it unifies the attributes into one. It also refracts universal nature into its various properties (depicted by Ibn ʿArabi according to the neo-Aristotelian tradition of the ten categories)[38] and unifies them back into the pure receptivity of nature. The place of the complete human as polishing of the mirror can be diagrammed as shown in figure 1.

Insān: Human Being, Pupil of the Eye

In the final part of this hymnic opening to *Ring Settings of Wisdom*, Ibn ʿArabi introduces a key pun on the word *insān*, which can mean both "human being" and "pupil of the eye." The complete human, then, is the pupil of the eye of reality, the mode of perception. As *khalīfa* or regent, it is also the "seal" by which the order of reality is maintained. Were it to be removed, the articulated world would collapse in upon itself:

> that one was named *insān* [human being, pupil of the eye]
> and *khalīfa* [regent]
>
> he is named *insān* because of the universality of his nature
> encompassing all realities

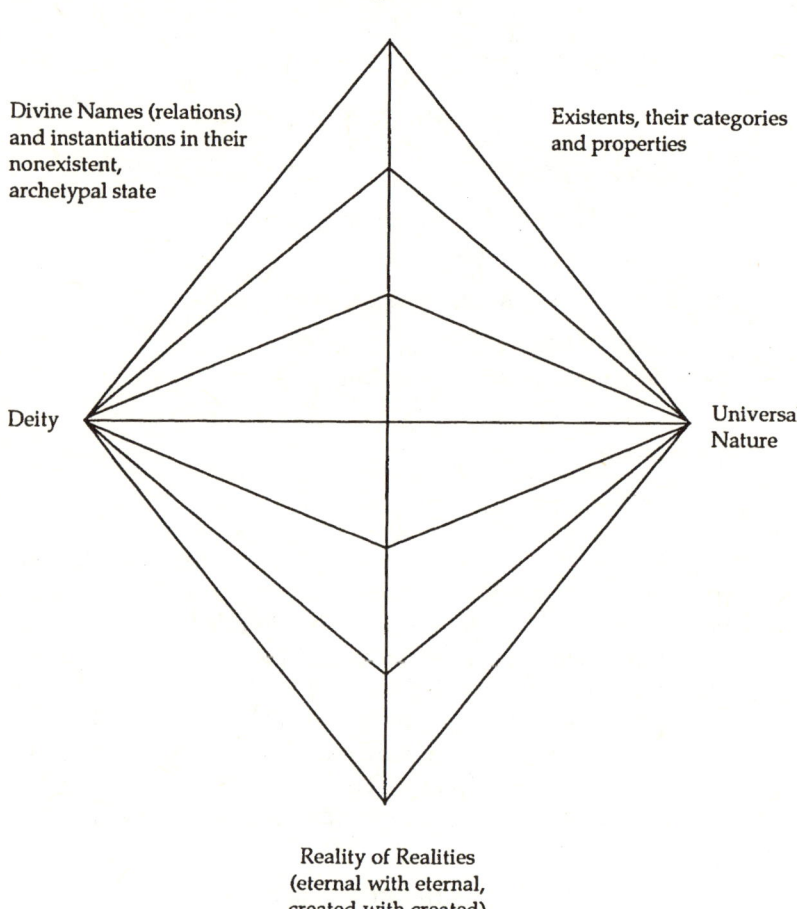

Fig 1. *dhāt al-haqq* (the incommunicable reality beyond all names and distinction, including that of creator and created)

> he is to the real
> as the *insān* is to the eye
> the medium of vision and perception
>
> so he is called *insān*
> because through him the real views its creation
> and extends them compassion
>
> he is *insān*, originated and eternal

> he is the living being, without beginning, without end
>
> he is the word, discriminating and integrating
>
> he is to the world
> as the ringstone of the ring is to the ring
>
> the plane of inscription
> the sign by which the king seals his coffer
>
> he is called *khalīfa* then
> since the transcendent guards through him his creation
>
> as long as the seal guards the treasure chest
> as long as it bears the seal of the king
> no one dares open it without his permission
>
> so he made him his *khalīfa*
> charged with the safeguarding of his property
> and the world is preserved
> as long as the complete human being remains in it
>
> don't you see that if he were no more
> or were broken off from the treasure chest that is the world
> the contents, which the real placed there, would spill out
> the parts would interfuse
> and the entire order would vanish into the afterworld
>
> where he would be the eternal seal on the treasure chest
> that is the afterworld.

In this last section, the text has finally returned to and completed the image of the polishing of the mirror. The complete human being is seen as fulfilling two roles: that of *khalīfa* (regent), the informing and caretaking agent of the cosmos, and that of *insān*, the reflection of the divine, its medium of self-perception.

The complete human is the word (*kalima*) which is both discriminating and integrating. For Ibn ʿArabi it is discursive intellect (*ʿaql*) that differentiates the real into various forms. His criticism of binding which was alluded to in the discussion of angels, is a criticism of the mistaken use of intellect. Binding leads to a world of conflicting beliefs, each of which sees the real in its own form and denies the form appearing in other beliefs. What is necessary is the dialectically complementary activity of synthesis or reintegration that Ibn ʿArabi associates with the heart (*qalb*). Through the perceptual shift (*taqallub*—a morphological play on *qalb*) symbolized by the polished mirror, forms no longer encompass the real but serve as manifestations of it, freed from binding.

The passage consists of a series of dialectical statements (that the complete human is both eternal and originated), a dialectic flowing directly from the perceptual shifts and split references that preceded. This dialectic is explained more fully in the third section of the Adam chapter. Attributes such as knowing or living are said to be eternal from the divine perspective and temporal or originated from the human perspective. In the polished mirror, the act of knowing is the one act that occurs in the eternal moment. Insofar as the human really knows, its knowledge is the divine self-knowing. Insofar as the divine knows, the divine name (knowing, the knower) is actualized through the knowing of the complete human. In a later passage from the Adam chapter, Ibn ʿArabi directly refers to the famous hadith that Adam was created "in his image":

> Because the order appears, as we said, *in his image* [*bi ṣūratihi*],
> the transcendent turns us to the originated for knowledge of
>   him. . . .
> We cannot describe him by any quality unless we are that
>   quality,
> with the exception of intrinsic necessity.
>
> When we know him in ourselves and through ourselves
> we attribute to him everything we attribute to ourselves.
>
> Thus divine sayings have come down to us
> through the tongues of their interpreters.
>
> He described himself to us, through us.
>
> When we witness him, we witness ourselves.
> When we witness ourselves, we witness him.[39]

The complete human, as the comprehensive locus for the divine names, is identical to the real except in one important aspect. The real exists in itself. In the language of the Islamic philosophers, it is necessarily existent (*wājib al-wujūd*). The complete human being can be said to exist necessarily only through the real, not through itself.

THE TWO HANDS OF REALITY

The divine attributes come into actuality in the polished mirror. The attributes are actualized at the point of intersection of human and divine, cosmologically in the role of Adam as the polishing of the mirror, mystically in the polishing of the mirror of the heart that occurs in mystical union or *fanāʾ*. The Adam chapter ends its meditation on these themes by returning to the Qurʾanic expression "my [Allah's] two hands." The controversial expression serves both as an example of a divine attribute that is actualized in this manner and as a prototype of the entire theological dispute over attributes vs. unity, anthropomorphism vs. the "explaining away" through the *taʾwīl* of figurative language. Ibn ʿArabi was particularly dismissive of theological attempts to explain away the expression "my two hands" as a figurative reference to divine power. Such an explanation fails to do justice to the Qur'anic literary context, the deity's chastising of Iblis for refusing to prostrate himself before "what I have created with my two hands." The expression "my two hands" must refer to something unique to Adam, but all creation originated from divine power. Following earlier criticisms of the theological explanations of the "two hands" as a metaphor for divine power, Ibn ʿArabi maintains that to explain away the two hands in such a way does justice neither to the special quality referred to in Adam as the regent (*khalīfa*) nor to the specifically dual grammatical form (two hands).[40]

In his own interpretation of the "two hands," Ibn ʿArabi gives a sequence of polarities that characterize the human being. The complete human encompasses both the hidden and the manifest. It exists in simultaneous states of intimacy (*uns*) and awe (*hayba*) in its relation to the real. From the point of view of the transcendence of the real (the real's ontological necessity as opposed to the contingency of all creatures), the human can never attain or comprehend the real, not through reason, not through Sufi unveiling, not through "taste" or mystical witness. Reality is hidden. Yet, from the point of view of the attributes, it achieves "similarity" to the real, containing all the attributes of the real, even as it reflects all the attributes of the world (and thus relates the real to the world). The human thus reflects two modes of the divine, the manifest mode of witness (*shahāda*) and the hidden pole of the unknowable (*al-ghayb*).[41] These two modes are dialogical rather than analogical. Insofar as the mirror is polished, the human reflects the divine attributes completely, with the exception of necessary existence. Yet within that polished reflection is a simultaneous reflection of unknowability, and the reflecting medium passes away, so that there is no human subject at that moment that can be said "to know." Other polarities also reflect the human's "two-handed" creation: benevolence and anger, fear and hope, intimacy and awe. In a final summation Ibn ʿArabi returns to the theme of knowledge and attributes. The two hands "stretch out over the complete human being," who is both completely reflective of the divine attributes (as regent or *khalīfa*) and yet, insofar as it is of the originated world, can never know the real as the real knows itself, because "originated being has no way there." Iblis did not understand the two handed creation of Adam.

Ibn ʿArabi's critique of the error of binding, into which Iblis and the other angels fell, suggests that humans are susceptible to the same error. Humans bind when they fail to understand that the complete reflection of the divine in the polished mirror of the human heart occurs simultaneously with the utter transcendence of the divine beyond any human grasp. Insofar as the mirror is polished, the human has "passed away" in *fanāʾ* and it is the real (beyond or between the polarity of divine and human) that sees, hears, and speaks to itself within itself. Ibn ʿArabi not only affirms the divine attributes, including the apparently anthropomorphic ones such as the "two hands of Allah," but he performs his understanding of such attributes as pointing to the essential and distinctive polarities within the nature of the being created by those two hands. Adam, the being created with two hands, is a locus of coincidences of opposites. In perhaps the most powerful allusion to the hadith that Adam was created in his/His image or form (*ṣūra*), Ibn ʿArabi returns to the issue of the refusal by Iblis:

> so he asked Iblis
> "what prevents you from prostrating yourself
>   before what I created with my two hands?"
> this is the essence [*ʿayn*]
> of his bringing together of two forms
> the form [*ṣūra*] of the world
> and the form [*ṣūra*] of the real.
> These are the two hands of reality.[42]

The above passage plays upon the meaning of *ʿayn*. *ʿAyn* can mean essence, eye (reminding us of the depiction of Adam as the *insān* or pupil of the eye of the real), or wellspring. In Ibn ʿArabi, it also means the concrete instantiation of a particular reality. Finally, it can mean, in a colloquial sense, "the same" as in "X is the *ʿayn*—the very same as—Y." The two-handed creation (Adam as the complete human being) is the very *ʿayn* of the bringing together of two images or forms, the form of the real and the form of the world.

Ibn ʿArabi goes on to tie this union of two forms to the crucial union-hadith "I am the hearing with which he hears, the seeing with which he sees, the hands with which he touches, the feet with which he walks, the tongue with which he speaks." This hadith, the repeated use of the key term *ṣūra* (image, form), and the play upon the word *ʿayn* raise the shift symbolized by the polished mirror to its strongest pitch:

> So he constructed his apparent form [ṣūra]
> from the realities of the world and its forms
> And he constructed his hidden form [ṣūra]
> upon his own transcendent form [ṣūra],
>
> Saying in this regard:
> "I was his hearing and his sight."[43]

The myth of first creation and the mystical eternal moment of passing away are brought together in the polishing of the mirror. At the moment of polishing, the image appears, even as the ego-self of the human passes away. Thus Ibn ʿArabi has performed the Qur'anic phrase of the "two hands" of Allah. Rather than explaining it away as allegory for another paraphrasable meaning in the manner of the scholastic theologians, or taking it literally in the manner of the anthropomorphists, he has placed it performatively at the moment of the polishing of the mirror. The "two hands" symbolize the human role in the polishing of the mirror, even as the meaning of the hands (like all attributes of the divine) can be understood only through that polishing in which the divine and human form one another.

IDENTITY SHIFT AND MEANING EVENT

In the Hermetic text *Poimandres* the complete human being (*anthropôs*), bearing the form (*eikôn*) of his divine father, looks down upon nature and sees his divine form reflected in it as in a mirror. Becoming infatuated with it, he falls into the embrace of nature.[44] In this myth the mirror serves as a metaphor for separation and alienation, and the love of the image reflected within the mirror is interpreted along the lines of the Narcissus myth. With Ibn ʿArabi the mirror reflection occurs only when the narcissism of the ego-self passes away. At the moment of passing away, mystical reunion as divine self-revelation occurs "in his image." The antecedent of "his" in the famous hadith is not given a theological solution by Ibn ʿArabi, any more than the issue of divine attributes is given a theological solution. Although Ibn ʿArabi gives a wide variety of possible positions on the question of "in his image," the crucial position from the perspective of this chapter is the position that is not stated but performed through apophatic discourse. That performance is a linguistic reenactment of the polishing of the mirror. Just as the question "Who reveals to whom in whom whose mystery?" refracts into a double possibility for each pronoun, so the antecedent of "his" in "in his image" can be either Allah or Adam. Or rather, we should say it is both the divine and the human at the moment of the polishing of the mirror. The polishing of the mirror, from a mystical perspective, represents an "identity shift" in two senses. In the first place, the individual, in passing away from her ego-self, no longer exists as a separate ego-entity, but rather the deity hears, sees, walks, touches, and speaks through her. Her "identity" has shifted from an ego-self in a dualistic relationship to a divine other, to a being-in-union with the divine. In the second sense of "identity shift," then, a self-other relationship has shifted to one of identity, i.e. oneness with the real. In this moment of polishing of the mirror, the divine names are "realized." The semantic reenactment of this identity shift and realization is the "meaning event," in which, by fusing the antecedents of "in his image," or of the pronouns associated with the revelation of the mystery in the mirror, the language reenacts and performs the polishing of the mirror.

The theological issues of divine names and divine image cannot be resolved through rational speculation, but the image can be glimpsed in the polished mirror through that "art of apprehension" that originated in divine unveiling (*kashf*). In mystical terms, the image appeared at the moment of mystical union. In semantic terms, it is "apprehended" as the meaning event when the dualisms of self-other, time, and space are temporarily fused through the collapse of the semantic structures that reflect them. In other kinds of discourse, or other moments of apophatic discourse, we can distinguish the event (the act of predication) from the meaning (as sense and reference, the "what" and the "what about"). In mystical dialectic, when predication and reference become realization, there can be no distinction between meaning and event. The divine names, as Ibn ʿArabi explains, are not ontological items (*ʿumūr wujūdiyya*); they have no existence independent of the world and the polishing of the mirror.

Ibn ʿArabi has often been treated as the author of a monistic metaphysical system. It is true that his followers, in trying to give more systematic shape to his thought, invented the term "unity of existence" (*waḥdat al-wujūd*), which was subsequently applied to Ibn ʿArabi's own thought by Orientalist scholarship. Yet, although Ibn ʿArabi might agree that all existence is one, such a statement, on the objective level, would be of little interest to him. In bringing together the cosmological notion of the complete human with the mystical notion of *fanāʾ*, Ibn ʿArabi attempts a dynamic, performative notion of existence. From the divine perspective the polishing of the mirror always has occurred and always is occurring. From the human perspective it is eternal but also a moment in time, an eternal moment that cannot be held onto but must be continually reenacted. The polishing of the mirror marks a shift in which the two perspectives are combined. The fusion of perspectives marks an identity shift in both senses of the word "identity." The identity *between* human and divine is realized in the image in the polished mirror, and the identity of *both* human and divine is constituted within that image; the divine name is realized and a language of predication becomes a language of realization.

The term *sirr* (mystery) in the statement "To reveal to it(self) through it(self) its mystery" is the hinge of that shift. What is the mystery that is revealed? On one level, it is the unmanifest identity that reveals itself through the divine names and the complete human being. However, insofar as it reveals itself it is delimited within a particular manifestation. Thus the true mystery can never be revealed, even to itself. Or we could say that the very question, "What is the mystery?" is misleading. The mystery is a mystery because it is beyond "whatness" or quiddity. Though revealing itself in a continuing flow of images and manifestations, it is confined to none.

The realization is an event. The continual shift from predication to realization prevents the mind from fixating upon any single "object," from reifying the real into a single form. The infinite regress built into the narrative leads the reader deeper into the aporetic meditation. The "two hands" are both a symbol of this process and an example of it. They symbolize the human position between the comparability of the divine and its incomparability and total transcendence. They symbolize the human position as locus of opposites. Yet in Ibn ʿArabi's text, their precise meaning "slides" or shifts each time they are evoked. The two hands can be the simultaneous intimacy (*uns*) and awe (*hayba*) of the human in relation to the real. They can be the human's reflection of the real and simultaneous inability to reflect and know reality's hidden identity, thus reflecting the mode of witness and mode of the unknowable. They reflect the beauty (*jamāl*) and majesty (*jalāl*) of the deity. They reflect fear and hope. They reflect the eternal realm and the mortal realm, at the intersection of which the human is situated. The constant tropological refiguring of this one divine attribute with Ibn ʿArabi's texts performs his central notion of "perpetual transformation." To understand why Ibn ʿArabi created a discourse that transforms itself so relentlessly, it is necessary now to turn to his critique of religious dogmatisms and his theory of perpetual transformation. It is in his theory of perpetual transformation that the joyful affirmation of the complete human that can receive each divine name and form is balanced by the sadness of the human condition in which the divine image—in poetic terms, the beloved—is continually being lost.

CHAPTER FOUR

Ibn ʿArabi's Garden among the Flames: The Heart Receptive of Every Form

*Wonder,
a garden among the flames!*

*My heart can take on
any form:
a meadow for gazelles,
a cloister for monks,*

*For the idols, sacred ground,
Kaʿba for the circling pilgrim,
the tables of the Torah,
the scrolls of the Qurʾān.*

*My creed is love;
wherever its caravan turns along the way,
that is my belief,
my faith.*[1]

These verses are among the more widely quoted passages in Sufi literature and have been used as an epitome of Ibn ʿArabi's thought in many modern accounts of Sufism.[2] Yet the intricate and highly interesting theory on which these verses are based—the theory of the heart that takes on every form—has been given less attention. In discussing Ibn ʿArabi's theory of the heart and its forms, special attention will be given to how Ibn ʿArabi's apophatic discourse poses questions, defers answers, and finally transposes into a new key the grounds on which the questions are based.[3]

BINDING OF THE INTELLECT, TRANSFORMATION OF THE HEART

The immediate context of the theory is the Sufi critique of rationalism. The Islamic philosophers had associated knowledge (ʿilm) with the intellect and maintained that the path to knowledge was rational argument. The scholastic theologians put the revealed text at the center of their search for knowledge, but they developed a rational discourse (*kalām*), based on the intellect, in order to solve problems of Quranic interpretation and Islamic belief.[4] The Sufis emphasized that intellectual knowledge alone was insufficient; they pointed to the heart (*qalb*) as the seat and faculty of *maʿrifa* (a continually transformative knowing).

Though Ibn ʿArabi's theory is partially rooted in the controversy among the various models of Islamic thought, it extends far beyond these original bounds. *Al-ḥaqq* (the real, the true) manifests itself to itself through innumerable forms or images but is confined to none. The forms of its manifestation are constantly changing. Through an etymological play, he relates the intellect (*ʿaql*, root meaning, rope) to definition, the "binding" (*taqyīd*) of the real into fixed and limited categories or forms. Such a function is necessary because the purely indeterminate cannot be known or made manifest. A fundamental error arises, however, when the partial categories or individual forms are taken as fixed and total. This error leads to a world of conflicting beliefs, each of which denies the other. And it leads to an individual's fixation on a particular viewpoint, conception, or experience. In either case, the error is serious, since a belief which denies all other beliefs denies the common root of them all, and an individual who is not in a state of constant change can no longer be said to know and reflect the constantly changing manifestations of the real. Thus Ibn ʿArabi's critique of the intellectual error of binding goes beyond a criticism of rationalist philosophy and dogmatic scholasticism and extends to any context in which a form or image (*ṣūra*) of the real appears: religious, scientific, aesthetic, or even mystical. The Sufis themselves are guilty of *taqyīd* when they stop at a particular station or experience, however exalted, and bind the real to it. In binding, they mistake meaning, polyvalent and dynamic, for the husks of the forms it has already shed. A preliminary indication of Ibn ʿArabi's critique was encountered in the previous chapter where the angels' refusal to prostrate themselves in prayer before Adam served as an example of binding. As the complete human being Adam is the microcosm on whose form the cosmos is patterned, the prism through which the undifferentiated divine light is refracted into its various attributes, and the faculty of perception through which reality discloses its forms and attributes to itself.[5]

In *Ring Settings*, the critique of binding and the theory of the "heart that is receptive of every form" is elucidated in the chapters on the ancient Arabian prophet Shuʿayb and on the Qur'anic Noah. As opposed to the intellect, which analytically differentiates the real into limited, fixed forms, the heart is synthetic—or rather dynamically integrative. Ibn ʿArabi previews his understanding of dynamic integration in a play upon the Arabic radical *q-l-b* ("heart," "change") which he relates through etymology to the notion of "perpetual transformation" (*taqallub*). The heart receives, shapes itself around, and becomes each form of the perpetually changing forms in which the real appears. In each moment the heart encounters a new form of manifestation (*tajallī*, manifestation, unveiling). In another etymological play, Ibn ʿArabi relates the discursive intellect *ʿaql* to its root meaning of "binding." Without the knowledge of the heart, the intellect binds the manifestation into fixed, mutually exclusive images. When the same images are no longer seen as fixed and mutually exclusive, but rather as perpetually changing forms of manifestation, they become transparent and revelatory. At this point, Ibn ʿArabi maintains that these forms are the self-disclosure of the divine within the human and the human within the divine—the forms of the mutual construction of divine and human.

After this very brief summary, I now turn to Ibn ʿArabi's own texts. With Ibn ʿArabi, one is always *in medias res*. The first citations may seem confusing. However, like one backing away from an impressionist painting, we should find the picture gradually coming into focus.[6]

The Breath of the Compassionate, The Heart of the Knower

Chapter 12 of *Fuṣūṣ* presents the ancient prophet Shuʿayb as the archetype of the heart that is receptive of every form. The chapter begins with a question concerning the relationship between the divine compassion (*al-raḥma al-ilāhiyya*) and the heart of the mystic knower (*al-ʿārif*). The evocation of compassion is an allusion to the myth of the breath of the compassion, that is, the "dilation," emanation, or manifestation through which the divine names are actualized. Ibn ʿArabi asks which is greater, the divine compassion or the heart of the mystical knower into whom the compassion flows. He first takes one position, then the other, using the rhetorical opposition of the two positions as a discursive guise under which the central argument develops.[7]

In the passage below, the myth of "the breath of the compassionate" is interwoven with the modal dialectic concerning the real. The first mode of the real is *al-dhāt*, unmanifest, undifferentiated, absolute unity. The second mode is made up of the manifest facets of the real: divinity (*al-ulūhiyya*), lordship (*al-rubūbiyya*), and the divine names. The divine names, divinity, and lordship are all dependent on a polar complement (e.g., lordship's dependence on the existence of a servant). The identity (*dhāt*) is beyond duality. The relationship between the two aspects is dialectical; they are radically distinguished from one another, and yet they are said to be the same. The narrative myth (the breath of the compassionate) is based on linear, dualistic logic and distinctions (cause-effect, before-after, here-there) that are destabilized by the dialectic. The tension between the myth narrative and the dialectical relationships forms a discourse of "mythic dialectic" that will now be traced through several key passages:

> Allah described himself as breath [*nafas*]
>   which is from *tanfīs* [relief]
>
> The divine names are the same
>   as that which they name
> They are nothing but he
>
> But they demand the realities
>   which they express
>
> And the realities that they demand
>   are nothing other than the world
>
> For divinity requires that over which it is divine
>   and lordship requires the servant
>
> Otherwise they would have no meaning or existence
>
> The real, in the inner identity,
>   is independent of the worlds
>
> But lordship does not have such independence
>
> So the order lies between
>   what lordship requires
> and the independence from the world
>   to which the real holds title
>
> But in reality lordship is the same as the identity
>
> Though when the situation contradicts itself in relations
>   He describes himself as having compassion on his servants:
>
> First he relieved the lordship with his breath
>   related to the compassionate

> By creating the world required in its nature by lordship
> and by the totality of divine names
>
> From this perspective his compassion embraces everything
> Including the real
>
> And is just as encompassing, or more so, than the heart.[8]

This passage begins and ends with allusions to the "breath of the compassionate" which imply a distinction between the breath and the heart that receives it, between content and vessel. That distinction is in tension with a dialectic in the central section of the passage that breaks down dualities. The dialectic operates on two planes simultaneously. On the first plane, the dialectic occurs between the unmanifest identity and the manifest aspects of the real (deity, divine names, lordship) which are distinguished from one another yet somehow said to be the same. On the second plane, the dialectic occurs between the correlative terms of polarities (lord/servant, divine/human). The result is an oblique, double dialectic indicated enigmatically by Ibn ʿArabi's statement that "the order lies between" the absolute unity of the identity and the polarity of the manifest correlatives.

The breath of the compassionate is an unfolding of the potentialities of the names that need a correlate (the world) to be actualized. This unfolding is mythologized in the breath of the compassionate's "relieving" of the lordship. Lordship is a classic case of the interdependency of correlates. Without a servant, a lord is not a lord. Lordship, then, comes to symbolize the correlation dependency within all the divine names, and the inherent tension within the divine realm without or before the creation of the world. Ibn ʿArabi's dialectic here begins to transform the mythic "before the world" by showing how lordship and divine names presuppose servanthood and creation—a logical presupposition ironically dramatized in the myth of the divine names (discussed in chapter 3 above) who complained of their "tension" before the breath of the compassionate relieved them through creation.

Rather than trying to explain what he means by "the order lies between," Ibn ʿArabi will go on to construct a series of apophatic transformations. The oblique dialectic is Ibn ʿArabi's distinctive version of the apophatic aporia in any attempt to bring the identity-beyond-relation into a relation: once it has been brought into relation, it is no longer the identity, and a new transcendent identity must be posed, ad infinitum. The energy of the infinite regress is harnessed within the dialectic and will form the central dynamic principle of the succeeding passages.

At this point, Ibn ʿArabi shifts the focus of discussion from the "breath" to the "heart" of the mystic, and from the mythic paradigm of the primordial breath to the mystical paradigm of the passing away of the individual self in union with the real. In doing so, he refers to the two most famous early Sufi figures, Abū Yazīd al-Bisṭāmī (died ca. 261/874) and Junayd (died 297/910), both of whom were instrumental in developing and refining the Sufi doctrine of *fanā'* or passing away.

> Then know that the real ( )[9]
> as is confirmed in the tradition
> transforms itself from form to form
> in its manifestations
>
> And that the real ( )
> when the heart embraces it—
> then the heart can embrace nothing else whatsoever—
> as if it were filled by the real
> To look upon the real when it manifests itself
> is to be unable to look upon anything other
>
> Concerning the breadth of the mystic knower's heart
> Abu Yazid al-Bistami said:
> If the divine throne and what it contained
> existed one hundred million times
> in the heart of the mystic knower
> he would not be aware of it
>
> And Junayd said in the same regard
> When the originated is related to the eternal
> no trace remains of the originated
>
> When the heart encompasses the eternal
> how can it feel the existence of the originated?[10]

The passage begins with a reference to the perpetual transformation (*taqallub*) of the real. This central notion of Ibn ʿArabi is then related to two classical Sufi ideas: the heart being "filled" by the divine emanation and Junayd's language of "passing away" (*fanā'*). Junayd's notion that the Sufi passes away from the individual self during the mystical experience and that only divine consciousness remains (the complementary notion of *baqā'* or remaining) is used here to effect the identity shift from the dualisms of language and linear logic to an absolute unity.

Because the unity cannot be stated directly in language, itself inherently dualistic, it is drawn into the same kind of apophatic practice found in Plotinus and Eriugena. A statement in dualistic terms (cause and effect, act and being, before and after, subject and predicate) is followed by a fusion of the two terms or an abstraction of one of them from the proposition. The practice is especially effective when combined, as it is here, with a metaphor such as the vessel-content image. The normal dualism that the image requires is undermined by the shift of "passing away" so that the vessel is the content or, stated otherwise, there is no longer vessel but only content. This metaphoric dialectic will achieve its greatest dynamism as it is in turn combined with the concept of perpetual transformation.

The question then arises whether the divine manifestation determines the form that the heart takes or whether the predisposition (*isti'dād*) of the heart determines the form of the manifestation it receives. Ibn 'Arabi defers an answer by posing a new simile: the heart that receives a manifestation is like a setting for a ringstone. Ultimately the question of whether the heart determines the manifestation or the manifestation determines the form of the heart is taken up into the identity shift of *fanā'*: in passing away, the very duality of heart and manifestation, vessel and content, setting and stone, is transformed.[11] Ibn 'Arabi poses the issue as a question, then continually displaces any monolithic answer. In the aporia of the identity shift (in which heart and manifestation, vessel and content are one), the question is not solved, but deepened.

This shift involves a double process: a downward regression to pure receptivity (*materia prima*, empty vessel, blank mirror) and a complementary mystical union in the universal consciousness of the complete human being. When one realizes (in both senses of the term) one's pure receptivity by giving up the ego-self and all its images, she realizes the divine self-reflection. Conversely, when she realizes the self-reflection, her ego-self passes away. It might be more accurate to say that the reflection realizes itself, insofar as in the moment of passing away, there is no "one" there (in the sense of ego-self) to be the subject of the realization. In the identity shift of *fanā'*, the one manifesting itself (*al-mutajallī*) becomes (is) the one receiving the manifestation (*al-mutajallā lahu*), as the deity becomes the hearing with which the Sufi hears, the seeing with which he sees, the tongue with which he speaks. This shift is not described in Ibn 'Arabi's text but rather enacted as a meaning event. Here the focus will be upon the necessity for the Sufi (and for Sufi language) to continually reenact the identity shift of *fanā'*, the polishing of the mirror. Though on the mythic level it is one primordial act, on the mystical level that act must be recreated in every moment.

GODS OF BELIEF

Ibn ʿArabi goes on to suggest that the precise relationship between heart and manifestation is to be found in a distinction between the "visible manifestation" (*tajallī al-shahāda*) and the paradoxical "hidden manifestation" (*tajallī al-ghayb*, literally, "manifestation of the hidden"). The visible manifestation is the image in which each individual sees the real. The hidden manifestation is the inner reality or secret (*sirr*) of the heart which is at once universal and undifferentiated and, at the same time, determines the particularity and individuality of each individual. On another level of dialectic, this hidden manifestation or predisposition is said to be identical to the visible manifestation it determines (just as the real is dialectically identical to the divine names and to each divine name). Ibn ʿArabi uses the dialectical interplay between the hidden and visible manifestations to set the context for his critique of rationalistic binding and dogmatism. At the core of this critique is the God of belief (*iʿtiqād*) within the visible manifestation. The God of belief is visible insofar as it contains a delimited intellectual form or shape constructed within the intellectual and cultural parameters of that belief. Such a deity can accurately reflect the real, but a serious error occurs when the real is bound and limited to it. In the passage below, the critique of binding is performed through the transformation of grammatical and referential structures within the identity shift of mystical union. The breakdown of standard grammatical divisions between self and other culminates in the words: "He gives him(self) of him(self) in accordance with the image in which he appears to him(self)." As we asked concerning the statement "It reveals to it(self) through it(self) its mystery," here we can ask with each case who is giving whom to whom. In each case the antecedent of the Arabic pronoun *hu* can be either the divine party or the human party, and the action can be either reflexive or nonreflexive. The old convention of capitalizing pronouns thought to be referential to the divine would lead us to both mark and challenge the upper-case, lower-case distinction, through graphic signs such as "Him/him" or "It/it."

> The real which resides in the belief
>   is that whose form the heart encompasses,
> what reveals itself to the heart to be known
>
> The eye sees nothing but the real of its belief

And there is no secret about the variety of beliefs

Whoever binds him [in a belief] denies him in any belief
 other than that in which he has bound him

And affirms him in the belief
 in which he bound him in his manifestation

But whoever liberates him from binding, denies him not at all

But affirms him in every image into which he transforms
 himself

He gives him(self) of him(self)
 in accordance with the image in which he appears to
 him(self)

Infinitely, since the forms of manifestation
 have no end at which to stop

And, likewise, knowledge of Allah has no limit for the knower
 at which he might stop

Rather, the knower asks in every moment for an increase
 in his knowledge of him

 "My lord, increase me in knowledge" [Qu'rān 20:116]
 "My lord, increase me in knowledge"
 "My lord, increase me in knowledge"

So it continues, perpetually, from both sides.[12]

The Qu'ranic sentence, "My lord, increase me in knowledge," is repeated three times, thus indicating that it is a *dhikr*. In Sufi practice, a *dhikr* is a constantly repeated phrase (often a Qur'anic phrase) that guides the Sufi through the various stages of contemplation. The *dhikr* can be repeated out loud or silently, alone or in a group ceremony. In some Sufi orders, the practice of *dhikr* is combined with bodily movements, poetry, music, and whirling dance. In modern group recitation, the *dhikr* gradually leads the group to a control of breathing patterns and a harmonization of inhalation and exhalation. In some cases people might link hands and move in a circle, or in two concentric circles, one moving clockwise, the other counterclockwise. Two individuals may then enter the center of the circle, grasp each other's hands, and whirl one another in a direction counter to the movement of the innermost circle. At that point the face of one's partner stands out powerfully against the whirling mass of chanters in the two circles.[13] By repeating three times "My lord, increase me in knowledge," Ibn ʿArabi embodies the meditative force and the circular movements of the *dhikr* within his apophatic language.

In this passage the *dhikr* serves discursively to indicate that true knowledge is always in a state of change and increase (and is, ultimately, that very change or increase itself). On the practical level, the *dhikr* is the chief means whereby the Sufi and (necessarily) the writer and reader of the text attempt to break the spell of binding and achieve perpetual transformation: through the incessant process of reminding, the text attempts a momentary release from binding that leads to an "increase" in knowledge.

The critique of binding is based finally on a redefinition of idolatry and infidelity. The individual image that one has of the real is the God of one's belief, a delimited God that one mistakenly worships as the transcendent and infinite. Idolatry is redefined as the worship of such an image. Because the real manifests itself everywhere, including within the beliefs of others, to categorically deny the doctrinal beliefs of others is to deny a valid manifestation of the real; it is a form of "denial" or infidelity to the one transcendent reality manifest in each belief. The reconception of idolatry and infidelity is made indirectly, through an allusion to the Qur'anic attack against the polytheists, of whom it is said that at the last judgment they will appeal to their gods, but the gods will not be able to help them: "They have no saviors" (Qu'ran 3:22, 56, 91; 16:38; 29:35; 30:29). Ibn ʿArabi's use of this Qur'anic phrase ("and they have no saviors") leaves no doubt that for him true idolatry is the worship of the delimited God of one's belief and infidelity, the denial of the God of the belief of another:

> "In that is a reminder [*dhikr*] for one who has a heart [*qalb*]" [Qur'ān 50:33] because of its constant transformation in forms and attributes.
>
> He did not say "for one who has an intellect" [*'aql*] For the mind binds [*qayyad*] and limits the matter in one characterization
>
> So it was not a reminder to one who has an intellect
>
> And they are the affirmers of a belief
>
> Who call one another heretics and infidels
>
> Who curse one another
>
> "And they have no saviors"
>
> The God of one has no authority over the God of the other.[14]

This view of the monotheist-polytheist controversy of the Qur'an is made more explicit in Ibn ʿArabi's interpretation of the story of Noah (Qur'an 71:21–27). Noah had called the polytheists to the one

God, but they stubbornly refused to renounce their Gods. Finally, Noah called on his lord to destroy the idolators lest they lead the people astray. In his commentary on this story, Ibn ʿArabi redefines the monotheistic-polytheistic struggle in keeping with the dialectical nature of his thought. The center of his interpretation is the issue of *makr* or deception. The Qur'an depicts Allah as being able to out-deceive his enemies. Ibn ʿArabi uses this reference to divine deception to suggest a complex hermeneutics of suspicion in which conventional notions of good and evil, pious and impious, are put under intense scrutiny and in some key areas inverted. At the heart of this apophatic hermeneutic is an exposé of the spatial reifications that inhere in Sufi discussions of stations and "lofty stations" of spiritual experience, and in the interpretation of prophecy as calls "to God."

The Station of no Station

Noah had accused the polytheists of *makr* (deception, guise), but according to Ibn ʿArabi, both Noah and his rival party practiced deception, hiding the true apophatic dialectic behind the polemic between monotheism and polytheism. Noah and the polytheists each represent one side of the dialectic of transcendence and immanence. In a formal poem Ibn ʿArabi suggests that neither side is sufficient in itself, that each side by itself is a binding:

> *If you affirm transcendence*
> *you bind*
> *If you affirm immanence*
> *you define*
>
> *If you affirm both*
> *you hit the mark*
> *You are an Imam in knowledge*
> *and a master.*[15]

Noah practiced deception by calling his people to Allah (as if Allah were absent from them, from their beliefs, or from any object in the world, including the wood and stones they worshiped). The polytheists practiced deception by insisting in their Qur'anic response to Noah that their idols were separate deities rather than manifestations of the one real. It is unclear whether Noah and his opponents realized their roles in this complex guise and deception. The mystic knower through the unveiling (*kashf*) can peel back the surface arguments and reveal (subjectively and objectively) the inner dynamic. In the following verses I use "it" rather than "he" to translate the Arabic pronoun *hu* in order to keep it from reifying into either a personal or impersonal sense:

You are not it
  You are it
You see it in the essence of things
  Boundless and limited.[16]

Applying the hermeneutic of *kashf*, Ibn ʿArabi proceeds to unveil the rest of the story. Noah's accusation that the polytheists lead people astray is actually a reference to the fact that they lead people into mystic perplexity or bewilderment (*ḥayra*). Bewilderment is caused by an abandonment of the linear, dualistic logic represented by Noah's calling his people "to" Allah.[17] Commenting on Noah's statement, "You [Allah] only increase them in delusion," Ibn ʿArabi reverses the value of bewilderment, turning it into the highest state of consciousness, that of the "Muhammadian" (*Muḥammadī*),[18] one who models himself personally upon the circular movement of the prophet Muhammad (symbolized in Sufism by the circumambulation of the *Kaʿba*) rather than on the linear intentionality of Noah. Like Muhammad, who was said in a famous hadith to have been given the "totality of words and wisdom," the Muhammadian through a continual circle of movement attempts to achieve all the various words and wisdom. The center of this circular motion is the *quṭb*, the pole or axis of reality:

That is the bewilderment [*ḥayra*] of the Muhammadian

"Lord, increase me in bewilderment in you . . ."

For the bewildered one has a round [*dawr*]
and a circular motion around the *quṭb*
which he never leaves

But the master of the long path
tends away from what he aims for
seeking what he is already in

A master of fantasies which are his goal

He has a "from" and a "to"
and what is between them

But the master of the circular movement
has no starting point
that "from" should take him over

and no goal
that he should be ruled by "to"

He has the more complete existence

And is given the totality of the words and wisdoms.[19]

The statement "My lord, increase me in bewilderment [*ḥayra*] in you" is a reformulation of the *dhikr* (and Qur'anic citation) seen above, "My lord, increase me in knowledge." The attempt to dispel *ḥayra* through a method leading to philosophical certainty was the explicitly stated goal of Islamic rationalist philosophers (*al-falāsifa*). Scholastic theologians used the logic and methods of rationalist philosophy to dispel perplexity or *ḥayra* in the interpretation of the Qur'an, particularly in the key areas of divine unity (*tawḥīd*) and justice (*ʿadl*).[20] As was shown in Chapter 3, Ibn ʿArabi used the theological arguments concerning the divine image and attributes and transformed them through the meaning event symbolized by the polished mirror. Rather than offering a logical solution to the key dilemmas, he pushed the theological arguments to their extreme to reveal the essential irresolvability of the dilemma outside of mystical union. By reciting "My lord increase me in bewilderment in you," Ibn ʿArabi makes plays upon the previous *dhikr* ("My lord increase me in knowledge of you") while at the same time standing on its head the explicit goal of rationalist philosophers and theologians. Through such intratextual and extratextual allusions, he suggests a higher knowledge that is a form of bewilderment. That bewilderment is achieved in the continual transformation from form to form and in the circular motion beyond the dualism of origin and goal.

Ibn ʿArabi then reinterprets the water and fire in which the polytheist opponents of Noah perished. The fire and water symbolize the universality in which the individual perishes in the experience of *fanāʾ*. In this interpretation, the notion of "savior" takes on a special twist. What seems to be a negative reference to the polytheists (they did not find any savior besides Allah and thus perished), Ibn ʿArabi reads positively. They perished in Allah, their only savior:

"They did not find any savior besides Allah"

Allah was their savior

In whom they perished eternally

If you had placed them on the shore
  [of the seas of knowledge-bewilderment],
the shore of nature

you would have taken them down from their high station

though everything [including the shore]
is Allah's, and in Allah, and is Allah.²¹

Noah called on his lord as if he could call on a fixed reality. The mystic knower, on the other hand, realizes the union of servant and lord ("To know one's self is to know one's lord")²² and realizes the merging of his particular lord with all the lords (all the personal aspects of divinity and individual essences). Thus there are two very different ways of addressing the lord, that of Noah and that of the mystic knower who chants, "My lord, increase me in bewilderment in you."²³

The critique of spatiotemporal reification and linear logic is not confined to the categories of religious belief, philosophical concept, and scholastic dogma. It extends to Sufism itself and to the Sufi hierarchy founded on the notion of *maqām*, the station. A station is a kind of plateau along the Sufi path (*ṭarīqa*). By the tenth century C.E., Sufis had developed a highly sophisticated moral psychology, with differing lists and definitions of the stations along the mystical path. The early Sufi theologian Abū Nasr al-Sarrāj (d. 988) lists seven stations in ascending order: repentance, moral vigilance, renunciation, poverty, patience, complete trust, and acceptance.²⁴ Sarrāj offers a dialectical analysis of each station based upon three degrees, the third degree often reaching the point of paradoxicality (a poverty so radical that it abandons even its own poverty). Sufi theologians agreed that stations were to be traversed in sequential order and that one could not achieve a higher station until the previous, lower station was mastered. The station is opposed to the *ḥāl*, the momentary condition. At a given moment one's condition may be above or below the station. (For this reason one cannot judge the station of another.) While the Sufi can intentionally enter upon a particular station, the momentary conditions "come upon" or "seize" the Sufi independently of the Sufi's intention or will.

For Ibn ʿArabi, even the Sufi station may be a binding. In questioning the creation of Adam, the angels had boasted of their "high station." To attribute to oneself a lofty station is to bind oneself into a spatially defined path and position in relation with the deity, and thus to bind the deity into the same spatially fixed relation. In the following passage, Ibn ʿArabi adopts the normal hierarchical positioning of the station of *quṭb* (pole or axis)—the axis of reality as it is instantiated within the closest realization of the complete human being in a particular individual existence. He then takes it to its extreme where the notion of station deconstructs itself. In discussing the relationship of each "pole" to a given prophetic wisdom, Ibn ʿArabi speaks of a

Muhammadian pole (a pole modeled on Muhammad's *rūḥ* or spirit-logos) as a station of perpetual transformation, *a station of no station*:

> Nothing is more universal in its distinction
> than the lack of limitation [*taqyīd*]
> to a distinguishing station
>
> The Muhammadian is distinguished
>   only by his lack of distinguishing station
>
> His station is that he has no station
>
> This means that a condition [*ḥāl*] can prevail on a person
> so that only through it is he known [or does he know]:
> he is related to it and determined by it
>
> But the relation of stations to a Muhammadian
> is like the relation of names to Allāh
>
> He is not determined in any station to which he may be related
>
> Rather, in every breath, in every time, in every condition
> he is the image of what that breath, time, or condition requires
>
> His limitation does not remain
>
> The divine decrees [*aḥkām*] vary in every moment
> and he varies in accordance with them
>
> For he ( ):[25] "Every day he is in a different state" [Qur'an 55:29]
>
> And so, similarly, is the Muhammadian
>
> Thus his word ( ): "That is a reminder [*dhikr*] for one who has a heart."
>
> He did not say "intellect" [*ʿaql*], something which would bind him
>
> The heart is named "heart" [*qalb*]
>   because of its perpetual transformation [*taqallub*]
>   in stations and orders
>   in accordance with the breaths . . .
>
> The Muhammadian pole or individual changes perpetually
>   with each breath
>   in knowledge
> just as each creature changes in condition (*ḥāl*)
>
> The Muhammadian increases in knowledge
> of what he is transformed in and through
> not of the transformation itself

For transformation pervades the world entire and pervades him.²⁶

Ibn ʿArabi's apophatic logic is contained in particularly condensed form in the statement that "Nothing is more universal in its distinction than the lack of distinguishing station."²⁷ By affirming transcendence without immanence, Noah limited his deity by marking it off from the world. He formed a spatial delimitation by calling the polytheists "to God" and thus placing the deity within a linear, spatial relation. He formed a temporal delimitation by fixing the deity in a static image and thus closing it off from all new manifestations. Simple transcendence, the affirmation that the deity is "beyond" the world is simply a more subtle and more dangerous mode of "binding." True affirmation of transcendence leads ironically to a transcendence of the normal notion of transcendence, to a dialectic of transcendence and immanence in which the "beyond" is simultaneously the "within." Similarly, the highest station is that which transcends the high-low polarity. The real is encountered only at that station of no station and at that point where the Sufi encounters and becomes one with the eternal deity in each of the constantly changing forms of its manifestation, in each moment, in each breath.

ETERNAL NOW: MOMENT, BREATH, *DHIKR*

In using the term *waqt* (moment), Ibn ʿArabi is drawing upon one of the more subtle and developed of Sufi concepts. At its most basic level, a "moment" is the duration of a given mystical condition *(ḥāl)*.²⁸ The relationship of this moment, which is often a time-out-of-time, with normal temporal duration was the subject of highly intricate analyses by early Sufis. Ibn ʿArabi's own powerful conception of the moment plays off against the scholastic notion of the instant *(ān)*.

The theory of the instant played a key part in theological attempts to vindicate the fullness of divine will against the naturalist position that traced chains of cause and effect within nature itself. For some Islamic theologians, such natural causality assumed a power beyond or in addition to the divine will by which all acts take place. The Ashʿarite school of theology developed an intricate atomistic metaphysics. The world was seen as made up of atoms and accidents which are destroyed and recreated by divine will in every instant. There is thus no causal necessity operating on a physical plane between one instant and the next. The instants themselves have the same characteristics as the atoms, since the temporal must be in keeping with the spatial. Instants are thus discrete, discontinuous, indivisible moments of time. One might call them temporal atoms. Although the divine will follows certain patterns within the perpetual creation (allowing for empirical prediction and scientific analysis), these patterns or habits can be broken at any moment. A miracle is simply a breaking of the pattern.[29]

Ibn ʿArabī placed the theory of the instant in a new context. The re-creation of the world in every instant was no longer only the perpetual re-creation of the objective, physical world by an exterior creator. The temporal atoms signify as well the continual passing away and re-creation that occurs in *fanāʾ* and *baqāʾ* and in the perpetually self-transforming, self-manifestation of the real. Alluding to the Quʾranic language about a "new creation"—interpreted in classical exegesis as a reference to the resurrection of the dead at the final judgment—Ibn ʿArabi accuses the scholastics of misunderstanding the mystical possibilities of Qurʾanic language and the real meaning of the theory of the instant. In his new interpretation, he unites once again mythic time (time beyond time) and the mystical eternal moment (the eternal within time). Mythic time includes the primordial creation of Adam as the polishing of the mirror as well as the final resurrection, the Qurʾanic "new creation" that marks the movement into the afterlife. The constantly renewed eternal moment or *waqt* is evoked through a direct reference to *fanāʾ* or passing away.

> And "they are in confusion about the new creation" [Qurʾan 50:15]
>
> But the people of unveiling [*kashf*]
> see that Allah manifests himself in every breath
>
> And that the manifestation never repeats itself
>
> And they see as witnesses that every manifestation presents a "new creation" and removes the old
>
> And its removal is nothing other than passing away [*fanāʾ*] which is implicit in the manifestation
>
> And the remaining [*baqāʾ*] is what is presented by the new manifestation—so understand.[30]

Just as the moment represents a combination of Sufi and scholastic notions of time, so the term "breath" is also complex. It refers on the first level to the primordial breath of the compassionate mentioned earlier. But here the mythic dualisms of time and causality are all but effaced. The one primordial breath by which the world flowed into actuality is seen now as the eternal breath that always has occurred, and always is occurring.³¹ The breath is the eternal moment in which Allah exhales into being a new form and inhales or contracts from the old form, even as the knower actualizes that process by receiving the new form and giving up the old. In Sufi meditation the knower pronounces a *dhikr* in each breath. In the following passage the complex terms *dhikr*, "moment," and "breath" are fused in a unified dynamic of re-creation and transformation, a dynamic where the moments vary with the subject, as opposed to the uniform instants of the physical theory on which the new theory has been superimposed. Once again, at the moment of identity shift and mystical union, grammatical antecedence breaks down, and the pronoun *hu* refers both to the divine and human breather:

> The seeker continues to say with every breath
> "My lord, increase me in knowledge"
> as long as the sphere of the universe turns in his breath
>
> So that he attempts to make the moment his/His breath . . .
>
> The moment lengthens or shortens
> in relation to the presence of its master
> The moment of some is an hour
> of others a day, a week, a month, a year, or once in a lifetime
> And some have no moment at all.
>
> For one who is heedful of the breaths has the hours in his
>   power,
>   and all that is beyond that
> And one whose moment is the presence of the hours loses the
>   breaths
> And one whose moment is the day loses the hours
> And one whose moment is the weeks loses the days
> And one whose moment is the year loses the months
> And one whose moment is his lifetime loses the years
> And whoever has no moment has no lifetime
>   and loses the afterlife.³²

The moment is the nexus for the *tajallī* (the self-manifestation of the real) and *kashf* (the human act of unveiling): the two acts are one act. The physical objectified re-creation of the scholastics is merely a shadow reality, a phantom (*shabaḥ*), the shadowy mirror that is the universe without the polishing of the complete human being.

By combining the classical Sufi doctrine of *fanā'* and *baqā'* with the dynamic notion of the moment of eternal now, itself an amalgam of Sufi and scholastic notions of time, Muhyi ad-Din forms his theory of perpetual transformation. Through the fusion of antecedents in the phrase "he attempts to make the moment his/His breath," the dichotomy between eternity and ephemerality is overcome. The primordial breath of the compassionate, through the fusion of grammatical antecedents, is performatively identified with the individual, momentary breath of the Sufi. To adopt a phrase Meister Eckhart will use, this breath "always has occurred and always is occurring."

Bewilderment, Love Madness

They swore, and how often!
they'd never change—piling up vows.
She who dyes herself red with henna
is faithless.

A white-blazed gazelle
is an amazing sight,
red-dye signaling,
eyelids hinting,

Pasture between breastbones
and innards.
Wonder,
a garden among the flames!

My heart can take on
any form:
a meadow for gazelles,
a cloister for monks,

For the idols, sacred ground,
Ka‛ba for the circling pilgrim,
the tables of the Torah,
the scrolls of the Qur'án.

I profess the religion of love;
wherever its caravan turns along the way,
that is the belief,
the faith I keep.

Like Bishr,
Hind and her sister,
love-mad Qays and his lost Láyla,
Máyya and her lover Ghaylán.[33]

In returning to the famous verses on "the heart that can take on every form," I have cited them with a previous verse from the same poem, the verse about the fickle lover, and the poem's final verse (the last four lines in the translation). These verses are usually left out of citations because they refer to the Arabic tradition of love poetry and to the most famous lovers from that tradition. Yet the erotic themes of the poem are critical for a full understanding of Ibn ʿArabi's heart that can take on every form.³⁴ It is within the language world of love poetry that Ibn ʿArabi's mystical apophasis achieves its final and most distinctive configuration; a configuration that draws together the major themes discussed in the chapter (binding, transformation, the heart of the mystic, the breath of the compassionate, passing away or *fanāʾ*, the mystical moment and breath, the station of no station).

The verses on the heart-that-can-take-on-any-form follow as a continuation of the combined themes of pilgrimage and journey of the beloved with the women of the tribe away from the poet. The verses are introduced by a reference to the faithless vows of the beloved and to her henna-stained hair. The lover's complaint of the faithlessness of the beloved who has left him is always matched in early Arabic poetry by his own inability to forget or actually disown her. The deep red of henna is used in this context to symbolize the "slaying" of the lover by the beloved, a slaying that the Sufis incorporate into the death of the ego-self (*nafs*) in the experience of passing away. The parallel between the passing away of the Sufi in mystical union and the passing away or perishing of the lover out of the intensity of his love (which Ibn ʿArabi plays upon throughout his poem) was by this time one of the central tropes of medieval Islamic culture.³⁵

With the mention of the henna-stained hair of the beloved and the meadow of gazelles, the classical tradition of Arabic poetry becomes another of the varied language worlds in which Ibn ʿArabi's thought takes form. Of the lovers and beloveds mentioned in the poem, the most famous are Qays and Laylā. In the poetry attributed to the poet Qays, said to have lived at the time of Muhammad, the poet speaks of being driven mad, *majnūn*, out of his unrequited love for Laylā. *Majnūn*, the term for "mad," means, literally, "jinned," i.e., taken over by *jinn* (genies), the semi-spirit denizens of the desert associated in early Arabic poetry with love, madness, and poetic inspiration. Because he was driven mad out of his love for the beloved, Qays was known as "Majnūn Laylā" (jinned for Laylā, driven-mad for Laylā). The legend Majnūn Laylā later became a central topos of Islamic romance. By Ibn ʿArabi's time, the groves, mountains, and wadis (river beds) that were the sites of the union and separation of the early Arab lovers have become fully inscribed within the cultural tradition. The name of one of these lovers, or one of the groves, mountains, or wadis associated with them, was enough to evoke the entire legend of Laylā and Majnūn.³⁶ Such sites were frequently recalled during the almost ritual recounting of the stations of the beloved in her journey away from the poet, a classical Arabic topos known as the *ẓa'n*.

The final seven verses of the poem, cited above in the form of seven stanzas, culminate a complex series of poetic transformations of the notion of "station." In the earlier part of the poem, the departure of the beloved was explicitly addressed. The stations of the beloved's departure *away* were then identified with the pilgrimage stations of the pre-Islamic and Islamic pilgrim in his movement *toward* the *ka'ba*. The final verses recount a third set of stations (a meadow for gazelles, sacred ground for idols, the *ka'ba* for the circling pilgrim, the tables of the Torah, the scrolls of the Qur'an) that expand out interculturally into various traditions and cultural modes. These stations are equated with the various forms that the heart can take on. They are also, still, the stations of the beloved's journey and the stations of the pilgrimage. This merging of various understandings of the station is intensified by the poetic shift in which the physical *ka'ba* is identified with the heart of the Sufi. In that shift, the stations or fixed sites are portrayed (through poetic allusion) as moving around the heart.

After publishing the set of poems known as *The Interpreter of Desires* (*Tarjumān al-ashwāq*) which included the "heart that can take on every form" poem, Ibn 'Arabi was criticized for writing erotic love poetry. He then wrote a commentary making more explicit the mystical connotations of the poem. In the commentary he gives a strong clue to the link between the poem's "heart that takes on every form" and the "perpetual transformation of the heart" (*taqallub*) that is central to the Noah and Shu'ayb chapters of the *Ring Settings of Wisdom*. Concerning the verse "My heart can take on every form," Ibn 'Arabi comments:

> "My heart can take on every form." Someone has said that the heart [*qalb*] takes its name from its own perpetual transformation [*taqallub*]. It changes with the influences that come upon it, which change with its conditions, which change with the divine manifestations to its heart-secret [*sirr*]. Tradition [*shar'*] calls this "alternation and substitution in forms" [*al-taḥawwul wa al-tabaddul fī al-ṣuwar*].[37]

The "someone" who has linked the heart (*qalb*) to perpetual transformation (*taqallub*) may well be Ibn 'Arabi himself, who, as seen above, draws this link in *Ring Settings of Wisdom*. The reference to "tradition" at the end of the above comment is a reference to the "hadith of the transformations," which describes the various forms in which the divine appears to Muslims in the afterlife, forms often in contrast with the forms they had expected.[38] The placement of the hadith reference to the alternation of forms *in the afterlife* within his discussion of the "heart that can take on every form" *in this life* achieves two effects. First, it gives an authoritative backing to the critique of binding by citing the deity's appearance in the afterlife and people's refusal to recognize the deity in a form other than that which they have imagined. Second, it brings the afterlife into the present mystical moment by presenting this transformation of forms as something that the mystic can encounter in the present now.

Concerning the list of famous lovers in the last verse of the poem, Ibn ʿArabi comments that "Allah dazed them with love [*hayyamahum*] for their fellow human beings as a rebuttal to those who claim to love him, but are not similarly dazed with love." He then expands on the motif of the love-dazed lover in language that brings the erotic and mystical together: "Love deprived these [unrequited lovers] of their wits. It made them pass away from themselves at the sight in their imagination of the beloved."[39] The reference to lovers being driven out of their wits (ʿ*uqūlihim*, pl. of ʿ*aql*) is a subtle but powerful evocation of the critique of binding by the mind (ʿ*aql*) and the theory of the heart that can take on every form. The lovers are then said to pass away in *fanāʾ* just as the mystic is made to pass away from his or her ego-self into the real.

Ibn ʿArabi's commentary on his love poem is not an artificial imposition of intellectualized allegory. The connections between the actual language of the poem and the expansions in the commentary are robust, and the terminological affinities between the poem and Ibn ʿArabi's philosophy are precise. Muhyi ad-Din suggests that the ancient Arabic lovers like Majnūn and Laylā are models for the Sufi in the intensity of their love. Yet like many Sufis, Ibn ʿArabi at some point refuses to rest at an easy and comfortable distinction between "earthly" love and "spiritual" love. Had the Arabic love-poetry tradition been merely an analogy for the intensity of the divine-human love relation, such an analogy could have been drawn without the profound and sustained appropriation of the classical poetic conventions of love, love sickness, love madness, and passing away in love. When it turns to the erotic mode and the identity of the beloved, Sufi discourse offers a distinctive apophatic perspective. To ask who she is, human or deity, would violate *adab*. It would be an indelicate question. The beloved, immanent within the heart-secret (*sirr*) of the poet and the Sufi, is also transcendent, beyond all delimitation, beyond any single static image. The ambiguity (earthly, heavenly) of the beloved is a central feature of much poetry within the Islamic (Arabic, Persian, Ottoman, Urdu) poetic traditions.

THE STATIONS OF DEPARTURE

For Ibn ʿArabi, the image in the polished mirror occurs when the divine and human know and form one another and the divine names are actualized. The image in the mirror is also the intersection of the mythic polishing of the mirror (as in the creation of Adam) and the mystical polishing of the mirror (in the heart of each mystic). The emphasis of the Adam chapter of *Ring Settings* was celebratory, the celebration of the complete human being in face of the criticism of the boastful angels. The emotive tone in the discussion of Shuʿayb and Noah, on the other hand, is elegiac. In this chapter, the mystical moment (*waqt*) or breath is again the intersection of the mythic (as the primordial breath of the compassionate and as the apocalyptic final resurrection or new creation) and the mystical (the passing away in *fanāʾ* and the filling of the heart with the divine seeing, hearing, and speaking). The constant giving up of binding and the achievement of transformation of the heart (*taqallub*) is particularly elegiac insofar as each image must be given up in turn if it is not to become a God of belief and an object of binding. By evoking the Arabic lyrical tradition and by identifying the love-dazed and love-perishing lover with the mystically bewildered Sufi passing away in *fanāʾ*, Ibn ʿArabi evokes the essential sadness of that tradition (the beloved is always already lost). A reevaluation of these themes (the dialectic between the absolute ineffable and the realm of the divine names, bewilderment, constant transformation, the intersection of the mythic and mystical) should allow a new look at some enduring controversies concerning Ibn ʿArabi.

The label "pantheism," for example,[40] neglects the oblique dialectic between a unity and reality independent of all relation and the polarity of its interdependent relationships. While it is true that the *dhāt*, the self beyond all relation, is ultimately the only reality, this ultimate state does not nullify the other part of the oblique dialectic. The dynamic polarity symbolized by the two hands of God is essential to the constantly changing form of the real. Terms like "pantheism" and "monism" reflect a category mistake by turning the linguistic movements of apophasis into static categories of being. The internally paradoxical claim that "all things are one" does not negate duality so much as it guides the fusions and shifts, based upon polarity, that constitute the meaning event.

The claim that Ibn ʿArabi destroyed the element of transcendence in Islamic mysticism fails to address the dialectic of transcendence and immanence: the most distinct is that which is distinct by its very lack of distinction; the highest station is the station of no station. If one is to claim that transcendence has been abandoned, it is first necessary to discuss Ibn ʿArabi's critique of nondialectical affirmations of transcendence and the dialectical logic that underlies his own affirmation of transcendence.[41] As with the other apophatic mystics, radical immanence with Ibn ʿArabi is affirmed through pursuing to its extreme the hypothesis of radical transcendence.

Controversy has also been generated by the poet's celebration of his own condition: "Wonder, a garden among the flames / my heart can take on every form!" On the one hand, Ibn ʿArabi can be understood to be alluding to his own experience or rank, that of a Muḥammadī (one who is modeled upon the prophetic wisdom of Muhammad, the wisdom of perpetual transformation). The establishment and even boasting of one's rank was part of Sufi life and involved sophisticated procedures for validation of these "credentials."[42] There is irony, however, in Ibn ʿArabi's "boast." To celebrate the station of no station is a very ambivalent assertion of high rank, since the very high-low dualism on which it is based is being abandoned. Because this station (of no station) can be achieved only through the passing away of the individual in *fanā*, the voice here cannot be simply identified with the ego-self of the author of the poem. The self-praise occurs when Allah becomes, in the heart of the mystic who has passed away, the hearing with which he hears, the seeing with which he sees, and the tongue with which he speaks. The entire theory of binding is brought to bear against the assertion of lofty spiritual ranks, and the very term "lofty spiritual rank" figures in Ibn ʿArabi's scathing critique of binding, where he exhorts his readers to learn from the angels' mistake that to claim a lofty rank is to fall from it. To claim a lofty station is to lack *adab*. No one bound within a station, however lofty, could achieve the heart that is receptive of every form.

Muhyi ad-Din has been caught up in the modern argument over experience and the modern focus upon the mystical as the realm of extraordinary, private, autobiographically related experience. The common stereotype of Sufi history is based upon the alleged opposition between the early Sufis such as Bistami, Junayd, and Hallaj, who spoke from their own experience, and intellectual theosophists and systematizers such as Ibn ʿArabi, who presumably did not write from experience. The modern preoccupation with personal experience misses the apophatic fusion, at key moments, between ideas and "life." From the perspective of that fusion, to live one's ideas is a redundancy. As with the other apophatic mystics studied here, this fusion allows the mystical to be identified with the most common activities of everyday living. In Ibn ʿArabi, giving up a God of belief and becoming receptive to a new manifestation, in however humble a context, is revealed as nothing less than the cosmogonic breath of the compassionate and the self-manifestation of reality. As Bistami said, as cited by Ibn ʿArabi, the heart of the mystic could encompass the divine throne and everything the throne contains a hundred million times without the mystic knower being aware of it. For Ibn ʿArabi, the cosmological and cosmogonic world symbolized by the divine throne, in itself, is unrealized. It is within the human heart that the cosmos is realized, and within that heart, at the moment of passing away, the human is no longer aware of what it contains. The form or image (ṣūra) of reality is that constantly changing form that appears in the polished mirror at the moment of fanāʾ. The form is ephemeral; outside the moment of mystical union, it becomes bound into a God of belief.[43]

Ibn ʿArabi's language works continually toward such a polishing of the mirror, as referential structures are transformed and the antecedents of pronouns are fused. The metaphors of the polishing of the mirror and transformation of the jewel and ring-setting of wisdom are the locus of the meaning event that, like mystical union, is fleeting from the point within time. With each semantic polishing of the mirror, the cosmogonic world with its mythic time and the eternal moment of mystical union are brought together.[44]

In his commentary on the famous lovers cited at the end of his poem, Ibn ʿArabi evokes the classical theme of the ẓaʿn, the beloved and the women of her tribe who enter into their howdahs (brightly decorated camel litters) and leave the lover. The women correspond to the "appearances" (ẓawāhir) of the real that appear to the mystic whose heart has become receptive of every form.[45] By exploiting the fact that the nonanimate plural form is grammatically feminine in gender, Ibn ʿArabi, like many Sufis, creates an intricately pitched gender balance in reference to deity. In the poetic mode, those references tend to be feminine. The heart that can take on every form must also be willing to let go of every form if it is not to freeze into binding.[46]

The form of the deity (the divine names) and the human is actualized in the polished mirror. The form cannot appear without the human heart, and the human really exists only in that image. Yet in the elegiac mode, the ephemeral nature of the appearances (and consequently of the "lives" of the viewer) is a source of halāk (perishing of the lover), bewilderment (*hayra*), and love madness. In the *Ring Settings*, the perpetual transformation of the heart that takes on every form is presented from a positive perspective. In each moment, in each breath the heart reflects a new manifestation and becomes one with the divine in that manifestation. In the elegiac mode of the poem and commentary, the other side of perpetual transformation is evoked. In order to constantly receive a new form, one must constantly give up the forms one has already received. These are the "appearances" that leave the mystic behind as the ancient beloved and her companions left the lover.[47] The more ecstatic is the reception of a new form, the deeper is the sadness of separation from the present form. It is characteristic for Ibn ʿArabi to insist upon both perspectives; Adam was made with "the two hands of God."

The polarity of the two hands (a polarity that continually takes on new forms in Ibn ʿArabi's writings) applies as well to the question of love and knowledge. While Muhyi ad-Din is intellectual in the sense that he is willing to consider seriously any thought or belief system, his is not an abstractly rational philosophy. To give up binding, to pass away in each new appearance or manifestation, demands neither a special gnosis (the secret is not an objective "known") nor high intellectual rank (the highest station is the station of no-station).[48] Ultimately, it means the merging of the way of knowledge and the way of love.

CHAPTER FIVE

Apophasis of Desire and the Burning of Marguerite Porete

Marguerite Porete was burned at the stake on the first of June, 1310, at the Place de la Grève in Paris. Porete, from Hainaut in northern France, belonged to that class of women known as beguines, whose status was midway between the laity and clergy. The beguines modeled their rule in part on the rules of the recognized monastic orders, but they were free to leave the cloister and marry. Porete followed in the distinguished line of beguine mystical writers that included Mechthild of Magdeburg (d. ca. 1294) and Hadewijch of Antwerp (fl. 1240).

Marguerite had written a book that was condemned and burned in her presence at Valenciennes by Guy II, bishop of Cambrai, in 1306. She was accused of circulating the book after its condemnation and was brought before Guy's successor, Philippe of Marigny, who turned her over to the inquisitor of Haute Lorraine. Finally, she was handed over to the Dominican inquisitor of Paris, Guillaume Humbert.

Marguerite refused to cooperate with the proceedings, to take the formal oath, or to testify. Lacking her own testimony, Humbert submitted a list of articles from her book, which was never referred to by name, to twenty-one regents of the University of Paris, who declared fifteen articles heretical. A panel of canon lawyers then declared her a relapsed heretic and handed her over to the provost of Paris to be burned along with a converted Jew also charged with relapse.[1] In 1309, Guiard de Cressonessart, a wandering contemplative who had declared himself "the Angel of Philadelphia,"[2] intervened on behalf of Marguerite. He was seized in turn, his case attached to that of Marguerite, and he was ordered to abjure both his teachings and the distinctive habit worn by his group.[3] After his initial resistance, the Angel of Philadelphia, unlike Marguerite, recanted under pressure and was condemned to perpetual imprisonment.[4]

Within a few years, Porete's name was being associated with what was called "the heresy of the free spirit." A series of suspect propositions was condemned in 1312 by Clement V in the Papal Bull *ad nostrum*, and in the bull *cum de quibusdam mulieribus* restrictions were imposed upon the beguines and the beghards (the male counterparts of the beguines), their houses and their habits. In 1317, Clement's successor, John XXII, promulgated the Clementine bulls and a major inquisition was begun in Strassburg by Bishop John of Dürbheim. In 1327, the Dominican friar, theologian, administrator, and preacher, Meister Eckhart, who had preached in Strassburg and whose ideas show strong beguine influence (see below, chapter 7), was condemned in the Papal Bull *in agro dominico*. For the next several decades, inquisitions were carried out throughout central Europe against alleged followers of the free-spirit heresy.

Much of what is known of the Porete affair comes from the chronicle of Nangis. Its author, an anonymous Benedictine monk of the Abbey of St. Denis, signals his loyalties by referring to Marguerite as a certain "pseudowoman" (*quaedam pseudomulier*), and to Guiard as "a certain pseudo" (*pseudo-quidam*).[5] He gives the following account of Porete's inquisition:

> Around the feast of Pentecost it happened that in Paris a certain pseudo-woman from Hainaut, Marguerite by name, called Porete, had composed a certain book, which, by the judgment of all the theologians who had carefully examined it, contained many errors and heresies, among others, that the annihilated soul in love of its founder can and should give to nature whatever it wishes and desires, without blame or remorse of conscience—which sounds manifestly heretical.[6]

In addition to this account, two of the fifteen condemned articles are preserved in the procès-verbal of the theological examination. The first declares that "the annihilated soul sets the virtues free and is no longer in their service, having no further use for them. Rather the virtues obey her will."[7] The fifteenth states that "Such a soul has no concern for the consolations of God nor for his gifts, nor should she have such a concern, because she is completely intent on God and her concentrations would be distracted by such concerns."[8]

For 650 years, these two articles and the account of the Nangis continuateur were all that was known about the teachings of Marguerite Porete. In 1946, Romana Guarnieri identified a French manuscript entitled *Le Mirouer des simples ames* (The Mirror of the Simple Souls) as a copy of Porete's lost work.[9] The manuscript published by Guarnieri turned out to be a late fifteenth or early sixteenth century version of the famous and until then anonymous mystical treatise of the same name which had been known for centuries in Latin, Italian, and Middle English translations. No other early vernacular mystical writing seems to have crossed linguistic boundaries and proliferated in translation to such an extent.[10] Thus it was discovered that a classic of Christian piety, which had even been published in 1911 by the Downside Benedictines in a modern English translation with the formal Church approvals of *nihil obstat* and *imprimatur*, was identical with the infamous work of the condemned heretic Marguerite Porete, a work burned in her presence in 1306, and burned along with her in 1310.[11]

The full title of Porete's book is: *The Mirror of the Simple Souls Who Are Annihilated and Remain Only in Will and Desire of Love (Le Mirouer des simples ames anienties et qui seulement demourent en vouloir et desire d'amour)*. The Mirror brings together the apophatic paradoxes of mystical union, the language of courtly love—as it had been transformed by the beguine mystics of the thirteenth century into a mystical language of rapture—and a daring reappropriation of medieval religious themes. The result is an apophasis of desire.

The apophasis of desire results in a radical reconception of selfless love, deity as love, and authenticity as involving acts that are ends in themselves rather than means. Any act done as a means (*moyens, intermedium*) or as a use (*usage, usum*) is a "work," which entails an enslavement to the will. What might seem an unexceptional doctrine of salvation through faith rather than works is then pushed to the extreme: the soul that gives up all will and works is no longer concerned with poverty or riches, honor or dishonor, heaven or hell, with self, other, or deity. Such a state of utter selflessness, of annihilation of the will and reason—both of which are concerned with works—cannot be achieved through works or effort. It occurs when the soul is taken up or ravished (*ravie, rapta, ravissee*) by its divine lover.

Many of Porete's themes may be difficult to capture in their full force, not because they seem alien, but because they seem familiar. Selfless love, rapture, the fall into love, abandon, freedom as having nothing, passing away of the lover in love, are all interwoven through Western literature and are the subject of innumerable popular songs and romances. The apophatic placement of the extraordinary within the ordinary recurs with Porete as a confluence of mystical apophasis with the most common vocabulary of erotic love. The most extraordinary language of mystical union reflects the perennial and quite popular theme of the loss of self in love. The counterreaction to this philosophy of love, a reaction Porete labels "the fear of love," may still be found at the heart of conflicts within Western societies today.

The Mirror of the Simple Souls is a book of 122 chapters, most of it a dialogue of courtly love carried out among a group of personified characters. The principal participants are Lady Love (*Dame Amour*), also called Her Highness Amour, and the Enfranchised Soul (*l'ame enfranchie*), also called the Annihilated Soul, or simply, the Soul.[12] Through this dialogue, Dame Amour expounds her doctrine of *fine amour*, courtly love, a love through which the soul becomes "refined" (*raffinée*) to the point of mystical union with the deity, who is love. Another dialogue takes place between Dame Amour and Reason, as Reason is continually perplexed and confounded by the paradoxes and antinomies, the "double words" that result from the apophatic dialectic. Reason is never explicitly defined, but it becomes clear what the personification represents. Throughout *The Mirror*, reason is associated with the masters of the schools and the monasteries and with the theological discourse over which they had charge, the very caste of clerical and lay masters that is reflected in the distinguished panel of twenty-one theologians who condemned Porete's book.[13] Reason's inability to understand the dialectic and paradoxes of love leads her to be called at one point "Reason who only understands gross things and leaves the fine behind."[14] Other characters, such as Pure Courtoisie, make brief speaking appearances. The major male character is FarNear (*Loingprés*), the divine lover of the annihilated soul. FarNear, whose name echoes the coming-and-going nature of divine love in both beguine and Sufi writings, is identified with the trinity.[15] He is a central character in the drama, but never speaks; for the most part women speak in this court of mystical love.

The Mirror was composed partially in the form of a play and was probably meant to be read out loud, since it refers to its "hearers" as often as it does to its "readers."[16] The central event of the drama is the death of Reason who, after continued questioning of Dame Amour over the paradoxes of love, finally dies (chap. 87), "mortally wounded by love." This theatrically constructed event marks a major transformation in the annihilated soul, who is now freed from reason and able to "reclaim her heritage."[17]

In this chapter, I will discuss Dame Amour's complex teaching on love, its similarity to other expressions of beguine mysticism and to Sufi love mysticism, its inversion and plays upon Christian theology, and its fate at the hands of the Inquisition. Porete's understanding of mystical union will intersect a number of topics, no single one of which is central: the "work" of love; the vocabulary of rapture; the "fall" of the soul into mystical union; the reversion of the soul to a state of preexistence; the soul's living "without a why"; the fire of love-madness that burns up all distinctions.

THE FEAR OF LOVE

Like the other apophatic mystics discussed in this volume, Porete both posits and retracts a hierarchy, in this case a hierarchy of states (*estats*) or beings (*estres*) of mystical ascent.[18] The soul rises through seven stages of spiritual ascent, stages that echo one of the most prevalent motifs of medieval mystical thought: the rising through various hierarchical stages of perfection.[19] In Porete's version, the soul first rises through the stages of grace, supererogatory devotion, and good works. *The Mirror* is relatively unconcerned with these early stages, and passes over the seventh stage, the joy of the afterlife, in silence.[20] The fourth stage is the stage of spiritual poverty, comprising fasts, prayers, devotions, sacraments, ascetic practices, and martyrdoms. Dame Amour calls such ascetic piety the "sorrowful life" (*vie marrie, vita maesta*) and criticizes it as an enslavement to works (i.e., the "works" of the life of poverty and contemplation). Union with the divine is achieved through faith, she states, not works. She raises the stakes on this preference of faith to works by turning it against the very forms of medieval monastic piety that were thought to embody such a life of faith.

Within this critique of the piety of works is the paradox of will. A work is any act carried out through one's own will. Even the conventional life of piety, the life of the fourth station, is subject to enslavement by the will. Such piety can be only a stage on the road to the loss of self-will. The harder the soul attempts to transcend will, the more she becomes entrapped in it; the more she works to transcend works, the more she is enslaved to works. From such a dilemma, reason can find no way out. The answer can be found only in moving from the fourth stage to the fifth and particularly the sixth stages— the stages of mystical union—that are the central concern of *The Mirror*.[21]

The notion of grace, which one might expect to mitigate this dilemma, intensifies it instead. Dame Amour conceives of grace as divine love, which is nothing other than deity itself. This love allows the soul to become "disencumbered" of its will and works, and thereby, of its own self. Only when the soul's own being and will are annihilated can the deity work through and in it. When Dame Amour takes these ideas to their extreme, Reason is taken aback and asks her to explain her "double words" (*doubles mots, duplicia nomina*) and remarkable statements (*grans admiracions*). Love asks, disingenuously, what the double words could be. In response, Reason cites an earlier chapter of *The Mirror*:

> It says—in the seventh chapter to be precise—that soul is concerned with neither shame nor honor, neither poverty nor riches, neither ease nor dis-ease, neither love nor hate, neither hell nor heaven. In addition, it says that this soul has all and has nothing, knows all and knows nothing, wills all and wills nothing, as is said in the ninth chapter, above. And she desires neither humbleness of station nor poverty nor martyrdom, nor tribulations, nor masses, nor sermons, nor fasts, nor prayers, and she gives to nature all that it demands of her, without remorse of conscience.[22]

Elsewhere, Dame Amour adds more items to the catalogue: the annihilated soul no longer wishes to do anything for God, or to refrain from doing anything for God,[23] no longer wishes not to have sinned,[24] no longer wishes to do God's will,[25] is no longer concerned with herself, with another, or with God.[26]

Reason, raising objections which despite their subservient tone ring hauntingly alongside the articles of Inquisition, states a religious ideal contradictory at every point to the mystical ideals of Lady Love. Reason's ideal is:

> To desire dishonor, poverty, and all manner of tribulations, masses, sermons, fasts, and prayers, and to fear all manners of love, whatever they might be, for the perils they might contain; to desire supremely paradise, to fear hell; to refuse all manners of honor and temporal things, all comforts, refusing nature what it demands, except for that without which it could not live, according to the example of the suffering and passion of our lord Jesus Christ.[27]

Reason's understanding of the example of Jesus can be interpreted two ways: either Jesus desired dishonor, poverty, and the world to come, or one should desire to imitate what he experienced even if he experienced such things without desiring them—neither of which would likely satisfy Dame Amour's understanding of gratuitous love. For Dame Amour, any will keeps the will enslaved to the objects it seeks and to the works with which it seeks them, even if the works are the staples of monastic piety. The piety of the fourth stage, the stage of spiritual poverty, is rooted in desire. Only the objects of desire have changed: dishonor, poverty, tribulations, and the world to come, instead of honor, wealth, comfort, and temporal things. In a later passage, this life of perfection of works receives further criticism. Those engaged in it must continually be at war with their own sensuality. Their bodies must act always against their will and pleasure, or they will "fall back" into the life of perdition.[28] Yet these same people take pleasure (*plaisance, complacentia*) in mortification of the body, works of virtue, martyrdom. These "good workers" live in a continual state of desire, the desire to continue in their good works. They perish in their good works because of the sufficiency they have in their desire, their will, and their being.[29]

Dame Amour associates being disencumbered of will and works with the giving up of means or medium (*moyens, intermedium*). The life of works is a life in which human acts are means to be used to attain blessedness in this life and reward in the next. They are the medium through which the human relates to the divine. Virtues are another aspect of works, means, and usage (*usage, usum*). Dame Amour suggests that to move beyond the fourth station, the soul takes leave of the virtues (*prent congé aux Vertuz, accepit licentiam a virtutibus*). When Dame Amour states that giving up the virtues will allow the virtues to remain in the soul even more perfectly than before, Reason objects that giving up and retaining virtues "are two contrary statements; it seems to me I cannot understand them."[30] Dame Amour responds: "I will calm you down, says Love. It is true that this soul takes leave of virtues, as to their usage [*usage, usum*] and as to the desire for that which they demand, but the virtues never take leave of her, for they are always with her."[31] The life of virtue enslaves the soul to the desire for what the virtues demand, and to their usage. Usage, like means, is an impediment to the soul that would act without means, whose activity would be an end in itself. Their continued existence and activity within the soul that has taken leave of them are the work of Love.

Reason states that she has been taught to "fear all manners of love, whatever they might be, because of their possible perils."[32] "License," a word that occurs in Dame Amour's Latin expression for taking leave of the virtues, *accepit licentiam*, embodies the fear her doctrine of love would engender. (A historical note: the chapters on Dame Amour's doctrine of love and Reason's fear of love are composed in a distinctive manner that suggests the intriguing possibility they may be Porete's response to earlier inquisitorial criticisms.)[33] In order now to evaluate the theological implications of Dame Amour's doctrine and Reason's fear, we need to examine the precise implications of the "work of love" within the soul.

THE WORK OF LOVE

According to Dame Amour, to disencumber oneself of one's will, works, means, usage, and virtues, is not to negate virtues and works but to remove the agency of those works from the soul. Who then carries out this work? Dame Amour names several agents. At times it is God (*dieu, deus*): "And that is a work for God, for *God works in me*. I owe him no work as he himself works in me and if I did something, it would be undoing his work" (emphasis added).[34] At times it is FarNear: "This FarNear is the trinity itself . . . The trinity *works in this soul* showing her his/her glory. Of this no one can speak, except the deity itself" (emphasis added).[35] At times it is the trinity by name: "this soul has given all through the freedom of the *work of the trinity*" (emphasis added).[36] Love also plays this key role. Reason asks how it can be true, as Dame Amour claims, that the annihilated soul has no concern for honor or dishonor, poverty or riches, comfort or discomfort, love or hate, hell or heaven. Dame Amour responds that an understanding of the annihilated soul cannot be found in scripture, that human sense (*sensus*) cannot apprehend it, nor human work merit it. It is a gift

> Given by the most high, in whom this creature is ravished [*ravie, perdita*] by the fullness [*planté*] of understanding and becomes nothing in her understanding. And such a soul, who has become nothing, has everything, wills nothing and wills everything, knows nothing and knows everything.
> And how can that be, Dame Amour, says Reason, that this soul can will what this book says, which has already said earlier that she has no will.
> Reason, says Love, it is not her will that wills it, but the will of God, who wills it in her. For this soul does not remain within love which makes her will it by some desire. Love remains in her who has taken her will, and thus *love does her will with her, and love works in her without her*. (Emphasis added.)[37]

This work within the annihilated soul is a nexus for various threads of Porete's thought and it is the point of transformation, the *dynamis*, of her apophatic discourse. It is also the point of union for her various divine personae: Love, the Trinity, FarNear. Though Love is female and FarNear is male, though Love speaks and FarNear holds his peace, in the work within the annihilated soul they are one. And in this one work, the annihilated soul becomes one with them: "Love dwells in her and transforms her into herself so that this soul herself is Love, and Love has no discretion. In all things one should have discretion, except in love."[38] This transformation of the soul into love and the peace of love, "in which the soul lives and endures and is and was and will be without being [*en laquelle elle vit, et dure, et est, et fut, et sera sans estre*]" is compared to the transformation of molten iron into fire by the action of fire,[39] and—more radically—to a transformation into fire so complete that the fire burns without any matter.[40]

The union between annihilated soul and deity is a union-in-act, the act being love's work within the soul. In the union the soul receives gifts from its divine lover as great as the giver. In one passage, the plural "gifts" suddenly changes, ungrammatically, to the singular. The divine gifts (*dons*) are as great

> As he himself who has given it [*cecy*], which gift transforms her into him. This is Love and Love can do what she wills. Fear, Discretion, and Reason can say nothing against Love.[41]

Although this change from the plural (gifts) to the singular (it, this) could be explained as a scribal error, something more serious may be involved. The gifts are identical to the giver. The divine gift of itself to the soul will become a central theme with Eckhart as well.[42] Porete cites in evidence of the greatness of this gift John 14:12: "Whoever believed in me will do the works I do and even greater."[43] This union is also spoken of as a union of form; in another passage with a precise analogue in Eckhart, the annihilated soul is imprinted (*emprainte, impressa*) upon the form of the divine, obtaining this impression from the union of love. The soul obtains the form of its exemplar as wax takes the form of the seal.[44]

The soul's abandonment of discretion reflects a paradox found within courtly love. The rules of courtly love or "courtesy" (*cortezia*) demand discretion, conforming to the conventions and norms of society, and *mezura*, avoiding of excesses of feeling and behavior. Yet the courtly lover (*fin aman*) continually violated these standards of cortezia and mezura and acted in a solitary, excessive manner.[45] Porete has combined this language of cortezia with an apophatic language of mystical union. The union-with-and-in-love is *rapture*. Rapture is the act and work of love. The language of rapture includes a complex of interdependent terms and figures of speech (disrobing, nakedness, loss of discretion, loss of shame, abandon) that reinforce the basic sexual metaphor. As Dame Amour said, there is no "discretion" in love. The soul gives up her honor, her shame. She disrobes herself of will.[46] Her union with the divine lover occurs in nakedness. She gives herself over to abandon. She "falls" (in an expression that will have many levels of meaning) into love.

Similar themes are to be found in other beguine mystics of the thirteenth century. The metaphor of nakedness is central to the writings of Mechthild of Magdeburg and Hadewijch.[47] In Hadewijch's great poem "The Seven Names of Love," Love is said to "work" in each name. Union is figured through metaphors of physical contact and mingling. However, the language continually pulls against the limits of the physical metaphors. A tension is engendered in which the metaphors are stretched and ultimately shattered under the demand for a union beyond that which the metaphor can convey.[48] Even those names that seem gentle turn violent. "Dew," for example, assuages with a kiss the torment of Love's names of Live Coal and Fire. But Hadewijch portrays that kiss as becoming increasingly voracious, until it results in a eucharistic devouring of flesh and blood and final trans-physical union that is the trinity:

> When the loved one receives from her beloved
> The kisses that truly pertain to love,
> When he takes possession of the loved soul in every way,
> Love drinks in these kisses and tastes them to the end.
> As soon as Love thus touches the soul,
> She eats its flesh and drinks its blood.
> Love that thus dissolves the loved soul
> Sweetly leads them both
> To the indivisible kiss—that same kiss which full unites
> The three persons in one sole being.[49]

Particularly close to *The Mirror* in vocabulary of love are some of the poems previously attributed to Hadewijch or to an anonymous "Hadewijch II." Because of the difficulty in dating these poems, they may well have been composed before Porete's *Mirror*, or after it and possibly under its influence. Here, the eroticism and lyricism are intertwined with a more abstract vocabulary in a manner reminiscent of *The Mirror*. Hadewijch II depicts understanding as being "in your mirror / always ready for you. // It is a great thing to see / In nakedness, without intermediary."[50] She depicts mystical union as occurring in the "wild and vast simplicity" beyond all form and accident:

> Naked Love who spares nothing
> In her wild overpassing,
> Stripped of all accident
> Finds again her simple nature . . .
>
> For Love strips of all form
> Those she receives in her simplicity.
>
> The poor in spirit are then free of all modes,
> strangers to all images."[51]

The erotic tension in Hadewijch's "Seven Names of Love" is in the tension between apophatic union and the physical metaphors of union that are unable to contain it. The tension pulls against spatial paradigms. The erotic tension in Porete is primarily temporal and is located between the fifth and sixth station. From the fifth station of annihilation the soul is rapt (*ravie, rapta*) into a sixth station of union by FarNear (*Loingprés*). However, "It lasts but a little time for her. It is an opening like a flash, quickly closing. No one can remain there for long. No one who has a mother can speak of this."[52] The instantaneous nature of rapture is evoked again in a passage of great lyrical beauty:

> The ravishing opening and expansion of this opening makes the soul, after its closing, of the peace of its work so free and so noble and so disencumbered of all things, as long as the peace which is given in the opening lasts, that she freely remains after this opening in the fifth station, without falling into the fourth, for in the fourth there is will while in the sixth there is no will. Thus in the fifth station of which this book speaks there is no will—there the soul remains after the work of ravishing FarNear which we call a flash because of the suddenness of its opening and loosening. No one can believe, says Love, the peace upon peace of peace that this soul receives, unless he be she.[53]

In some cases, Porete will evoke the spatial tension as well. Referring to her divine lover, the soul speaks of "The exalting ravisher who takes me and unites me with the middle of the marrow of divine love in which I am melted."[54] More often, it is the temporal paradigm that prevails. Like the *waqt* or eternal moment for Ibn ʿArabi, the sixth station is the intersection between time and eternity. From the temporal perspective, which is all that can be evoked (the eternal perspective of the seventh station being passed over in silence), eternity is perceived as a flash, both timeless and in time, both permanent and evanescent.

THE FALL OF LOVE

In regard to the fifth and sixth station, Dame Amour had said that once the soul has been rapt into the sixth station (of clarification and rapture), it stays in the fifth station (of annihilation) without "falling" into the fourth. Those in the fourth station cannot have peace unless they act against their own will and pleasure. "Such people do the opposite of the sensual, otherwise they fall back into the perdition of this life if they do not live contrary to their pleasure."[55] Up until this point, the spatial metaphor of mystical ascent is consistent. Those in the fifth station are rapt into the sixth. They return to the fifth without danger of "falling" into the fourth. Those in the fourth must continually fight their own will, sensuality, and pleasure lest they "fall back" into the earlier stages. Then in a sudden inversion, the ascent is figured as a fall. In contrast to those in the fourth station, the life of the spirit, who must fight their own will,

> Those who are free [*frans*] do the opposite. For, just as it is proper in the life of the spirit to do the opposite of the will, if one does not wish to lose peace, so—in contrast— the free souls do whatever pleases them, if they do not wish to lose peace, because they have come to the state of freedom [*franchise*], that is, they who have fallen back [*soient cheuz*] from the virtues into love and from love into nothing.[56]

This fall back from the virtues into love and from love into annihilation and freedom is related to Dame Amour's statement that freed souls give to nature whatever it demands. *The Mirror* assures us that the freed soul, though it can do what it wishes, will never wish anything contrary to the laws of the Church (though some of these assurances are later interpolations).[57] Even if these explicit disclaimers are not interpolations, however, by themselves they cannot resolve the issue. In order to evaluate Dame Amour's claim that the soul is "excused" from everything, it is necessary to examine the view of agency upon which it is based. Those who act contrary to their own will and pleasure act through a kind of counter-will that is just as much tied to human will and works as the natural will. Such action is only another form of enslavement to will. As will be shown below, at the point of mystical union, the soul is free precisely *insofar as it is not the soul who is acting*. The divine (FarNear, Amour, or the Trinity) is acting in and through her.[58]

The sudden inversion of the metaphor of mystical ascent into one of descent is not unknown in medieval mystical texts. It occurs in the Jewish Hekhalot literature, where the ascent to the Merkevah or divine chariot can be replaced by a language of descent.[59] Sufis also offer some striking inversions of spatial metaphors.[60] In Eriugena, redemption was seen as a reversal of the fall in a way that inverted the *temporal* metaphor. There could be no fall until the redemption, because had humankind actually occupied paradise they could not have fallen from it. There is no paradise from which to fall until they return to it. Porete's reversal is distinct in the particular theological and cultural implications of sudden change in paradigm from ascent to descent. She associates the "fear of love" with the fear of nature. In this inversion of the Christian language of the fall, Porete brings together and affirms woman, love, the fall, and nature, four elements whose combination received a sharply negative light in medieval Christianity.[61]

In the mystical hierarchy, the mystic who ascends through the various stations can reach the "station of no-station," in Ibn ʿArabi's terms, in which the hierarchy is folded back into itself. Similarly, the soul who ascends through the first five states undergoes a series of deaths and rebirths that end in a folding back into itself of the telescope of hierarchical articulations. Porete speaks of the death of sin and the life of grace, the death of nature and the life of the spirit, and finally of the death of the spirit and the "death of the life of works" as leading to the most genuine form of life.[62] The apophasis of desire includes the admonition to give to nature all that it desires, but that admonition applies to the annihilated soul in which nature and will and spirit have died. After the death of the will and life of works, the soul no longer needs to work contrary to her will and pleasure. As Dame Amour will suggest, the soul no longer is the worker; the deity works in her.

This self-abandon results in a dialectic of nothing and everything. The soul shrinks to a smallness where she can no longer find herself. She has "fallen" into the certainty of knowing nothing and willing nothing:

> Now this soul has rights [*droit*] to nothing in which she stays. And because she is nothing, she has no care of anything, not of herself nor of her neighbors nor of God himself. For she is so small, that she cannot find herself. Everything created is far from her, so far that she cannot

feel it. God is so great that she cannot comprehend. And through such nothing, she is fallen into the certainty of knowing nothing and into the certainty of willing nothing. And this nothing, of which we speak, says Love, gives her all.[63]

The freed soul is disencumbered of all things and has no care for anything, self, neighbors, or *Dieu mesme*. The soul is liberated (*enfranchie, libera*) in complete abandonment of all will and all its "usages." Love tells her that she is "passed away in love and remains dead" (*estes vous pasmee et more demouree; in nihilo syncopyzastis et mortua remansistis*),[64] and thus is able to live truly.

In addition to will, reason also dies. The death of reason had been intimated earlier when the annihilated soul was said to be

> dead to all the feelings of within and without, insofar as such a soul engages no further in works, neither for God nor for herself, and has lost her senses [*sens, sensus*, wits] in the usage, that she knows not how to seek God nor find him nor guide herself.[65]

In this stage, reminiscent of the Sufi perplexity (*ḥayra*) and love madness, discursive reason passes away. In *The Mirror*, the death of Reason is acted out theatrically. Love states that this soul is "lady of Virtues, daughter of Deity, sister of Wisdom, and spouse of Love" (*dame des Vertuz, fille de Deité, soeur de Sapience, et espouse d'Amour*).[66] Soul predicts that Reason will not be able to bear the paradoxes of these marvels (*merveilles*), even as she declares herself "nothing but love." Reason then cries: "O God! how can anyone say such things? I do not dare to hear them. I fail, Lady Soul, in hearing you. My heart has failed. I live no more."[67] Lady Soul laments at the death of Reason, but her lament carries a ruthless twist; her lament is that Reason had not died long before. Only now is she able to reclaim her freedom. She formally announces Reason's death, whereupon Love graciously goes on to ask the question that Reason would have asked were she still alive:

> "Alas!" says the Soul, "why didn't this death occur before? For as long as I had you, I was not able to claim my heritage in freedom, which was and is mine. But now I claim it freely, because I have mortally wounded you with love."
> "Now Reason is dead," says the Soul.
> "Then I will say," says Love, "what Reason would say were she alive in you, what she would have asked of you,

beloved of ours"—says Love to this soul who is Love itself and nothing other than Love, since Love through her divine bounty has taken her reason and her works of virtue and thrown them under her feet, bringing them to death without return.[68]

Love's takeover of the function of Reason contains an interesting implication, beyond the necessity of someone to take on Reason's role if the dialogue is to proceed. Although Porete does not give a formal exposition of her understanding of "reason," Dame Amour had identified Reason with the intellectual establishment of natural philosophers, scriptural exegetes, and monastic leaders.[69] And as was shown above, Reason's questions echo those of Porete's inquisitors, and we can deduce from them Reason's premises and logic. With Love's assumption of the role of Reason, discursive thought (as regulated by the intellectual establishment of Porete's time and personified in Reason) is not so much rejected as it is brought into contact with the apophatic logic of the unlimited and ultimately subsumed into it at the point of mystical union. The questioning according to conventional logic and behavior continues, but the questioning is no longer an obstacle to the union. Reason has been subsumed into that higher knowledge called in *The Mirror* "entendement d'amour."[70]

In Plotinus and Eriugena, abandon and absolute trust are figured primarily as ontological, the giving up of being. As was shown above, at the point of mystical union, this nothingness or beyond-beingness cannot be distinguished discursively from mere nothingness. Apophatic mysticism entails a moment of letting go of such distinctions. With Porete's apophasis of desire, figured in terms of rapture, there is a similar moment of risk. Rapture entails complete abandon—abandon of will, of works, of reason, of self-vulnerability. It can occur only in a context of absolute trust. At the moment of abandon, the soul gives up all defenses, control, security. The soul annihilated in love of the divine no longer exists in the formal sense as a subject that wills and acts—the only will and act are the will and act of the deity.

The mystical union occurs at the moment that will is abandoned, but that abandonment of will (the theological implications of which will be examined below) does not entail a lack of consent. In the past two decades, the more sinister aspects of the courtly love tradition have been explored, particularly the way rape has been both exploited and disguised within the romance.[71] In appropriating the language of courtly love, Porete was not merely borrowing conventions and tropes but in many cases was transforming them. A language of "rapture," which in the courtly tradition could become a code for violation and disenfranchisement, is transfigured in *The Mirror*. For a closer look at the inversions and transformations within Porete's apophasis of desire, we turn to Dame Amour's distinctive understanding of the soul's reversion to what she was "as she was before she was."

As She Was Before She Was

The annihilation of the soul (with its reason, will, and works) entails a reversion to a precreative state of being, to what the soul was "when she was not." The reversion is evoked through puns made upon the word *pourquoy* (for what; i.e., why) and related terms such as *de quoy* (of what, concerning what). The annihilated soul has no "why," and acts "without a why,"[72] without a "what."

Dame Amour states that one who truly believes "is said to live and to be" what he believes. "He has no more to do with himself or with another or with God himself, not more *than if he were not*, though he is [emphasis added]."[73] In another passage, the paradigm shifts from the conditional (than if he were not) to the temporal (when she was not). Out of its overflowing good (*bonté*) the deity gave free will to the soul. But this freedom is only realized when the soul gives up her will and gives back her free will to the divine. There, where she was before she was, the soul has no "of what" (*de quoy*) for the deity to reprehend. She participates with the deity in many works, but always flows back into the deity where "I was created of him without me." There the deity and the soul carry out works together as long as the soul continues to reflow (*refluss*) back into the divine. The deity's act of giving "without a why" (*sans nul pourquoy*) echoes the soul's acting without a why.[74] Just as through its *bonté* the deity gave the soul her free will freely, without a why, and just as the freed soul acts without a why, so the deity takes back the free will from the soul without a why.[75]

Porete combines here the Neoplatonic emanation paradox of procession and return, her own inversion of the language of the fall, and a distinctive notion of "exchange of wills."[76] The exchange of wills occurs after the soul has fallen from the virtues into love, from love into nothingness, and from nothingness into divine clarification. At the moment of divine clarification, as the soul returns to its precreated state, the deity dissolves into its three actions of self-seeing, self-loving, and self-knowing. The soul no longers sees, loves, or knows the divine: the actions are now reflexive. At this point the deity, which had given over its freedom to the soul in making her "lady," receives back its freedom as the soul abandons her own will. In this courtly exchange, the divine "cannot take this free will back from himself without the pleasure of the soul."

> She has fallen from grace into the perfection of the work of the virtues, and from the virtues into love, and from love into nothingness, and from nothingness into the clarification of God who sees himself with the eyes of his majesty, who at this point has clarified her through himself. She is so returned into him that she sees neither herself nor him. He sees himself alone from his divine *bonté*; he is of himself in such *bonté* that he knew of himself when she was not, before he entrusted his *bonté* to her and made her lady of it. This was free will, which he cannot take back by himself without the pleasure of the soul. Now he has it, without a why, at that point that he had it before she was lady. There is no one else. No one else loves but he, for no one is outside of him and he alone loves and sees and praises from his own being.[77]

This freedom is ecstatic; the soul lives and is without itself, outside itself, or beyond itself. The ecstatic freedom occurs simultaneously with two events: (1) a highly erotic version of the mystical union of the lover and beloved (in which the two parties are now only one party), and (2) the courtly exchange whereby the deity entrusts the soul with its goodness and the soul hands back her will to the deity. Dame Amour dramatizes this radical freedom through complex puns on the word *pourquoy* (why, for what). To the implicit question, "why [*pourquoy*] should the soul live or act," Dame Amour states that the soul has no what (*quoy*) for (*pour*) which or on account of which it might act.[78] Dame Amour's colloquial language of living "without a why" contains within it the notion that the annihilated soul lives without means (*moyens*; or, in the Latin, *intermedium*). The term *moyens* can be read two ways: as a living without means or usages, a living without will, in other words, without a why; and as a lack of a medium between the divine and human, a complete immediacy of contact. Ultimately the two meanings are fused in Porete's thought. One aspect of this "why" consists of the rewards of heaven and the punishments of hell, neither of which, Dame Amour insists, are of any concern whatsoever to the freed soul. Similarly, the Virgin Mary lives without her will. She lives the life of the trinity without any *entredeux* or "go-between."[79]

The stage of "clarification" of the soul in Porete can be viewed along two vectors of comparison. One vector reaches toward the strikingly similar conception in the Sufism of the twelfth to fourteenth centuries, while the second moves through the courtly and theological context of thirteenth-century Europe, and particularly the beguine tradition. The reversion to the precreative state in which one "was before one was" has a close analogue within the classical Sufi exposition of mystical union. For Junayd (d. 911), the goal of the mystic is to reach that state where he is "as he was when he was before he was."[80] Behind Junayd's formula was the theory of the early Sufi, Sahl al-Tustari, in which this precreative state is identified with a Qur'anic passage in which the preexistent souls of humankind pledge their allegiance to their lord.[81] By the twelfth century C.E., Tustari and Junayd's theory of reversion to the precreative state was thoroughly integrated into Sufi understanding of mystical union. Another key element was the shift from vision to self-vision as elaborated in the Sufi mystical union and depicted through the imagery of the polished mirror (above, chap. 3). Of course, Porete was drawing upon a long European tradition of mirror imagery in her *Mirror of the Simple Souls*. However, the combination of that imagery with three specific themes dominant in Sufi literature of her time—the annihilation of the soul, the soul's reversion to the precreative state, and the shift from vision to self-vision—raises questions about the relationship of Porete's mysticism with Sufi thought.

The fundamental doctrine of Sufism is the annihilation (*fanā'*) and subsequent abiding (*baqā'*) of the self. These mystical states are compared to a polished mirror. When the heart of the Sufi is "polished" and the ego-self of the Sufi passes away, the divine is said to reveal to it(self) through it(self) its mystery; or to use a different convention, to reveal to Him/him through Him/him His/his mystery. At this point the referential distinction between reflexive and nonreflexive, self and other, human and divine, breaks down. For Porete, a similar dynamic occurs in the annihilation and the clarification that take place in the fifth and sixth stations respectively. However, the ambivalence of referential antecedence in Ibn ʿArabi is more muted in Porete's *Mirror*. Although referring to an absolute unity, the gender distinction between the annihilated soul (feminine) and the divine lover (masculine) makes the fusion of pronominal antecedents less likely, even at the point of mystical union. At times, however, we can see signs of stress in this distinction. Thus, the Latin text, which for the most part echoes faithfully the French, diverges from it in the depiction of the "clear" life. One particularly difficult problem here is that the French text is late (fifteenth century) and probably does not reflect the pronouns that Porete may have used in her thirteenth-century dialect. In earlier French, the gender distinction within the dative pronouns was fragile and could be ambiguous.[82] The composers of the later French text and the Latin may have been trying to interpret an older French in which the gender distinctions, already fragile, are breaking down at the point of mystical union. One example of this frequent breakdown can be found in the following passage. I have marked the discrepancies between the Latin and French versions with a slash:

> I call [this life] clear [*clere*] because she has surmounted the blindness of the life of annihilation. . . . She does not know who she is, God or humankind. *For she is not, but God knows of himself in him/her for her of her/himself.* Such a Lady does not seek God. She has no "of what" [*de quoy*] with which to do that. She need not do that. For what [*pourquoy*, why] would she seek then? [83]

In this context, the term "annihilated soul"—which I can find used nowhere else in previous Christian literature—its combination with the reversion to the precreative state, and the reference fusions that take place at the point of mystical union show a multifold affinity to Sufi thought that can hardly be dismissed as pure coincidence. The issue is not whether the beguine "borrowed" the concept from Sufi-influenced writings or developed it out of the courtly love tradition on her own—for the courtly love tradition itself was implicated with Arabic and Islamic culture.[84] No claim is made here of any particular textual influence; these ideas must have been circulating freely, probably more through oral traditions and conversations than the translations of particular texts. On the one hand, Porete's understanding of mystical union is remarkably close to the formulations of her Sufi contemporaries. On the other hand, it is grounded within the European milieu, particularly within the beguine appropriation (going back at least to Mechthild of Magdeburg) of courtly love, with the themes of the nakedness of the soul, the union of the lover with the divine beloved. Her writing seems situated at the matrix of beguine and Sufi traditions. Her originality and genius are one major testimony to the simultaneous culmination of apophatic traditions in Judaism, Chrisitianity, and Islam. They also suggest that at this particular moment in the history of Western mysticism, Sufism and European Christian mysticism were part of a larger multireligious cultural entity.

Daughter of Deity

The distinctiveness of Porete's apophatic language is found not only in the subtle way in which she configures the various themes just discussed, particularly her version of the "fall," but also in her reinterpretation of biblical and theological themes from the perspective of Dame Amour's court. The moment of annihilation in love of the divine is represented not only by the Virgin Mary but also by Mary Magdalene in the desert. When she began seeking God, Mary Magdalene lost God because the "of which" (her will, her work) interposed itself.[85] Just as Ibn ʿArabi had criticized Noah for calling people "to" the divine, as if the divine were not everywhere, so Dame Amour says of Magdalene that she "did not know when she sought him that God was everywhere and that she had, without any intermediary, the divine work within herself."

> But when she was in the desert, love took her and annihilated her and thus love works in her through her without her. She lived, then, the divine life which gave her the life of glory. Thus she found God in her, without seeking him, and also she did not have any "of which" since Love had taken it.[86]

In another pun, Dame Amour contrasts the sorrowful soul (*marrie, maesta*) with Marie (the Virgin Mary, but perhaps with allusions to Magdalene and Martha's sister—these latter two Marys were identified with one another in Porete's time—who also represent the life of the soul annihilated in love). Those in the fourth stage live the sorrowful life, the life appropriate for a fallen nature and a fallen world. A further aspect of the pun may be the association of this sorrowful life with the married life, but loss of the original French text and the fluidity of accents makes this supposition difficult to demonstrate.[87]

Porete's distinction between the sorrowful life of works and the life of the three Marys can be seen as conventional. She takes up the very popular contrast between Martha, busy about many things and thus representative of the active life, and Mary, who represents the contemplative life. Yet she uses this contrast as she uses the themes of courtly love, with a sudden reversal; in this case a reversal of the contemplative piety that saw itself as embodying the life of Mary, the life of contemplation. For Dame Amour, what others might call a life of contemplation is only a different form of enslavement to will and works. Such a life is caught up in the pleasure of its own mortification of the body, in the "pleasure" it takes in acting contrary to its own pleasure. A similar critique is to be found with Meister Eckhart.[88]

An unconventional twist underlies Porete's conventional use of the Martha and Mary figures. Similarly, beneath what appears to be a conventional understanding of the Christian trinity is a truly radical implication. In several places within *The Mirror* Porete takes up the issue of the trinity more explicitly and seems to be taking pains to show that her trinitarian position is traditional.[89] These passages on the trinity from a beguine with no formal theological training, sensitive as they are, were unlikely to have impressed her inquisitors. The bull *Cum quibusdam mulieribus* shows particular contempt for beguines who would presume to engage in discussions of the trinity.

It is in the relationship of the trinity to the personae of Dame Amour's court of love that Porete achieves one of her most important breakthroughs. Porete identifies FarNear with the trinity both implicitly (when she uses the trinity and FarNear interchangeably as the agent that works in the freed soul) and explicitly. Her use of triadic formulations for the divine work in the soul (self-seeing, self-knowing, self-loving) could also be interpreted in trinitarian terms. Despite Porete's care to repeat the traditional credal formulations of trinity, another trinity appears within *The Mirror*, though it is never named as such, that of Dame Amour, FarNear, and the Freed Soul, the three prime actors in the court of love. Dame Amour and FarNear are by nature divine and, as mentioned above, are identified with one another. The Freed Soul that is born of the death of the spirit is divine within them, or within their work within her. Heralding the death of Reason, Lady Love announces that the Freed Soul is nothing less than the "daughter of divinity" (*fille de deité*). It is through these three persons (who are yet one) that Porete's reconception of deity within Christianity unfolds, a deity who is gendered male and female and who speaks through the female voice. This voice speaks on the margins of institutional theology and its categories of reason, which Dame Amour refers to as "Holy Church the little."

The triad of Dame Amour, FarNear, and Freed Soul is not a trinity in the formal sense; the soul is not divine by nature. As Love declares: "I am God, for love is God and God is love, and this Soul is God by condition of Love; I am God by divine nature and this Soul is so by right of love, so that this precious friend of mine is taught and led by me without herself for she is transformed into me."[90] Even so, the three persons are placed in a suggestively analogous position to the trinity of the Church fathers. They each have a particular personality and yet are identical with one another as the agent of divine movement and work. The result is a daring vision of a gender balance in the deity. This was a period in which gender dynamics within the deity were being explored; the extraordinary symbolism of gender within the Zoharic *sefirot* (the ten divine emanations or manifestations) is a case in point. But in constructing a parallel to the trinity, in making the female voice the voice of divine speech, and in its difference from the Gnostic and Kabbalistic paradigms in which the female elements—however important and powerful—are particularly prone to sin and exile, Porete's vision may be unique within the classical and medieval Western world.

No One Can Harm Them

Porete's burning at the stake in 1310 can be seen as a turning point. The inquisitorial process was gaining momentum. It intensified with the prosecution of the alleged heresy of the free spirit and culminated (at least in central Europe) with a century and a half of witch-burning. Our discussion of the apophasis of desire in Porete will end with a contrast between the symbolism of fire in her writings and its symbolic meaning in the Inquisition. Hadewijch had already established a strong beguine fire symbolism in her poem on the seven names of love. She said of the name "Live Coal" that it makes the proud timid, the horseman go by foot, the vassal proud, the pauper a king. The live coal "sets afire and extinguishes" all contraries by the madness of love.[91] The fifth name, "Fire," burns to death good fortune and adversity since "All manners of being are the same to fire." Among the opposites that are collapsed or annihilated by fire are love and hate, winning or forfeit. Hadewijch then extends the idea to more radical grounds:

> Gain or loss, honor or shame,
> Consolation at being with God in heaven
> Or in the torture of hell:
> This Fire makes no distinction.
> It burns to death everything it ever touches:
> Damnation or blessing no longer matters."[92]

The burning away of opposites and distinctions in love is expressed by Porete's Dame Amour in another way:

> He who burns has no cold, and he who drowns has no thirst. Now this soul so burns in the furnace of the fire of love, that she becomes fire itself, through which she no longer senses fire, she who is now the fire itself by virtue of love who has transformed her into the fire of love. This fire burns in all places and in all moments without taking any matter, nor is it able to take any matter other than itself. For whoever feels God through matter which he sees or hears outside himself, or through the labor that he makes of him(self), he is not all fire and thus has matter with the fire.[93]

The annihilation of the soul, the annihilation of opposites and distinctions, the annihilation of the will, the annihilation of reason are all intertwined in Porete's book, and are brought together in this image of a fire that is completely self-consuming, a fire that has no exterior matter or fuel to burn. Elsewhere, the love is said to be the union of love and a blazing fire that burns without air (*souffler*).[94]

Despite its historical importance, the practice of burning at the stake has generated little serious discussion of its symbolic intent. Burning was the prevalent punishment for heretics from the twelfth century on, and the association of burning with the punishment of heretics was so strong as to be self-evident to those who practiced it. Yet explicit discussions of the symbolism of burning tended to be rare. This rarity seems to be due in part to the specific division of labor within the Inquisition. The Church authorities would convict the heretic and then would "relax" or relinquish her (*relinquari*) to the secular arm for the "merited penalty" (*animadversione debita*) as the euphemism of Gregory IX's bull *Excommunicamus* put it. The Church authorities would not specify death in the sentence, but works such as Innocent IV's bull of 1252, *Ad extirpanda*, made it clear to the secular arm how the language should be interpreted, and the penalties that would ensue for the secular authorities if the sentences (as intended, not as stated) were not carried out. Aquinas was equally explicit. In his argument that stubborn heretics should be put to death, he left little doubt about the consequences of being relinquished to the secular arm: "The Church provides for the salvation of others by separating him [the stubborn heretic] by excommunication and, beyond that, relinquishes him to the secular justice to be put to death [*exterminandum per mortem*]."[95]

The specific language of condemnation used against Marguerite Porete is the same language that was standard in the condemnation of those convicted of relapse:

> *Te, Margaretam, non solum sicut lapsam in heresim, sed sicut relapsan finaliter condempnamus et te relinquimus iusticie seculari, rogantes eam ut citra mortem et membrorum mutilationem tecum agat misericorditer, quantum permittunt canonice xanctiones.*[96]

> You, Marguerite, not only as lapsed into heresy, but as definitively relapsed, we condemn and hand over to the secular authority, requesting it to act mercifully short of death and mutilation of bodily parts, insofar as the sanctions legally allow.

The expression "requesting it to act mercifully short of death [*citra mortem*] and mutilation of bodily parts insofar as the sanctions legally allow" is difficult to place within the language of literary tropes. It is not a euphemism like "merited penalty," since a euphemism is related more directly to the word it displaces. This particular inquisitorial expression comes close to meaning the exact *opposite* of what it intends—only the sly qualifier "insofar as the sanctions legally allow" keeps it from such a purely oppositional intent. The expression has been called "a legal fiction," a "hypocrisy," and "a miserable equivocation."[97] However it is characterized, the expression both enjoins (implicitly) and denies (explicitly) at the same time the capital act, and denies the Church's responsibility for it. Such a denial left little room for theological speculation on the symbolic merit of the practice of burning at the stake; it was, allegedly, the concern of the secular arm alone. We are forced, then, to turn to popular accounts.

In the twelfth-century literature we find accounts of mobs rushing forward to burn the accused heretic who is protected from their wrath by a Church leader who suggests other, less radical penalties.[98] These accounts—even if they are considered an attempt to deflect responsibility from the ecclesiastic authorities to the mob—suggest an unspoken, automatic "fitness" between heresy and burning. While the Romans had a panoply of modes of execution, by the thirteenth century the association of burning and heresy had become dominant within Europe. Despite the lack of explicit theoretical discussion, several symbolic associations between burning and heresy can be found in popular literature.

1. The scriptural source used par excellence is John 15:6: "if a man abide not in me, he is cast forth as a branch, and is withered, and they shall gather them and cast them into the fire and they are burned." In itself, the passage demands no such immediate action and historically we might ask why burning became prevalent in this particular corner of Christendom at this particular time.

2. Thomas Aquinas suggested that there is no connection between hell fire and stake fire, agreeing with the argument that while the fires of hell burn the appropriate sins of the sinner, the fires of the stake are governed merely by the laws of humidity and moisture. The fires of hell punish the wicked not out of interior necessity but because they are directed to do so by the deity. At the popular level, however, burning at the stake could well be viewed as a preview of hell fire, and this connection was made explicitly in one of the medieval accounts in which the fires of the stake are treated almost as if they are raging up out of hell itself.[99]

3. The accounts explicitly connect burning at the stake to trial by fire and water.[100] In some cases, heretics were given over to burning only after being rejected by the water in the water test. Further study of the logic of the medieval trial by fire and water might well indicate an important aspect of the symbolic nexus of burning at the stake.

4. Burning at the stake was a method of utter annihilation which served several functions: prevention of relic collection and devotion; denial of ritually proper burial (an early alternative to burning was the depositing of the heretic's body in a Jewish cemetery, or burning it in a Jewish cemetery), and the cauterization and sterilization of society's disease or wound, a metaphor still used to justify political execution and torture in modern times.[101] In his argument in favor of executing heretics, Aquinas cites St. Jerome's famous string of contagion metaphors. The heretic should be cut off like a piece of dead flesh, expelled from the fold like a sheep with scabies, lest the entire household, body, or flock should burn or rot. Jerome ends (ironically in view of the medieval solution) by depicting heresy itself as a raging fire: "Arius started in Alexandria as a spark, but because he was not immediately suppressed, his flames consumed the entire earth."[102]

Some accused heretics, especially among the beguines, saw themselves in the tradition of the Christian martyrs, and it is clear that they had integrated their trial and execution into their own spiritual path. The popular accounts of heretics using magic to escape from or to become invulnerable to fire reveal an overarching anxiety on the part of the burners of heretics: that in the burning process the heretic might be vindicated through a pseudo-miracle. In one such account, the populace is ready to attack the bishop after two attempted burnings have left the accused heretic uncharred. Finally the bishop sprinkles holy water on the heretic's home and it is set ablaze, but this time nothing in the home is burned except the body of the heretic, which is utterly annihilated—the medieval equivalent of the neutron bomb.[103]

5. Finally, the stake seems to represent a kind of demonized image of the cross and the burning at the stake a demonic version of the crucifixion.[104]

The worry that a heretic should escape punishment through sorcery (interpreted as a miracle by the crowd) was not the only worry for the inquisitor. The Inquisition also feared that the courageous behavior of the heretic might place her in the company of the martyrs in the eyes of the crowd. The concern that the heretic's death might be interpreted as a martyrdom appears in the accounts of the burning of Porete. The chronicles suggest that the immense crowd that witnessed the burning was moved to Porete's favor by her comportment during her ordeal:

> *Multa tamen in suo exitu poenitentiae signa ostendit nobilia pariter et devota, per quae multorum viscera ad compatiendum ei pie ac etiam lacrymabiliter fuisse commota testati sunt oculi qui viderunt.*
>
> Many were the signs of penance, both noble and devoted, that she showed in her departure from life, through which those who witnessed the event testified that the *viscera* of the crowd were moved toward pious, even tearful compassion with her.[105]

The Chronicler, a partisan of the French Inquisition, must account for the sympathetic reaction of the crowd, a reaction the contrary of what was desired. His explanation, that the signs that moved the crowd were signs of penance (*poenitentiae signa*) is contradicted by the evidence on many levels. In this period any sign of penance whatsoever often was enough to stop the proceedings. The unrepentant heretic was a defeat for the Inquisition. In some cases, heretics were pulled half-charred from the fire at the first sign of repentance.[106] In Marguerite's case, the canon lawyers who condemned her, specified that on her repentance, before or after her sentencing, her death penalty should be commuted and she should be condemned to perpetual imprisonment.[107] Porete's behavior is consistent: from the authorship of the book, to her arrest, to her refusal to cooperate at various stages, she never wavers. Furthermore, after years of defiance, a sudden turnaround at her execution would likely have been considered a retreat in the face of death and a vindication of her original conviction and sentence. It would not likely have earned sympathy for her. Yet the Chronicler, openly sympathetic to the Inquisition, could not acknowledge her courage and persistence without placing her in the company of martyrs—a placement that Peter the Venerable feared when he complained that only heretics seemed to show the courage and resolution that used to be the hallmark of Christians. Of particular interest is the phrase the Chronicler uses to depict the emotional reaction of the crowd: the eyes of the spectators are said to bear the witness of the *viscera* (insides) that were moved to compassion—a highly personified depiction of perception and feeling, almost as if the faculties of perception and feeling had taken on lives of their own.

Within Porete's apophasis of desire, the fire of love melts distinctions: distinctions between human and divine, between heaven and hell, between honor and dishonor, between self and other, between joy and sorrow. The fire of the stake, by contrast, reinforced distinctions.[108] The anti-beguine pronouncements at Vienne show anxiety over the status of beguines. They were neither lay nor clergy. They did not work yet they were not authorized to live a mendicant life. They wrote in vernacular what should be kept in Latin. They lived a contemplative life but frequently traveled rather than remaining in the cloister. They engaged in theological questioning viewed as the prerogative of the male. Porete's challenge to such distinctions earned her the inquisitorial epithet of "pseudo-woman" (*pseudomulier*).

The tales of illicit sexual behavior in popular accounts of the Inquisition—both before Porete, and after her in connection with alleged members of the free-spirit heresy—dramatize further this concern with distinction. Porete's statements about the freedom of love and taking leave (*congé, licentia*) from the virtues—taken out of the context of the divine work within the soul—could not help but resonate with such fears. Within the apophasis of desire, the moment of freedom cannot be easily distinguished in a discursive manner (discursive reason at this point is dead) from what in contemporary language is disparagingly called "license." Medieval accounts of heresy are obsessed with the mingling of the sexes, with bestiality (the breakdown of the distinction between the animal and human), with homosexuality (the breakdown of distinction between male and female), and with incest (the breakdown of the distinction between parent and child).[109] To the stories of sexual abandon were added tales of ritual murder of infants and ritual consumption, as a "sacrament," of their ashes.[110] In the inquisition of Porete and Guiard, Guillaume Humbert is called by the common expression "the inquistor of the depravity of heresy" (*pravitatis heretice*). The language of perversion and depravity, associated in modern times primarily with sexual activities, shows strong parallels with the language of the Inquisition, but there the prime perversion was intellectual, with the sexual activities being a presumed inevitable concomitance of perverted theology. The charges of sexual license, as a literary figure applied automatically to those accused of heresy, in a way parallels the use of the blood libel during persecutions of Jews.[111] The impulse to impute, without evidence, sexual "perversion" to those accused of heresy is still with us. A recent historian ties together the concerns with several different "boundaries" when he charges that, because Porete seems to have traveled a good deal, she "*must have* been an unattached beguine, with no fixed residence, regarding mendicancy as a means of livelihood, pursuing a life of moral laxity, and refusing to submit to authority."[112]

In both mystical fire and inquisitorial fires, the fire annihilates.

Through burning at the stake, the reburning of the charred remains of the victim, the scattering of the ashes, and the burning of all copies of the condemned works of the heretic, the Inquisition sought total annihilation of all material aspects of the heretical being. Porete's fire of love burned with no material for fuel, self-consuming, at a point in which all distinctions between heaven and hell, the blessed and the damned are consumed, a point in which all works, including martyrdom, are burned away.

"Relinquishment" offers another contrast between Porete and the Inquisition. For Porete, relinquishment is necessary for the annihilation of the soul. It entails the giving up of all usage, works, and will. For the Inquisition, relinquishment is the turning over of the heretic to the secular arm, an act whereby the Inquisition disowns its responsibility for the execution (even to the point of explicitly asking for the heretic's life to be spared), while carefully assuring that the secular arm carries out the death sentence.[113]

In the present century, Porete has been called the "high priestess" of the free-spirit heresy, and a "heresiarch," and her work has been called "a work of heresy, written by a teacher of false doctrine skilled in concealing her unorthodoxy behind ambiguity and imprecision."[114] On the other hand, the very existence of a free-spirit heresy, in the sense of an organized movement with a defined ideology, has been called into question.[115] The notion that Porete attempted to conceal her unorthodoxy behind ambiguity and imprecision is at odds with the insistence with which she repeated her most controversial statements. Equally blunt are Dame Amour's contrasts between "Holy Church the little," trapped in its own will and works and its "rude scriptures," and "Holy Church the great" made up of those annihilated in divine love. The same scholars who accuse Porete of "concealment," write inconsistently (and more accurately) of her "audacity" and "obstinacy" in propounding her views even in the face of inquistorial prohibition.[116] Porete could have had no illusions about where her actions might lead, given the history of persecution of beguines that stretched back to the career of Robert le Bougre.[117] As Dame Amour said concerning the union of the annihilated soul with Love: "Loves transforms her into herself, so that she is Love, and Love has no discretion. In everything one should have discretion, except in love."[118]

At this point we might reflect upon Porete as author and upon the title of her book. The phrase "mirror of the simple souls" is ambiguous: it could be a subjective genitive (the mirror that the simple souls have) or an objective genitive (the mirror in which the simple souls appear).[119] The mirror was an extremely common topos in medieval European literature of all kinds, commonly used in the titles of books. Some suggest that the mirror in European literature is not an instrument of perfect reflection but one of reflection "as through a glass darkly."[120] In Sufism, however, the mirror was frequently associated with the polished reflection that occurs at mystical union. Porete's authorial voice within the book is ambivalent. In chapter 96, *The Mirror* comments upon its author. She is a "begging creature" (*mendiant creature*) who wishes that others find God in her through writings and words. The apophatic critique of the posing of reified entities is here turned by the text against its author. She is subjected to the same critique that *The Mirror* applies to all good workers, all those who are slaves (*serfs*) to their own will. Then, in chapter 97, the issue is complicated further. In the midst of what seems like a continuation of *The Mirror*'s relentless critique of its own author, another possibility is suddenly offered. The Soul refers to herself as foolish (*socte*) at the time she made the book, "or when Love made it for me." She then immediately shifts back to the more critical view, speaking of her authorship as self-encumbering.[121] The possibility that the book might be the work of the Dame Amour in her, that she might be an oracular voice, was a strong one. Yet Porete refused to privilege the oracular position. She chose a more ambiguous and problematic view of authorship, seeing her work in both negative terms, as a product of a begging creature trying to persuade others and using her work as means to do so, and in positive terms, the divine self-revelation in the annihilated soul.

Her stubborn (*contumax*) refusal—in the face of repeated urgings—to acknowledge the authority of the Inquisition, and her refusal to be moved by the threat of execution, are consistent with what Dame Amour says of those who are overtaken by love (*sourprin d'amour*)":

> But those who are always loyal to him [*Loingprés*], are always *sourprins d'amour* and annihilated by love and all disrobed by love, and have no care outside of love, no care even for suffering and enduring for all time all torments, however great, even if they are as great as God in his majesty. The soul does not love finely [*finement*] who doubts that this is true.[122]

The themes of abandonment of will, gender harmony, and living "without a why," introduced in this chapter, will be considered in more detail in chapter 7 in comparison with parallel themes in

Eckhart's writings. As a closing for these preliminary discusssions of Marguerite Porete and the apophasis of desire, here are Dame Amour's words on the souls annihilated in love.[123]

> They have no shame, no honor, no fear for what is to come. They are secure. Their doors are open. No one can harm them.
>
> Ce sont ceulx qui n'ont en terre ne honte ne honnour ne crainte pour chose que adviengne. Telles gens, dit Amour, sont segurs, et si sont leurs portes ouvertes, et si ne les peut nul grever.

CHAPTER SIX

Meister Eckhart: Birth and Self-Birth

Little is known of the early life of Meister Eckhart. He is believed to have been born in a village called Hocheim (two of which existed in the province of Thuringia) around the year 1260. At some point, Eckhart became a novice with the Dominican friars. For most of his life he moved back and forth between Germany and Paris: to Paris around 1277; to Cologne around 1280 to pursue theology at the school founded by Albert the Great; to Paris for more studies; to Thuringia, where he was vicar of the Dominican houses and prior of a particular house. In 1302 he was back in Paris where he was awarded the title of *magister* (master). The title, in its German form of *Meister*, completely displaced his given name. The Meister was soon called back to administration, first as "first provincial" of Saxonia, where he was put in charge of Dominican houses and convents, then later as director of the reformation of Dominican houses in Bohemia. In 1311 he returned once again to Paris, staying in the same Dominican house as Marguerite Porete's inquisitor, where he may have had access to a copy of her book. In Strassburg (1314–16) he was given the responsibility of spiritual direction for Dominican nuns in Teutonia. Sometime after 1323 he was preaching in Cologne. There began the troubles with the Inquisition which were to follow Eckhart the rest of his life.

In a letter to the pope in 1327, Eckhart lodged a complaint against his prosecution for heresy at the hands of Henry of Virneburg, the bishop of Cologne, who was later to lead persecutions against beguines in Strassburg. Virneburg had set up an inquisitorial commission to examine Eckhart's teachings. Sets of articles (*articuli*) were taken out of Eckhart's writings and subjected to theological scrutiny. Eckhart's responses to two of the sets (the first a set of forty-nine articles, the second a set of fifty-nine articles from the vernacular sermons) provide our best information on Eckhart's reaction to his inquisition. In addition to defending the propositions (in those cases where he acknowledged that they were indeed his), Eckhart criticized an inquisitorial process that took isolated propositions out of context, without regard for the central principles of his discourse. He also made a public declaration of his innocence at the Dominican church in Cologne. His appeal denied, he traveled to Avignon to appeal directly to the papacy. By the time the papal commission had cited twenty-eight articles from his writings as heretical, Eckhart was dead. On March 27, 1329, Pope John XXII issued his bull, *In agro dominico* (in the field of our lord) condemning seventeen of the articles as heretical and eleven as dangerous and suspect.[1]

The writings of Eckhart are varied in style and genre. His Latin works were for the most part associated with a massive project called the *Opus tripartitum* (Tripartite Work). Of the first part, a book of propositions that was to contain over a thousand philosophical demonstrations, there survives only the prologue and a sketch of the first proposition, "existence is God" (*esse est deus*). The second part is completely lost, unless some surviving disputations of Eckhart in Paris were meant to be included within it. Of the third part, the work of commentaries (*Opus expositionum*), significant portions remain of the commentaries on Genesis, Exodus, Ecclesiasticus, Wisdom, and John. Finally, a number of Latin sermons remain, some in the forms of outlines and sketches, others masterworks of Eckhartian preaching.

Eckhart's Latin writings are frequently composed in formal, consecutive propositions. However, his apophatic discourse with its double propositions destabilizes the static, point-by-point apparatus. Eckhart's writings in Middle High German, by opening up the vernacular to theological, philosophical, and literary dimensions formed a key moment in the history of the German language.[2] The German works include counsel literature written for the Dominican monks and nuns under Eckhart's spiritual guidance, a book of consolation, a number of short treatises, and the German sermons for which Eckhart is most famous.

Self-Birth (*Parturitio Sui*)

Eckhart's discourse, like that of Ibn ʿArabi, is situated between the unmanifest realm of absolute unity and the self-revelation of the deity. Eckhart refers to the unmanifest unity in a variety of ways: as the desert; nothingness (*nihtheit*); the godhead (*gotheit*); the ground (*grunt*) of the soul which is also the ground of the deity; the spark (*vünkelîn*) of the soul; naked (*blos*) being, the castle (*castellum*) into which Jesus was received. The distinctiveness of Eckhart's mystical discourse is in part due to his strategies, to be examined below, for keeping such references from hardening into false names for the unnameable.

The realm of self-revelation is identified by Eckhart with the procession of the divine son and word. In writing about the procession of the son or word, Eckhart combines his mystical language of saying and unsaying with his distinctive trinitarian theology. Two metaphors are central to this trinitarian apophasis. The first metaphor, "bubbling" (*bullitio*), is an Eckhartian version of emanation. *Bullitio* is the bubbling up of the trinity within itself, a bubbling that takes the specific form of the emanation or procession of the son. The second metaphor for divine self-revelation is birth. In the birth of the son, the deity not only reveals itself, but because the son is one with the father (mother) that gave it birth, the deity gives birth to itself. Eckhart's placement of a birth metaphor within the context of trinitarian procession destabilizes traditional trinitarian gender configurations. The traditional language of "begetting" or "proceeding" and "emanating" fits in well with masculine metaphor, but the language of birth, even in its paradoxical form as self-birth, cannot help but raise the issue of a mother. The language of the birth of the son, and even of the birth of the divine son within the soul, was not new to Eckhart. What is new, and what will be a major theme in this chapter, is the Eckhartian location of birth, self-birth, and virgin birth within a specifically apophatic treatment of trinitarian emanation.

The birth of the divine son (which is also the self-birth of the divine) takes place "in eternity" (*in aeternis*). In speaking of the eternal, Eckhart's challenge is to keep the language of eternity from reduction into a temporal category of "before" time or "after" time, in which the "before" and "after" evoke a temporal category even in the attempt to use them to distance the eternal from the temporal. In engaging this dilemma, Eckhart's language violates the normal grammatical division between perfect or completed action, and imperfect or action in progress: the one and only-begotten son always *has been born* and always *is being born*. It is the one divine "work" which always has occurred and always is occurring. This eternally occurring birth also takes place in the human soul. Eckhart insists that the birth of the son in the soul is the very same eternal birth that always has occurred and always is occurring within the trinity.

Bullitio as a purely interior movement is contrasted to *ebullitio* (bubbling out, boiling over), the procession of the divine outside of itself that Eckhart associates with the creation of the world. Eckhart uses the terms "univocal" and "equivocal" to distinguish between *bullitio* and *ebullitio*. The interior relations within *bullitio*, the relations among the persons of the trinity, are univocal, implying a relation of both equality and identity. The son is both equal to the father and one with the father. The relations between the deity and the world of creation (*ebullitio*) are equivocal. By equivocal, Eckhart means a relationship of inequality and opposition. If the deity is characterized by life, for example, then the world is dead. If the world is characterized by life, then the deity is beyond life. A similar double-sided opposition applies to other attributes such as being, justice, and truth.[3] Eckhart uses the term "analogical" to indicate the equivocal relationship of inequality and opposition.

The challenge for Eckhart is to link the realm of *bullitio*, the relationships of equality and identity within the trinity, with the analogical or equivocal realm of *ebullitio*, in which the created world is seen as unequal and opposite to the deity as creator. Even more so than John the Scot Eriugena, Eckhart employs the "insofar as" (*in quantum*) principle to indicate a transformation from one relation to another. In Eckhart, the transformation from analogical relationships of inequality and opposition to univocal relationships of equality and identity occurs when the divine son is born in the human soul. It is through this "birth-of-the-son-in-the-soul" that attributes such as life and justice take on meaning in both human and divine spheres. Any just work, *insofar as it is just*, is nothing other than the birth of the divine son within the soul, the one and only birth of the son of God that always has occurred and always is occurring. Any living, insofar as it is genuinely life, is nothing other than this same birth. Insofar as the soul participates in this birth, it is taken up (*assumptum*) into the univocal realm of divine self-birth where what gives birth is equal to and identical with what is given birth. In the divine (*in divinis*) what proceeds or is begotten or is born is equal to and the same as its principle.

When the gap between the univocal and equivocal is suddenly overcome with the birth of the son, there occurs a particularly Eckhartian version of the dialectic of transcendence and immanence. There is a point in the writing of all the mystics discussed in this book where the truly transcendent can be known only through its self-revelation as the absolutely immanent. Eckhart applies this dialectic to the language of distinction and indistinction. The realm of absolute unity is radically distinct from the rest of the world. Yet to adequately affirm that distinction, the mystical discourse is led to the paradox that what is absolutely distinct is distinct by virtue of its utter lack of distinction. It is only when the distinction is overcome that it can be genuinely affirmed.[4] The analysis below will pay special attention to the manner in which this paradox emerges within Eckhart's discourse and the manner in which it becomes intelligible.

The birth of the son in the soul collapses the hierarchical world of unequal or analogical relations: any work of justice—however humble, seemingly insignificant, unnoticed by the world or powers it may be—insofar as it is just, it is nothing other than the birth of the "only begotten" son of God that always has occurred and always is occurring. Conversely, the only just work, the only justification, that can ever occur is this one birth. The most extraordinary, the most cosmic activity—the self-birth of the deity and the procession of the son of the deity—is within and identical with the most common act of justice.

Eckhart's language of saying and unsaying will transform the temporal and spatial categories it must use. In treating the divine son or word, Eckhart's language continually equates the person of the son with the event of the birth of the son. The son as event—the event of the self-birth of the deity—is manifested in an eternal moment. The birth of the son always has occurred and always is occurring. Thus, while eternal, it is, from the human standpoint in time, an event that must recur in each new moment. In each new moment the soul becomes "virgin" (defined by Eckhart as free of attachment to images of the deity and desires), and insofar as it becomes virgin, the son is born within it.

In a spatial metaphor, Eckhart distinguishes between the realm of *bullitio* (trinitarian procession), where what proceeds from a principle somehow remains "within" its principle, and the realm of *ebullitio* (creation) where what proceeds becomes distinguished from and less than its principle. As with Eriugena, Eckhart's language hinges upon transformations at the microlevel of the preposition. In speaking of the birth of the son "in" the soul, Eckhart will place the "in" at the intersection of the two major modes of mystical union. Upon the transformation of the temporal and spatial senses of the word "in," the procession of the son into the soul and the breakthrough of the soul back into the ground of being become one. This is Eckhart's distinctive version of the strong Neoplatonic paradox that the procession is the return. In the following pages, I locate as precisely as possible the apophatic transformations at the level of prepositions such as "in." The first part of the chapter will focus upon the birth of the son in the trinity. The second part will take up the birth of the son in the soul. The key to Eckhart's mystical language of unsaying is to be found in his assertion that both cases involve one and the same birth.

BULLITIO AND SELF-BIRTH

In his *Exodus Commentary* Eckhart suggests that two names are particularly fitting for the divine. The first name is the tetragrammaton, a name that is unpronounceable and thereby, through its silence, protects the one so named from linguistic reification.

The second name is the divine self-revelation of Exodus 3:14: *ehyeh asher ehyeh* ("I am that I am," or "I am who I am"). Eckhart follows Maimonides in interpreting this self-revelation as a "negation of negation." In a general sense, Eckhart's approach implies the common scholastic distinction between essence (*essentia*: what a thing is, its quiddity) and existence (*esse*: that something is). The "I am that I am" identifies quiddity (*quiditas*: what is) with existence (*anitas*, the act of existence: that something is). This identification of essence and existence is an attempt to affirm a transcendence beyond delimitation and prevents the deity from being reduced to what Eckhart calls "a this or a that."[5] Rather than attempting to fit Eckhart's *Exodus Commentary* more explicitly into his notoriously complex scholastic ontology, I will focus instead upon Eckhart's linguistic strategies, particularly his use of the metaphors of *bullitio* and *self-birth*. It is through the temporal and spatial transformations within these metaphors that Eckhart's distinctive contribution to apophatic language can be found.

In chapter 1 of this book, Plotinian metaphors of emanation were read in part as reflections upon the nature of Plotinian apophasis; with the turning back (*epistrophe*) corresponding to the apophatic turn of the discourse against its own reification. In the Eckhart commentary, the movement of language and the movement of emanation are more explicitly joined. The reduplication of the "I am" in "I am that I am" is read as both an ontological and a semantic "turning back" of the divine existence into and upon itself. This turning back is then read into the metaphors of *bullitio* and self-birth. Through such a reading Eckhart establishes a definition of life that he will deepen into a multivalent and recurring symbol.

> Indeed, the essence is the existence, which is fitting only for God, whose "whatness" [*quiditas*] is his "thatness" [*anitas*], as Avicenna said, and who has no whatness beyond his thatness, which is his existence [*esse*]. . . .
> Note that the repetition of "am" in "I am who I am"

> indicates the purity of affirmation, along with the exclusion of everything negative from *deus*; as well as a certain turning back and reversion of its existence [*esse*] into and upon itself, and its dwelling and inherence in itself; all this, as well as a certain *bullitio* and self-birth [*parturitionem sui*]—seething in/into itself [*in se*], and in and into itself melting and bubbling. Light in light and into light, utterly interpenetrating itself, turned completely upon itself and reflected upon itself from all sides. As the wise man said: "Monad begets—or begat—monad, and reflected its love or ardor into itself."
>
> For this reason it is said in the first chapter of John: "In him was Life." "Life" indicates a certain pushing out [*exseritionem*] by which something, swelling up in itself, pours itself into itself, whatever of it into whatever, before pouring out and boiling over. So it is that the emanation of the persons in the deity is a reason [*ratio*] and a precursor [*praevia*] of creation. Thus, in John 1 it is said: "In the beginning was the word," and a little later on: "all things were made through it."[6]

The speaker of "I am who I am" does not become a "what," or a "this or a that." The semantic and ontological turning back of existence onto itself is read in terms of metaphors of *bullitio* and self-birth (*parturitionem sui*). The second paragraph brings the prologue of John's Gospel into a more explicit apophatic exploration of "life" as self-birth. Life is a certain pushing out (*exseritionem*), by which something "swelling up in itself" (the same phrase we had seen in the earlier *bullitio* passage) pours itself into itself. The word *quodlibet* is used to express this pouring of self into self without dividing the self into a pouring part, a poured part, and a receiving part. Part-language, even when used with explicit disclaimers, can serve to reduce apophatic dynamic into a static sum-of-the-parts view of unity. The *quodlibet*, literally "whatever you wish," or "whatever you might choose to call it," takes on a distinctive precision, ironically calling into question its own language of "whatness" (*quod, quid*) and the tendency of that language to delimit.[7]

Eriugena used a paradox of procession and return to effect a series of transformations at the level of prepositions such as "into": the emanation both is, and transcends, the "all things" that it flows into. It overflows all things. Eckhart's language of *bullitio* effects the same transformations, with a twist. *Bullitio* is a purely interior process, with no pouring out. Eckhart cannot, in the manner of John the Scot, assert the emanation *out and into* all things and then move toward a transformation of the spatial implications of the "out" and "into." With bullitio, the tension between the "within" and the "without" is more immediate: "in an into itself melting and bubbling." "Into" implies a motion from the outside to the inside, and a receptacle of the motion. "In" implies a remaining within. Similarly, while the "turning back" of the existence into and upon itself implies an initial separation or distinction of the self from the self, the "dwelling and inherence" (*mansionem et fixionem*) would contradict such a separation.

The immediacy with which spatial categories are destabilized in Eckhart's *bullitio* is clearly illustrated in his definition of *bullitio* as a formal emanation (*emanatio*), with "everything exterior [*extrinsecus*] excluded."[8] Yet *emanatio* means, literally, "*out*-flowing" (*e-manatio*). The tension between the interiority and exteriority implied by the paradox of a purely interior emanation is further reflected in Eckhart's language of something "swelling up out of itself and in itself." In this commentary on Exodus 3:14, Eckhart grounds his conception of "life" in the apophatic critique of a substantialist deity, the spatial transformations of a distinctive version of emanation, and the metaphors of *bullitio* and self-birth as expressions of those transformations.

Analogical and Univocal

Eckhart ended the above passage on Exodus with references to the opening of the Gospel of John. In his own *Commentary on John* Eckhart places *bullitio* and self-birth within the context of a trinitarian theology focusing upon the procession of the son from the father. The key passage takes the form of an interpretation of the words *principium* (principle, beginning), "life," and "light" in the famous opening passage of John:

> In the *principium* was the word, and the word was with God, and the word was God. It was with God in the beginning. Through it all things were made. Without it nothing was made. What was made was life in it, and the life was the light of humankind. The light shines in the darkness and the darkness has not comprehended it.[9]

The commentary begins with the relationship of a product to its principle (*principium*) or producer (*producens*), from which it is said to proceed (*procedere*). That which proceeds is "in" its producer as a seed is in its principle, as a word is in its speaker, as a product is in its producer in the form of an idea (*ratio*).[10] The expression "in the beginning was the word" is here being interpreted in several ways: the word is in its *principium* (beginning or principle) as a generative cause (seed in its principle); as potential expression (word in the speaker); and finally as a formal cause (as the idea through which something is produced).

Eckhart then states that that which proceeds from anything is distinguished from it (*quid procedit ab alio, distinguitur ab illo*). The sentence from John, "and the word was with God," indicates for Eckhart that the word was distinguished from, but "equal" to, its source. The notion of equality enables him to link the language of emanation or procession to his distinctive understanding of the analogical and the univocal:

> In the analogical realm what is produced is always inferior, less, more imperfect, and unequal to the producer. In the univocal realm, however, it is always equal, not just participating in the same nature, but taking the entire nature, simply, wholly, and equally, from its principle.[11]

Eckhart integrates his notions of "procession" and analogy within his distinctively apophatic employment of the conventional trinitarian distinction between the sameness of nature and distinction of persons. "What proceeds is the son of the producer. For a son is that which becomes other in person, not other in nature" (*Procedens est filius producentis. Filius est enim qui fit alius in persona, non aliud in natura*). In Eckhart's interpretation of the Johannine "the word was God" (*deus erat verbum*), he stresses the sameness of nature: "The son or word is the *very same thing* as the father or principle" (*sit id ipsum filius sive verbum, quod est pater sive principium*).[12] Thomas Aquinas draws a similar line between the distinction of persons, indicated by the masculine pronouns for other (*alius*) and one (*unus*), and the sameness of nature or essence, indicated by the neuter pronouns for other (*aliud*) and one (*unum*). "Because distinction in the divine is according to persons rather than essence, we say that the father is other [*alius*] than the son, not other [*aliud*]; and conversely, we say that they are one [*unum*], not one [*unus*]."[13] This is exactly the distinction Eckhart plays upon when he uses the neuter pronouns *id ipsum* (the same thing) to say that the father and the son are one. What separates Eckhart from Thomas here is not a difference in doctrine but a difference in discourse. Eckhart will go on to use the oneness located in the neuter terms to dislocate grammatical and semantic structures within his notions of self-birth and univocal relations. If what proceeds is *the same thing* as that from which it proceeded, then the procession is a self-begetting (or self-birth). The paradox of self-causality destabilizes the logical and grammatical distinction between self and other, reflexive and nonreflexive action.

Eckhart now ties his theory of analogy and his self-transformative use of prepositions into the key *inquantum* (insofar as) principle. In analogical relations, what descends *from* its producer is *under* the producer, not equal to it. Taking the example of a chest in the mind of its maker, Eckhart states that "*Insofar as* it is in it [its producer] it is not other than it in nature." This chest in the mind of the craftsman is not a chest, Eckhart tells us, but the life and understanding of the craftsman.[14] The *inquantum* principle allows Eckhart, as it allowed Eriugena, to link the interior movements of formal causality within the trinity to the movement outside of the trinity, to creation. The principle will become for Eckhart the link between the apophatic logic of double propositions and the traditional logic of single propositions. In the interior relations of trinity, the causality is purely formal, with no efficient, final, or material cause. Eckhart, like other writers influenced by Neoplatonism, uses the metaphor of emanation to explore the concept of a purely formal causality. He also uses it to support his paradoxical use of terms like *emanatio* and *processio* that imply a movement out, but that somehow allow the product to remain within the producer, since the product exists within the producer as an idea in the mind.

Emanation as purely formal causality destabilizes not only the spatial sense implied in the language of procession, but also the basic grammatical distinction between perfect or completed action and imperfect or ongoing action. What is *within* its principle, such as a chest within the mind of the carpenter, is beyond corruption. As a purely formal and interior procession, production, or emanation (*processio sive productio et emanatio*) is atemporal. It does not "slip into the past" (*labitur in praeteritum*). "It is always in the principle, always being born, always being generated" (*et si semper in principio, semper nascitur, semper generatur*). "Either it never happens or it always happens."[15] The language of "always being born" is radicalized by being placed together with the language of "always having been born." The son in the divine realm (*in divinis*) or the word in its principle "Is always being born, and always is already born" (*semper nascitur, semper natus est*).[16] The grammatical distinction between perfect and imperfect tenses is a reflection of time. To glimpse the meaning of the eternal from a standpoint in time requires a transformation of temporal categories.

The first treatise on John ends with a discussion of life and light. John's expression "and what was made in him was life" indicates that the chest in the mind and art of the maker is neither a chest nor is it "made" (*factum*) but is the art itself, the *life*, and the vital conception of the craftsman.[17] The product in the mind of the maker is intelligible and this intelligibility is symbolized by light: "In created things nothing shines except their ideas" (*in rebus creatis nihil lucet praeter ipsarum rationes*).[18] This Eckhartian formula dramatizes the relation of objects to the ideas: insofar as objects are "in themselves" they are darkness; insofar as they are "in their ideas" and "are their ideas," they are taken up into purely formal causality and univocal relations. As such, they are life (*bullitio*, self-birth). They are light and intelligibility because insofar as they are in their ideas and are their ideas they take on the purely formal causality of the divine word in which the ideas reside and with which the ideas are one.

In this short section, Eckhart presents a number of concepts, all of which intersect, but each of which operates on a different plane of discourse:

1. Procession as emanation that remains "in" its principle.
2. The distinction of "in" and "from" and the beginning of the transformation of their spatial sense.
3. Example of the chest in the mind of its maker.
4. *Analogical* relations (whereby what proceeds is below, inferior to, and in many cases contrary to that from which it proceeds) and *univocal* relations (whereby what proceeds remains within its principle, equal to it, the same thing as it).
5. Trinitarian theology:
    a) distinction between difference of persons, sameness of nature;
    b) identification of that which begets and that which is begotten as "the same thing."
6. The *inquantum* (insofar as, inasmuch as) principle: insofar as what proceeds remains within its principle, it is equal to it, univocally related to it, the same thing as it.
7. Time:
    a) insofar as it remains in its principle, it does not slip into the past;
    b) the word "was" in the prologue to John's Gospel combines substance with perfect and imperfect senses;
    c) the word always has been born and always is being born.

8. Life: the chest in the mind of its maker is its "life," life as self-birth, self-generation (where what is born is equal to and identical with and remains within what gives it birth); life as purely formal causality and self-causality.
9. Theophany: the light of all things is their idea in the mind of their maker.

Each of these points, operating on different levels of metaphor and abstraction, recurs throughout Eckhart's writings. Each is propositionally unstable, that is, each involves a paradox that prevents it from freezing into a stable proposition. As with Ibn ʿArabi, the various points can never be definitively articulated but must be reconfigured continually. Eckhart deepens his employment of these themes in the very next series of propositions from the *Commentary on John*. In it, the trinitarian deity is figured as "justice," with a dialectical relationship between unbegotten justice (the father) and begotten justice (the son).

Begotten Justice, Unbegotten Justice

For Eckhart, the just person (*iustus*),[19] is begotten justice itself, the divine son. The divine son, as was seen above, is identified with the event of his own birth, the birth that always has occurred and always is occurring. However, any person, *insofar as he is just*, is *in* justice, in a univocal relationship to it, equal to it, identical with it. There is a univocal relationship between the just person "in justice" and justice itself.

Early in the essay, in a key passage, Eckhart speaks of the just person being "taken up" (*assumptum*) into justice:

> The just person is the word of justice, that by which justice speaks itself and manifests itself. If justice did not justify, no one would have knowledge of it, but it would be known only to itself, as when it is said: "No one has seen God; the only-begotten who is in the heart of the father has announced him" (John 1:18) or "no one knows the father except the son" (Matt. 11:27), or "No one knows who does not receive" (Rev. 2:17). It is universally the case that no one knows divine perfection "who does not receive." Thus justice is known to itself alone and to the just person taken up [*assumptum*] by justice. This is the meaning of the authority that says that the trinity, God, is known to itself alone and to one who is taken up in it. The Psalm

says: "Blessed is the one you have chosen and taken up" (Ps. 64:5).[20]

"If justice did not justify, no one would have knowledge of it, but it would be known only to itself." The act of justification is an act of revelation. Furthermore, that person who "receives" and knows justice has been "taken up" into justice—and therefore insofar as that person is *in* justice, he is equal to and identical with justice. The act of justification is a self-revelation of deity of itself to itself. Matthew's "No one knows the father, but the son" is ramified through this apophatic meditation upon the trinity.

That meditation on the trinity generates an oscillation between the perspectives of sameness and otherness: identity in nature and the distinction in person between unbegotten justice and begotten justice. Eckhart begins with the perspective of distinction. The son and the father are distinct in person, because "nothing gives birth to itself." The claim that "nothing gives birth to itself" is true by normal logic. It is also in contradiction to Eckhart's central metaphor of self-birth.

Next, the voice of the commentator, Eckhart, becomes assimilated to the quoted voice of Jesus and, in a shift that will occur often in the German sermons, the speaker speaks from the perspective of the just person *insofar as* he is just:

> "The father and I are one" (John 10:30)—we are distinct in person, because nothing gives birth to itself; we are one in nature, because otherwise justice would not beget the just, nor would the father beget the son as other, nor would generation be univocal. That is what is meant by "The word was God."[21]

The perspectives of distinction of persons and sameness of nature are interdependent correlates. The oneness of nature exemplified by the *unum* is explained by the principle that if there were not a oneness of nature, justice would not beget the just. In formal terms, without the oneness of nature, the word would be in an analogical rather than univocal relationship to its principle, justice. However, the oneness in nature demands a distinction of persons which is exemplified by the phrase "the father and I." This ambivalent perspective then yields to the perspective of sameness of nature:

> If the father and son, justice and the just, are one and the same in nature, it follows (in the seventh place) that the just person is equal to justice, not less than it. Nor is the son less than the father. "The word was with God." The word "with" signifies equality, as said earlier.[22]

In bearing and justifying the just man, justice does not cease to be justice, and—like life and light—justice is not subject to movement in time. In an echo of the earlier grammatical paradox, he states: "The just person is always being born from justice itself in the same way that he was born from it from the beginning of the time he became just."[23] Elsewhere he radicalizes the expression "in the same way as" by stating it is the *very same* birth. At this point, the *inquantum* principle and the principle of univocal relations mark the reversion of the various stages of emanation back into their primal source.

> Begotten justice itself is the word of justice in its principle, the justice that gives birth. This is what it says here: "All things were made through him, and without him nothing was made." (In the twelfth place) the just person in justice itself is not yet [*iam non est*] begotten nor begotten justice, but is unbegotten justice itself. This is what is meant by "what was made," or produced by any form of production, "was life in him," that is, "principle without principle." Only that which is without principle lives in the proper sense, for everything that has the principle of its operation from another, insofar as it is other, does not live in the proper sense.[24]

In the second half of this passage, Eckhart shifts from justice to life, linking the two concepts through their identity with the trinitarian *bullitio* and self-birth. In speaking of life, he again shifts from the perspective of distinction ("nothing can give birth to itself") to the perspective of identity, that is, "life" as "principle without principle," that which has its principle of operation within itself—or as he has said in the *Exodus Commentary*—"self-birth" (*parturitio sui*).

The notion of a procession that does not proceed outside, that remains within, in a kind of interior welling up of life, is of course not unique to Eckhart. As was seen earlier, it appears in Aquinas in similar terms. What is distinctive here is the way in which Eckhart's apophatic discourse on the trinity enacts or performs that interior unity. It takes the perspective of distinction of persons (nothing gives birth to itself) and then *reads it back through the perspective of the identity of nature*, in which the word and its principle are the same thing. The "reading back" generates the metaphor and paradox of self-birth. The vitality of Eckhart's notion of life as "self-birth" depends upon the continual reading back of distinction into indistinction. The condition for such a reading back is Eckhart's move toward a nonsubstantive conception of deity as opposed to Thomas's emphatic affirmation of divine substance.[25]

Eckhart's emphasis upon the moment of radical unity has been read by some as a challenge to the ultimate status of the trinity. Such criticism has been countered by a reading of distinction and indistinction as dialectically reinforcing one another.[26] Eckhart's treatment of justice gives us a clear sense of how he saw distinction and indistinction as mutually reinforcing. Without distinction of persons, justice would not justify. The self-revelation of justice would yield to a solipsistic stasis. But without the unity of nature, justice would not justify, because it would not produce the just; it would proceed outward into analogical relationships of inequality and absolute difference. By reading back the distinction of persons through the identity of nature, Eckhart intensifies the dislocations of the temporal and spatial senses of prepositions like "in" and "not yet." It is as if the apophatic semantics were pushing the distinction of persons back into the identity of nature. We recall Plotinus's statement that "it is because nothing is *in the one* that all things are from it." The apophatic dialectic in Eckhart is similar. The more distinction is pushed back into sameness, the more semantically explosive is the counteremergence of the persons into distinction. As with Plotinus and Eriugena, emanation for Eckhart is not merely an explicative metaphor. Emanation as a metaphor turns back upon itself to reveal among other things the nature of the discourse in which it is embedded. The overflowing, the "pouring forth of a vast power" (with Plotinus), the welling up of life within and into itself, self-birth (with Eckhart) all have a semantic parallel in the overflow of meaning that occurs at this moment in apophatic discourse.[27]

The spatial dynamic, the "pushing back" of the persons "into" their oneness, has a parallel in the temporal dynamic. The just person in justice is *not yet* begotten nor begotten justice, but is unbegotten justice itself. The temporal sense of "not yet" is destabilized as was the spatial sense of "in." The key claims underlying the transformation of the "not yet" are the following:

1. A person, insofar as he has proceeded *from* justice into creation, is related analogically to the word. If we say that the word is light, life, intelligibility, or justice, then we must say that a person, like any other created thing, in himself is the opposite of all those characteristics. In other words, nothing shines in created things except the idea (the word): in themselves created things are darkness.

2. A person, insofar as he is just, is in the word and is the word. Since the word is life, intelligibility and, light, the just person, insofar as he is just, is life, intelligibility, and light. Insofar as he is just, he is "taken up" from the analogical relation to the univocal relation. Thus

he is equal to justice, the principle. He is the son which is begotten by justice.

3. By the fact that the son is begotten, he is distinguished from what gives him birth. For nothing can give birth to itself.

4. However, since the son is equal to the father, he is of the same nature, and thus from another point of view, he is "the same thing." The son is life, i.e., principle without principle, self-birth. Everything that has the principle of its operation from another, *insofar* as it is other (*ut aliud*), does not live in the proper sense. Here the *insofar as* principle governs the same/other dialectic within the univocal relations. This is the meaning of *bullitio*, of self-birth, of absolute interiority and sameness. "Thus the just person in justice is not yet begotten nor begotten justice but is unbegotten justice itself."

What does Eckhart mean by saying that in justice the just person is *not yet* begotten justice when he had insisted that the son or begotten justice is *always being born* and is *always* already born? Within the apparently innocent expression "not yet" is to be found a temporal aporia.

The German sermons express this aporia with particular starkness. The oneness of nature is not expressed in formal, trinitarian language, but as a spark, a light, a little castle, a desert, godhead, naked being, and nothingness. It is also called the "ground [*grunt*] of the deity" which is identical with the "ground of the soul." A reference to this ground, the godhead, in a German sermon, contains the same, strange "not yet": "He is a father of all godhead. I am talking about a godhead which is not yet flowing out."[28]

Eckhart offers two paradigms concerning the ground of deity.[29] In the first perspective, the ground of the deity is identified with the father or even placed beneath it, as when Eckhart speaks of the father as "origin of the godhead."[30] Similarly, the term "father" can be privileged over the word "God" (*got*); the intellect of the highest part of the soul "does not want God as he is God" but rather "as he is father."[31] In a particularly striking example, Eckhart reverses the gender imagery of fatherhood: "The name of 'father' means to give birth, there where the godhead shines forth from its primal brightness."[32]

The second paradigm places the godhead and the ground of deity beyond the trinitarian persons, including the father. Father and son are correlatives; there can be no father if there is not yet a son.[33] Eckhart speaks of a little castle (*bürgelîn*) that is so simple and so "one" and so far beyond every manner and power, that not even God can look into it. The deity, in order to attain a glimpse of this little castle, needs to give up the *eigenschaft* of his persons. The word *eigenschaft* has two meanings here. It refers to the quality or property of the persons. It can also refer to attachment: the attachment of the soul to its own images and desires, and, by extension, the attachment of the deity to its own properties and person. The passage reads:

> This is as true as it is that God lives! God himself never glimpses it and never has glimpsed it, as long as he has himself in the manner and according to the *eigenschaft* of his persons. It is good to take note of this, for it is an absolute one without manner and without property. Therefore, if God is ever to glimpse it, it must cost God all his godly names and the *eigenschaft* of his persons.[34]

Elsewhere the godhead is depicted as the "silent desert where distinction never gazed, where there is neither father nor son nor holy spirit."[35]

This double paradigm—with the ground of the deity sometimes characterized as the father, sometimes as a unity beyond all trinitarian persons—reflects a similar double paradigm in Plotinus.[36] With Plotinus, emanation devolves into a double paradigm of self-causality. In vertical emanation the one generates *nous*. In horizontal emanation *nous* generates itself out of the primal ground of the one. The two paradigms operate simultaneously and implicate one another. Either paradigm in itself is unstable: the one cannot generate *nous* since the one is beyond the subject/object duality of "it generates." *Nous* as self-act generates itself? But if *nous* generated itself, what was it before it made itself to be? The answer can only be an infinite regress leading back toward an unreachable self prior to its self-making. It may seem strange that such a double paradigm in Eckhart would echo Plotinus in this sensitive area. After all, in Plotinus, *nous* is inferior to the one, while Eckhart is discussing the realm of *bullitio*, equal relations. Yet an apophatic treatment of emanation has its own dynamic which asserts itself despite differences in cosmological frameworks. With Eckhart, the ground of *bullitio* is the father, but from another perspective a father is only a father insofar as he has a son, and thus both father and son are aspects of *bullitio*. The ground must be beyond fatherhood and sonship.[37] When Eckhart swears that what he is saying is as true as it is that God lives, he is not merely being emphatic. The unity and distinction of *bullitio* loop back upon and generate one another in exact accordance with Eckhart's formal understanding of life as self-birth. It is through the apophatic pushing of the trinitarian deity back into the primal ground that the persons well forth with a new semantic vitality. It is through the letting go of the divine being and properties (*eigenschaft*) that Eckhart's dynamic trinitarian understanding of life as self-birth achieves a nonsubstantialist understanding of deity. The double paradigm of self-causality creates an open or unlimited semantic force that cannot rest on a single paradigm and continually works toward transforming the temporal sense of the "not yet."

Mirror, Medium, without a Why

The transformation of the "not-yet" parallels the transformations of the spatial sense of "in." The apophatic transformations of "in" are in turn radicalized in Eckhart's sermons on the-birth-of-the-son-*in*-the-soul. Eckhart gives a number of differing accounts of the placement, the "in-ness" of this birth: in the soul, in the spark of the soul, or in the tiny castle that is identical with the godhead, or beyond all "in-ness," beyond all place. The three basic paradigms show the three major stages of the collapse of the "in." The first paradigm implies locus and containment: the son is born "in" the soul. The second paradigm insists that the birth can occur only insofar as the soul has become "equal to nothing," has emptied itself and gone out of itself. In doing so it becomes equal to its ground, to naked being, to nothingness. Such nothingness cannot serve as a place or locus. It is beyond place. With the third paradigm, the ground of the soul is identical with the ground of the deity, with the godhead. When the soul gives up its *eigenschaft* (properties, attachment), its images, its will, and becomes nothing, it is said to be virgin. It is "in" that virgin soul that the son is born, not only as contained in the soul, but as being "in" its principle. The son as an emanation flowing *out into* the soul, into the realm of creation, becomes identical with the son as proceeding only within its principle. The flowing out into creation that the birth of the son in the soul might otherwise imply is, through that very birth, transformed, or taken up (*assumptum*) into the interior *bullitio* of the trinity, where what gives birth is identical with what is given birth, and is the space for its own self-birth.

In what appear to be two versions of a single sermon (numbered 16a and 16b in the Quint edition), these transformations in the meaning of "in" occur within the paradox of self-containment that was seen in Eriugena. In the first passage below, from 16a, they occur in connection with the negation of all mediation or medium (*mittel*) in the paradox of self-containment, that each of two objects is "in" the other. In the second, from 16b, the transformations occur in connection with the two properties of any "vessel": that it receives and that it contains. The "unsaying" of the properties begins with the paradox of self-containment: "whatever is received in that [the spiritual vessel] is *in* the vessel and the vessel *in* it, and it *is* the vessel itself:[38]

> A master says, if all mediation were gone between me and this wall, I would be on the wall, but not in the wall. It is not thus in spiritual matters, for the one is always in the other; that which embraces is that which is embraced, for it embraces nothing but itself. This is subtle. He who understands it has been preached to enough.[39]

> Every vessel has two properties: it receives and it contains. Spiritual vessels are different from physical vessels. The wine is in the cask, the cask is not in the wine. And the wine is not in the cask as it is in the staves, for if it were in the cask as it is in the staves, we could not drink it. With a spiritual vessel it is different. Whatever is received in that is *in* the vessel and the vessel *in* it, and it *is* the vessel itself.[40]

In order to illustrate the lack of all mediation, Eckhart employs, in addition to the metaphors of the wall and vessel, the metaphor of the mirror. In his Latin *Commentary on Wisdom*, he interprets the divine word or wisdom, the "unblemished mirror" (*speculum sine macula*), as a "pure emanation" (*emanatio dei sincera*).[41] The mirror is a recurring theme with Eckhart and serves—as it did with Ibn ʿArabi and Marguerite Porete—as a central symbol of mystical union:

> There are many masters who claim that this image is born of will and intellect, but this is not so. I say rather that this image is an expression of itself without will and without intellect. I will give you a simile. Hold up a mirror before me and whether I want to or not, without will and without intellectual knowledge of myself I am imaged in the mirror. This image is not of the mirror, and it is not of itself, but this image is most of all in him from whom it takes its being and its nature. When the mirror is taken away from me, I am no longer imaged in the mirror. I am myself the image.[42]

As with Porete, when the soul gives up its *media*, that is its will and its intellect, it becomes a mirror in which the divine image appears. In Eckhart's use of the metaphor of the mirror we see an example of apophatic abstraction (*aphairesis*) similar to that found in Plotinus's metaphor of the glowing sphere. An initial image is depicted, and then one of the elements (the central mass, the mirror) is removed. The removal of the mirror as a medium of reflection is often implicit in apophatic mirror imagery; when we look at a polished mirror, the mirror as an object of sight disappears. Eckhart makes that disappearance more explicit. The paradox of self-containment (that X is in Y and Y is in X) becomes more dynamic in the paradox of procession and remaining: that what comes out stays within.

> Thus too I say of the image of the soul: what comes out is what stays within, and what stays within is what comes out. This image is the son of the father, and I myself am this image, and this image is wisdom. Therefore God be praised now and evermore. Whoever does not understand, let him not encumber himself with it.[43]

Throughout the German sermons, Eckhart exploits three key principles from Aristotle's *De Anima* (On the Soul) to illustrate his understanding of a medium: (1) the need for a sense faculty to be empty before it can receive the sense impression; (2) the necessity for a medium of perception between the faculty and the object perceived; and (3) the union between the perceiving faculty and the object perceived, which takes place in the act of perception.

The first principle is stated implicitly in Aristotle's wax analogy where sensation is compared to wax taking on the imprint of a signet ring:

> By a "sense" is meant what has the power of receiving into itself the sensible forms of things without the matter. This must be conceived of as taking place in the way in which a piece of wax takes on the impress of a signet-ring without the iron or gold.[44]

If there is already an impression on the wax it cannot take a clear new impression; for the impression to be made, the wax must be clear. For the eye to see, it must be clear of actual color.[45] According to the second principle there can be no perception if there is no medium between what is perceived and the perceiving faculty. Color cannot be seen, for example, unless there is a medium between the color and the eye. Eckhart denies the necessity of such a medium in the spiritual realm, and part of his apophatic technique is to remove the linguistic equivalent of the medium at key moments in his discourse.[46] A third principle, not mentioned explicitly by Eckhart in sermons 16a and 16b, is the union that occurs in the activity of sensation between the sensible object and the percipient sense. Aristotle offers the example of hearing:

> A person may have hearing and yet not be hearing, and that which has sound is not always sounding. But when that which can hear is actively hearing and that which can sound is sounding, *then the actual hearing and the actual sound are merged in one* (one might call these respectively hearkening and sounding). . . . Since the actualities of the sensible object and of the sensitive faculty are one actuality in spite of the difference between their modes of being, actual hearing and actual sounding appear and disappear from existence at one and the same moment.[47]

At the moment a guitar string is plucked, for example, there is a union between the player's act of sounding the guitar string and the listening act of hearkening to it; the two are united in one act when the sound is heard. Though Eckhart does not cite this last principle formally at this point, it is implicit in his treatment of the union of human will and divine will, of human work and divine work, of human intellect and divine intellect, in the one act with which Eckhart is concerned, the birth of the son in the soul. However, he will push the principle to the extreme by speaking of the reversion of creaturely being to its ground, which is one with the ground, of deity.

Eckhart's volitional aporia also resonates with that of Porete. The more one wills to abandon her will, the more one is willing and is caught up in her will. Eckhart compares the standard piety of those who will to do God's will or to gain paradise to the mentality of "knaves and hirelings" (*knehte und mietlinge*) in a manner reminiscent of Porete's characterization of the willing souls or "good workers" as *serfs*.[48] The mirror image, the "pure emanation," can only appear in the mirror when all media, all will and images, all intentions (however pious) that are to be purchased or traded for by the action, are absent.

Porete had expressed the state of will-lessness through a pun on *pourquoy*. The annihilated soul lives and acts without medium, that is, "without a why" (*sans pourquoy*), and "without a what" (*quoy*). Eckhart expresses this purely spontaneous act that is an end in itself through a similar pun. It is an act without "why" or "for what" (*warumbe*), and without a "therefore" or "for that" (*dar umbe*). In the following passage Eckhart turns the pun against his own rhetoric of sermonizing; the second instance of *dar umbe* places the first instance of *dar umbe* (Eckhart's own language of logical intention) in an ironic light. As with Porete, the giving up of medium is associated with the giving up of all works:

> The just person does nothing with his works, for those who seek something with their works are knaves and hirelings, or those who work for a wherefore [*warumbe*]. Therefore [*dar umbe*], if you would be in-figured and transfigured [*in- und übergebildet*] into justice, do not intend with your works and do not figure [lit. in-figure, *enbilde*] any wherefore [*warumbe*] in yourself, not in time or in eternity, neither reward nor blessedness, neither this nor that; for such works are all really dead. Yes, I say that if you image God into yourself [*ja, und bildest du got in dich*] whatever works you do for that [*dar umbe*] are all dead and you will spoil good works, and not only will you spoil good works, but you will sin.[49]

Like Aristotle's sense faculty that can receive a new sense impression only when it is empty of previous impressions, like a wax seal that cannot receive an imprint unless empty of previous imprints, the soul cannot receive the image or formal emanation unless it is empty of will and images. The paradox of will in Eckhart here finds a new expression. To give up will (in the radical sense of no longer even willing to do God's will, willing not to have sinned, willing blessedness, heaven, avoidance of hell) is to reach a point where the human will is voided and only the divine will remains, a kind of mystical union of wills. Yet at this moment of union of human and divine will, or the giving up of all will, the soul "compels" the divine. "Hold up a mirror before me, and whether I want to or not, without will and without intellectual knowledge of myself I am imaged in the mirror."[50] "When a face is cast before the mirror, the face must be imaged in it whether it will or not."[51] A most explicit passage in this regard is the following:

> When the will is so united with God's will that they become a single will, then the father begets his only-begotten son in himself and in me. Why in himself and in me? When I am one with him, he cannot exclude me; and in this act the holy spirit receives his being and his activity and his becoming, from me as from God. Why? There I am in God. If he, the spirit, does not receive it from me, he does not receive it from God either. He cannot shut me out, in no way can he do so.[52]

Two aspects of necessity are combined here. The first is the natural necessity whereby an image appears spontaneously, without will, in a polished mirror; a bubbling spring pours into an empty channel; or a sense impression is received by a sense that is emptied. The second is the necessity resulting from the soul's being "taken up" into the realm of univocal relations. As will be seen below, when the soul is "equal" to nothing, it reverts to that ground which is one with the divine ground, to the primordial nothingness "from" which and "in" which the procession or birth of the son occurs.

The language of natural necessity, whereby an image will necessarily appear in a polished mirror or water will fill a vessel, alternates with a more personal, dramatic, and intentional depiction of the deity:

> God works all his work for this, that we might be his only-born son. Whenever God sees that we are the only-born son, then God hurries so quickly and behaves just as if his divine being [*wesen*] wished to break into pieces and become nothing in himself, so that he can reveal to us all the abyss [*abgrunt*] of his godhead and the fullness of his being and nature.[53]

The ground of the soul is identical to the ground of deity, and it is "in" this ground that the "only-begotten" son is eternally born and eternally being born. When the soul is brought into this process it can receive nothing less than the only-begotten son. And if the only-begotten son that always has been born and always is being born is not born "there," then he is not born at all.

However, as long as the soul is intending, seeking, willing, and imaging the object of its will—even if that image is an image of traditional piety—as long as it works for a "why," its works are "dead." That such works are dead is not a decorative metaphor in Eckhart. The reference to the works being dead corresponds precisely to the formal definition of life articulated throughout the Eckhartian writings: life as that which does not have its principle in another as other, life as *bullitio*, life as self-birth. It is a commonplace in much medieval theology that in some sense the various divine attributes are one. In Eckhartian language, however, this unity is not so much asserted as it is performed. At the point of mystical union, attributes such as justice, equality, nobility, life, and love continually loop back one into the other. Each is a nexus of the apophatic dialectic. Each is grounded in the Eckhartian notion of *bullitio*, formal emanation, and the birth of the son.

Justi Vivent (The Just Shall Live)

Eckhart's great sermon "The just shall live in eternity" (*justi vivent in aeternum*) offers a dramatic performance of this unification of attributes. *Justi vivent* begins with the commonplace medieval definition of justice as "giving to each person his due." In a series of complex puns upon the word "equal" (*glîche*) the formal rigor of the Latin treatments of univocal and analogical relationships is united with a dramatic and poetic vernacular. The doctrine of equality is further explicated in terms of the union of human will and divine will. The sermon then shifts to an examination of "will live" (*vivent*), again in terms of equality. Then in a climactic passage, justice, life, and equality are performatively enacted and unified in the birth of the son in the soul. Haunting the entire sermon is the paradox of distinction and indistinction: that the most distinct of all things is that which is distinct by virtue of its utter lack of any distinction.

The sermon proclaims that those who give God what belongs to him are those who have gone completely out of themselves (*die ir selbes alzemâle sint ûzgegangen*) and who do not seek their own in anything, "whatever it might be, whether large or small" (*swaz ez joch sî, noch grôz noch klein*). In an echo of Porete's annihilated souls, those who are just

> Look neither under themselves nor over nor beside nor at. They intend neither good nor honor nor comfort nor pleasure nor use nor inwardness nor holiness nor reward nor the kingdom of heaven.[54]

God takes such pleasure in these just souls "as if his blessedness and his being, his sufficiency and his well-being, were hanging in the balance."[55] As will be seen below, the sermon will go on to radicalize and literalize this "as if"; from the perspective of trinitarian procession, the being and well-being of the deity do hang in the balance. To prepare the ground for this shift, the sermon applies the language of equality to the soul unconcerned with its own will. The just are those who

> Accept every thing equally [*glîch*] from God, whatever it may be, be it large or small, sweet or sorrow, all equally [*al glîch*], less or more, one thing or the other. If you weigh one thing more than another, that is not right. You ought to go completely out of your own will.[56]

The unity of the human will with the divine will is addressed explicitly. Different stages of separation and unity are posited. The first stage belongs to those who look for their own will in everything. The second belongs to those who want what God wants, but who want God to want what they want. The final stage belongs to those who consider everything "the same" to them, equal (*glîch*), however much distress it might cause.

The evocation of distress (*ungemach*) signals a shift to a series of starker claims about equality. Those who are just love justice so much that, if God were not just, they would not give a bean (*bône*) for God. They have gone so completely out of themselves that they have no concern for the pains of hell or the joys of heaven or anything else. Heaven and hell are the same to them. If all the pains of those in hell, whether humans or demons, or all the pains that have ever been suffered were joined to justice, it would not matter to them. The concept of pain is then reformulated: "Nothing is more painful or more difficult to the just that that which is against justice" (*Dem gerehten menschen enist niht pînlîcher noch swaerer, dan daz der gerehticheit wider ist*).[57] Repeating yet again the central principle of equality, the sermon states that if one thing can make them rejoice and another grieve, or if they rejoice more at one time than another, they are not truly just. Union in love (*minne*) is invoked: "Whoever loves justice stands so fast by it that whatever he loves, that is his being" (*Swer die gerehticheit minnet, der stât sô vaste dar ûf, swaz er minnet, das ist sîn wesen*).[58]

At this point the sermon turns to the biblical citation upon which it is constructed: "The just shall live" (*die gerehten suln leben*), and defines "life" in terms of equality. As with justice, life is a value in itself. It is sought for itself. In an apostrophe to the reader, the implied speaker states: you know why (*war umbe*) you eat and why you sleep: in order (*umbe daz*) that you might live. But why do you live? "In order to live, and you still do not know why you live. So desirable is life in itself, that one seeks it on account of itself."[59] This punning apostrophe, in which the speaker of the sermon turns to the audience and states that "you ask how/why [*dar umbe*] you should live," and responds by stating that true life is lived without a how/why (*umbe*), is repeated throughout Eckhart's sermons. The sermon *Justi vivent* goes on to state that however painful life is, in this life or even in hell, those who live wish to continue living. Life is so noble (*edel*) that it flows without medium from God into the soul (*daz ez sunder allez mitel vliuzet von gote in die sêle*). Just as there is only one just work, there is only one life, the life that is divine overflowing and divine being: "What is life? God's being [*wesen*] is my life. If God's being is my life then must it be that God's be-ing [*sîn*] is my be-ing and God's is-ness is my is-ness, neither more nor less."[60]

The mention of "neither more nor less" brings back with striking vernacular language the theme of equality that was central to *The Commentary on John*. Those who live "with God" live equally with God (*glîche bî gote*), not under or above. In an expression that echoes Porete's statements on works, they are said to work their works in God and God in them. The sermon then returns to its interpretation of John's "with God" as the relationship of equality and applies it to gender; Eve was created from Adam's rib, not his head or his feet. Similarly, the just are "equal with God," not "under or over God." At this point the entire sermon is brought together in a paradox: those who are equal in this way are those who are equal to nothing, just as "Godly being is equal to nothing." Though the German would be more literally translated as "those who are not equal" (*die niht glîch*)—I have followed the example of Edmund Colledge in translating the expression as "equal to nothing," in order to bring across the play Eckhart is making upon his central paradox of distinction and indistinction: the most distinct of all is that which is distinct by virtue of its utter lack of any distinction. This paradox entails the dialectic of transcendence and immanence: that which is absolutely transcendent is that which is simultaneously absolutely immanent.

Yet the paradox of distinction and indistinction entails more than the dialectic of transcendence and immanence. It also entails a dialectic of nothingness and everything (identical with that found in Porete): that which is equal to nothing is equal to all things. Finally, it entails a dialectic of self and other: whoever attains such equality is as equal to another as she is to herself. These three dialectics, which weave themselves through Eckhart's writings, come together in the paradox of equality. The paradox plays upon the equivocal use of "nothing" found in the famous syllogism: (A) Nothing is better than God; (B) anything is better than nothing; (C) therefore, anything is better than God. But the play is grounded within an apophatic and nonsubstantialist discourse that transforms the normal semantics of being and nothingness. Morally and mystically (with the focus upon justice, the moral and the mystical have become the same), the transformation pushes the values of life, justice, and equality to the extreme. These values are in turn equated with the birth of the son of God.

> Who are those who are equal in this way? Those who are equal to nothing are alone equal to God. Godly being is equal to nothing; in it there is neither image nor form. To souls that are equal, the father gives equally and holds nothing back. Whatever the father can do, that he gives to this soul equally, yes, if it stands equally, not more for itself than for another, and it should be not closer to itself than to another. Its own honor, use, or whatever is its own—it

should desire or consider no more than that of a stranger. Whatever is anyone's, bad or good, should not be alien to this soul or far from it.[61]

By this point in the sermon, the paradox of distinction and indistinction has been used as a point of intersection for the central concepts of justice and life. The paradox of distinction and indistinction is related to the principle of equal or univocal relations developed in Eckhart's Latin works, whereby what proceeds is equal to and thereby identical with its principle. The birth of the son in the soul, that is, the same birth of the same only-begotten son of God that always has occurred and always is occurring, is then evoked. At this point, the speaking voice of the sermon is transformed:

> The father gives birth to his son in eternity, equal to himself. "The word was with God, and God was the word" (John 12:1). It was the same in the same nature. Yet I say more: he has given him birth in my soul. Not only is the soul with him and he equal to it, but he is in it, and the father gives his son birth in the soul in the same way as he gives him birth in eternity, and not otherwise. He must do it whether he likes it or not. The father gives birth to his son without cease; and I say more: he gives me birth, his same son. I say more: he gives me birth not only as his son, but he gives birth to me as himself and himself as me and to me as his being and nature. In the innermost source, there I spring out in the holy spirit, where there is one life and one being and one work. Everything God works is one; therefore he gives me, his son, birth without any distinction.[62]

As was the case with Sufi language of mystical union, the "I" of such a passage undergoes a transformation. The voice of Eckhart the preacher is transformed into the voice of the just person, insofar as he is just. We hear echoes of Eckhart's discussion of justice and the just person in his commentary on John, particularly the statement that the just person, insofar as he is just, is taken up (*assumptum*) from the world of analogical relations into the realm of equal relations, the world of the trinity in which the son is equal to the father and is the same as the father, the world of self-birth (*parturitio sui*). The birth occurs in the soul that is equal to nothing, that is devoid of all will and all images. Just as the divine reveals itself in the heart of the thirteenth-century Sufi who has passed away in *fanā'*, so with Eckhart the divine reveals itself and gives birth to itself in the soul that has become equal to nothing, that has let go of, or gone out of, its own will and images.

With the shift in voice from Eckhart the preacher to Eckhart the just person insofar as he is just, the seemingly trivial preposition "in" explodes into its full semantic range. The birth occurring "in" the soul does not at all occur *in* the soul, Eckhart tells us elsewhere, since it occurs where there is no place. The birth is said to occur "in" the soul, but this "in" is transformed into the "in" of "in the ground" of the soul which is also the ground of the deity: "in" nothingness, the desert, the godhead. Through a series of apophatic shifts and transformations, the birth of the son in the soul has been performatively identified with the birth of the son in the trinity. The soul is the mirror, which, when it reflects perfectly, disappears. The disappearance is enacted through language with the reversal in meaning of the "in." The "in" of "in the soul" is identified with the "in" of the son that proceeds while remaining "in" its principle. The various attributes—life, justice, equality, nobility, and love—are also fused with one another in this one event that has always occurred and always is occurring.

Finally, by placing the birth metaphor at the heart of his trinitarian theology, Eckhart has completely destabilized the gender relations within the trinity. "The father gives birth to his son in eternity equal with himself . . . and the father gives his son birth in the soul in the same way as he gives him birth in eternity, and not otherwise." Such language raises questions about the status of the mother of this divine son. Eckhart's reconfiguration of trinitarian gender relations are so far-reaching that they will require a separate discussion. In the next and final chapter, Eckhart's language of unsaying will be compared with that of Porete, with special emphasis upon gender issues in Porete and Eckhart's interpretation of the virgin birth. Before turning to that subject, however, I would like to mention Eckhart's extraordinary understanding of grace and love.

As Oneself

It is common to view the birth of the son in the soul as a result of the process of *abegescheidenheit*, the letting go or self-abandon through which the soul gives up its attachments, desires, works, and becomes "equal to nothing." This "letting go" is frequently depicted as the "breakthrough" back into the primal ground. However, there is a dilemma involved here. At times Eckhart speaks of the birth of the son in the soul as the *result* of the breakthrough back into the primal ground (as in the sermon *Justi vivent*), but at other times he speaks of the birth as the *precondition* for the breakthrough. Causality loops around upon itself into what can be called self-causality, an acting out or performing of that central principle of self-birth that is at the heart of Eckhart's *bullitio* and of his understanding of life.

The paradox of self-causality becomes the center for Eckhart's deeper reflections on grace and free will. The son cannot be born in the soul unless the soul becomes empty of its own will and images, unless it "sinks back into nothingness," or breaks through to the divine ground where the soul's ground and God's ground are one. On the other hand, how is it to achieve this state of emptiness? Clearly *not* through its own works and will, since the emptiness is precisely an emptiness of works and will. "Grace" might be a traditional answer, but Eckhart's concept of grace is complex and tends only to heighten the dilemma. He does speak at times of grace as that which prepares the soul for the fruition of birth. But there is a more radical and more paradoxical discussion of grace. In his sermon *Ave Gratia Plena*, Eckhart speaks of grace in a manner strikingly parallel to his depiction of the procession of the son from the father and the birth of the son in the soul. Grace does not perform works, for example. Eckhart uses extravagant language to hint at the power of this pure self-generation without any works other than the one eternal work that is the birth of the son. The work of an angel "in God" is so powerful that when a chip falls from it, there falls from that chip a lightning flash from which there "shoots and blossoms and springs into life everything that is in the world."[63]

Eckhart then writes that there are two springs. One is the spring from which grace gushes forth, which is the same spring in which the father bears forth his only-begotten son. The other is the spring from which creatures flow forth. These two springs are clearly identifiable as *bullitio* and *ebullitio*. By identifying grace with the spring of *bullitio*, Eckhart makes it difficult to distinguish grace from the actual procession and birth of the son. Both grace and the birth of the son are aspects of same emanation. Eckhart then goes on to characterize grace in terms that further challenge the distinction between grace and the procession of the son. Grace is an in-being (*innesîn*) and a clinging (*anehaften*) and a oneness with God.[64] Elsewhere grace is characterized as an indwelling (*înwonen*) and a "with-dwelling [*mitewonen*] of the soul in God."[65] Taken together with the claim made elsewhere, that the birth of the son of God cannot occur in the trinity unless it occurs in the soul, these statements further intensify the paradox of self-causality.

Grace allows the birth of the son, but it is an aspect of that very same emanation that is the birth of the son. The dilemma can be resolved partially by viewing grace as the conceptualization in time, the gradual ripening of the soul, of the eternal event that is conceptualized as the one birth that always has occurred and always is occurring.[66] Ultimately the dilemma is unresolved; it is a truly apophatic aporia. At the moment of birth, the "in" of "in the soul" refers both to the son's reception and containment by the soul, and to the existence of the son (and by extension the soul which is "taken up" into equal relations) *in* its principle. The birth (the procession) is the breakthrough back to the ground (the return). As Eckhart says, God is an "indwelling in self" (*insiczen in sich selber*) and the virgin soul also attains this "nobility [*edelkeit*] of dwelling in self."[67] Consistent with the Eckhartian dialectic of *bullitio*, however, the more something dwells within itself, the more powerfully it bursts forth. Conversely "God's outgoing is his ingoing."[68] Through the dialectic of distinction and indistinction, the outgoing—procession and birth of the son in the (ground of) the soul—is the ingoing, the breakthrough back into primordial unity. Both meanings are contained in Eckhart's "in."

The dialectic of distinction and indistinction pushes to its extreme the equality of honor and dishonor, heaven and hell, the honor of one's self and that of another. The following proposition was condemned in the papal bull *in agro dominico*:

> The twenty-fifth article. When it says, "Simon, do you love me more than these men?" [John 21:15], it means, that is, more than these others—and indeed well, but not perfectly. In the case of what is more and less there is an order and a degree, but there is no order and degree in the one. Therefore, whoever loves God more than his neighbor, loves well, but not yet perfectly.

As Eckhart wrote in *Justi vivent*, equality abolishes degree (the less and the more) and distinction. The love of God that is placed above the love of the neighbor, or a loving of the neighbor as a kind of duty taken on with loving God, are for Eckhart loves based upon distinction. Eckhart's language strives to unsay the love of God as a reified idol. Just as a God who is not born in the soul is a God who is not born, so for Eckhart the love for God that is not simultaneously and equally the love of the neighbor is not the perfect love. In another proposition cited during the Inquisition, in this case in the trial at Cologne, Eckhart states that one should love one's neighbor not on account of God but truly *as oneself*.[69] Mystical interpretation is often associated with symbolic and allegorical modes of interpretation, but in this case Eckhart seems to be using the principle of equality to retrieve the literal meaning of Mark's definition of love. In another sermon he makes this connection explicit, saying that whoever loves God

> must love his neighbor as himself, rejoicing in his joys as his own and desiring his honor as much as his own and loving a stranger as one of his own. This way a person is always joyful, honored, and advantaged, just as if he were in heaven.[70]

The dialectics of distinction and indistinction, nothingness and all, self and other, work toward a radicalization of the "as oneself" in the love of the neighbor. The achievement of equality breaks down the distinction between self and other within the birth of the son in the soul. For Eckhart such a birth is more compelling than any conception of heaven as a reward for works.

The principle of equality is the ground not only for Eckhart's understanding of life and justice but also for his understanding of suffering. In his extended treatise on the consolation of suffering, Eckhart transcends the normal boundaries of consolation by identifying the suffering of the disencumbered soul with the suffering of the deity. Rather than identifying merely the suffering of individual humans with the suffering deity, Eckhart grounds the union-in-suffering in the same union that occurs in justice, equality, and life.

> And the seventh teaching from the saying that God is with us in suffering and suffers with us is that we should be mightily comforted by God's attribute, that he is the purely one, without any accidental admixture of distinction, even in thought; that everything that is in him is God himself. And because that is true, therefore I say, everything the good person suffers for God's sake, he suffers in God and God is suffering in him in his suffering. But if my suffering is in God and God is suffering with me, how then can suffering be sorrow to me, if suffering loses its sorrow and my sorrow is in God and my sorrow is God? Truly as God is truth and I find the truth, I find my God the truth there; and too, neither less nor more, as I find pure suffering for the love of God and in God, I find God my suffering.[71]

This treatise breaks with the notion of the impassivity of the divine and the suffering of the humanity of Jesus. Here the deity is said to suffer and to suffer in and with humankind.[72] Eckhart's meditation on this issue is not Christocentric in the sense of focusing upon the passion of Jesus in the manner of Eckhart's followers, Tauler, Suso, and the author of the *Theologia Germanica*. Yet in another sense it is deeply and distinctively Christian, a full realignment of centuries of trinitarian thought and centuries of religious meditation upon the meaning of suffering. Eckhart suggests a Christian theology built upon the vulnerability of the divine and its interrelation and interdependence with humanity. The divine being depends upon the deity's self-birth, but that birth is the same as the birth of the son in the soul. If the soul doesn't receive the divine emanation, if it doesn't let go, if it cannot give birth to the divine act, not only the happiness but the being of divinity is threatened. And the human loyalty to this divinity is not dictated by reward or punishment but by equality, in which the pains of hell and the pleasures of heaven are equal and where the birth of the son in the soul can be experienced in terms of joy or suffering alike, "without a why."

The notion that the deity might be vulnerable, dependent upon its self-birth within the human soul, is shocking to some. It would be a mistake, I believe, to deny the radical nature of Eckhart's position. Yet such a position is not at all indefensible according to the criteria of apophatic logic. In one sense, the dependence of the deity upon the soul's reception is a function of a purely contrary to fact condition; if there were no justice in the soul (i.e., in the ground of the soul which is the ground of deity), the deity, as justice, would not give birth to itself. Yet this birth, by definition, always has occurred and always is occurring. When Eckhart speaks of the divine being depending upon the birth in the soul, he is speaking from within the imperfect "always is occurring." From within the imperfect, the birth is a matter of faith and risk. Eckhart appears to have believed that honesty entailed this moment of risk, in which the deity and the human soul are mutually vulnerable and mutually dependent upon the birth of justice in the soul. By fusing perfect and imperfect (always is already born and always is being born) and by then speaking from within the continuous action (being born), from the very point of being born, Eckhart attempts to keep the birth from "fading into the past," from becoming a matter of fact (in both senses of "matter of fact"). Similarly, he refuses to put the birth off until a future in which it would become a reward for works. The drama of creation and redemption is funneled into the present moment.

This refusal to make an easy predetermination of the issue of justice can be seen as well in Eckhart's shifting priority in using divine names and attributes. In some places it is deity that is the absolute first principle. In other places it is justice. As with the other apophatic mystics, Eckhart is capable of a deep mystical agnosticism. A God without justice in the world is of little interest to Eckhart. Justice without the principle of justice—the father that begets/gives birth to the son in the soul—is inconceivable. Justice and deity, love and deity, life and deity, come together in the birth of the son in the soul. That birth always has occurred and always is occurring, but it is not to be presumed.[73]

Epilogue

Eckhart's conduct during his inquisition was controversial. At times he was defiant. At other times he was ready to admit errors, though never heresy, which he viewed as a matter of intent as well as error. Sometimes he argued "to the point" (*ad propositum*). Sometimes he digressed. Eckhart's conduct contrasts with that of Porete at her inquisition. Porete never faltered. Her behavior and stance were consistent throughout. She neither sought martyrdom nor fled it. She was an outsider, a *pseudo-mulier* in the eyes of the Inquisition. Though she fought to have her book validated by theological authority, she had no illusions about the outcome of her inquisition.

The inquisitors formulated their articles of suspect propositions carefully. Indeed, their lists (*rotuli*) are so accurate that they have been invaluable for establishing a critical edition of Eckhart's writings. However, that kind of accuracy does not imply that the inquisitors were fair to Eckhart. In his defense of the first set of forty-nine suspect articles at Cologne, Eckhart outlined the principles needed for interpreting his thought. His outline relies upon the *inquantum* (insofar as) principle. That principle, as applied to our discussion of justice, would insist that when we speak of the act of the just person as the birth of the son in the soul, we speak of the just person *insofar as he is just*. The premise of this book is that apophatic language is a language of double propositions in which no single proposition can stand by itself as meaningful. The inquisitorial method of abstracting single propositions into lists of articles that must then be defended one by one, each on its own merits, is based upon a logic of single propositions. It was the *inquantum* principle that was, in all of Eckhart's work, the principle that connected the apophatic movement of double propositions to the normal semantics and logic of single propositions. Without it, apophatic logic and inquisitional logic are incompatible languages. The Inquisition refused to acknowledge the *inquantum* principle.

In addition to disallowing the *inquantum* principle, the inquisitorial authorities misrepresented it. Eckhart used the principle to reduplicate the attribute: "The noble or good human *to the extent that* he is noble . . . is the only-begotten son of God." The inquisitorial commission turns the *inquantum* into a reduplication of the human subject: "the good human to the extent that he is a human [*secundum quod homo*] can be called the only-begotten son." [74] What occurs here goes beyond a rejection of the *inquantum* principle; it is a perversion of it, turning it into the opposite of what it wishes to affirm.

Recently, major parallels have been discovered between one of Eckhart's last sermons and Marguerite Porete's *Mirror*. It has been suggested that, after his vain attempts to defend his writings, he may have authored the sermon *Beati pauperes spiritu* (Blessed are the poor in spirit)—a sermon on willing nothing, knowing nothing, and having nothing—as a final gesture to Porete. It is to this sermon and to Eckhart's famous sermon on the virgin birth that we now turn. The final chapter of this study will explore how Eckhart's sermons turn back upon the hierarchy presupposed in the sermon genre as Eckhart's authoritative persona as the "master" yields to a variety of voices in continual critical conversation. It will also suggest that in regard to "poverty of the spirit" and gender issues, Eckhart's writings and Porete's writings complement and deepen one another.

CHAPTER SEVEN

Porete and Eckhart: The Apophasis of Gender

The 1946 discovery that Marguerite Porete was the author of *The Mirror of the Simple Souls* has provoked new interest in *The Mirror*. It has also raised intriguing questions concerning the relationship between *The Mirror* and the writings of Eckhart. When Eckhart returned to Paris in 1311, only a year after Porete's execution, he stayed at the same Dominican house as William Humbert, Porete's inquisitor, where he may have had access to a copy of *The Mirror*.[1] Particularly strong thematic parallels have been drawn between Porete's *Mirror* and Eckhart's German sermon, *Beati pauperes spiritu* (Blessed are the poor in spirit).[2]

In this final chapter I review the parallels between the works of Porete and Eckhart that have already been noted, and proceed to add a number of further parallels. I argue against the hypothesis that Eckhart corrected and put into cogent form the more confused language of Marguerite Porete. The writings of Eckhart and Porete will be heard to echo, answer, and deepen one another when read together (whether or not the affinities between the two are due to a direct influence of one upon the other). The goal of the comparison is a specification of the literary and theological matrix of the two sets of writings. Within that matrix the apophasis of both Porete and Eckhart reaches its culmination. The chapter concludes with a more wide-ranging exploration of central issues (freedom, authenticity, and gender) from within the space between the two great mystical texts. From this vantage point, the apophatic unsaying of the substantialist deity will be shown to be at one with the apophatic unsaying of gender essentialism.

Willing Nothing

Points of comparison include affinities between the writings of the two mystics as well as specific affinities between Eckhart's famous sermon on spiritual poverty, sermon 52 (*Beati pauperes spiritu* / Blessed are the poor in spirit) and Porete's *Mirror*. The affinities center around the complete abandonment of the will (willing nothing) and the radical apophatic dialectic to which it leads.

1. The refrain of Eckhart's sermon 52 ("willing nothing, knowing nothing, and having nothing") appears in almost the exact same form in *The Mirror*. In both cases, the three versions of nothingness are part of an apophatic dialectic whereby that which is equal to nothing is equal to everything. In both cases, the soul's achievement of the three forms of nothingness is the occasion for mystical union.[3]

2. The litany of things for which Porete's annihilated soul shows no concern is almost identical, in form and content, to that of Eckhart. Porete's annihilated soul desires "neither humbleness of station, nor poverty, nor martyrdom," nor "shame nor honor, poverty nor riches, ease nor dis-ease, love nor hate, hell nor heaven." She seeks God neither by "penances, nor sacraments, nor holy church, nor justice, mercy, glory, divine recognition, divine love, or divine praise." Eckhart's emptied soul looks "neither under nor over nor beside, nor is she intent on possessions, honors, ease, pleasure, profit, inwardness, holiness, reward, or heavenly kingdom."[4]

3a. Both Eckhart and Porete state that only those who are equal or identical to the truth can understand it. Both employ the rhetorical technique of apostrophe, suddenly addressing the reader or audience directly, to make that point. Porete's Lady Love states: "Gloss these verses, if you wish to understand them, or you will misunderstand them, because they seem contradictory."[5] At another point she says: "Gloss this, if you wish, or rather, if you can. If you cannot gloss it, *you are not it*."[6] Eckhart proclaims: "Now I beg you *to be that*, that you might understand this speech. I say to you in the eternal truth that if you are not equal to this truth, of which we are now speaking, you cannot understand me."[7]

3b. Eckhart's apostrophes contain a distinctive play on the notion of "encumbering." The reader should not "encumber" herself if she doesn't understand. Eckhart states: "and if you do not understand it, then do not encumber yourself with it, for I want to speak of such a truth as few good people will understand."[8] The same injunction is repeated at the end of the sermon: "If anyone does not understand this speech, he should not encumber his heart with it. As long as a person is not equal to this truth, so long will he not understand this speech. This is an unclothed truth which has come from the heart of God without medium."[9] Eckhart uses the expression elsewhere in his sermons as well.[10] The expression "encumber yourself," (*enbekûmbert iuch*) is the same expression employed by Porete throughout *The Mir-*

ror for the soul encumbered by will, works, and the limitations of discursive reason.[11] Eckhart's statement that one must be equal (*glîch*) to the truth in order to understand it is a verbal play upon his dialectic of equality-in-nothingness that was examined in chapter 6. Similarly his statement about not "encumbering oneself" may be a play on the parallel notion in Porete—when the soul is disencumbered of all will and all works and becomes nothing, it is given all.

4a. Eckhart and Porete use similar rhetoric to characterize those who, by conventional standards, might be considered pious. Porete characterizes those who cannot give up the the counsel of reason and will as "such beasts and asses,"[12] while Eckhart calls "asses" those who think poverty of the will resides in penance and outward practices.[13]

4b. Porete and Eckhart cast in similar terms those who have not achieved the state of willing nothing. In *The Mirror*, Reason had argued that the soul should will to gain the rewards of paradise, to avoid the pains of hell, and should will, retrospectively, not to have sinned. Porete portrays such willers as "good workers," and as *serfs*. Eckhart compares those who will such things to "hirelings and traders" (*knehte und mietlinge*). In both cases, the terms of disparagement are bound up in an apophatic dialectic of nobility and commonality, although Eckhart's barbs are more tinged with allusion to commercial and urban transactions.[14]

5. Both Porete and Eckhart create a paradox around the place of the deity's work in the soul; the soul that has nothing no longer has any place for God to work.[15]

6. The paradox of poverty of the will culminates in both Porete and Eckhart with the statement that the poor of will no longer will to do God's will. Porete's 48th chapter begins with the following title and statement:

> How the soul is not free which desires that the will of God be done in her to her honor—the 48th chapter. Thus the Soul wills nothing, says Love, because she is free; for no one is free who wills anything from within his own will, whatever he might will. For he is still a slave to himself, because he has the will that God do his will for his honor.[16]

This same claim is repeated in Eckhart's sermon 52 in almost identical fashion:

> Were someone to ask me now, what a poor person who "wills not" might be, I would answer: As long as one has this, that he wills to fulfill the most dearly beloved will of

> God, that person does not have the poverty of which we wish to speak. He has a will with which he wishes to be sufficient to the will of God, and that is not true poverty. If a person would truly have poverty, he should stand as free of his created will as he did when he was not. I say to you by the eternal truth: as long as you have will to fulfill the will of God, as long as you have desire for eternity and God, you will not be poor. A poor person is one who wills not and desires not.[17]

These parallels range from central conceptual resonances to precise correspondences in rhetoric and terminology. It has been suggested that Eckhart's sermon on the poverty of the spirit was composed after his condemnation, shortly before he disappears from history. Such a chronology would explain why the sermon's radical propositions appear neither in the final articles of condemnation nor in the preliminary Cologne proceedings against Eckhart. *Beati pauperes spiritu* can then be given a human interpretation as a final gesture by a Meister no longer concerned with defending his position or orthodoxy.[18] In such a scenario (plausible, but unamenable to demonstrative proof), the textual parallels to Porete suggest an Eckhart who, after a long effort to defend himself and maintain his position in the Church, had lost all. Willing nothing, knowing nothing, having nothing, no longer concerned with anything that would come, he would have acknowledged in a final masterwork his affinity with the condemned heretic Marguerite Porete, a *pseudomulier* (pseudo-woman) in the eyes of the Inquisition.

WITHOUT A WHY

These preliminary affinities between Eckhart and Porete lead to deeper and wider convergences around the dialectic of nothing and everything, and the dialectic of naming and namelessness. Central to these dialectics are five interdependent themes common to *The Mirror* and Eckhart's sermon 52, "Blessed are the Poor in Spirit": (1) the reversion to the state of precreation;[19] (2) living "without a why"; (3) the relinquishment of all medium or mediation; (4) the nakedness of the soul that has given up all will and reason; and (5) the giving up of all works.

Sermon 52 asserts that one who would be poor of will must stand "as free of his created will as he did when he was not." The expression "as he was when he was not" echoes throughout the sermon. The human reversion to a state of pre-creation parallels the reversion of deity to the state before it was deity. Sermon 52 goes on to proclaim that "before creatures were, God was not God; he was what he was."[20] The "I" of the sermon at this point is speaking from that point beyond the distinction of deity and creation, from the pre-creative perspective when creatures were not creatures and God was not God:

> When I stood in my original source, I had no God then, and I was my own source. Then I willed not and desired not, since I was a free being and a knower of myself in enjoyment of the truth. Then I willed myself and nothing else. What I willed, I was, and what I was, I willed. Here I stood free of God and all things. But when I went out from my own free will and I received my created being, then I had a God. Before creatures were, God was not God; he was what he was. But when creatures came to be and received their created being, then God was not God in himself, he was God in creatures.[21]

The speaker has "gone out" from his own free will. This "going out" parallels *ebullitio*, the outpouring of the deity into creation, but from the point of view of the absolute unity (*unum*) personalized as a speaking "I." From the divine perspective the going out from free will suggests that the deity turns over a certain amount of its own "free will" to the human creature. From the human perspective, the going out from free will suggests a devolution into creaturehood from which one becomes free (*ledic*) only in giving up all will, by willing nothing—in giving the will back. The deity gives the soul its free will in the act of creation, and the soul, insofar as it gives back its own free, created will, then reverts to its pre-created state of nothingness in which there is true freedom.

Porete spoke of this reversion in the third person rather than the first-person "I" of Eckhart. The annihilated soul gives up its will entirely and reverts to the state where "it" was before creation. In some passages, the "it" refers to the deity that becomes as it was before creation. In other passages, the "it" refers to the soul which becomes as it was before creation, before it was made "lady" over the divine overflowing or *bonté*. Creation entails the deity handing over its free will—a more transitive version of the "going out from its own free will" in Eckhart. The deity cannot "have back" (*ravoir, rehabere*) its will until the soul gives up her will in union with the divine lover and reverts to the pre-creative state.

This giving and giving back of free will unsays yet again the "what" or "which" in *pourquoy* (for what). In an apostrophe, the reader or hearer is told that she will not understand as long as she has an "of which" (*de quoy*) to hear. The soul also reverts to the pre-creative state, to "what she was before she was," to a state of nakedness and nothingness.

> This soul has been given all by the noble freedom of the work of the trinity. In this trinity such a soul plants its will so nakedly that she cannot sin as long as she does not uproot it. She has no "of what" [*de quoy*] to sin, for without will no one can sin. Now she has no need to be on guard against sin, as long as she leaves her will there where it is rooted, that is, in him who gave it to her freely from his *bonté*. Thus he wishes by his prayer to take it back [*ravoir, rehabere*] from his beloved, nakedly and freely, without a why for her [*sans nul pourquoy pour elle*].²²

In a second passage, the speaker is named as "Forfeited Will." When Forfeited Will speaks of herself as "having back" herself, she is using the same terminology that is usually applied to the divine lover, who cannot "have back" his will until the soul hands it back through the annihilation of her will. This passage is one of the richest and most difficult in Porete's *Mirror*. The complexity of issues, the highly wrought character of the language, the radical nature of the apophasis, and the temporal gap between the single French manuscript and the old French original, make any conclusive reading difficult:

> I cannot be, says Forfeited Will, what I must be, until I am again there where I was at that point where I was as naked as I was when I was not, as I was naked as he is who is, as naked as I would be when I am not. It would be appropriate for me to have myself, if I wish to have back [*ravoir*] my own, otherwise I will not have it back. Gloss this, if you wish and if you can. If you cannot, you are not it. If you are, it will open for you. You will not be profoundly annihilated as long as you have an "*of which*" to hear. Otherwise I would not say this. If goodness takes hearing from you, I will not veil myself.²³

Porete refers to the moment of creation, in which the deity gives the soul her free will, as the moment in which the soul is "made lady" over the divine *bonté*. The radical freedom of the good had been figured by Plotinus as a good that overflows neither out of its own will nor out of necessity. In Porete this overflow is figured in a more personal representation: the deity hands over its will, a relinquishment that, in contrast to Plotinian emanation, puts the divine lover in some sense at the mercy of the human soul. It cannot have back its will until the soul gives it up. At this point in Porete's language, the imagery of the mirror comes implicitly into play. Two parties are realized to be one, as the soul becomes a pure reflection. The phrases that commonly appear at the point of mystical union—"in itself," "through itself," "of itself"—are generated. Here Dame Amour is speaking after the soul has given back her will, after the divine has received it back at the pleasure of the soul, at a point "without a why":

> It is true, says Love, that her will is ours. She has passed through the Red Sea, her enemies remain behind. Her pleasure is our will, by the purity of the unity of the divine will, wherein we have enclosed her. Her will is ours, for she is fallen from grace to perfection of the work of the virtues, and from virtues into love, and love into nothingness, and nothingness into the clarification of God, who sees himself with the eyes of his majesty—who at this point has clarified her. And she is so returned into him that she sees neither herself nor him. He sees himself alone from his divine *bonté*; he is of himself in such *bonté* that he knew of himself when she was not, before he entrusted his *bonté* to her and made her lady of it. This was free will, which he cannot take back by himself without the pleasure of the soul. Now he has it, without a why, at that point that he had it before she was *lady*. There is no one else. No one else loves but he, for no one is outside of him and he alone loves and sees and praises from his own being.[24]

In contrast to Porete, Eckhart does not state explicitly that the divine cannot have back its will until the soul gives it up. He places the restriction upon the divine in a different key. The divine blessedness, happiness, and being depend upon the soul's becoming virgin (which includes giving up her will). If the soul is not virgin, then the only-begotten son of the divine cannot be born in her. And since this birth is the self-birth of divinity itself, its very being is dependent upon that birth. For Eckhart, a divinity that is not realized in the soul as the just act, as life, as equality, is an abstraction; deity's very being depends upon its being born in the soul.[25] Insofar as the soul gives up her will, the divine must give her all that it has and is; this giving is nothing other than the self-birth of the divine.[26] Despite their distinctive approaches to the exchange of wills, both Porete and Eckhart make that exchange central to a number of key themes: the dialectic of will; procession and return; living without a why; and the reversion (of the will, the soul, the deity) to a state where it was before it was. In each case the divine is said to be "compelled," a compulsion that is at least apparently scandalous from both Plotinian and traditional Christian perspectives. Each portrays the all-powerful divine as giving over to the human creature a free will, but with emphasis upon the way in which such a free will puts the deity in a position of vulnerability. Each portrays the human as gaining true freedom in giving back the will—a traditional claim—but each associates this giving back of will with reversion to the state of pre-creation where deity and soul were before they were.

In the passages cited above, Porete links the soul's abandoning of will with a reversion to living "without a why." Eckhart makes a similar link in a variety of sermons (though not so specifically in "Blessed are the Poor in Spirit"). The two writers are using highly colloquial expressions which nevertheless reflect the formal notions of willing nothing and pre-creation. Each breaks down the term ("why" or "wherefore": *pourquoy, dar umbe*) into its components, "for" (*pour, umbe*) and "what" or "that" (*quoy, dar*). The "what" is then unsaid, exposed as a "some-thing," "a reason," "a means" (*moyen, mittel*) or "use" (*usage*, being useful or *nutz*).

The "what" in "for what" is the being "for which" an action is selfishly undertaken. To give up such intentionality, to give up the "what," is to give up being-something, a reversion to the pre-creative state of nothingness in which one is not a creature, not a deity, but is simply that one is. This state is symbolized by Eckhart through the "I am what/that I am" of Exodus, and by both Porete and Eckhart as the nothingness and nakedness of the soul. In becoming nothing, the soul becomes equal (*glîch*) to everything (in Eckhart) and everything is "the same [*égal*] to it" (in Porete).[27] In both cases, the notion of equality is pushed, through the dialectic of distinction and indistinction, to the extreme sense of identity.

Praying God to Be Free of God

To measure this radical "poverty of the will" in Porete and Eckhart, we return to the issue of rewriting Eckhart's texts with which this book began. The modern editor of Eckhart's German works interpolated inverted commas in selected places in the text around Eckhart's word *got*. Modern translations have either followed this interpolation,[28] extended it (by placing inverted commas around other instances of "God" not altered by the editor of the German text),[29] or interpolated into Eckhart's text an upper-case/lower-case graphic distinction between "God" and "god."[30] One translator explains that the

German editor "devised a method, not suggested by any of his manuscripts, of interpretation *ad meliorem* [for the better], by placing the word *got* sometimes in inverted commas."[31] Here is the passage in translation without editorial alteration:

> Now we say that God, with that whereby he is God, is not a perfect end of creatures, so great is the richness that the least creature has in God. Were it the case that a fly had reason and could rationally seek the eternal abyss of the Godly being from which it came, we say with all that whereby he is God, he would not be able to fulfill or suffice the fly. Here we pray God that we might be free of God [*her umbe sô biten wir got, daz wir gotes ledic werden*] and that we might grasp the truth and enjoy it eternally. There where the highest angel and the fly and the soul are equal, there I stood and willed what I was and was what I willed. We also say if someone would be poor of will, he must will and desire as little as he willed and desired when he was not. And in these ways a person is poor who does not will.[32]

The use by modern editors and translators of interpolated inverted commas or the equivalent occurs in the following key propositions from this passage:

> 1. But when of my own free will I went on, and became aware of my created being, then I had a "God" (*sic*).
> 2. For before there were any creatures, God was not "God" (*sic*), but he was what he was.
> 3. So we pray God to free us of "God" (*sic*).

These rewritten expressions are explained by one translator as offering "the commonplace scholastic distinction between God as he is in himself and 'God' as he is in creatures." The interpolation of inverted commas into Eckhart occurs not only in the modern edition and translations, but in modern interpretive paraphrases as well, where the reader without access to the original manuscript is unable to know that the inverted commas have been added.[33]

These "inverted commas" may seem innocuous. After all, modern editions of classical texts commonly add punctuation and capitalization, which themselves can become controversial in cases of syntactical ambiguity. From the perspective of this study, however, the selective interpolation of inverted commas into editions and translations amounts to a censorship of the fundamental principle of apophatic discourse. That principle—stated in the introduction and employed throughout this study—is *the refusal to resolve the apophatic dilemma by posing a distinction between two kinds of names.* The apophatic writer does not hesitate to make such a distinction. Indeed, Eckhart makes it quite clearly, without having to resort to inverted commas: "But when creatures came to be and received their created being, then God was not God in himself, he was God in creatures." (*Aber dô die crêatûren gewurden und sie enpfiengen ir geschaffen wesen, dô enwas got niht got in im selben, mêr: er was got in den crêatûren.*)

The key problem with the interpolations is that the apophatic writing does not rest with the distinction between God-in-himself and God-in-creatures, and indeed, will unsay the distinction. In the case of "Blessed are the Poor in Spirit" the unsaying is signaled by an apophatic marker, the expression "now we say" (*nû sprechen wir*). This expression is a condensed version of a longer statement: "We said *before* that . . . but *now* we say." The significance in "Blessed are the Poor" of the "now we say" as an apophatic marker becomes clearer through a comparison with other examples.

Sermon 48 in the Quint edition is titled, significantly, *Ein meister sprichet* (a master speaks, or a master says). Toward the end of that sermon, Eckhart says that he has spoken of an uncreated light within the soul, a light that comprehends deity without medium, uncovered, naked. This comprehension occurs during the birth of the son in the soul. After these statements, the text turns apophatically back upon them with the expressions "Here I may truly say . . ." and "I say truly."[34] These expressions mark a shift to indistinction, wherein this same light is no longer concerned with fruitfulness and generation (the birth of the son) but seeks the "simple ground" or "quiet desert" into which distinction and the divine persons (father, son, and spirit) have never gazed.[35] In another sermon, Eckhart states that he has spoken of a free "power in the spirit," "guard of the spirit," "light of the spirit," or "spark." He then immediately unsays these names: "But now I say [*Ich spriche aber nû*] it is neither this nor that. . . ."[36] When "a master speaks" in Eckhart's sermon, whether the master is Eckhart or another authority, the saying is never unprotected from a later "but now I say," turning back upon it, not to deny it, but to unsay it. The "now we say" unsays both the previous statement and the authoritative closure associated with the statements of a master.

The "now we say" in "Blessed are the Poor" is used precisely in this way as an apophatic marker. Eckhart has just made the distinction between God as he is in himself and God as he is in creatures (or in "historico-cultural-linguistic effects"). Immediately after making that statement, he begins the famous passage "Now we say that God, whereby he is God, is not a perfect end for creatures." This new passage is signaled by the "Now we say" as *contrasting* with the previous distinction between God in himself and God in creatures. If it did not contrast with the previous distinction, then the entire passage—including the prayer to God to be free of God—would be a redundant statement of the distinction already made; and this redundancy is in fact what the interpolated inverse commas make of the text. The rewriting of the passage through selective interpolation is an imposition upon it of the commonplace scholastic (and largely Thomistic) distinction between God in himself and God in creatures that Eckhart has already made. That imposition neutralizes the entire following passage with its unsaying of that distinction, cutting the raison d'etre out from under it.

The issue here is not that what Eckhart is saying in the "now we say" passage is different substantially from what he said in making the previous scholastic distinction. At the moment of unsaying, the discourse is shifting away from the "what" (as quiddity, as creation, as intentionality, as distinction between creator and created) to the nothingness of the ground of the soul and the ground of the deity. From the perspective of this no-thingness, this "what-less-ness," God is not the perfect end for creatures.

That the modern editors, translators, and interpreters would feel compelled to rewrite the text *ad meliorem*, would feel authorized to rewrite it at all, and would be for several decades unchallenged in doing so, illustrates the discomfort the modern world finds with apophatic language and to what lengths it will go to transform it into an analogical pattern based upon the distinction between two kinds of names. The rewriting betrays a reification of the generic word "God," as if letting go of that word were somehow inconceivable. The central principle of apophatic discourse is the letting go of the generic name.[37]

The rewriting of Eckhart's discourse is a manifestation of a larger phenomenon: modern and postmodern writers construct a monotonic God and project it back upon the medievals. Eckhart's sermon *Quasi stella matutina* (Like the morning star) has been used as an example of the "hyperbeings" within Eckhartian apophasis. The center section of that sermon is a counter version of the key passage from "Blessed are the Poor." In both passages, Eckhart indulges in extravagant analogies regarding a "fly" and deity. In "Like the Morning-

Star," however, the "fly" analogy is used to dramatize the hierarchical ontology rather than to collapse it:

> Before there was being, God worked; and He brought about Being when there was no Being. Unrefined masters say that God is a pure Being; He is as high above Being as the highest angel is above a fly. I would be speaking as wrongly in calling God a being as I would in calling the sun pale or black. God is neither this nor that.[38]

This passage does indeed posit an ontological hierarchy, with the deity as a hyperbeing or a being beyond the beings we can conceive. Such hierarchies are intrinsic to the apophatic writings studied in this volume. They abound in Eckhart. What is apophatic in Eckhart is the continual motion toward the unsaying of such hierarchical ontologies through the dialectic of indistinction and distinction, whereby that which is most distinct is distinct by virtue of its lack of distinction. The dialectic of distinction and indistinction grounds the key passage, cited above, from "Blessed are the Poor." In the hierarchic ontology—selectively chosen to illustrate the hierarchy—God is as far beyond "being" as an angel is beyond a fly. In the unsaying of that hierarchic ontology at the point of nothingness in which all things are equal—which was selectively ignored—"God, with all that whereby he is God, would be unable to fulfill or suffice the fly":

> Were it the case that a fly had reason and could rationally seek the eternal abyss of the Godly being from which it came, we would say that with all that whereby he is God, he would not be able to fulfill or suffice the fly. Here we pray God that we might be free of God and that we might grasp the truth and enjoy it eternally. There, where the highest angel and the fly and the soul are equal, there where I stood and willed what I was and was what I willed. We also say if someone would be poor of will, he must will and desire as little as he willed and desired when he was not. And in these ways a person is poor who does not will.[39]

Eckhart's words "We pray God to free us of God" perform a praying and an unpraying reminiscent of the antisermonic nature of his sermons. Just as he turns the sermon form back upon itself by refusing to tell people how they should live (since true life is lived without a "how" or a "why"), so his prayer turns back upon itself. Both Porete and Eckhart put into question the notion of prayer as petition. At one point Porete states that the annihilated soul which is beyond usages and will does not pray. Throughout his sermons, Eckhart strongly critiques prayer as petition, stating that, as long as the soul is trying to get something from the deity, it has not reached a virgin state free of its own self-will. Eckhart's prayer to God to free him of God asks freedom from the very deity that would grant the petition. In both Porete and Eckhart the prayer as petition is a preliminary act. In order for the soul to give up its will entirely, it must make a sacrifice of its petition, and in order to sacrifice petition it must give up the deity (named and substantial) that grounds petition. Without the interpolated inverted commas, Eckhart's praying God to make him free of God becomes a charged statement that, like some of the Dionysian formulas in Eriugena, contains within it the entire apophatic dialectic. Porete and Eckhart do not deny the importance of petition, nor the importance of "will" upon which petition is based. At the moment of unsaying, the volitional aporia is operative: to become free of will, it is necessary to become free of the will (expressed through petition) to become free of will. And that can happen only when the soul is free of deity as a being that grants petitions.

One Work, One Gift

For Porete and Eckhart, when the virgin soul gives up all works, she allows the deity to work within her. This theme unites the other strong correspondences (the reversion to the pre-creative state, the living without a why, the dialectic of nothing and all, the utter abandonment of will). Both authors reject salvation through works and both raise the stakes on the critique of works, turning the critique back upon the medieval monastic piety that sought contemplation over works. For Porete, monastic asceticism, this self-named life of the spirit, is in fact an enslavement to works and to will. Those who retain their works, the good workers, "perish in their works"; and "their works are really dead."[40]

When works are given up, then the deity can work in the soul—whether that divine work is considered as the work of Dame Amour, FarNear, God, and the trinity, as in Porete, or as the birth of the son in the soul, as in Eckhart. The text performs the transfer from the false agency of the creaturely actor to the true agency of the divine actor. In his discussion of this "work," the voice of Eckhart the preacher suddenly becomes the first person voice of the divine: "There I spring out in the holy spirit where there is one life and one being and one work. The father performs one work and therefore his work is me, his only begotten son, without any difference."[41] For both Porete and Eckhart, the place of the work "in" the soul is ultimately given up and the "in" is transformed as the soul reverts to a state of nothingness.

Dame Amour is calling not so much for the abandonment of activity as for a reinterpretation of its meaning and its agency.[42] As she said earlier, the soul is concerned neither to do anything nor to refrain from doing anything for God. For Porete and Eckhart there is only one authentic work, the eternal divine work that in Eckhart's definition of eternal, "always has occurred and always is occurring."[43] Such a radical rejection of "works" has little to do with quietism. Neither Porete nor Eckhart led quiet lives, neither abandoned human activity, neither were passive. The act of giving up activity would be considered "a work" by Porete and Eckhart. The rejection of human "work" is not a rejection of activity, but of the identification of the agent with the ego-self. Insofar as a work is just (i.e. carried out without self-interested attachment), the true actor is the divine who works in the soul. The giving up of creaturely agency does not result in a lack of productivity. For Eckhart, as will be shown below, it results in a "thousandfold fruitfulness" in which the soul is bearing fruit (the divine son) in every new moment. For Porete, the union with the divine occurs in a "flash"; the "work" of love in the soul is continually recurring.

Central to both Porete and Eckhart is the notion that *in this work, the deity gives the soul nothing other than itself*. Alluding to John 14, "whoever believes in me, he will do the works I do and even greater,"[44] Porete speaks of divine gifts to the soul, gifts "as great as he himself who has given it."[45] This statement by Porete contains a shift from the plural (gifts, *dons*) to the singular: "has given it [*cecy*]." This one gift is then said "to transform him [the divine giver] from him(self) within him(self)." Porete images the divine work in erotic terms, in terms of sexual union. Her passages on the ravishment of the annihilated soul in union with FarNear exploit the tension between the metaphor of sexual union and the logic of apophatic, mystical union.

Eckhart figures the gift as the birth and self-birth of the divine within the soul.[46] That self-birth constitutes life, equality, and the one just act that has ever occurred and is ever occurring (with both senses of "ever," as both unique and continuous). That self-birth is in turn expressed as Neoplatonic procession through the metaphor of emanation. It is also the "procession of the son" within classical trinitarian theology. Finally it is a birth and self-birth of the son or word in the soul, thus embodying—with some radical transformations—the Christian notion of the virgin birth.[47]

In both Eckhart and Porete it is the soul's abandonment of all possessions (in the form of will, means, medium, and works) that allows deity to work within her and to give itself to her.[48]

Freedom, Nobility, and Equality

"To live without a why" for Porete and Eckhart is to be free. Freedom in turn is defined through a dialectic of nobility and equality. Porete's understanding of freedom and nobility is mediated through her transformation of courtly love.[49] For Dame Amour, freedom (*franchise*) is linked to nobility and opposed to serfdom or slavery; the noble holy-church-the-grand opposed to the servile holy-church-the-little. Yet even this counterhierarchy is dissolved in Lady Love's teachings concerning the annihilated soul; for the annihilated soul, all (honor, dishonor, heaven, hell, joy, sorrow) is equal (*égal*).

With Eckhart, the freedom and nobility of the soul contrast not so much with serfdom as with commercialism, with buying and selling. His term for "without medium" (*âne mittel*) could also mean "without money." Eckhart is also more explicit than Porete in collapsing the hierarchical notion of nobility. His German treatise "On the Nobleman" begins with an affirmation of hierarchy in all its aspects, yet it ends with one of Eckhart's most sustained evocations of equality. The nobility beyond means is identified with the common, with those who have nothing and are equal to nothing. At the beginning of Sermon 6 "The Just will live forever" (*Justi vivent in aeternum*), Eckhart remarks that what he says will sound "common" or "lowly" (*gemeine*), but that it is in fact noteworthy (*merklich*).[50] In the dialectic of the noble and the common, hinted at here through what might seem a homiletic commonplace, the most noble soul is equal to everything and everyone. In chapter 6 above, the paradox of distinction and indistinction was shown to be at the heart of Eckhart's apophasis. That paradox allows a hierarchy of virtues and standards and, at a key point, the transcending of that hierarchy in a manner similar to Ibn ʿArabi's notion of the "station of no-station."

Justice and life are the attributes that dominate Eckhart's densest apophatic explorations, while for Porete love is the prime attribute of the annihilated soul (though Porete is willing to give up the name "love" along with everything else). For Porete the soul disencumbered of all attributes—including justice—would endure eternal torment out of loyalty to the divine lover. For Eckhart, the virgin soul—empty of everything, even God, if God is not justice—would endure eternal torment for the sake of justice. Eckhart, in applying his dialectic of equality to the suffering of the deity itself, breaks with the tradition of the impassivity of God in his claim that insofar as the soul suffers without self-interest that suffering is the suffering of God. Porete affirms a more conventional distinction between the suffering humanity of Jesus and the divine nature of Christ which cannot suffer, yet in her discussion of "Forfeited Will" she offers a powerful intimation of mutual interdependence between deity and humanity.

The act (of love, justice, or equality) is no longer a means, but an end in itself. It is a self-birth. The apophatic language of Porete and Eckhart ties human "nobility" or authenticity to an acceptance, beyond all consolations, of the no-thingness that underlies human existence. This nobility is taken to its logical extreme in both authors. It is achieved only when all things are "equal" to the soul: heaven and hell, reward and punishment, honor and dishonor. Intentionality, with its hierarchical structures of being, is inscribed within the theological language Porete and Eckhart inherited and used. That intentionality allows for a vision and a goal. But at a critical moment—when nobility is revealed as equality, when freedom is viewed as the letting go of self-will and being itself—intentionality is momentarily displaced and enslavement to a fixed ontology averted.[51]

Mary, Martha, and Mary

Mention has been made of the difference between the figuring of the divine work in the soul as birth (by Eckhart) and as erotic union (by Porete). For both writers, the divine "work" within the soul transforms the monotonically male "He-God" of the onto-theological tradition into an open and dynamic series of gender relations. At the same time, Porete and Eckhart unsay both medieval and modern gender essentialisms that tie the character of writing to the biological sex of the author.

Porete's Dame Amour suggests the three Marys as models for the annihilated soul: the Virgin Mary, Mary Magdalene in the desert, and Mary of Luke's Martha and Mary story (the latter two frequently identified in medieval writings). Each is virgin, empty of works. While Porete's writings turn back sharply upon the ideals of medieval ascetic piety, her interpretation of Martha and Mary keeps the conventional medieval associations: the preference of Jesus for the silent Mary over the busy-about-many-things Martha is read as a preference for the life of contemplation over the life of works. The revolutionary aspect of Porete's interpretation resides in her defining the life of works to mean what would normally be considered a life of contemplation. Eckhart, in a move that may be unprecedented in medieval spirituality, reverses the equation and favors Martha. Both authors use the story to exemplify the soul devoid of will, works, and medium. Both authors ultimately challenge the distinction and hierarchy between contemplation and works.

Four areas of contemporary feminist thought help bring the gender dynamic in Porete and Eckhart (and between them) into higher relief: (1) the critique of trinitarian theology as a theological archetype for an all-male society of "processions";[52] (2) the critique of conventional Christian symbolism of the Virgin Mary as a religious paradigm for the passive, subservient female;[53] (3) the recent critical attention given to the association in many medieval Christian writings, mentioned above, of woman, nature, fall, birth, and sexuality; and, most important, (4) the critique of the Martha and Mary story in the Gospel of Luke and its use within Christianity as a paradigm for spiritual choices.

> Now as they went on their way, he entered a village and a woman named Martha received him into her house. She had a sister called Mary who sat at the Lord's feet and listened to his teaching [*ton logon autou*]. But Martha was distracted with much serving [*diakoinian*]; and she went to him and said: "Lord, do you not care that my sister has left me to serve alone. Tell her to help me." But the Lord answered her: "Martha, Martha, you are anxious and troubled about many things; one thing is needful. Mary has chosen the good portion, which shall not be taken away from her." (Luke 10:38–42)

In an important feminist discussion, this story is seen as a later reaction (by the author of Luke) against the active role of women in the primitive Church. The story puts woman against woman in competition for the approval of a male authority, and places women within roles easily controlled and defined by the male authority. A history of interpretation finds the story engendering four hierarchical polarities: *abstractionist* (Martha and Mary as abstract principles—works against faith, Judaism against Christianity, worldly against spiritual, this world against the world to come, active against contemplative); *nonabstractionist* (good woman against bad woman, woman serving God against woman serving man, nun against housewife); *apologetic feminist* (the supposed acceptance by Jesus of a contemplative and scholarly role for women as opposed to the alleged rabbinic rejection of the same); and *psychological* (sibling rivalry and sexual rivalry, in which women are defined by the relation to men). In each of the four, hierarchical structures predominate. Christian is lauded over and against Jew. The independent Martha who approaches Jesus (as constructed by the author of Luke) as an equal is rejected in favor of the deferential Mary. Mary—who sat and listened in apparent silence—is praised. The outspoken Martha is put in her place.[54]

When viewed from the perspective of the four feminist positions listed above, the achievement of Porete and Eckhart's apophatic discourse becomes clearer. Porete's court of love, while offering homage to the traditional trinity, in effect displaces it with a new divine triad (Dame Amour, FarNear the Annihilated Soul) whose interactions form the central mythic and literary dynamic of *The Mirror*. The deity is given a thoroughly interactive gender configuration in terms of Dame Amour, FarNear and the Annihilated Soul. The divine speaker, Dame Amour, is feminine. The tradition of courtly love is reconfigured. Common medieval notions of the fall, woman, nature, and sexuality are inverted in the figuring of the last stages of mystical ascent as a "fall of love."

By placing virginity above marriage, Mary above Martha, Porete had adopted the standard hierarchical paradigm of medieval piety that is the object of feminist critique. Yet by incorporating this paradigm into the mythos of courtly love, she also subverts that paradigm. While Mary is praised by Luke's Jesus for sitting at his feet and listening—in contrast to the outspoken Martha—in the court of Dame Amour it is primarily females who speak. FarNear, the major male character in the drama, is silent.

The tension over the role of speaking is reflected in Porete's ambivalence about her own status as author. She refers to her act of writing *The Mirror* as the "work" of a poor begging creature and as an "encumbrance." Yet she also suggests that the work may be nothing other than the reflection and work of the divine within the annihilated soul. However we interpret *The Mirror*'s complex portrayal of Porete as author, within her life her position is clear. It was her unbreakable resolve to continue writing and circulating her book that led to her execution at the stake.

Eckhart's trinitarian, processional theology could be viewed as a reaction against the rich gender dynamic among Dame Amour,

FarNear, and the annihilated soul.[55] By placing the "work" of the divine within the language of trinitarian processions rather than that of Lady Love and FarNear, Eckhart may be thought to risk losing that dynamic. Eckhart's language at times seems to dwell repetitively on the "fatherly heart."[56] A central danger in Eckhart's birth imagery would be that it represents yet another appropriation by the male power (in this case the deity) of female power and creativity. However, the birth imagery occurs when and only when the univocal maleness of the deity is most radically undone.

The unsaying of the monotonically male deity begins, as is often the case with apophatic discourse, at the semantic microlevel; in this case with the preposition "in" of "in the soul." A theology in which a series of processions descend from the divine source to fill the emptied, passive soul (figured as feminine) would be yet another example of androcentric discourse—with its movement of male processions into a passive receptacle figured as feminine. Yet the receptacle paradigm is undone with the transformation of "in the soul." The "in" also refers to the principle that what proceeds, insofar as it remains "in" its principle, is equal to and identical to that principle. At the moment of mystical union, the "in" refers not to the descent of a procession into a lower vessel but to the higher reality of something "in" its principle.

As with Eriugena, this notion of "in" is the basis for the reversions of the various hierarchical strata back up into a point of absolute equality. This concept of "in-ness" is the principle of disontology within the language of Eriugena and Eckhart. At the moment of the birth of the son in the soul, however, the "in" of "in the soul" is revealed *to be the same* as the "in" of "in the principle." The procession is the return. For the deity, as Eckhart states strongly, does not give birth to itself in the soul as a place, or locus, or receptacle: it becomes the place of its own self-birth, its own "work."[57] In other words, the self-birth takes place really within the ground of the soul, which is identical to the ground of the deity, that primal source of reality, naked-being, nothingness. When the soul becomes "equal to nothing" then the divine gives itself to it, but by becoming "equal to nothing" the soul has reverted to the nothingness of the ground of reality. This is the paradox of *bullitio*, the bubbling out (of, in and into itself) into which the virgin soul is taken up (*assumptum*). This "assumption" then is not the "assumption" of a passive Mary, nor is it the "assumption" of human nature by a salvific male, but rather a theological inversion in which the virgin soul becomes the ground and source of the one real work that always has occurred and always is occurring. At this point, the virgin soul, the Virgin Mary, has a real role in the birth of the deity. She is revealed to be the mother of God in a literal sense, rather than the "catatonic" virgin whose motherhood of God is so often treated as a kind of purely formal honor.[58]

The power of Eckhart's theology of birth and self-birth is due to the transformation of the meaning of "in-ness." By translating the language of procession into a paradigm of self-birth, Eckhart displaces the male autogenesis that can be read in other examples of processional and generational theology. The deity is both a self-birth and a self-genesis. Birthing becomes the central event in divine and cosmic history. When the son is born in the soul, and the soul is taken up through that birth into equal relations or—to use the alternate paradigm—when the soul becomes "equal to nothing" and the son is thereby born "in" the nothingness that is the ground of reality—at that moment the gender components of deity become fluid. The soul (in its ground) is the mother of deity and gives birth to it but is also equal to (and identical to) the son and therefore the father in the process. Eckhart does not stress the feminine components of the trinity here in explicit terms; he remains faithful to traditional language in his formulations. But his paradigm of self-birth shatters traditionally monotonic gender paradigms from within.

The gender implications of Eckhart's apophatic writings can be found most clearly in his German sermon 2, which begins, fittingly, with the Martha and Mary story: "Jesus entered into a certain little town and a certain woman, Martha by name, took him up into her home" (*Intravit Jesus in quoddam castellum et mulier quaedam, Martha nomine, excepit illum in domum suam*). Eckhart rephrases this citation in German as: "Our master Jesus Christ went up into a little castle and was received by a *virgin who was a wife*."[59] Martha becomes the symbol for the virgin wife and for the mystical reconception of the virgin birth. The reconception is signaled by two expressions in the German rewording of the Latin text on Martha and Mary. The first expression is "up in" (*ûf in*), which alludes to transformation of "in-ness" and the paradox that the procession is the return, discussed above as central to Eckhart's apophasis of gender. The second expression is the term *enpfangen* which Eckhart used to translate the Latin "excepit," a term that can mean both receive and conceive, and that paves the way for Eckhart's discussion of the wife who gives birth.[60]

The explication of the virgin who was a wife begins with the figuring of virgin as lacking all images. There is a further wordplay; the term for free, *ledic*, also means unattached in the sense of unmarried:

> Now then, pay close attention to this word: it was necessarily by a virgin that Jesus was received/conceived. "Virgin" designates a person who is free of all foreign images, as free as he was when he was not yet.[61]

Switching to the first person, the voice in the sermon speaks of being as free of images "as I was when I was not"—the familiar theme of reversion to the pre-created state.[62] Eckhart is combining both intellect and will in his notion of foreign images. By refusing all foreign images and all attachment to images, the soul is free and virginal. At this point the soul is ready to receive the impression, which in this sermon is compared to the fruit which the soul bears. The analogy of "bearing" evokes the birth of the son in the soul. The sermon then moves on into a passage in which this birth takes place in an eternal moment that, just as in Ibn ʿArabi's conception of mystical union, must be reenacted in each new moment in time. The passage is constructed around an opposition between "spouses" who give birth only every year and a "wife" who is perpetually giving birth each new moment. "Spouses" are defined as those who carry out their own work with *eigenschaft*. I have translated *eigenschaft* as "attachment," but it also connotes "possessiveness" and "self [*eigen*] regard." In more abstract philosophical terms, *eigenschaft* denotes a quality or property of a thing, and Eckhart is playing upon that sense as well. Later in the same sermon, he will speak of the spark of the soul. The deity, in order to see the spark, must give up its *eigenschaft*, its attachment to and its quality of persons.[63] Those who are attached are those who still have their own qualities; they have not yet become nothing. Such attachment takes a period of time before it can bear fruit, a period Eckhart calls "a year." By contrast, those who are free are said to be those who have, will, and can (do) nothing other than what the divine wills for them in each new moment—a phrase that recalls the "willing nothing, having nothing, knowing nothing" of Eckhart's sermon on the poor in spirit.

> Any attachment to any work that takes from you the freedom to wait upon God in this present now [*disem gegenwertigen nû*] and to follow him alone in the light in which he informs you what to do and what to let be, in each now free and new [*in einem ieglîchen nû vrî und niuwe*], as if you possessed, desired, and were capable of nothing else—

any such attachment and every proposed work [*vürgesetzet werk*] which takes from you this freedom that is new in each moment [*alle zît niuwe*]—I now call a year.⁶⁴

The sermon then turns in apostrophe to the reader to delineate the consequences of such attachment. Precisely as with Ibn ʿArabi,⁶⁵ to live in long periods (with attachment to a particular work or image) is contrasted with the giving up of works and images in a kind of perpetual birth and rebirth in every moment.

> Your soul brings forth no fruit until it has accomplished the work to which you were attached. You trust neither God nor yourself, until you have carried out the work that you have seized upon with attachment; otherwise you have no peace. So you bear no fruit unless you complete your work. I consider this a "year" and even then the fruit is small, for it comes from attachment to the work and not from freedom. I call such people spouses [*êlîche liute*] because they are bound to attachment.⁶⁶

The sermon then turns to the wife (*wip*) that gives birth in each moment. This short passage applies all the major elements of Eckhartian apophasis to the gender dynamic. The virgin who is a wife is "equally close" (*glîche nâhe*) to God and herself—and the dialectic of equality, distinction, and indistinction (those who are equal to nothing, are equal to all) is evoked. This virgin who is a wife is bearing fruit in each moment, neither more nor less than God—and the notion of eternity as the birth that always has occurred and always is occurring is evoked. In its specific language, in which the virgin who is a wife bears "a hundred or thousand times a day" the sermon gives a direct response to tradition, extending from Jerome to Augustine to Aquinas, that places the virgin over, against, and above the wife. Aquinas, in his affirmation of the superiority of virginity to other forms of chastity, had offered a succinct summary of that tradition:

> Hieronymus [Jerome] attributes a hundredfold fruit to virginity, on account of its superiority to [the chastity] of widowhood, to which he attributes sixty-fold; and to that of matrimony, to which he attributes thirty-fold. However, according to Augustine, a hundred-fold fruit is for martyrs, sixty-fold for virgins, and thirty-fold for spouses.⁶⁷

For Eckhart, the virgin who is a wife bears a hundred or thousand times daily and bears forth the only begotten son from the noblest ground of all (*ûz dem aller edelsten grunde*). Here the dialectic of nobility and equality, the noble and the common, is evoked.

> A virgin who is a wife is free and unbound with attachment, is at all times equally close to God and herself. She bears much fruit, which is great, neither more nor less than Godself. This virgin who is a wife brings about this fruit and this birth, and brings forth fruit, a hundred or a thousand times a day, countless fruit, giving birth and by becoming fruitful from the most noble ground of all. To say it even better: from the same ground from which the father is bearing his eternal word, she is fruitfully bearing with him.[68]

The virgin who gives birth to the son of God is clearly to be identified with the Virgin Mary—what other virgin birth of the son of God occurs in Christian tradition? However, the virgin mother of God is not to be identified with the natural or prescribed role of women. Any soul, of male or female, that is empty of attachment to its own images and desires is the virgin that gives birth to the son.

Eckhart does not evoke the name of the Virgin Mary at this point. Instead, his reinterpretation of the Virgin Mary as the actual source or ground of the deity—in the most radical, literal sense—is superimposed upon his inversion of the standard interpretation of the Martha and Mary story. That reinterpretation was effected through the very subtle play upon the translation of the sermon's introductory quote from the Martha and Mary account in which "going up to a little town" was rephrased as being "received by a virgin who was a wife." Contemplation, as figured by the empty, silent, virgin soul, is no longer placed above activity (as figured by the wife who gives birth). The silent Mary is no longer put above the silenced Martha. Martha is now the prototype of the virgin who is a wife, the *wip*, who represents the fullest life (for male or female), or life itself, as birth (and self-birth) in every moment. Contemplation and proclamation are part of the same moment, as dialectically linked as are letting go and giving birth. The just act is the birth of the son in the soul, the only just act that ever has occurred and ever is occurring. The contemplative and the active are fused into the one eternal work and birth that always has occurred and always is occurring. Mystical union is not an experience of the extraordinary, it is a new vision of the ordinary; the most humble act of justice, insofar as it is just, is nothing other than the birth of the "only-begotten" son of God. It is not some grand one-time experience, but a work that must be realized anew in each moment.

At the end of the sermon, the virgin soul and virgin wife are identified once again with the virgin/wife who received/conceived (*enp-*

fangen) Jesus into her little town (*bürgelîn*). In that little castle, God is "blooming and growing as he is in himself." He is bringing to birth his only begotten son as truly as in himself. In that little town, "God is gleaming and shining with all his richness."[69] The "in" is transformed from an indication of containment to an indication of the existence of something in its principle. Again we see that the "procession and receptacle model" (where the male deity begets himself) is countered by the gender dynamic operative on this mythic level where the little town and the virgin who is a wife are decoded as the ground of reality and the mother of deity.

The "Pseudowoman" and the Meister

From what we know, Porete had no formal training in theology and was considered unqualified to engage in theological discussion, while Meister Eckhart was placed in the prototypical position of patriarchal authority as spiritual and intellectual guardian of women. He was an intellectual champion of the Dominicans, sent by them to Paris to do battle with the Franciscan Gonsalvo. His honorific, "meister," became so attached to him that we do not even know for certain what his given Christian name was. He was placed in a position of authority over nuns and other women; yet both the nature of his sermons and the history of their transmission suggest that, rather than controlling the powerful currents of women's spirituality, he was part of them. After his death, many of his sermons were passed on in an oral tradition by nuns and beguines. Eckhart was a preacher and many in his audience would have been nuns or beguines. Yet instead of telling them how they should live, his sermons subverted the question of "how to live" by turning to a discourse of living "without a how" or "without a why," without a *dar umbe*. When his sermons reach the point of "without a why" they collapse the hierarchical structure from which the preacher gains his teaching authority. As shown above in the discussion of Eckhart's expression "a master says," this collapse of hierarchy into radical equality is signaled by the transfiguration of the monolithic voice of the "meister" into a continual conversation in which each statement of a meister is subject to an apophatic turn by the statement of another meister: "now we say." At other key points, the voice of the preacher is transformed into the voice of the just person insofar as he or she is just. This transformation echoes and validates key themes (nakedness of the soul, abandonment of works and will, the work of the deity in the soul, the dialectic of nothingness and everything, the reversion to pre-creation, living without a why) of the great women mystics (Mechthild, Hadewijch, Beatrice, Hadewijch II, Porete) even as it links them, in often revolutionary ways, to the classical traditions of Neoplatonic mysticism and Christian trinitarian theology.

From the perspective of this conversation between Porete and Eckhart, it would seem futile to try to rank the two. Porete's apophasis of desire and mysticism of love find a complement in Eckhart's mysticism of birth. In appropriating, combining, and inverting the mythos of courtly love and the paradigms of Martha, Mary, and the Virgin Mary, Porete may have also run up against the limitations within traditional understandings of those paradigms. Yet she succeeded in creating a court of love with an exceptionally rich gender dynamic within the divine, within the human, and between the two. She figured the deity in terms of both male and female, and she figured the voice of the deity as feminine. In her passages on the "fall of love" she transformed the themes (interlinked in medieval Christianity) of fall, femininity, nature, and desire. And by making the divine lover dependent upon the annihilated soul (he cannot have back what he has given except at her pleasure), she achieves a sense of interdependence that transcends the original metaphor associating the naked soul with pure receptivity.[70] Eckhart's gender dynamic is less explicit. Yet in its reinterpretation of the virgin birth (as occurring in the ground of any soul—male or female—which is the ground of God), transfiguring of the Martha and Mary paradigm, and refiguring of trinitarian processions in terms of birth and self-birth, his apophatic discourse stands besides that of Porete as a reconception of gender in divine and human realms. His validation of birth and his emphasis upon the fruitful *wip* (wife) breaks with a tradition of associating birth with the fall and sin of Eve. It also collapses the hierarchy that places contemplation in opposition to and over works; contemplation and works are united in the one genuine work, the birth of the son.

Porete's writings and her life as a beguine (neither clergy nor lay, neither married nor cloistered) threatened established social, intellectual, and theological boundaries and acquired for her the inquisitorial epithet of "pseudowoman." Eckhart, as a Dominican "meister," was placed in a position of administrative and theological control over nuns and other women, but rather than controlling the expressions of late thirteenth-century women's spirituality, he embraced them. But the gender roles that Porete and Eckhart challenged were not only the gender roles as defined at their own time. Contemporary historians have also attempted to define gender roles for medieval authors: how medieval "women" and "men" wrote. Medieval women focus on images of feeding, nourishment, the body, discipline of the body (fasting and flagellation), while men focus upon more abstract, disembodied concepts.[71] There is historical fact behind these generalizations. Yet the generalizations do not do justice to late thirteenth-century mystical writings—of Mechthild, Hadewijch, Hadewijch II, Beatrice, and most particularly, Porete and Eckhart. From the apophatic perspective, authorial protestations that the named God is not bound in space and time are impotent in the face of the power of language and the implicit temporal, spatial, and substantialist categories created within it. Protestations that the terms "male writers" and "female writers" are not meant to essentialize gender difference can be equally ineffective against the practical effects of language. In addition, the historical categories of "male writer" and "female writer" may well replicate the medieval gender roles prescribed and enforced by inquisitorial repression, thereby ignoring a revolution against such prescriptions as widespread and as radical as any within the history of Christian discourse.

At the intersection of the languages of Eckhart and Porete three unsayings occur: the unsaying of essentialist deity; the unsaying of monogendered deity and monotonic gender relations between divine and human; and the unsaying of prescribed roles for male and female writers. The three unsayings imply and reinforce one another.[72]

Epilogue

. . .

The goal of this study has been the exposition of mystical apophasis as a cross-cultural mode of discourse, emerging out of a variety of religious and cultural traditions and sharing key semantic features. Although most mystical writings employ both kataphatic and apophatic modes, the emphasis here has been upon those texts and passages in which the apophatic tendency is most pronounced. In each of the preceding seven chapters or readings, the principles of apophatic language have been encountered as grounded in specific texts and in the individual cultural contexts of each writer's tradition.

At certain times I have pointed out similarities across traditions, without belaboring the obvious doctrinal contrasts. For Meister Eckhart, mystical union and the true affirmation of divine unity occur with the generation and birth of the divine son in the soul. For the Muslim Ibn ʿArabi, the primal affirmation is: "He is Allah, one, Allah the perduring. He does not beget and is not begotten" (Q 111: 1–3). Yet despite such stark doctrinal contrast, the two mystics show remarkable affinity in their respective use of apophatic language to speak of an eternal moment of mystical union that always has occurred and always is occurring.[1] Such contrasts might be partially explained by the historical culmination of the larger Abrahamic and Graeco-Roman metaculture of which Eckhart and Ibn ʿArabi were a part and which was soon to break up. The contrast in doctrinal positions does put into high relief, however, the working of apophatic language and apophatic thinking across specific religious and cultural barriers.

As a way of thinking and a way of writing, apophasis can be given a purely formal description. I present the following outline with some reservations. Such outlines, taken out of context, can resemble a mechanism. The intention of the seven readings that precede has been to show how, in each case, apophatic language emerges out of the writer's struggles with the basic principles of his or her own theological and mystical tradition. It is not a formula than can be applied. Yet given the absence of studies of apophasis as a literary mode and the tendency, discussed previously, for the modern commentator to transpose apophatic language into a nonapophatic paraphrase, it is worth taking the risk to present a schematic and formal outline.

Principles of Apophatic Language

1. The Aporia of Transcendence
   a) X transcends all names and referential delimitation.
   b) If the major premise is true, it must also be false or incomplete, because if X is ineffable in this rigorous sense, it cannot be called X.
   c) This dilemma leads neither to silence nor to a distinction between two kinds of names (*deus* in itself, *deus* in our minds; God in himself, God in creatures; God and "God"; or God and god).
   d) The aporia yields an open-ended process by which the original assertion of transcendence continually turns back critically upon itself.
2. A Language of Ephemeral, Double Propositions
   a) No statement about X can rest as a valid statement but must be corrected by a further statement, which itself must be corrected in a discourse without closure.
   b) The meaningfulness of the apophatic moment of discourse is unstable, residing in the momentary tension between two propositions.
   c) The habits of language pull the writer and reader toward reifying the last proposition as a meaningful utterance. To prevent such reification, ever-new correcting propositions must be advanced.
3. The Dialectic of Transcendence and Immanence
   a) The effort to express and affirm transcendence leads to an affirmation of radical immanence. That which is beyond is within. That which is other, is the non-other.
   b) The transcendent cannot be known as an object by a creaturely subject. It is known through itself. As Eckhart says: "None knows the father but the son."
   c) It is known then only at that point where the subject-object, self-other dichotomies are undone.

      d) The undoing of self-other dichotomy occurs in mystical union.
      e) In mystical union, the divine attributes are not known but realized, simultaneously actualized and understood in the polished mirror of the heart.
      f) While the mystical experience of the self-revelation of the transcendent in the annihilated heart is called a realization, the semantic re-enactment of that realization—what the writer and reader encounter in the act of writing and reading—is a meaning event.
      g) This study makes no presuppositions about the exact relationship of the meaning event to the mystical experience of realization (such a relation is defined by each reader).

4. Disontology and Nonsubstantialist Deity
      a) The transcendent is not a thing, an entity. It is not being, a being, or substance. It is no-thing, nothing.
      b) Yet any naming or nondialectical description will inevitably lead to an object reified in temporal, spatial, and ontological categories.
      c) Because it must be named and reified if we are to use language, the language of unsaying continually turns back upon the spatial, temporal, and ontological reifications it has posed.

5. Metaphors of Emanation, Procession, and Return
      a) These metaphors are often used nonapophatically as causal explanation.
      b) In the apophatic use of the metaphors, causal explanation is displaced as the metaphor turns back upon itself in the hard version of paradox: the emanation *is* the return.
      c) This turning-back (*epistrophê*) entails a folding of the multitiered hierachy of being back into itself to a moment of equality.
      d) The result of such a turning back is a rich set of grammatical transformations.

6. Semantic Transformations
      a) At the moment of mystical union, the undoing of self-other, before-after, and here-there distinctions is reflected in radical grammatical and semantic transformations.
      b) The possible antecedents of the "his" or "its" can

be fused so that the pronoun refers to both the human and the divine party.
   c) The grammatical distinction between reflexive and nonreflexive can be undone, so that the action is both reflexive and nonreflexive at the same time. It reveals to it(self) in it(self) its (own) mystery.
   d) At the microlevel of prepositions, words such as "in" and "before" are brought through a series of transformations that destabilizes the temporal and spatial dualisms upon which they are based.
7. Meaning Event
   The above formal principles make up the meaning event of apophatic language as a literary mode. The meaning event is a reenactment (within grammar, syntax, and metaphor) of the fusion of self and other within mystical union.

The meaning event with apophatic language includes a moment that is nihilistic or "anarchic"[2]—without *archē* or first principle. The anarchic moment is intimated in the turning back of the second proposition upon the first in order to remove the delimitation. In terms of Plotinus's metaphor of the glowing mass within the illuminated sphere, the anarchic moment occurs upon the removal of the glowing mass, which serves as the beginning, source, or principle of the light. This moment was found in Eckhart's prayer to God to be free of God, in Porete's annihilation of the self and its will to do anything or refrain from doing anything for God, Eriugena's nothingness of God, Ibn ʿArabi's continually letting go of every image of self and deity, and Plotinus's awakening without an awakener.

When taken out of context, the nothingness of the deity is indistinguishable discursively from "mere nothingness"; the freedom of the soul from license; the disinterestedness of the soul from indifference; the bewilderment of the soul that knows nothing from irrationality. To attempt to interpose discursive distinctions by claiming that the mystic doesn't *really* mean "nothing," when she says nothing, or doesn't really mean she gives up all will, including the will to do God's will, when she says she does, is to explain away the anarchic moment. To explain away the anarchic moment is to turn apophatic language into conventional theology. Yet to insist upon the integrity of the anarchic moment is to highlight certain moral and intellectual risks.

Three areas of contextualization can better frame the evaluation of the risks entailed by the anarchic moment: (1) the directionality of its context; (2) the manner in which the apophatic language functions; and (3) the importance of performance. The common communication event of the joke offers an analogous series of contextual keys.

1. At a certain moment, the joke will violate accepted standards of propriety, expectation, or appropriateness.

2. While violating those accepted standards, the joke is dependent upon them. Without the accepted standards the joke could not exist; a good humorist will understand the conventional expectations of her audience.

3. A joke is performative. Its effectiveness as a communication is dependent not only upon the content of the joke but upon the manner of its telling, as anyone who has tried to explain a badly timed joke will understand.

4. The anarchic moment of a joke can be used either to reinforce or to challenge the conventions upon which it plays.[3]

Will and Will-lessness

The first relation between the performance of apophasis and its context centers upon will. Porete's Dame Amour speaks of the soul-annihilated-in-love as giving up her will entirely. She no longer wills to do or refrain from doing anything for God. The context of that statement is the transition from the fourth stage, the stage of works, to the fifth and sixth stages of mystical union. The seven-stage pattern of ascent is kataphatic and directional. Each stage leads to a higher stage, and no stage can be skipped. The abandonment of will takes place in the context of the striving to do good works and to follow the divine will. It is from within that striving that the soul realizes the apophatic aporia of desire, that even the desire to do good works or follow the divine will contains an egoism that must be given up in order to arrive at the fifth station of annihilation. At the moment of abandonment of the self, of will, and of works, Dame Amour tells us, the deity (as trinity, Dame Amour, or FarNear) will work within the soul.[4] A similar, directional context can be found in the other apophatic writings, as well as in the taken-for-granted directional context of the milieu in which they wrote or preached. Thus Ibn ʿArabi's station of no-station is placed within the Sufi context of a gradation of stations of practice and discipline.

Precisely because of the ethical principles with which the mystic is concerned, and the directionality they provide, the moment of complete abandon entails an ethical risk. In itself it has no ethical guarantee. It demands trust in the directional context. Although from the kataphatic perspective, the reader is assured that a sincere willlessness will result not in quietism or license but in the divine working within the soul, from the apophatic perspective we are placed at the moment of loss of all will. To will or expect the divine work in the soul is to fail to abandon all will. The apophatic mystic brings the reader into the eternal moment in which—in Eckhart's terms—the divine is giving birth to itself in the soul. As Eckhart says, the being of the divine, and its well-being, depend upon that birth which is the same birth that always has occurred and always is occurring. For that birth to occur, the soul must be completely empty. But to be completely empty, the soul must be free of everything, including its desire and expectation of the birth. To give up such desire is to risk nothingness.

The erotic language of writers such as the beguines and the Sufis intensifies the sense of ethical risk. The deliberate refusal by many Sufis to specify whether the beloved is earthly or spiritual and Porete's provocative combination of fall, nature, ravishment, and the giving up of virtues challenge the compartmentalization of love into safe and easily defined categories such as earthly and spiritual. At the moment of complete self-abandon, the soul, as Dame Amour states repeatedly, is no longer concerned with such distinctions. Indeed, for the Sufis, to ask about the beloved would be to ask an indelicate question. Eckhart's emphasis upon birth may have been equally provocative, given the medieval tendency to associate birth with Eve's fall. Birth and sexual union are two human experiences that have commonly been associated with the overcoming of subject-object dichotomy. Although Dame Amour assures us that the enfranchised soul who has taken leave of virtues (which presupposes a previous stage of complete servitude to the discipline of the virtues) will never do anything contrary to the teachings of the church, such a statement belongs to the directional, kataphatic context. Dame Amour assures the annihilated soul that when she (the soul) abandons all works and will and takes leave of virtue, divine love will "work" within her. Yet, in this context as well, the apophatic anarchic moment occurs at the point beyond all will and expectation, beyond assurance.

Bewilderment and Rationality

The anarchic moment is embedded as well within a rational context. The paradoxes and contradictions of apophatic language proceed logically from the original aporia of ineffability. The apophatic moment of anarchy—the withdrawal of the glowing mass within the illumined sphere—occurs within the context of the original affirmation of transcendence. Indeed, the original kataphatic element in the affirmation of transcendence (the use of the name "X" to state that X is beyond all names) is necessary to begin the apophatic critique of the name. The affirmation of transcendence—when taken with full apophatic seriousness—then turns back upon itself. The paradoxes of transcendence and immanence, the coincidences of opposites, the displacement of the grammatical object—all are in violation of the conventional logic that functions for delimited entities. It is when language encounters the notion of the unlimited that conventional logic, not illogically, is transformed. The apophatic paradoxes are constructed upon a foundation of conventional logical distinctions; the more highly tuned the rationality of the kataphatic context, the more successful will be the apophatic paradox.

This moment in which the transcendent reveals itself as the immanent is the moment of mystical union. At this moment, the standard referential structures of language are transformed: the breakdown of the reflexive/nonreflexive grammatical distinction in the antecedence of a pronoun [It sees it(self) through it(self) in it(self)]; the breakdown of the perfect/imperfect distinction (it always has been occurred and always is occurring). At the moment of mystical union, the divine attributes are not known to a nondivine subject, the distinction of deity and creation and the duality of lover and beloved are undone. The attributes appear in the mirror, and the image in the mirror is divine in human and human in divine. As soon as the attributes are "known" (perceived as objects by a subject other than them) they harden into idols. They can be realized only through union and self-manifestation. For Eckhart the relevant scriptural citation is: "No one knows the father but the son." For the Sufis, the relevant hadith is: "I [Allah] become the hearing with which he hears. . . ." This realization is both timeless and utterly ephemeral.

The moment in which the ego-self passes away entails a "bewilderment," "love-madness," a "being driven out of one's wits." Conventional rationality is built upon the very structures that are momentarily superseded in mystical union. For Eriugena, it is reason that divides nature into what is (what can be known to reason) and what is not (what exceeds the grasp of reason); and the movement from what is to what is not is a movement of reason. Reason moves to transcend itself. For Porete, Lady Reason is more closely linked to conventional logic, which abhors the coincidence of opposites, and it is the "understanding of love" which can move beyond the death of reason. In the case of all five writers, apophatic nonknowing is an essential feature of understanding, won with difficulty. Yet to give up the self-other dichotomy upon which reason is based entails a risk of its own. It is—if we take Porete and Ibn ʿArabi seriously—madness. The status of that madness depends upon its placement within the directional context. As Ibn ʿArabi suggests, conventional logic has a "from" and a "to," a starting point and a goal. With such logic Noah can call people "to" the transcendent deity. But in the act of calling, Noah reifies the transcendent into spatially delimited images. In opposition to Noah is the "master of the circular path" who—from the context of the directional Sufi path (*ṭarīqa*)—abandons linear directionality to find the transcendent in the immanent, the beyond in the within. Ibn ʿArabi's own discourse is a combination of the linear and the circular, which would yield—to extend Ibn ʿArabi's spatial metaphor—a spiral motion.

Event, Experience, and Unsaying

In both the moral and the intellectual domains, apophatic language affirms hierarchies, and then collapses them from within the directional context; the highest station becomes the station of no-station; the most noble becomes the most common. A radical equality works within the language. For Eckhart and Eriugena, the link between the perspective of equality and the perspective of gradation is the *insofar as* principle; insofar as the soul is equal to nothing, it becomes equal to the nothingness that is the ground of the deity. The hierarchies provide the directional context and the possibility of moral and intellectual distinction (in which not all things are equally right or equally true). The apophatic anarchic moment provides a continual challenge to the directional context and hierarchy, keeping them from hardening into a fixed system.

To attempt to place a guarantee within the anarchic moment is to transform apophatic discourse into nonapophatic discourse. For the apophatic mystic, within his or her kataphatic religious or philosophical context, the risk of the anarchic moment is worth taking. The moral alternative, continued enslavement to the subtle forms of self-will within the will to do or be good, is ultimately (to use the nutritor's language) the death of the ethical spirit. The intellectual alternative, the worship of images constructed from beliefs, is ultimately the death of the rational spirit.

The apophatic mystic wrote for an immediate audience that shared her religious and cultural heritage, directional context (stages of discipline, stages of knowledge), and meditative practices. Insofar as any individual human was able (from a context of willing and knowing) to abandon will and knowing, the realization of mystical union took place. The *insofar as* principle (in Eckhart and Eriugena), the principle of ephemerality and perpetual transformation (in Plotinus, Eckhart, Porete, and Ibn ʿArabi), and the notion that such union occurs only when the ego-self passes away (in Porete, Eckhart, and Ibn ʿArabi especially) attempt to prevent mystical union from hardening into an ego-claim, a presumption, or a binding.

The nonintentional aspect of apophasis runs up against the modern concept of experience:

> Religious experience is the experience of something. It is intentional in that it cannot be described without reference to a grammatical object. Just as fear is always fear of something, and a perceptual act can only be described by reference to its object, a religious experience must be identified under a certain description, and that description must include a reference to the object of experience.[5]

If the nonintentionality claims of apophatic mystics are taken seriously, and if experience is, by definition, intentional, it necessarily follows that mystical union is not an experience. All experience must have a grammatical object, but the prime motivation of apophatic language is to subvert or displace the grammatical object. Similarly, the notion of the unmediated at the heart of apophatic mysticism (particularly that of Eckhart and Porete) contradicts the common opinion that all experience is mediated. If it is true that all experience is constructed, it is equally true that the concept of experience is a modern construct. None of the mystical writers discussed in this book speaks directly of "experience." The apophatic mystic speaks of the birth of the son in the soul, of annihilation, of an awakening without an awakener, but does not speak of "the experience" of such a birth, annihilation, or awakening.

There are at least three possible reactions to the conflict between the apophatic displacement of the grammatical object and the notion that all experience is intentional: (1) to dismiss the apophasis and supply an object of experience;[6] (2) to reconceive experience to include the nonintentional;[7] and (3) to bracket the concept of experience and choose a concept that fits apophatic language but opens that language onto a field of critical inquiry. I have chosen the third.

For Eckhart or Porete to say to their immediate audience that they cannot know what is being spoken of, unless they *are it*, is a valid form of intrareligious discourse which presumes an audience embarked upon the same religious path, sharing the same tradition, engaged in the same meditative, ritual, and social practices. Questions arise when these writings are read by a less immediate audience, by those who do not participate so completely in the writer's cultural and religious world. The appreciative reader can participate in some way in that world; the non-Sufi can understand how the Sufi "stations" might apply to her life even outside the context of observant Islam and might make those stations her own through the act of reading. The central moment in the act of reading is the meaning event, the mimetic reenactment at the semantic level of subject and object of the fusions of self and other that occur in mystical union.

As with the realization of mystical union, the meaning event entails the undoing of basic dualisms of thought and language (self and other, before and after, here and there). As with mystical union, the meaning event in itself has no meaning in the sense of a "what," no paraphrasable or descriptive content; meaning is a function of the kataphatic context in which the event is embedded. The meaning event is constantly being repeated. It cannot be possessed. The continual shift from predication to realization keeps the mind in constant activity, continually displacing the "object," as the infinite regresses built into the discourse lead the reader deeper into the aporetic meditation. The meaning of narrative, philosophical, mythological, and poetic language (the kataphatic aspect) is not negated, but "what" is meant becomes one with the event of the perspective shift.

The meaning event occurs within a kataphatic theological context. The apophatic language itself contains a strongly mimetic aspect, that is, through particular strategems (such as "withdrawing" the subject from a subject-predicate proposition), it aims to induce within the reader an event that will emerge from the kataphatic context (such as the notion of awakening), but which in itself refuses subject-predicate dichotomy (an awakening without awakener). The moment of fusion of subject and predicate is ephemeral; the awakening without awakener soon reifies into just another object of experience. The writer must continually turn back to unsay the previous saying.

Does one have to be a mystic to understand mystical language? The audience of a tragedy must in some sense experience the tragedy in order to understand it. The implication of Aristotle's notion of catharsis is that without a participation in catharsis one cannot really understand the play. Yet one doesn't necessarily have to be a tragic hero (in the literal sense) to participate in the cartharsis event of the drama. Similarly, the reader of mystical apophasis will need to participate in the meaning event in order to understand the text in its own distinctive literary mode. The meaning event is just beneath the semantic surface and within the dualistic narrative and expository framework. It is a secret or mystery that the reader continually uncovers in the act of reading. Whether or not the meaning event, as a mimetic reduplication of mystical union, is in some sense itself mystical is not a decision for the critic to make.

To return to the question of the extended audience of apophatic discourse—what does a work like *The Mirror* mean to us who are not beguines, for example?[8] The anarchic aspect, in terms of both will and reason, need not make this discourse inaccessible to a readership that can participate (albeit from the outside) in the ethical and rational commitments within the tradition of a given writer. Like poetry, apophasis is not a discourse that everyone will appreciate immediately. Like poetry, apophasis resists paraphrase into other linguistic modes; paraphrases can only be partial. When we write about a poem, we do not attempt to express the meaning of the poem—if the meaning could be expressed discursively, it would not have required a poem. In trying to understand how the poetry works, we are led more deeply into the event of reading the poem. What that event means to different readers may well differ strongly from one to another. Yet what has been commonly accepted for poetic discourse—a resistance to semantic reduction—is frequently viewed as a form of mystification in apophasis.

No attempt has been made here to discuss a common religious experience, or a common mystical experience. The goal of this study has been an understanding of a similarly structured semantic event that takes place within various versions of the apophatic mode of discourse. I have tried, apophatically, to refrain from defining this event. But perhaps some positive language, however tentative, would be helpful. We might call the event, then, the evocation of a sense of mystery. This apophatic sense of mystery is not a mystery in the sense of a secret known only by an initiated few. It is not a doctrine that is to be accepted as true but which is held beyond rational explanation. Rather, it is a basic human response—at least among apophatic writers and their appreciative readers—to the nothingness in which being is situated (that what is might have not been). It is a sense of wonderment (*thauma*, in Plotinian terms), bewilderment (*ḥayra*, in Ibn ʿArabi's terms), that is rediscovered not outside of, but within, our cultural, religious, theological, and philosophical worldviews at the horizon where they point beyond themselves. This mystery might be viewed through the prism of three "names": the mystery of being, the mystery of being alive, and the mystery of being aware (the mystery of consciousness). Such an experience of mystery does not insulate the worldviews in which it is found from criticism or scrutiny; on the contrary it is an invitation for continual reevaluation of them as the limited constructions they are.[9]

To evaluate mystical union as an experience of mystery is a kataphatic judgment. The experience has a grammatical object (mystery). From the apophatic perspective such analysis is partial, even misleading, if left without the apophatic complement. Mystery would then become reified into another name, another God of belief. The category of mystery is useful insofar as writer and reader turn back upon it to withdraw the glowing mass and unsay the name.

To arrive at the kind of unknowing spoken of by the five mystics in this volume is not an easy task. On the literary level, unsaying demands a full utilization of the literary, theological, and philosophical resources of the tradition. Its achievement is unstable and fleeting. It demands a rigorous and sustained effort both to use and free oneself from normal habits of thought and expression. It demands a willingness to let go, at a particular moment, of the grasping for guarantees and for knowledge as a possession. It demands a moment of vulnerability. Yet for those who value it, this moment of unsaying and unknowing is what it is to be human.

NOTES

• • •

Introduction

1. Quint 2:493 (see below, chap. 7, for full discussion and references): Waere daz sache, daz ein vliege vernunft haete und môhte vernünfticlîche suochen den êwigen abgrunt götlîches wesens, ûz dem si komen ist, sô spraechen wir, daz got mit allem dem, daz er got ist, sô enmöhte er niht ervüllen noch genuoc tuon der vliegen. Her umbe sô biten wir got, daz wir gotes ledic werden.

2. Edmund Colledge and Bernard McGinn, *Meister Eckhart: The Essential Sermons, Commentaries, Treatises and Defense* (New York: Paulist Press, 1981), p. 200. See the more detailed discussion of these issues, including the rewriting of this text, the prayer in connection with the rest of Eckhart's sermon, and Colledge's full argument in chap. 7 below.

3. "We find ourselves in an *aporia*, in pangs over how to speak." Plotinus, *Enneads* 5.5.6.23 (see below, chap. 1).

4. See Augustine, *On Christian Doctrine* 1:6: "Have I spoken or announced anything worthy of God? Rather I feel that I have done nothing but wish to speak: if I have spoken, I have not said what I wished to say. Whence do I know this, except because God is ineffable? If what I said were ineffable, it would not be said. And for this reason God should not be said to be ineffable, for when this is said something is said. And a contradiction in terms is created, since if that is ineffable which cannot be spoken, then that is not ineffable which can be called ineffable. This contradiction is to be passed over in silence rather than resolved verbally." Augustine, *On Christian Doctrine*, trans. D. W. Robertson, Jr. (Indianapolis: Bobbs-Merrill, 1958), pp. 10–11.

5. For an example of such a theory of names, see Thomas Aquinas, *Summa Theologiae*, 1a, 13 (Blackfriars edition,1963): 3: 47–97. Cf. n. 24, below. For a more detailed discussion of the Thomist underpinnings of the God/"God" distinction, see chap. 7, below.

6. One of the more explicit discussions of the mutual interdependence of *apophasis* and *kataphasis* occurs in Dionysius. See below, chap. 2.

7. See for example, the work of Stephen Gersh, cited in chap. 2.

8. Other texts that would correspond to the characterization of apophasis given here would include the Taoist *Chuang Tzu*, the Ch'an *Platform Sutra*,

the collection of popular Hindu mythology, the *Yogavasistha*, the *Katha Upanishad*, the *Chandogya Upanishad*, the writings of Dogen, to mention only a very few examples.

9. *The Holy Teaching of Vimalakīrti*, trans. R. F. Thurman (University Park: The Pennsylvania State University Press, 1976).

10. By Emmanuel Levinas and Edmond Jabès, to mention two examples. Wittgenstein's statement in the *Tractatus* that unsayable things do exist, followed by the statement that this previous statement "must be thrown away " is a classically apophatic move, but one that comes as a kind of postscript, rather than being inscribed within the *Tractatus* as a whole. Ludwig Wittgenstein, *Tractatus Logico-Philosophicus*, 6.5222, 6.54.

In a separate study, James Webb and I offer several areas of comparison between classical apophasis and what might be called, by extension, the apophatic trend in psychoanalysis as exemplified by W. Bion and J. Lacan. We are not claiming that classical apophatic mysticism and the apophatic trend in psychoanalysis are "the same thing" or seek "the same thing." But the languages, the aporias, and the strategies have some comparable elements. In both instances the effort to engage "the real" in language leads to a continual turning back of language upon itself. The real is unknowable, yet that unknowability, rather than resulting in silence, becomes the dynamic of a new discourse. The real is best approached when intentionalist perspectives (salvation, healing) are, at least momentarily, set aside—Bion and Lacan's critique of intentionalist psychoanalysis, with its emphasis upon goals, expectations, progress, recalls Porete and Eckhart's critique of intentionalist Christianity (with its heavens and hells). The real's location (in the soul, in the deity, in the unconscious, in the analysand) is placed into an apophatic transformation of "in-ness" and distinction of place. The real is ultimately not locatable in the self or the other (soul and deity, self and neighbor, analysand and analyst), but is "radically dialogic." James Webb and Michael Sells, "Lacan and Bion: Psychoanalysis and the Mystical Language of Unsaying," *Theory & Psychology* (in press).

11. While the strongest apophatic writings have generated traditions of commentaries, the commentaries themselves seldom contain the intensely apophatic discourse found in the primary writing.

12. Such elements could be found in the dynamism of Heraclitus's view of constant change, in the paradoxes of Plato's Parmenides, in Plato's assertion that the good was "beyond being," in the implications of Aristotle's notion of mind (*Nous*) as thought thinking itself.

13. We find such efforts in the writings of Marius Victorinus. See Hadot, *Porphyre et Victorinus* (cited in chap. 1, below, n. 32).

14. Although Arabic and Judaeo-Arabic versions of Plotinian writings circulated widely in medieval Jewish and Islamic circles, many Islamic apophatic texts developed as much in competition with Neoplatonism (which was interpreted nonapophatically for the most part in Islamic philosophy) as in sympathy with it. Ironically, then, Plotinus may have been at least as influ-

ential on apophatic performance in Latin Europe, where he was known only indirectly, as in the Arabic and Judaeo-Arabic contexts, where he was read in translation. Plotinus's writings were translated into Arabic and Judaeo-Arabic as the "Theology of Aristotle." Ironically, however, the *Theology of Aristotle* omits the passages that will be discussed in this study as exemplifying Plotinian apophasis at its most intense. And although the authors of the masterworks of Islamic apophasis may have had direct or indirect contact with the *Theology of Aristotle*, there is no evidence that they were dependent upon it in creating their apophatic discourse, or that they should be considered part of some medieval Plotinian tradition. Indeed, Plotinus seems to have been appropriated by rationalist philosophers (*falāsifa*) who were often hostile to the performatively apophatic language of the mystics. Even in the West, it remains a question whether Neoplatonism was a necessary condition for the mystical apophasis of Eckhart and Porete. Porete may have had little formal contact with Neoplatonic writings, and though Eckhart may have known Eriugenean and Dionysian writings, one wonders whether he would not have composed apophatically even without the influence of his Neoplatonic predecessors.

15. A convenient end-date for this common world would be 1492, the year Jews and Arabs were expelled from Spain, the colonial age began, and the civilization held in common by Jewish, Christian, and Muslim cultures began to break apart into increasingly separate spheres.

16. This brief sketch of the historical and geographical parameters of this study is not meant to foreclose the attribution of "apophatic" to any writer not discussed or mentioned in this study. As mentioned above, the relationship of apophasis to particular historical traditions is complex. The combination of apophatic discourse or moments of apophatic discourse with other modes of theological, poetical, and discursive languages complicates further efforts at definition.

17. The kind of reading engaged in in this book requires close attention to the word-play within the texts in their original languages. For practical reasons, therefore, I have not been able to include readings from the Aramaic, Hebrew, and Persian works of Moses de Leon, Abraham Abulafia, Rumi, or Hafiz, to mention a few important examples. This study cannot be and is not intended to be a comprehensive treatment of the historical manifestations of apophasis in the classical Western tradition. Nor can it hope to give a broad treatment of mysticism or mystical literature; the goal is a clearer understanding of only one kind of mystical writing, the apophatic, as it appears in a variety of texts. The intense focus upon apophatic language here is meant to help clarify an aspect of mystical language which has often been marginalized or neglected. It is not meant to imply that other forms of mystical language, or nonapophatic aspects of some of the same traditions discussed here, are not important in their own right.

18. It is beyond being (*epekeina ontos*) in Plotinus, "nothing" (*nihil*) in John the Scot Eriugena, the "no-limit" (*ayn sof*) or "nothing" (*ayin*) in the *Zohar*

(depending upon whether one views the Ayn Sof or the first of the sefirot, Keter, as the source of emanation), that which is beyond the distinction between the divine and the nondivine (in Eckhart and Ibn ʿArabi). Cf. "*Ayin:* The Concept of Nothingness in Jewish Mysticism," in R. Forman, ed., *The Problem of Pure Consciousness* (Oxford: Oxford University Press, 1990), pp. 121–62.

19. A. Lovejoy's influential book, *The Great Chain of Being* (Cambridge: Harvard University Press, 1936), presents a strong and very nonapophatic picture of hierarchy and ontology. The popularity of the book, and the transformation of the its title into a truism, has tended to obscure the apophatic elements of disontology within the classical, Western tradition.

20. The previous tendency to deny the existence of mystical union within the Kabbalah of the *Zohar* has been countered by Moshe Idel. See M. Idel, "Universalization and Integration: Two Conceptions of Mystical Union in Jewish Mysticism," in Idel and McGinn, eds., *Mystical Union and Monotheistic Faith* (New York: Macmillan, 1989), pp. 27–58; and M. Idel, *Kabbalah: New Perspectives* (New Haven: Yale University Press, 1988).

21. Paul Ricoeur, *Interpretation Theory: Discourse and the Surplus of Meaning* (Fort Worth: Texas Christian University Press, 1976).

22. For some works within the large and vibrant controversy over the issue of experience, see Wayne Proudfoot, *Religious Experience* (Berkeley: University of California Press, 1985); G. William Barnard, "Explaining the Unexplainable, Wayne Proudfoot's *Religious Experience,*" *Journal of the American Academy of Religion* 60.2 (1992): 231–56; and Robert Forman, "Introduction: Mysticism, Constructivism, and Forgetting," pp. 3–49, and the essays that follow in Forman, *The Problem of Pure Consciousness*; Sallie King, "Two Epistemological Models for the Interpretation of Mysticism," *Journal of the American Academy of Religion* 56 (1988): 257–79. I return briefly to the issue of experience in the epilogue, below, but should emphasize here once again that this study is primarily *literary* and will be bracketing for the most part the psychological issues that have been prominent in the controversy over experience. It is hoped, however, that a clearer understanding of apophasis as a literary mode will contribute to the wider discussion of mysticism, including the psychological aspects. For a new study that approaches mysticism from a historical and theological framework and moves beyond emphasis upon autobiographical experience, see Bernard McGinn, *The Presence of God: A History of Western Christian Mysticism*, vol. 1, *The Foundations of Mysticism: Origins to the Fifth Century* (New York: Crossroad, 1991). Cf. M. Sells, "From a History of Mysticism to a Theology of Mysticism," review essay on B. McGinn's *The Presence of God*, in *Journal of Religion* 73.3 (1993): 390–99.

23. For examples, see below, chaps. 4, 5. On capitalizing of pronouns interpreted as referential of deity see the *Chicago Manual of Style*, 14th ed. (Chicago: University of Chicago Press, 1993), Sec. 7.80.

24. Aquinas argues strongly that *deus* is a common, not a proper, name. He offers a theological explanation of why and how it is not a proper name in the Christian tradition. *Summa Theologiae* 1a, 13, 9, response, point 2: "The

name *deus* is a common name, not a proper name, because it signifies the divine nature in concrete" (*Hoc nomen, deus, est nomen appellativum, et non proprium*). Here Aquinas is speaking of the word as it is in our mind (*in cognitione nostra*). In itself it is incommunicable. In which case the apophatic might ask: "How then can we know it as the name *deus*?"

25. Resistance to the modern hypertrophy of the word "God" should allow a better access to apophatic discourse. It should also allow the more specific and complex languages of deity to emerge into higher relief. In the *Zohar*, *elohim*, *hokhma*, and the dynamic world of the sefirotic names emerge as a multivalent world of semantic correspondences. The inherently apophatic nature of the unpronounceable tetragrammaton (YHWH), and its intensification in Kabbalistic discourse, emerges with particular power when no longer covered by the generic God. In Eckhart, the central terms of Christian scripture and theology (such as father, son, word, mother of God), emerge and combine with a meditation upon the attributes to which they correspond (such as life, justice, understanding, love). In Ibn ʿArabi, the removal of the generic God reveals the vital distinction between *al-ḥaqq* (reality) and Allah (the personal creator and revealer) across which Islamic language of divinity is generated, and retrieves the semantic intimacy and gender balance generated by the Sufi understanding of deity as the divine beloved. In Marguerite Porete, the generic deity yields to a unique gender dynamic among three divine personas.

26. The point of any possible commonality would not be located in the "what." Respect for the referential openness of any potential commonality might help contribute to a more non-threatened and detailed attention to the specific languages of each tradition, while avoiding the particularist fallacy that interpolates a "what" into the mystical language and then distinguishes the "what" of one tradition from the "what" of another.

The cul-de-sac to which the purely nonapophatic language of "what" has led is shown in a recent discussion of the differing cases of experience of "nothingness" in the mysticisms of differing traditions. There it was argued that "the difference between cases is a difference between *what* is experienced, not just how *something* is experienced [emphases mine]." S. Katz, "Language, Epistemology, and Mysticism," *Mysticism and Philosophical Analysis* (New York: Oxford University Press, 1978), p. 52. The substantialist presuppositions of the question of "what" are revealed in the phrase "how something is experienced." An argument that presents itself as defending the contextual distinctiveness of differing traditions against would-be homogenizers has, in the space of one sentence, changed the specific language of "nothing" into a language of "something."

Though the assertion that differing religions uphold the "same God" is a common beginning to interreligious conversation, it has not led to productive results. If, for example, Islam and Christianity affirm the same God, that same God either has a son or does not have a son. The move toward interreligious conversation ends in stark contradiction, which can only be explained by the hypothesis that the writer's own tradition has the correct understanding. For a vivid example of this devolution of dialogue into apologetics, see Hendrik M. Vroom, "Do All Religious Traditions Worship the Same God?" *Religious Studies* 26.1 (1990): 73–90.

If the commonality is *not* "the same thing" or "the same God," then each tradition is encouraged to examine the god-language of the other, to see what Allah and sonship mean within the Qur'an, and what sonship and *deus* mean within the Christian Bible. Because the two language systems are not placed in competition, a more detailed understanding of the religious language world of the other poses no threat, and the presumption that one tradition must be the correct one, and that other traditions must have a false or at best distorted view, may at least have to compete with other possibilities.

27. See Jacques Derrida, "How to Avoid Speaking: Denials," trans. Ken Frieden, in Sanford Budick and Wolfgang Iser, *Languages of the Unsayable: The Play of Negativity in Literature and Literary Theory* (New York: Columbia University Press, 1989), pp. 3–70; reprinted in H. Coward and T. Foshay, eds., *Derrida and Negative Theology* (Albany: SUNY Press, 1992), pp. 79–142. For the original French version, see "Comment ne pas parler: Dénégations," in Jacques Derrida, *Psyché: Invention de l'autre* (Paris: Galilée, 1987), pp. 535–95. For Derrida's reading of a specific Eckhartian text, see chap. 7 below. Cf. Robert P. Scharlemann, ed., *Negation and Theology* (Charlottesville: University Press of Virginia, 1992), which includes essays by David Klemm, Mark Taylor, Edith Wyschogrod, Jane Mary Trau, Langdon Gilkey, and Masao Abe; Kevin Hart, *The Trespass of the Sign: Deconstruction, Theology, and Philosophy* (Cambridge University Press, 1989); and Antony Dugdale, "Silent Prayers: Derridean Negativity and Negative Theology" (Master's thesis, McGill University, 1993).

In a response, John Caputo argued that Derridean deconstruction itself, when it is not purely parasitic on other texts, is liable to being read as posing a hidden God. See John Caputo, "Mysticism and Transgression: Derrida and Meister Eckhart," in *Continental Philosophy II: Derrida and Deconstruction*, ed. Hugh Silverman (New York: Routledge, 1989), p. 30: "Deconstruction requires a prior hermeneutics, the anterior work of addressing one another as about the matter at hand. Deconstruction lies in wait for 'discourse' to stake its claims and then it pounces on it. . . . In classical terms, the Being of deconstruction always exists *in alio*, by inhabiting the discourse of others." For a discussion of Caputo's paraphrase of Eckhart as a distinction between God and "God," see below, chap. 7.

28. In discussing the need for prayer in Dionysius, Derrida writes: "Why? No doubt, to attain union with God" ("How to Avoid Speaking," p. 45). This "no doubt" signals the unquestioning authority with which some contemporary writers seize the referent of apophatic language. Derrida twists the mystical metaphor of the nakedness of deity (shared by the beguines and Eckhart) into a metaphor of flagellation: "The strategy of his sermons puts to work a multiplicity of voices and of veils, which he superimposed or removed like skins or garments, thematizing and himself exploring a pseudo-metaphor until reaching that extreme flaying of which one is never sure that it allows

one to see the nakedness of God or to hear the voice of Meister Eckhart himself" (p. 44). For nakedness as a metaphor in the mystical language of the beguines and its reflection in Eckhart, see below, chaps. 6–8. For a different and more open Derridean reading of classical apophasis, see J. Derrida, "Post-Scriptum: Aporias, Ways and Voices," trans. by John P. Leavey, Jr., in Coward and Foshay, *Derrida and Negative Theology*, pp. 283–323.

29. For a more detailed discussion of this issue, see M. Sells, "Bewildered Tongue: the Semantics of Mystical Union in Islam," in Idel and McGinn, *Mystical Union and Monotheistic Faith*, pp. 169–73.

30. See chap. 6 below.

31. Classical apophasis does posit, despite itself, substantialist deities. Its integrity resides not in a realm free of contamination from reification and linguistic idolatry but rather in a self-critical stance, an acknowledgment of its own reifications, and a relentless turning-back to unsay them. The apophatic mystic is engaged in a continual struggle with her own tradition. That tradition supplies the cultural and mythic hierarchies that ground ethical choice, the choice between affirming life over inflicting death, for example. Yet, if the *being* that grounds those hierarchies is not subject to criticism, it becomes the center of domination, exclusion, and the manipulation of power. Apophasis is the continually-in-process turning of language back upon and beyond its own reifications.

Chapter One

1. An earlier version of this chapter appeared as "Apophasis in Plotinus: A Critical Approach," *Harvard Theological Review* 78: 3–4 (1985): 47–65. It was first presented at the panel of the International Society for Neoplatonic Studies, American Philosophical Association, Western Divison (Chicago, 25 April 1985). I owe special thanks to Aryeh Kosman for his comments and suggestions.

2. Most of what we know of Plotinus's life is dependent upon Porphyry's biography. Some of the elements of the biography, such as the long search by Plotinus for a teacher, seem to fit a common hagiographical pattern. Porphyry's life of Plotinus is included at the beginning of most editions and translations of Plotinus. See *Plotinus* (vols. 1–7), ed. A. H. Armstrong (Cambridge, Mass.: Loeb, 1966–88), vol. 1.

3. The following from Harold Bloom, *Kabbalah and Criticism* (New York: Seabury Press, 1975), p. 18, is typical: "To most modern sensibilities, Gnosticism has a strong and even dangerous appeal, frequently under other names, but Neoplatonism scarcely moves anyone in our time. William James reacted to the Neoplatonic Absolute or God, the One and the Good, by saying that 'the stagnant felicity of the absolute's own perfection moves me as little as I move it'. No one is going to argue with James now."

4. Just a few examples will be mentioned here. John Caputo in a response to Jacques Derrida writes: "I do not deny that there is a wide streak of this in Eckhart, a streak of Neoplatonic, henological metaphysics." See "Mysticism and Transgression: Derrida and Meister Eckhart," in *Continental Philosophy II:*

Derrida and Deconstruction, ed. Hugh Silverman (New York: Routledge, 1989), p. 32. He later returns to the same comparison: "What Eckhart taught had little to do with a Neoplatonic One or a super-essential presence" (ibid., p. 39). For a more theologically toned assertion of Eckhart's superiority to the perceived Neoplatonic monodimensionality, see James Clark, *Meister Eckhart: An Introduction to the Study of His Works* (Edinburgh: Nelson, 1957). Dermot Moran is similarly concerned to separate Eriugena from the rigid ontological hierarchy depicted by Lovejoy as a great chain of being, and imputed as an invariable to "Neoplatonism." See Dermot Moran, *The Philosophy of John Scottus Eriugena* (Cambridge University Press, 1989), pp. 94–96.

5. *Enneads* 5.5.6.11–17: Τὸ γὰρ ἐπέκεινα ὄντος οὐ τόδε λέγει—οὐ γὰρ τίθησιν—οὐδὲ ὄνομα αὐτοῦ λέγει, ἀλλὰ φέρει μόνον τὸ οὐ τοῦτο. Τοῦτο δὲ ποιοῦν οὐδαμοῦ αὐτὸ περιλαμβάνει· γελοῖον γὰρ ζητεῖν ἐκείνην τὴν ἄπλετον φύσιν περιλαμβάνειν· ὁ γὰρ τοῦτο βουλόμενος ποιεῖν ἀπέστησεν αὐτὸν καὶ τοῦ ὁπωσοῦν καὶ κατὰ βραχὺ εἰς ἴχνος αὐτοῦ ἰέναι.

All references are to Plotinus, *Plotini Opera*, ed. Paul Henry and Hans-Rudolf Schwyzer, 3 vols. (Paris: Desclée de Brouwer, Leiden: Brill, 1951, 1959, 1971), cited by standard *Ennead*, treatise, section, and line number. My translations are indebted to those of A. H. Armstrong (Cambridge, Mass., 1966–88); Bréhier (Paris, 1924–38); V. Cilento (Bari, 1947–49); and R. Harder (Hamburg, 1956–62). They are particularly indebted to the translation of Stephen MacKenna (London, 1921–30). Though in some ways superseded by more recent translations based upon better editions, MacKenna's translation remains a compelling literary interpretation, bringing across the spirit of the *Enneads*, the dramatic sense of searching, the late Platonic lyricism, and the apophatic intensity. Plotinus speaks of his first principle with the personal, masculine pronoun (*autos*), and with nonpersonal terms such as "the good" (*to agathon*), "the one" (*to hen*), and "the beyond-being" (*epekeina ontos, epekeina ousias*). In order to emphasize his effort to go beyond delimitation, I vary between masculine and neuter forms in my translations. There is a large modern literature on Plotinus and Platonism. For a recent discussion of Plotinus in the context of the development of the Platonist tradition in late antiquity, see John Peter Kenney, *Mystical Monotheism: A Study in Ancient Platonic Theology* (Providence: Brown University Press, 1991), pp. 1–128. Kenney includes an excellent bibliography on Plotinian studies. Cf. J. Dillon, *The Middle Platonists* (Ithaca: Cornell University Press, 1977). For a summary treatment of Neoplatonism, see R. T. Wallis, *Neo-Platonism* (London: Duckworth, 1972). Of the studies devoted to Plotinus, that of E. Bréhier, *La Philosophie de Plotin* (Paris: Boivin, 1928), trans. J. Thomas as *The Philosophy of Plotinus* (Chicago: University of Chicago Press, 1958), is particularly sensitive to the apophatic aspects of the *Enneads*.

6. I have translated *to on* and *ousia* throughout as "being," and *ta onta* as "beings." For Plotinus, "being" is implicated in any form of referential entification.

7. A more mundane but nevertheless operative difficulty will result from the decision not to capitalize terms such as "the one." This is simply an effort

to reflect more accurately the original text, from which such capitalizations were absent. We have become habituated to the ease with which uppercase letters mark out and define as divine or transcendent certain words. Especially with simple terms like "the one," the possibilities of semantic confusion can be expanded when the capitalization is relinquished. Yet the richness of apophatic discourse resides in its working with and against such semantic intertwinings. As was mentioned in the introduction concerning the term "God," the Plotinian uppercase "One" is a construct of modern scholarship.

A much more problematic construct of modern scholarship is the Plotinian "God," commonly identified with Plotinus's *to hen*. This translation can result in a serious distortion of Plotinian language, especially by ignoring the fact that *nous* is treated by Plotinus as divine, described with the language of *theos*. If a God is to be found in Plotinus, it needs to be very carefully related to the extraordinarily complex relationship between *nous* and *to hen*.

8. *Enneads* 5.5.6.26–33: Τάχα δὲ καὶ τὸ 'ἓν' ὄνομα τοῦτο ἄρσιν ἔχει πρὸς τὰ πολλά. Ὅθεν καὶ Ἀπόλλωνα οἱ Πυθαγορικοὶ συμβολικῶς πρὸς ἀλλήλους ἐσήμαινον ἀποφάσει πῶν πολλῶν. Εἰ δὲ θέσις τις τὸ ἕν, τό τε ὄνομα τό τε δηλούμενον, ἀσαφέστερον ἂν γίνοιτο τοῦ εἰ μή τις ὄνομα ἔλεγεν αὐτοῦ· τάχα γὰρ τοῦτο ἐλέγετο, ἵνα ὁ ζητήσας, ἀρξάμενος ἀπ' αὐτοῦ, ὃ πάντων ἁπλότητός ἐστι σημαντικόν, ἀποφήσῃ πελευτῶν καὶ τοῦτο.

9. *Enneads* 5.5.6.33–37.

10. For Plotinus's concept of *theōria*, see Ennead 3:8 and John Deck, *Nature, Contemplation and the One: A Study in the Philosophy of Plotinus* (Toronto: Toronto University Press, 1967).

11. See Walter Ong, *Orality, Literacy: The Technologizing of the Word* (London: Methuen, 1982).

12. See 5.9.5.1–13 for a particularly explicit statement by Plotinus on this subject. Our dealing with the things of the world generates the habit of separating out entities even when we are trying to conceive of a realm (in this case self-reflective *nous*) where such separations should not apply. This critique of the habits generated by dealing with things of the world can be found throughout the *Enneads* as an implied premise of much of the apophatic discourse.

13. See H. A. Wolfson, "Albinus and Plotinus on Divine Attributes," *Harvard Theological Review* 45 (1952): 115–30; John Whittaker, "Neopythagoreanism and Negative Theology," *Symbolae Osloenses* 44 (1969): 109–25; idem, "EPEKEINA NOU KAI OUSIAS," *Vigiliae Christianae* 23: 91–104; R. Mortley, *From Word to Silence* (Bonn, 1986), vol. 2; idem, "Negative Theology and Abstraction in Plotinus," *American Journal of Philology* 96 (1975): 363–77; idem, "What is Negative Theology? The Western Origins," in *Prudentia*, supplementary number, 1981: *The Via Negativa*; and John Peter Kenney, *Mystical Monotheism*, pp. 84–85. Kenny distinguishes between two views of *aphairesis*, a narrow one based upon rules concerning "what notions should be discarded in the identification of the highest divinity," and "a more general notion of negation" that Kenney associates with the term *apophasis*. In this book, I will use the term *apophasis* to refer to the more general process whereby

discourse attempts to unsay its own reification, and "abstraction" to refer to the particular technique of removing or abstracting an element out of a previous proposition. Apophasis will include various forms of paradox, the dialectic of immanence and transcendence, and the various forms of *aphairesis*. R. Mortley states that Plotinus does not use the word *apophasis* to refer to his method of abstraction: "Now it is indeed striking that the term apophasis is not used by Plotinus in relation to negative theology—he seeks a term which connotes stripping off." This assumption becomes the basis for Mortley's distinction between *aphairesis* (abstraction) and *apophasis* (negation). Mortley's strict division between the two terms is puzzling, given the *Ennead* 5.5.6.26–33 (translated and discussed below) where *apophasis* does refer to a method of abstraction or *aphairesis*. See R. Mortley, "Negative Theology and Abstraction in Plotinus," p. 375. *Apophasis* as it is used in this book, and as it was used by Plotinus in 5.5.6, could not be termed a form of negation. As pointed out throughout the readings in this study, negative propositions fall to the apophatic critique just as strongly as affirmative statements. See below, where Plotinus states of his transcendent reality that neither the "thus" nor the "not thus" can apply to it: 6.8.9.38–39. For a fine examination of apophasis in Gnosticism, see R. Mortley, "The Name of the Father Is the Son," in R. Wallis and J. Bregman, eds., *Neoplatonism and Gnosticism* (Albany: SUNY Press, 1992), pp. 239–52.

14. *Enneads* 6.4.7.32–38: φέρε, εἴ τις τὸν ὄγκον τοῦ σώματος ὑφέλοι, τηροῖ δὲ τὴν τοῦ φωτὸς δύναμιν, ἆρ' ἂν ἔτι εἴποις που εἶναι τὸ φῶς, ἢ ἐπίσης ἂν εἴη καθ' ὅλην τε τὴν ἔξω σφαῖραν; οὐκέτι δὲ οὐδ' ἀπερείσῃ τῇ διανοίᾳ ὅπου πρότερον ἦν κείμενον, καὶ οὔτε ἔτι ἐρεῖς ὅθεν οὔτε ὅπῃ, ἀλλὰ περὶ μὲν τούτου ἄπορος ἔσῃ ἐν θαύματι ποιούμενος.

15. *Enneads* 6.8.9.38–48: Ἀλλ' οὐδὲ τὸ οὕτως· οὕτω γὰρ ἂν ὁρίσας εἴης καὶ τόδε τι· ἀλλ' ἔστι τῷ ἰδόντι οὐδὲ τὸ οὕτως εἰπεῖν δύνασθαι οὐδ' αὖ τὸ μὴ οὕτως· τί γὰρ ἂν εἴποις αὐτὸ τῶν ὄντων, ἐφ' ὧν τὸ οὕτως. Ἄλλο τοίνυν παρ' ἅπαντα τὰ οὕτως. Ἀλλ' ἀόριστον ἰδὼν πάντα μὲν ἕξεις εἰπεῖν τὰ μετ' αὐτό, φήσεις δὲ οὐδὲν ἐκείνων εἶναι, ἀλλά, εἴπερ, δύναμιν πᾶσαν αὐτῆς ὄντως κυρίαν, τοῦτο οὖσαν ὃ θέλει, μᾶλλον δὲ ὃ θέλει ἀπορρίψασαν εἰς τὰ ὄντα, αὐτὴν δὲ μείζονα παντὸς τοῦ θέλειν οὖσαν τὸ θέλειν μετ' αὐτὴν θεμένην. Οὔτ' οὖν αὐτὴ ἠθέλησε τὸ οὕτως, ἵνα ἂν εἴπετο, οὔτε ἄλλος πεποίηκεν οὕτως.

16. For discussions of "being" in Greek and Christian thought, see Ivor LeClerc, "God and the Issue of Being," *Religious Studies* 20 (March 1984): 63–78, and Christopher Stead, *Divine Substance* (Oxford: Clarendon Press, 1977).

17. The apophatic critique is commonly foreclosed. W. Christian states, for example, that "In most conceptions of God He transcends the world but is not utterly or absolutely transcendent, *since* He is immanent in the world also [emphasis mine]." William A. Christian, Sr., *Meaning and Truth in Religion* (Chicago: University of Chicago Press, 1964, 1978), p. 190. The implicit logic of this statement allows no possibility for an apophatic, dialectical understanding of transcendence and immanence.

18. *Parmenides* 137c–155d. See E. R. Dodds, "The Parmenides of Plato and the Origins of the Neoplatonic One," *Classical Quarterly* 22 (1928): 129–43.

19. The usual translations of *nous*, "thought" and "intellect," are not fully satisfying. I will be using the term *nous* throughout, but italicize it here only on the first formal usage.
20. See the fine exposition by Kenney, *Mystical Monotheism*, pp. 112–28 and passim. Cf. P. Merlan, *Monopsychism, Mysticism, Metaconsciousness* (The Hague, 1963). For a recent discussion from within Plotinian studies of the relationship of nous to the one, see John Bussanich, *The One and Its Relation to Intellect in Plotinus* (Leiden: Brill, 1988).
21. *Enneads* 6.8.13.1–9: Ἀλλ' εἰ καὶ τὰ ὀνόματα ταῦτα ἐπάγειν δεῖ οὐκ ὀρθῶς τοῦ ζητουμένου, πάλιν αὖ λεγέσθω, ὡς τὰ μὲν ὀρθῶς εἴρηται, ὅτι οὐ ποιητέον οὐδ' ὡς εἰς ἐπίνοιαν δύο, τὰ δὲ νῦν τῆς πειθοῦς χάριν καί τι παρανοητέον ἐν τοῖς λόγοις. Εἰ γὰρ δοίημεν ἐνεργείας αὐτῷ, τὰς δ' ἐνεργείας αὐτοῦ οἷον βουλήσει αὐτοῦ—οὐ γὰρ ἀβουλῶν ἐνεργεῖ—αἱ δὲ ἐνέργειαι ἡ οἷον οὐσία αὐτοῦ, ἡ βούλησις αὐτοῦ καὶ ἡ οὐσία ταὐτὸν ἔσται. Εἰ δὲ τοῦτο, ὡς ἄρα ἐβούλετο, οὕτω καὶ ἔστιν.
22. A. H. Armstrong in *The Architecture of the Intelligible Universe in the Philosophy of Plotinus* (Cambridge University Press, 1940) took these passages as affirming a positive one, a being with attributes of freedom, will, knowledge, love, and goodness, in contradiction with a negative one mentioned in other Plotinian passages. Armstrong's later work has taken the apophatic aspect of Plotinian writing more seriously and treated it more favorably. See, for example, "The Escape of the One," *Studia Patristica* 13 (1975). Cf. R. T. Wallis, "The Spiritual Importance of Not-Knowing," in *Classical Mediterranean Spirituality*, ed. A. H. Armstrong (New York, 1986): 460–80; and Mortley, "Negative Theology and Abstraction in Plotinus," 363–77.
23. *Enneads* 6.8.16.1–39: Ἐπεὶ δέ φαμεν καὶ δοκεῖ πανταχοῦ τε εἶναι τοῦτο καὶ αὖ εἶναι οὐδαμοῦ, τοῦτό τοι χρὴ ἐνθυμηθῆναι καὶ νοῆσαι, οἷον δεῖ καὶ ἐντεῦθεν σκοπουμένοις θέσθαι περὶ ὧν ζητοῦμεν. Εἰ γὰρ μηδαμοῦ, οὐδαμοῦ συμβέβηκε, καὶ εἰ πανταχοῦ, ὅσος ἐστὶν αὐτός, τοσοῦτος πανταχοῦ· ὥστε τὸ πανταχοῦ καὶ τὸ πάντη αὐτός, οὐκ ἐν ἐκείνῳ ὢν τῷ πανταχοῦ, ἀλλ' αὐτὸς ὢν τοῦτο καὶ δοὺς εἶναι τοῖς ἄλλοις ἐν τῷ πανταχοῦ παρακεῖσθαι. Ὁ δ' ὑπερτάτην ἔχων τάξιν, μᾶλλον δὲ οὐκ ἔχων, ἀλλ' ὢν ὑπέρτατος αὐτός, δοῦλα πάντα ἔχει, οὐ συμβὰς αὐτοῖς, αὐτῷ δὲ τῶν ἄλλων, μᾶλλον δὲ περὶ αὐτὸν τῶν ἄλλων, οὐ πρὸς αὐτὰ βλέποντος αὐτοῦ, ἀλλ' ἐκείνων πρὸς αὐτόν· ὁ δ' εἰς τὸ εἴσω οἷον φέρεται αὐτοῦ οἷον ἑαυτὸν ἀγαπήσας, αὐγὴν καθαράν, αὐτὸς ὢν τοῦτο, ὅπερ ἠγάπησε· τοῦτο δ' ἐστὶν ὑποστήσας αὐτόν, εἴπερ ἐνέργεια· μένουσα καὶ τὸ ἀγαπητότατον οἷον νοῦς. Νοῦς δὲ ἐνέργημα· ὥστε ἐνέργημα αὐτός. Ἀλλὰ ἄλλου μὲν οὐδενός· ἑαυτοῦ ἄρα ἐνέργημα αὐτός. Οὐκ ἄρα ὡς συμβέβηκέν ἐστιν, ἀλλ' ὡς ἐνεργεῖ αὐτός. Ἔτι τοίνυν, εἰ ἔστι μάλιστα, ὅτι πρὸς αὐτὸν οἷον στηρίζει καὶ οἷον πρὸς αὐτὸν βλέπει καὶ τὸ οἷον εἶναι τοῦτο αὐτῷ τὸ πρὸς αὐτὸν βλέπειν, οἷον ποιοῖ ἂν αὐτόν, οὐχ ὡς ἔτυχεν ἄρα ἐστίν, ἀλλ' ὡς αὐτὸς θέλει, καὶ οὐδ' ἡ θέλησις εἰκῇ οὐδ' οὕτω συνέβη· τοῦ γὰρ ἀρίστου ἡ θέλησις οὖσα οὐκ ἔστιν εἰκῇ. Ὅτι δ' ἡ τοιαύτη νεῦσις αὐτοῦ πρὸς αὐτὸν οἷον ἐνέργεια οὖσα αὐτοῦ καὶ μονὴ ἐν αὐτῷ τὸ εἶναι ὅ ἐστι ποιεῖ, μαρτυρεῖ ὑποτεθὲν τοὐναντίον· ὅτι, εἰ πρὸς τὸ ἔξω νεύσειεν αὐτοῦ, ἀπολεῖ τὸ εἶναι ὅπερ ἐστί· τὸ ἄρα εἶναι ὅπερ ἐστὶν ἡ ἐνέργεια ἡ πρὸς αὐτόν· τοῦτο δὲ ἓν καὶ αὐτός. Αὐτὸς ἄρα ὑπέστησεν αὐτὸν συνεξενεχθείσης τῆς ἐνεργείας

μετ' αὐτοῦ. Εἰ οὖν μὴ γέγονεν, ἀλλ' ἦν ἀεὶ ἡ ἐνέργεια αὐτοῦ καὶ οἷον ἐγρήγορσις οὐκ ἄλλου ὄντος τοῦ ἐγρηγορότος, ἐγρήγορσις καὶ ὑπερνόησις ἀεὶ οὖσα, ἔστιν οὕτως, ὡς ἐγρηγόρησεν. Ἡ δὲ ἐγρήγορσίς ἐστιν ἐπέκεινα οὐσίας καὶ νοῦ καὶ ζωῆς ἔμφρονος· ταῦτα δὲ αὐτός ἐστιν. Αὐτὸς ἄρα ἐστὶν ἐνέργεια ὑπὲρ νοῦν καὶ φρόνησιν καὶ ζωήν· ἐξ αὐτοῦ δὲ ταῦτα καὶ οὐ παρ' ἄλλου. Παρ' αὐτοῦ ἄρα αὐτῷ καὶ ἐξ αὐτοῦ τὸ εἶναι. Οὐκ ἄρα, ὡς συνέβη, οὕτως ἐστίν, ἀλλ' ὡς ἠθέλησεν αὐτός ἐστιν.

24. Enneads 6.8.20.1–6: Τί οὖν; Οὐ συμβαίνει, εἴποι τις ἄν, πρὶν ἢ γενέσθαι γεγονέναι; Εἰ γὰρ ποιεῖ ἑαυτόν, τῷ μὲν ἑαυτὸν οὔπω ἐστί, τῷ δ' αὖ ποιεῖν ἔστιν ἤδη πρὸ ἑαυτοῦ τοῦ ποιουμένου ὄντος αὐτοῦ. Πρὸς ὅ δὴ λεκτέον, ὡς ὅλως οὐ τακτέον κατὰ τὸν ποιούμενον, ἀλλὰ κατὰ τὸν ποιοῦντα, ἀπόλυτον τὴν ποίησιν αὐτοῦ τιθεμένοις.

25. See Henry and Schwyzer's apparatus for 6.7.16.15–16, 6.7.8.16.37, 6.8.13.54–55, 5.2.1.12–15, 5.1.7.10 for a few examples of the controversy over whether the reflexive or nonreflexive is meant. For a more extended view of the controversy in a particular instance, see V. Cilento, *Enneadi*, vol. 3, part 2, p. 32. A close reading of these passages is beyond the scope of this volume and will entail a study of its own.

26. For similar shifts in Ibn ʿArabi, see chaps. 3 and 4, below. Ibn ʿArabi refers to the *fanā'*, the passing away of the ego-self in the contemplation of the divine beloved, through the image of the polished mirror. When the Sufi passes away, his heart becomes a polished mirror. The mirror is no longer "seen"; only the divine image reflected in the mirror is seen. The question "Who sees whom in whom?" then involves an infinite regress of shifting referents, which I attempt to translate as "It (divine subject, human subject) sees it(self) through it(self) in it(self)". Again, normal linguistic distinctions between reflexive and nonreflexive, between self and other, are split or fused.

27. Enneads 6.8.19.12–20: Χρὴ δὲ ἴσως καὶ τὸ ἐπέκεινα οὐσίας καὶ ταύτῃ νοεῖσθαι τοῖς παλαιοῖς λεγόμενον δι' αἰνίξεως, οὐ μόνον ὅτι γεννᾷ οὐσίαν, ἀλλ' ὅτι οὐ δουλεύει οὐδὲ οὐσίᾳ οὐδὲ ἑαυτῷ, οὐδέ ἐστιν αὐτῷ ἀρχὴ ἡ οὐσία αὐτοῦ, ἀλλ' αὐτὸς ἀρχὴ τῆς οὐσίας ὢν οὐχ αὑτῷ ἐποίησε τὴν οὐσίαν, ἀλλὰ ποιήσας ταύτην ἔξω εἴασεν ἑαυτοῦ, ἅτε οὐδὲν τοῦ εἶναι δεόμενος, ὃς ἐποίησεν αὐτό. Οὐ τοίνυν οὐδὲ καθό ἐστι ποιεῖ τὸ ἔστι.

28. Enneads 5.2.1.1–16: Τὸ ἓν πάντα καὶ οὐδὲ ἕν· ἀρχὴ γὰρ πάντων οὐ πάντα, ἀλλ' ἐκείνως πάντα· ἐκεῖ γὰρ οἷον ἐνέδραμε· μᾶλλον δὲ οὔπω ἐστίν, ἀλλ' ἔσται. Πῶς οὖν ἐξ ἁπλοῦ ἑνὸς οὐδεμιᾶς ἐν ταὐτῷ φαινομένης ποικιλίας, οὐ διπλόης οὑτινος ὁτουοῦν; Ἢ ὅτι οὐδὲν ἦν ἐν αὐτῷ, διὰ τοῦτο ἐξ αὐτοῦ πάντα, καὶ ἵνα τὸ ὂν ᾖ, διὰ τοῦτο αὐτὸς οὐκ ὤν, γεννητὴς δὲ αὐτοῦ· καὶ πρώτη οἷον γέννησις αὕτη· ὂν γὰρ τέλειον τῷ μηδὲν ζητεῖν μηδὲ ἔχειν μηδὲ δεῖσθαι οἷον ὑπερερρύη καὶ τὸ ὑπερπλῆρες αὐτοῦ πεποίηκεν ἄλλο· τὸ δὲ γενόμενον εἰς αὐτὸ ἐπεστράφη καὶ ἐπληρώθη καὶ ἐγένετο πρὸς αὐτὸ βλέπον καὶ νοῦς οὗτος. Καὶ ἡ μὲν πρὸς ἐκεῖνο στάσις αὐτοῦ τὸ ὂν ἐποίησεν, ἡ δὲ πρὸς αὐτὸ θέα τὸν νοῦν. Ἐπεὶ οὖν ἔστη πρὸς αὐτό, ἵνα ἴδῃ, ὁμοῦ νοῦς γίγνεται καὶ ὄν. Οὗτος οὖν ὢν οἷον ἐκεῖνος τὰ ὅμοια ποιεῖ δύναμιν προχέας πολλήν — εἶδος δὲ καὶ τοῦτο αὐτοῦ — ὥσπερ αὖ τὸ αὐτοῦ πρότερον προέχεε.

29. John Kenney has shown how the Plotinian position on the correlativity

of being and nous grows out of Plotinus's grappling with the earlier nous theology of Middle Platonism. Cf. Kenney, *Mystical Monotheism*, pp. 112-28.

30. Plotinian discourse is filled with correlative dyads (beauty-life, unity-multiplicty, rest-motion), which, again, become the locus of an apophatic play on reciprocal causality. A particularly striking example occurs in *Ennead* 6.7.17.13-16. In that passage, life, multiplicity, and determination are generated through the *epistrophē*, with the kind of double paradigms and aporias of self-causality mentioned here in connection with nous and being in 5.2.

31. *Enneads* 6.7.41.8-17, 6.7.40.22-30. Plotinus considered himself a disciple of Plato and a critic of Aristotle. Yet it may have been in part through Plotinus's unraveling the hidden dynamic within Aristotelian formulations of nous that the infinitely receding referent evolved. See Aristotle, *Metaphysics* 1074b 33-1075a, *De Anima* 3.4.429b-430a. The term "Neoplatonism" may grant too much to Plotinus's rhetorical self-positioning, and may neglect the profound impact upon him of certain Aristotelian texts. The more general problem with terms like Neoplatonism, in connection with apophasis, is the implication that what defines a text is its metaphysical doctrine alone, without reference to its mode of discourse.

32. See Stephen Gersh, *Kinesis Akinetos: A study of Spiritual Motion in the Philosophy of Proclus* (Leiden: Brill, 1973); and idem, *From Iamblichus to Eriugena: An Investigation of the Prehistory and Evolution of the Pseudo-Dionysian Tradition* (Leiden: Brill, 1978); and P. Hadot, *Porphyre et Victorinus*, 2 vols. (Paris: Etudes Augustiniennes, 1968).

33. To treat emanation as an explanatory concept is to risk losing its coherence and integrity. For example, as in this early judgment by A. H. Armstrong, one of Plotinus's foremost modern readers: "The difficulty is to see what the precise philosophical meaning of this conception [emanation] is, or rather, as it is fairly clear that it has not got any precise philosophical meaning, to explain how a great and subtle thinker like Plotinus came, at a most critical point in his system, to conceal a confusion of thought under a cloud of metaphor. " Another reader treats the *Enneads* as an attempt at philosophical explanation that failed because Plotinus did not have available to him or could not discover, on his own, the notion of *creatio ex nihilo*, as it was formulated in the nonapophatic theology of the Abrahamic traditions. See J. M. Rist, "The Problem of 'Otherness' in the *Enneads*," in *Le Néoplatonisme*, ed. P. Schul and P. Hadot (Paris, 1971): 77-87, and idem, *Plotinus: The Road to Reality* (Cambridge, 1967).

34. *Enneads* 3.8.10.26-32: εἰ δὲ τὸ τῶν κατ' ἀλήθειαν ὄντων ἕν, τὴν ἀρχὴν καὶ πηγὴν καὶ δύναμιν, λαμβάνοι, ἀπιστήσομεν καὶ τὸ μηδὲν ὑπονοήσομεν; ἢ ἔστι μὲν τὸ μηδὲν τούτων ὧν ἐστιν ἀρχή, τοιοῦτο μέντοι, οἷον, μηδενὸς αὐτοῦ κατηγορεῖσθαι δυναμένου, μὴ ὄντος, μὴ οὐσίας, μὴ ζωῆς, τὸ ὑπὲρ πάντα αὐτῶν εἶναι. Εἰ δὲ ἀφελὼν τὸ εἶναι λαμβάνοις, θαῦμα ἕξεις.

35. *Webster's Ninth New Collegiate Dictionary* (Springfield, Mass., 1991), p. 736, "meaning"; definitions 1a and 1b. Meaning in these two formulations is depicted as purport and import respectively.

36. For an excellent account of Porphyry and the issue of the intellect with-

out object, see Hadot, *Porphyre et Victorinus*. Hadot (1:96) gives a quotation from the late Neoplatonist Damascius that effectively summarizes the issue: "Are there, before the first intelligible, two first principles: the absolutely ineffable principle and the principle uncoordinate with the triad? This is the opinion of the great Jamblichus, in the 28th book of his *Very Perfect Chaldean Theology*. Or, as most of those who came after him thought, does the first triad of intelligibles come directly after the intelligible cause? Or again, must we turn from this hypothesis and say with Porphyry that the father of the intelligible triad is the unique principle of all things?"

37. Gershom Scholem, "Emanation," in his short encyclopedia of Jewish mysticism, *Kabbalah* (Jerusalem: Quadrangle, 1974).

Chapter Two

1. See Acts 17: 22–32. The Acts passage depicts Paul's conversion of Dionysius and a few others at the court of the Areopagas. Standing before their altar "to an unknown God," Paul declares to the Athenians, "What you worship but do not know—this I now proclaim." As we will see later in this chapter, the status of God's unknowability becomes an ironically crucial issue in the writings attributed to and influenced by "Dionysius the Areopagite."

2. In 536 the writings were translated into Syriac by Sergius of Reshaina. (The Syriac translations raise the question of whether the Dionysian writings were ever translated into Arabic, especially given the role of Syriac translations as an intermediary between Greek and Arabic philosophy and the central place of the issue of divine names in Islamic theology.) In the early sixth century, John of Scythopolis, a Byzantine priest and opponent of Monophysitism, wrote a commentary upon them. See D. Knowles, "The Influence of Pseudo Dionysius on Western Mysticism," in *Christian Spirituality: Essays in Honour of Gordon Rupp*, ed. P. Brooks (London: SCM Press, 1975), pp. 79–84; J. Pelikan, "The Odyssey of Dionysian Spirituality," and K. Froehlich, "Pseudo-Dionysius and the Reformation of the Sixteenth Century," both in *Pseudo-Dionysius: The Complete Works* (New York, Paulist Press, 1987), pp. 11–24 and 33–46.

The history of suspicion of the authenticity of Dionysian authorship is an intriguing story. As early as 532, Hypatius of Ephesus had challenged the authenticity of the Dionysian corpus on the grounds that it was not known to or cited by earlier Church fathers. In 1457, Lorenzo Valla's challenge to the early dating of the corpus was published by Erasmus (Paris, 1505). In 1895 independent studies by H. Koch and J. Stiglmayr established that the writings were post–fifth century. See the *Dictionnaire de Spiritualité*, pp. 244–57, and *The New Catholic Encyclopedia*, 11: 943; J. Stiglmayr, "Der Neuplatoniker Proclus als Vorlage des sogen. Dionysius Areopagita in der Lehre vom Übel," *Historisches Jahrbuch* 16 (1895): 253–73, 721–48; H. Koch, *Pseudo-Dionysius Areopagita in seinen Beziehungen zum Neuplatonismus und Mysterienwesen* (Mainz: Franz Kirchheim, 1900). For the claim that the works were composed by the Monophysite patriarch of Antioch, Severus (ca. 465–538), see J. Stiglmayr, "Der sogenannte Dionysius Areopagita und Severus von

Antiochien," *Scholastik* 3 (1928): 1–27, 161–89. Another candidate for authorship is Stephen Bar-Sudhaile (d. ca. 550), the Syrian mystic, theologian, and author of *The Book of Hierotheus* later attributed to the Hierotheus mentioned by Pseudo-Dionysius as his teacher. See Stephen Bar-Sudhaile, *Works*, ed. and trans. F. S. Marsh (London, 1927); H.D. Saffrey, "Nouveaux liens objectifs entre le Pseudo-Denys et Proclus," *Revues scientifiques philosophiques et théologiques* 63 (1979): 3–16, translated as "New Objective Links between the Pseudo-Dionysius and Proclus," *Neoplatonism and Christian Thought*, ed. Dominic O'Meara (Albany: SUNY Press, 1982), pp. 64–74.

3. The earlier conflation of the Areopagite with Dionysius the first bishop of Athens was made by Eusebius.

4. There is some confusion about the name. He is commonly called Joannes (Johannes) Scottus but I prefer the English "John the Scot" to avoid the common confusion with John Duns Scottus (d. 1308). The name Eriugena also occurs under the forms Erigena and Scottigena. The word "Scottus" or "Scotus" designated at the time of Eriugena an Irishman, which is also what the term Eriugena (or Erigena) means: of Erin, Eire.

5. An earlier example of Christian Neoplatonic writing in Latin is the work of the fifth-century theologian Marius Victorinus. For studies on Victorinus, see P. Hadot, *Porphyre et Victorinus* (Paris: Etudes Augustiniennes, 1968). For the Neoplatonic textual tradition, see S. Gersh, *From Iamblichus to Eriugena: An Investigation of the Prehistory and Evolution of the Pseudo-Dionysian Tradition* (Leiden: Brill, 1978), and *Middle Platonism and Neoplatonism: The Latin Tradition*, 2 vols. (Notre Dame: University of Notre Dame Press, 1986). For Eriugena's doctrine of the nothingness of God, see D. Duclow, "Divine Nothingness and Self-Creation in John Scottus Eriugena," *Journal of Religion* 57 (1977): 109–23.

6. The other two main treatises, *The Ecclesiastical Hierarchy* and *The Celestial Hierarchy*, were to exercise a major influence on Latin Christianity. Pseudo-Dionysius also refers to a treatise of his called the *Symbolic Theology*, but no such work survives.

7. This brief summary can cover only those points directly related to the question of apophatic language in Eriugena, and cannot possibly do justice to the richness of Dionysian thought. For a lucid introduction to Dionysius, see B. McGinn, *The Foundations of Mysticism*, vol. 1 of *The Presence of God: A History of Western Christian Mysticism* (New York: Crossroad, 1991), pp. 157–82. For detailed studies, see René Roques, *L'Univers dionysien, structure hiérarchique du monde selon le Pseudo-Denys* (Paris: Aubier, 1954); Paul Rorem, *Biblical and Liturgical Symbols within the Pseudo-Dionysian Synthesis* (Toronto: Pontifical Institute of Mediaeval Studies, 1984); Jan Vanneste, *Le Mystère de Dieu* (Brussels: Desclée de Brouwer, 1959). All texts cited from Dionysius are taken from the new edition, *Corpus Dionysiacum*, I and II, ed. Beate R. Suchla, G. Heil, and A.M. Ritter, Patristische Texte und Studien, 33 and 36 (Berlin: de Gruyter, 1990 and 1991). An invaluable resource is the collection of texts published as *Dionysiaca*, ed. Ph. Chevallier, 2 vols. (Paris: Desclée de Brouwer, 1937–49).

8. "[T]he holiest and highest of the things perceived with the eye of the body or the mind are but the rationale which presupposes all that lies below the transcendent one. Through them, however, his unimaginable presence is shown, walking the heights of those holy places to which the mind at least can rise. But then he [Moses] breaks free of them, away from what sees and is seen, and he plunges into the truly mysterious darkness of knowing. Here, renouncing all that the mind may conceive, wrapped entirely in the intangible and the invisible, he belongs completely to him who is beyond everything. Here, being neither oneself nor someone else, one is supremely united by a completely unknowing inactivity of all knowledge, and knows beyond the mind by knowing nothing." Dionysius, *The Mystical Theology*, trans. Colm Luibheid in collaboration with Paul Rorem, in *Pseudo-Dionysius: The Complete Works*, p. 137. *Corpus Dionysiacum*, 2:144 , De Mystica Theologia 1 (1000D–1001A): Καὶ τότε καὶ αὐτῶν ἀπολύεται τῶν ὁρωμένων καὶ τῶν ὁρώντων καὶ εἰς τὸν γνόφον τῆς ἀγνωσίας εἰσδύνει τὸν ὄντως μυστικόν, καθ' ὃν ἀπομύει πάσας τὰς γνωστικὰς ἀντιλήψεις, καὶ ἐν τῷ πάμπαν ἀναφεῖ καὶ ἀοράτῳ γίγνεται, πᾶς ὢν τοῦ πάντων ἐπέκεινα καὶ οὐδενός, οὔτε ἑαυτοῦ οὔτε ἑτέρου, τῷ παντελῶς δὲ ἀγνώστῳ τῇ πάσης γνώσεως ἀνενεργησίᾳ κατὰ τὸ κρεῖττον ἑνούμενος καὶ τῷ μηδὲν γινώσκειν ὑπὲρ νοῦν γινώσκων. Dionysius's technical language parallels the Plotinian play upon *theôria* and various terms for vision and its notion of how the contemplator is freed (*apoluetai*) of all objects.

9. See J. Pelikan, *The Christian Tradition* (Chicago: University of Chicago Press, 1971), vol. 1, pp. 201–67, for trinitarian and christological dogma and the issue of *ousia*. *Ousia* was translated into Latin as either *substantia* (substance) or as *natura*. Cf. R. Jenson, *The Triune Identity* (Philadelphia: Fortress Press, 1982); C. Stead, *Divine Substance* (Oxford: Clarendon Press, 1977); and John Marenbon, *From the Circle of Alcuin to the School of Auxerre* (Cambridge University Press, 1981).

10. See H. A. Wolfson, "The Identification of *ex nihilo* with Emanation in Gregory of Nyssa," in *Studies in the History of Philosophy and Religions* (Cambridge: Harvard University Press, 1973), pp. 199–221. Dermot Moran points out, that within Carolingian circles, Fredegisus's *Epistola de nihilo et tenebris* (treatise on nothingness and darkness) comes close to identifying the *nihil* of *creatio ex nihilo* with the deity itself. See Moran, *The Philosophy of John Scottus Eriugena*, p. 215. For an introduction to this superessential nothingness in Kabbalah, see Gershom Scholem, *Major Trends in Jewish Mysticism* (New York: Schocken, 1941, 1961), p. 25 and n. 24 (in which he refers to Dionysius and Eriugena).

11. See Book 1: 441A—442B; SW 1: 37–38. All citations are from the recent edition of Books 1–3 by I. P. Sheldon-Williams, *Iohannis Scotti Eriugenae, Periphyseon, De Divisione Naturae* (Dublin: Dublin Institute for Advanced Studies, 1968, 1972, 1981), hereafter, SW. The SW edition also lists the column numeration from the older Floss edition: Joannis Scoti, *Opera Quae Supersunt Omnia*, ed. H. Floss (Paris: Patrologiae, 1865). The *Periphyseon* takes up columns 441A–1022D in the Floss edition of the complete works. All citations

from SW will be followed by the Floss column notation and the SW pagination. For a good abridged translation, see John the Scot, *Periphyseon: On the Division of Nature*, trans. Myra Uhlfelder (Indianapolis: Bobbs-Merrill, 1976). See also *Periphyseon: The Division of Nature*, trans. I. P. Sheldon-Williams and John O'Meara (Montréal/Paris: Bellarmin-Vrin, 1987).

12. De Praed. 1.1, trans. Willemien Otten in *The Anthropology of Johannes Scottus Eriugena* (Leiden, Brill, 1991), p. 22. For an excellent discussion of the relationship of nature to reason, see pp. 7–39 of Otten. I have chosen the latinate "resolution" rather than "analysis" here because of the tendency in other contexts to use analysis in the sense of division and to oppose it to synthesis.

13. Ibid., p. 39.

14. For this tension in Dionysius and its relation to the Dionysian concept of *eros*, see McGinn, *Foundations*, pp. 164ff. Like "mystical theology," the word "hierarchy" was coined by the pseudo-Areopagite, one of the more successful neologisms in Western thought. Dionysius, seeker of the beyond-the-name, certainly had a way with names.

15. One cannot help but wonder if the relation between the alumnus and the nutritor may perhaps mirror that between Eriugena and Dionysius.

16. Et notandum quod participatio significantius expressiusque et ad intelligendum facilius a Graecis dicatur, in quorum lingua METOXH vel MEΘOYCIA participationem significat, METOXH autem quasi METAEX-OYCA, hoc est post-habens vel secundo-habens, METOYCIA quoque quasi METAOYCIA, hoc est post-essentia vel secunda essentia. Hinc facillime datur intelligi nihil aliud esse participationem nisi ex superiori essentia secundae (post eam) essentiae derivationem et ab ea quae primum habet esse secundae ut sit distributio, et hoc exemplis naturae possumus argumentari (632b; SW 3:56).

17. Siquidem ex fonte totum flumen principaliter manat et per eius alveum aqua quae primo surgit in fonte in quantamcunque longitudinem protendatur semper ac sine ulla intermissione deffunditur. Sic divina bonitas et essentia et vita et sapientia et omnia quae in fonte omnium sunt primo in primordiales causas defluunt et eas esse faciunt, deinde per primordiales causas in earum effectus ineffabili modo per convenientes sibi universitatis ordines decurrunt, per superiora semper ad inferiora profluentia, iterumque per secretissimos naturae poros occultissimo meatu ad fontem suum redeunt (632b-c; SW 3:56–57).

18. *Bonitas* is clearly related to the Plotinian *to agathon* and will be echoed later in Porete by *bonté*. In each of these cases, what is referred to is the Platonic notion that the good inherently overflows and gives itself.

19. I translate *omnia* as "all" rather than the common "all things" in order to avoid the sense of reality as a sum of items that can be implied by the term "things." At times, however, the context seems to make "all" ambiguous and I use the expression "all things."

20. The SW translation of this phrase seems to lose the point by negating the force of the double negative with a "but what": "For It encircles all things

and there is nothing within It but what, insofar as it is, is not Itself, for It alone truly is." The issue is important since it concerns a crucial statement of the Eriugenan principle that whatever truly is, is the cause *in which* it exists. Insofar as it is, it is its cause.

21. Summae siquidem ac trinae soliusque verae bonitatis in se ipsa immutabilis motus et simplex multiplicatio et inexhausta a se ipsa in se ipsa ad se ipsam diffusio causa omnium, immo omnia est. Si enim intellectus omnium est omnia et ipsa sola intelligit omnia, ipsa igitur sola est omnia quoniam sola gnostica virtus est ipsa quae priusquam essent omnia cognovit omnia et extra se non cognovit omnia quia extra eam nihil est sed intra se habet omnia. Ambit enim omnia et nihil intra se est in quantum vere est nisi ipsa quia sola vere est. Caetera enim quae dicuntur esse ipsius theophaniae sunt quae etiam in ipsa vere subsistunt. Deus itaque est omne quod vere est quoniam ipse facit omnia et fit in omnibus, ut ait sanctus Dionysius Ariopagita (633a; SW 3:58). Cf. *Corpus Dionysiacum*, 2: 202–3, *Epistula* 9:3 (1109C). The Greek text is given below, n. 38.

22. For a useful definition of syntagm, see Philip Pettit, *The Concept of Structuralism: A Critical Analysis* (Berkeley: University of California Press, 1975), p. 8:

> The syntagmatic relationships of a word are those it has with words which can occur in its neighborhood in a sentence. There is a syntagmatic relationship between 'John' and "dances' which allows the words to appear in the sentence 'John dances . . .' The relationship in question is like that between any two words, the first of which can appear as subject to the second: for example, between 'he' and 'plays', 'river' and flows', 'dog' and bites'. Such a relationship does not exist between two nouns or two verbs since we do not get 'Dog river . .' or 'Plays flows . . .'. Also it does not exist between every noun (or pronoun) and every verb: we do not normally find '(The) river bites . . .' or '(The) dog flows . . .'.'

While the words "dog barks" and "river flows" are syntagmatically compatible, the expression "dog flows" harnesses two syntagmatically incompatible words together. If it has meaning, it has meaning as a metaphor, as an explicit alteration of a syntagmatic pattern. In Eriugena the syntagmic alteration is implicit. The normal understanding of "encircles" and "all things" presupposes the act of going around a preexistent object. But the context has established that this "going around" creates the things it goes around. There is no longer a relation of motion or space between verb and already existing object; the relationship is causal. The sentence "it encircles all things" uses categories of space and motion inherent in the verb's implication of relation to a preexisting object but transforms those categories through the apophatic collapsing of the levels of being in upon one another. The result is a contexted metaphor and a paradox. The metaphor is contexted because the transformations of normal sense are glimpsed only from the context. Unlike the expression 'the dog flows," the expression "encircles all things" is on the surface unexceptional. The bending of normal syntagmatic possibilities is only glimpsed from the apophatic context.

The expression "it knows all things before they are" is a latent contexted metaphor. It is only later in the treatise that the nutritor states that there can be no temporal priority and that the divine maker makes by knowing. Though the reader can infer such a principle from the context, the explicit clue is not given until later. For another discussion of metaphor and mystical language, see T. M. Tomasic, "Neoplatonism and the Mysticism of William of St. Thierry," in P. Szarmach, *An Introduction to the Mystics of Medieval Europe* (Albany: SUNY Press, 1984), pp. 53–76.

23. Omne enim quod intelligitur et sentitur nihil aliud est nisi non apparentis apparitio, occulti manifestatio, negati affirmatio, incomprehensibilis comprehensio, ineffabilis fatus, inaccessibilis accessus, inintelligibilis intellectus, incorporalis corpus, superessentialis essentia, informis forma, immensurabilis mensura, innumerabilis numerus, carentis pondere pondus, spiritualis incrassatio, invisibilis visibilitas, illocalis localitas, carentis tempore temporalitas, infiniti diffinitio incircunscripti circunscriptio et caetera quae puro intellectu et cogitantur et perspiciuntur et que memoriae sinibus capi nesciunt et mentis aciem fugiunt (633b; SW 3:58).

24. My characterization of apophatic "dialectic" here is in keeping with the use of the term throughout this study. It does not correspond to the understanding of the term among many Carolingian writers, Alcuin, for example. Cf. Moran, *The Philosophy of John Scottus Eriugena*, pp. 123–54, who argues (p. 125) that Eriugena went well beyond Alcuin's more restricted view of dialectic. For Alcuin, dialectic was "an amalgam of logical interests, which includes *divisio*, division into genera, species, and individuals; *partitio*, partition into whole and parts; *diffinitio*, the nature of definition; substance and the categories; the relation between what is found in a subject and what is said of a subject (*in subiecto et de subiecto*), as well as the nature of the syllogism and the square of opposition; and also logical argument and the fallacies."

25. Quae ineffabilis diffusio et facit omnia et fit in omnibus et omnina est (6334a; SW 3:61).

26. Intellectus ut dicis vehicula illa in quibus ad aliorum sensus invehitur de materia extra se creata et facit et suscipit. Divina vero bonitas extra quam nihil est non de aliquo apparitionis suae materiam sumpsit sed de nihilo. Sed cum audio vel dico divinam bonitatem omnia de nihilo creasse non intelligo quid eo nomine quod est nihil significatur: utrum privatio totius essentiae vel substantiae vel accidentis an divinae superessentialitatis excellentia (634a–b; SW 3:60). Here and elsewhere I translate the Latin compounds of *super* with hyphenated terms built upon "beyond." The term "super" has become debased in modern English, and both "hyper" and "super" in contemporary English can imply an intensification of a particular category rather than the movement to a new category.

27. The nutritor states that matter (ʿ*ule*) is another one of the "all" that are eternally made in the wisdom of the father (636d–638a; SW 3:66–71). Since matter is likewise eternal in the wisdom of the father, it cannot be the solution

to the problem—we cannot say that the temporal meaning of "from nothing" refers to a temporal creation of matter.

28. Qua ratione et omnia in sapientia dei aeterna sunt et de nihilo facta, hoc est priusquam fierent non erant (636b; SW 3:66–67).

29. "But since he [*deus*] is prior to the universe which he created solely for the reason that he is the cause, it follows that the creation of the universe is not accidental to God but is in accordance with a certain mysterious reason on account of which caused things subsist always in their cause."

Quoniam vero ea sola ratione qua causa est universitatem ab eo conditam praecidit sequitur universitatis conditionem non esse deo secundum accidens sed secundum quandam ineffabilem rationem qua causativa in causa sua semper subsistunt (639b; SW 3:72–73).

SW translates *deo secundum accidens* as "not in God as an accident," a translation that confuses the important Eriugenean play upon spatial and temporal meanings of "in." It might be argued that change from noncreative to creative deity occurs through divine will, not through accident, but then the question would be asked in turn, is not a deity that does not will to create and then does will to create subject to change and accident?

30. Totius ergo creaturae universitatem aeternam esse in verbo dei manifestum est (639c–d; SW 3:72). "It is therefore clear that the entire universe of created beings is eternal in the word of God." The nutritor here presents God-as-cause under the rubric of the divine word.

31. Nihil enim aliud nos sumus in quantum sumus nisi ipsae rationes nostrae aeternaliter in deo substitutae (640a–b; SW 3:74).

32. 640c–41a; SW 3:74–76. One representative sample: "If we take account of these and similar examples and testimonies, we are given to understand most clearly that all are not only eternal in the word of God, but also are the word itself."

His atque huius modi exemplis ac testimoniis in unum collectis apertissime datur intelligi omnia in verbo dei non solum aeterna verum etiam ipsum verbum esse (641a; SW 3:76).

33. "[The word is] simple, because the universe of all things is in it an indivisible and inseparable one, or rather the indivisibile and inseparable unity of all things is the word of God since it is all; and it is understood not incorrectly to be multiple because it is diffused through all things to infinity, *and that diffusion is the subsistence of all things* [emphasis mine]."

Simplex quidem quia rerum omnium universitas in ipso unum individuum et inseparabile est vel certe individua et inseparabilis unitas omnium dei verbum est quoniam ipsum omnia est, multiplex vero non immerito intelligitur esse quoniam per omnia in infinitum defunditur et ipsa diffusio subsistentia omnia est (642c–d; SW 3:80).

34. [I]ndiminutum ut omnia in se ipso superans et supermanans secundum unam et incessabilem per se superplenam et non minoratam largitatem (643a; SW 3:80).

See *Corpus Dionysiacum*, 1: 227, *De Divinis Nominibus* XIII:1 (977B–C): ὡς πάντα ἐν ἑαυτῷ προέχον καὶ ὑπερβλύζον κατὰ μίαν τὴν ἄπαυστον καὶ ταύτην καὶ ὑπερπλήρη καὶ ἀνελάττωτον χορηγίαν.

35. 643a–b; SW 3:80–83. The metaphor of running was first introduced in book 1 through a pun on the Greek *theos* (God) and *theomai* (to run): SW 1:60.

36. [F]usio sapientiae vel extensio vel cursus vel quoquo alio modo infinita verbi multiplicatio dicatur non quasi in ea quae prius erant quam funderetur vel extenderetur vel curreret verbum patris et sapientia sed ipsius fusio vel extensio vel cursus praecedit omnia at causa existentiae omnium est et omnia. Quis enim veritatem consulens crediderit vel cogitaverit deum praeparasse sibi locos per quos sese diffunderet qui nullo loco continetur dum locus omnium communis sit ac per hoc locus locorum ullo loco capitur? Aut sibi praeparasse spatia localia seu temporalia per quae sese extenderet cursuue suo curreret qui omni spatio caret et omnia tempora sua aeternitate superat? At quis dixerit quod incredibilius est, ipsi deo dico ab alio veluti principio praeparata fuisse locorum temporumque spatia seu qualiumcunque quantitatum intervalla quae sua diffusione impleret vel suo cursu perageret vel sua extensione solidaret? Haec enim de natura ineffabili et superessentiali non solum dicere verum etiam cogitare falsisque imaginationibus fingere et ridiculossissimum est et perniciosissimum. Non enim alia mors rationalis animae turpior peiorque est quam talia monstra abhominandaque idola de creatore omnium cogitare (643b–d; SW 3:82).

37. This understanding of reason is reminiscent of Gregory of Nyssa's concept of *epektasis*, the soul's infinitely deepening and never-ending pursuit of the divine. See McGinn, *Foundations*, pp. 139–42. The nutritor's stretching of reason beyond linear logic and argumentation parallels his expansion of "dialectic" beyond its Carolingian sense, again in a manner consonant with the Greek tradition of Gregory of Nyssa, Origen, and Pseudo-Dionysius. See Moran, *The Philosophy of John Scottus Eriugena*, pp. 123–53. Cf. Otten, *The Anthropology of Johannes Scottus Eriugena*, 40–47.

38. Primum, inquit, omnium illud dicere verum est ut bonitate universali superessentialis divinitas eorum quae sunt essentias substituens ad esse adduxit. Est enim hoc omnium causae et super omnia bonitatis proprium ad communionem suam ea quae sunt vocare ut unicuique eorum quae sunt ex propria diffinitur analogia. Omnia igitur participant providentiam ex superessentiali et causalissima divinitate manantem. Non enim fortasis essent nisi eorum quae sunt essentiae et principii assumptione. Existentia igitur omnia esse eius participant—esse enim omnium est super esse divinitas (644a–b, SW 3:82–84). The final phrase could also of course be translated as "the divinity beyond being."

For the passage from Dionysius translated here by Eriugena, see *Corpus Dionysiacum*, 2:20, *De Coelesti Hierarchia* IV:1 (177C–D): Πρῶτον δ' ἁπάντων ἐκεῖνο εἰπεῖν ἀληθές, ὡς ἀγαθότητι πάσας ἡ ὑπερούσιος θεαρχία τὰς τῶν ὄντων οὐσίας ὑποστήσασα πρὸς τὸ εἶναι παρήγαγεν. Ἔστι γὰρ τοῦτο τῆς πάντων αἰτίας καὶ ὑπὲρ πάντα ἀγαθότητος ἴδιον τὸ πρὸς κοινωνίαν ἑαυτῆς τὰ ὄντα καλεῖν, ὡς ἑκάστῳ τῶν ὄντων ὥρισται πρὸς τῆς οἰκείας ἀναλογίας. Πάντα μὲν οὖν τὰ ὄντα μετέχει προνοίας ἐκ τῆς ὑπερουσίου καὶ παναιτίου θεότητος ἐκβλυζομένης· οὐ γὰρ ἂν ἦν, εἰ μὴ τῆς τῶν ὄντων οὐσίας καὶ ἀρχῆς μετειλήφει. Τὰ μὲν οὖν ἄζωα πάντα τῷ εἶναι αὐτῆς μετέχει (τὸ γὰρ εἶναι πάντων ἐστὶν ἡ ὑπὲρ τὸ εἶναι θεότης).

See also *Hiérachie céleste*, ed. R. Roques, G. Heil, and M. de Gandillac, SC 58 (Paris, 1958), pp. 93-94. Edouard Jeauneau gives a detailed account of Eriugena's frequent use of this Dionysian formula and the problems entailed by translating it into Latin, in *Jean Scot: Homélie sur le prologue de Jean* (Paris, 1969), appendix 2, pp. 323ff.

39. . . . et in omnia procedit et in omni fit et continet omnia et iterum ipse in sese per excellentiam nullum in nullo per nullum est sed exaltatur omnibus (645a; SW 3:86). See *Corpus Dionysiacum*, 2:202–3, *Epistula* 9:3 (1109C): καὶ ἐπὶ πάντα πρόεισι καὶ ἐν τῷ παντὶ γίγνεται καὶ περιέχει τὰ πάντα καὶ αὖθις ὁ αὐτὸς ἐν τῷ αὐτῷ καθ' ὑπεροχὴν οὐδὲν ἐν οὐδενὶ κατ' οὐδέν ἐστιν.

Luibheid and Rorem (*Pseudo-Dionysius: The Complete Works*, p. 286) translate this passage as "Thus providence occurs everywhere. It contains everything and, at the same time, it is something in something, but in a transcending way; in no way is it nothing in nothing." It is clear that Eriugena is taking the *ouden* (nothing) as depicting providence; it proceeds into all things, is made in all things, but, *per excellentiam*, it transcends all things and is, therefore, nothing (no-thing). Dionysius' passage may bear both interpretations; but it is not clear why Dionysius would feel compelled to say that "in no way is it nothing in nothing" when he had been speaking of providence as being something in something. If Eriugena is correct in his translation, Dionysius may have arrived here at an explicit concept of the nothingness of deity, beyond his usual language of the beyond-being-ness of deity.

40. Tota principia et ordines destinans et omni principio et ordini supercollocata, et mensura est eorum quae sunt et saeculorum et super saecula et ante saecula (645c; SW 3:86–87). See *Corpus Dionysiacum*, 1:134, *De Divinis Nominibus* II:10 (648C): τὰς ὅλας ἀρχὰς καὶ τάξεις ἀφορίζουσα καὶ πάσης ἀρχῆς καὶ τάξεως ὑπεριδρυμένη. Καὶ μέτρον ἐστὶ τῶν ὄντων καὶ αἰὼν καὶ ὑπὲρ αἰῶνα καὶ πρὸ αἰῶνος.

41. *Corpus Dionysiacum* 1:189, *De Divinis Nominibus* V:10 (825B–C): πέρας πάντων καὶ ἀπειρία πάσης ἀπειρίας καὶ πέρατος ὑπεροχικῶς τῶν ὡς ἀντικειμένων.

42. "If then the word of God itself both *makes all things and is made in all things*—and this can be proved from the words of the aforesaid Dionysius and others . . . [emphasis mine]" (Si ergo ipsum verbum et *omnia facit et in omnibus fit*—et hoc ex verbis praedicti patris Dionysii aliorumque potest approbari—) (646c; SW 3:88).

43. Et his omnibus incomparabiliter altius et mirabilius mihi videtur quod sancti Dionysii Ariopagitae auctoritate utens asseris, ipsum videlicet deum et omnium factorem esse et in omnibus factum—hoc enim adhuc inauditum et incognitum non solum mihi sed et multis ac paene omnibus. Nam si sic est, quis non confestim erumpat in hanc vocem et proclamet: Deus itaque omnia est et omnia deus? quod monstrosum aestimabitur etiam his qui putantur esse sapientes (650c–d; SW 3:98).

44. Just before the theophany as apparition passages, there is a long Neopythagorean discussion of the procession of numbers from the *monad* (651a–661c). See Sheldon-Williams's Introduction, pp. 5–8, and Moran, *The Philoso-*

phy of John Scottus Eriugena, pp. 218–28. The discussion repeats the basic points concerning the procession of the word into all things, the existence of all things in the word, and the fact that all things are both eternal and made.

45. "For quantities and qualities, although through themselves they are incorporeal, yet when they come together they produce formless matter, which by the addition of incorporeal shapes and colours moves into various bodies."

Quantites siquidem et qualitates dum per se sint incorporeae sunt, in unum vero coeuntes informem efficunt materiam quae adiectis formis coloribusque incorporeis in diversa corpora movetur (663a; SW 3:126).

For a more detailed treatment of this aspect of Eriugena's thought, see the outstanding essay by Jean Claude Foussard, "Apparence et apparition: la notion de *'phantasia'* chez Jean Scot," in *Jean Scot Erigène et l'histoire de la philosophie*, vol. 561 of the Colloque internationaux du centre national de la recherche scientifique (Laon, 1975, and Paris: Editions du CNRS, 1977).

46. Et semper non erant; priusqam enim per generationem in formas et species loca et tempora inque omnia accidentia quae aeternae eorum subsistentiae in verbo dei incommutabiliter substitutae accidunt profluerent, non erant in generatione (665b 8–11; SW 3:132).

47. Another way to approach the problem here would be to see how the nutritor is changing the emphasis of his definition of being from the second mode of being (according to which the affirmation of one level of being negates the next level) to the third mode of being ("being as manifestation"). See the discussion of the modes of being in *Periphyseon* 443a–446a.

48. For an account of Eriugena's complex, paradoxical, and intriguing views on the fall, see Otten, *The Anthropology of Johannes Scottus Eriugena*, pp. 118–210. In the same work, Otten also explores the tension between atemporal perspectives and sacred history. See also, W. Otten, "The Dialectic of the Return in Eriugena's *Periphyseon*, *Harvard Theological Review* 84.4 (1991): 399–321.

49. Because the condemnation of *Periphyseon* was bound up in the affair of Amalric of Bene, we do not have a clear articulation of the Church position in the case of Eriugena. However, the condemnation of Eckhart's mystical dialectic, so similar in key ways to that of Eriugena, is a vivid example of institutional articulation of the alumnus's objections (see below, chap. 6).

50. Putasne igitur me docere voluisse omnia in quantum aeterna sunt in verbo dei unigenito aeterna esse, in quantum vero facta sunt extra verbum facta esse? (666c; SW 3:134).

51. 669a–b; SW 3:140.

52. [A] Grecis ΕΠΕΚΕΙΝΑ vocatur quia omnia tempora in se creat et circunscribit dum super omnia tempora sit aeternitate sua, omnia intervalla praecedens ambiens concludens (699c; SW 3:140).

53. Again, in attempting to discuss apophatic discourse, I am repeating the basic aporia. The word "it" in the above discussion is torn between the delimited subject it can actually denote, and the unlimited subject that lies beyond its linguistic range.

54. I have passed over the discussion of the word's self-diffusion into a variety of forms as a seminal force (672b–c; SW 3:146–47). The discussion of the seminal force repeats earlier assertions that the word makes all things and makes itself into all things.

55. At si voluntas eius visio eius est et visio voluntas, omne quod vult subtracto omni intervallo fit; at si omne quod vult fieri et faciendum videt, et non extra se est quod vult et videt sed in se, nihil in ipso est quod ipse non sit, sequitur ut omne quod videt et vult coaeternum ei intelligatur si voluntas illius et visio et essentia unum est (675b; SW 3:154).

Eriugena's contemporary, al-Farabi, took the same position on the unity of attributes. See Al-Farabi, *Mabādi ʿArāʾ Ahl al-Madīnat al-Fāḍila* [On the Perfect State], Revised Text with introduction, translations, and commentary by R. Walzer (Oxford, 1985), chap. 1, 57–87. However, while al-Farabi makes the same philosophical point about the unity of attributes, he does not employ the kind of tense apophatic strategies used by Eriugena.

56. Quid autem eo nomine quod est nihilum sancta significat theologia explanari a te peto.

Ineffabilem et incomprehensibilem divinae bonitatis inaccessbilemque claritatem omnibus intellectibus sive humanis sive angelicis incognitam—superessentialis est enim et supernaturalis—eo nomine significatam crediderim, quae dum per se ipsam cogitatur neque est neque erat neque erit—in nullo enim intelligitur existentium quia superat omnina—, dum vero per condescensionem quandam ineffabilem in ea quae sunt mentis obtutibus inspicitur ipsa sola invenitur in omnibus esse et est et erat et erit. Dum ergo incomprehensibilis intelligitur per excellentiam nihilum non immerito vocitatur, at vero in suis theophaniis incipiens apparere veluti ex nihilo in aliquid dicitur procedere, et quae proprie super omnem essentiam existimatur proprie quoque in omni essentia cognoscitur ideoque omnis visibilis et invisibilis creatura theophania, id est divina apparitio, potest appellari. Omnis siquidem ordo naturarum a summo usque deorsum, hoc est ex celestibus essentiis usque ad extrema mundi huius visibilis corpora, in quantum occultius intellegitur in tantum divinae claritati appropinquare videtur. Proinde a theologia caelestium virtutum inaccessibilis claritas saepe nominatur tenebrositas (680d–681b; SW3:166–67).

57. In quantum vero longius ordo rerum deorsum descendit in tantum contemplantium obtutibus manifestius se aperit, ideoque formae ac species rerum sensibilium manifestarum theophaniarum nomen accipiunt (681b; SW3:68).

58. Neque est hoc ut ait ille hoc autem non est sed omnia est (683b; SW3:170–71). See *Corpus Dionysiacum*, 1:187, *De Divinis Nominibus* 5:8 (824A–B): Καὶ γὰρ οὐ τόδε μὲν ἔστι, τόδε δὲ οὐκ ἔστιν οὐδὲ πῇ μὲν ἔστι, πῇ δὲ οὐκ ἔστιν, ἀλλὰ πάντα ἐστὶν.

59. In thinking of this interior circular self-movement before the circle completes itself in comprehension, we are reminded of the Porphyrian "intellection without an object." In the last part of book 3 and in book 4 of the *Periphyseon*, Eriugena will integrate the emanation perspective of his *de nihilo* section with an interpretation of Christian sacred history as a process of pro-

cession from and return to the incomprehensible nothingness of the source of being.

60. These aspects of Fredegisus' work, *Epistola de nihilo et tenebris*, are pointed out by Moran, *The Philosophy of John Scottus Eriugena*, pp. 11, 215.

61. See Dom Maïeul Cappuyns, O.S.B., *Jean Scot Erigène, sa vie, son oeuvre, sa pensée* (Brussels: Culture et Civilisation, 1964), for a general account of Eriugena's influence (pp. 233–69). For Honorius's letter, see the list of sources on p. 247.

62. Totus scatens vermibus heretice pravitatis. See Cappuyns, *Jean Scot Erigène*, p. 248 n. 2. See also, Moran, *The Philosophy of John Scottus Eriugena*, p. 86; and Jean Potter, introduction to *Periphyseon: On the Division of Nature*, xxiii.

63. See, for example, Eckhart's close approximation to Eriugena in the use of the *in quantum* principle in the context of an analysis of the perfect, imperfect, and material senses of "was" in the Johannine "in the beginning was the word." See chap. 6 below.

64. Guillaume, *Epistola ad Petrum*: Ubi, post aliquot annos, a pueris quos docebat grafiis perfossus, animam exuit, tormento gravi et acerbo, ut dum iniquitas valida et manus infirma saepe frustraretur et saepe impeteret, amaram mortem obiret.

See Cappuyns, *Jean Scot Erigène*, pp. 252–53, and p. 247 n. 4. Cappuyns goes on (pp. 253–60) to give other accounts of the legend and to trace the legend's origins.

65. For a discussion of this issue, see M. Sells, "Response," in M. Idel and B. McGinn, *Mystical Union and Monotheistic Faith* (New York: Macmillan, 1989), pp. 169–73.

Chapter Three

1. Part of this chapter was originally presented at the 1983 Middle East Studies Association, Classical Islamic Literature Panel, Chicago, Illinois, and was published subsequently as "Ibn ʿArabi's Polished Mirror: Perspective Shift and Meaning Event," *Studia Islamica* 67 (1988): 121–49. Among the many who have contributed to this study I owe special thanks to Larry Berman, Bernard McGinn, Fazlur Rahman, and Jaroslav Stetkevych.

I focus on a group of performative passages selected from the massive corpus of Ibn ʿArabi. I cross-reference these passages to other key texts of Ibn ʿArabi by citing other texts in Arabic and by referring to the following major sources in Western languages: S. Hirtenstein and M. Tiernen, eds., *Muhyiddin Ibn ʿArabī: A Commemorative Volume* (Oxford: Element Books, 1993); William Chittick, *The Sufi Path of Knowledge* (Albany: SUNY Press, 1989); Michel Chodkiewicz, ed., with the collaboration of W. Chittick, Cyrille Chodkiewicz, Denis Gril, and James W. Morris, *Ibn ʿArabi, Les Illuminations de la Mecque* (Paris: Sindbad, 1988); M. Chodkiewicz, *Le Sceau des saints: Prophétie et sainteté dans la doctrine d'Ibn ʿArabi* (Paris: Gallimard, 1986); Henry Corbin, *Creative Imagination in the Sufism of Ibn ʿArabi* (Princeton: Princeton University Press, 1977); and Toshihiko Izutsu, *Sufism and Taoism* (Berkeley: University of California Press, 1984).

2. Hereafter I use the shortened form Ibn ʿArabi instead of the more formal

Ibn al-ʿArabi, with its article (al) and transliteration indication of a quantitatively long "i" (ī). Ibn ʿArabi's given name was Muḥyī d-Dīn (Reviver of the Faith).

3. In Konya, he seems to have just missed meeting the other great Sufi of the time, Jalāl ad-Dīn Rūmī, who had made a journey in the opposite direction, eastward, from Balkh (in central Asia), through the area now part of Afghanistan, through the great Sufi heartland of Khurasan in Persia, down through the thriving cities of western Persia (Isfahan, Shiraz), to Konya, where Rumi's tomb is to be found, under the care of the Mevlevi order of "Whirling Dervishes" founded by Rumi.

4. For Ibn ʿArabi's biography, see Claude Addas: *Ibn ʿArabī ou la quête du soufre rouge* (Paris: Gallimard, 1989).

5. James Morris, "Ibn ʿArabi and His Interpreters," *Journal of the American Oriental Society* 106.3 (1986): 539–52; 107.1 (1987): 101–20. For a major study of Ibn ʿArabi's view of Islamic sacred history, see M. Chodkiewicz, *Le Sceau des saints*. Ibn ʿArabi's ideas also represent a strong permanent strain within Islam and have found vibrant Islamic expression in modern times. See Martin Lings, *A Sufi Saint of the Twentieth Century: Shaikh Ahmad al-Alawī* (Berkeley: University of California Press, 1961, 1973).

For the place of Ibn ʿArabi in contemporary Islamic societies, see Th. Emil Homerin, "Ibn ʿArabi in the People's Assembly: Religion, Press, and Politics in Egypt," *Middle East Journal*, 40:3 (1986): 462–77; Alexander Knysh, "Irfan Revisited: Khomeini and the Legacy of Islamic Mystical Philosophy," *Middle East Journal* 46.4 (1992): 631–53; and idem, "Ibn ʿArabi in Contemporary Arabic Literature: The Light Reflected and Refracted," *Journal of the Muhyiddin Ibn ʿArabi Society* 12 (1992).

6. Over two hundred works are attributed to him, one of which, *Al-Futūhāt al-Makkiyya*, will include more than thirty volumes in its new edition. See ʿUthmān Yaḥya, *Histoire et classification de l'oeuvre d'Ibn ʿArabi* (Damascus: Institut Français de Damas, 1964).

7. *Al-dhāt* can also be translated as "essence" or "self." However, essence implies quiddity but the *dhāt* is beyond quiddity. To translate it as "self" would be to risk confusion with the *nafs*, the ego-self. In previous articles ("Garden among the Flames" and "Polished Mirror," I translated *dhāt* as "Self," but have eschewed such a solution here for reasons discussed in the introduction. The *dhāt* corresponds to the Plotinian One and Eckhart's Godhead (*Gottheit*), in the sense that it is beyond all dualism, all name, and all quiddity.

8. Within a short time, there were hundreds of theological positions attempting to rationalize the plurality of attributes with the necessity of affirming divine unity. The disputation was pursued down to the level of the preposition. If we say that Allah "knows through his attribute of knowledge," does not the "through" indicate an instrumental quality, implying that the deity is dependent upon his attribute for his knowledge? Such disputes were more than hair-splitting; they set the theological groundwork for a Sufi critique of the temporal, spatial, and causal reifications within language

that—as with Eriugena—was most powerful and most sustained at the microlevel of preposition and pronoun.

Because Ibn ʿArabi's treatment of these issues transposes them into an apophatic dialectic, I have given only a schematized treatment of the positions of the scholastic theologians. For general treatments of the complicated world of Islamic scholastic theology, see: A. J. Wensinck, *The Muslim Creed* (Cambridge University Press, 1932); H. A. Wolfson, *The Philosophy of the Kalam* (Cambridge: Harvard University Press, 1976); L. Gardet and M. N. Anawati, *Introduction à la théologie Musulmane* (Paris, 1949); I. Goldziher, *Introduction to Islamic Theology and Law*, translated from the German, *Vorlesungen über den Islam* (Heidelberg, 1910), by Andras and Ruth Hamori (Princeton: Princeton University Press, 1981), pp. 67–116 (still valuable despite Goldziher's dismissive tone); A. S. Tritton, *Muslim Theology* (London: Luzac, 1947); M. Watt, *The Formative Period of Islamic Thought* (Edinburgh: Edinburgh University Press, 1973). For more focused discussions, see R. M. Frank, *Beings and Their Attributes* (Albany: SUNY Press, 1978); R. J. McCarthy, *The Theology of Al-Ashʿari* (Beirut: Imprimerie Catholique, 1953); D. Gimaret, *La Doctrine d' al-Ashʿari* (Paris: Cerf, 1990); D. Gimaret, *Les Noms Divins en Islam* (Paris: Cerf, 1988); Eric Ormsby, *Theodicy in Islamic Thought* (Princeton: Princeton University Press, 1984); and Josef van Ess, *Zwischen Ḥadīth und Theologie, Studien zum Entstehen prädestinationischer Überlieferung* (Berlin: De Gruyter, 1975). For a brilliant summary of various schools, see M. Shahrastānī, *Kitāb al-Milal wa al-Niḥal*, ed. M. Badrān (Cairo, 1951), the relevant portion translated by A. Kazi and J. Flynn as *Muslim Sects and Divisions* (London: Kegan Paul, 1984). For a Sufi "handbook" of theological positions, see Abū Bakr al-Kalābādhī, *Kitāb al-Taʿarruf*, trans. by A. J. Arberry as *The Doctrine of the Ṣūfīs* (Cambridge University Press, 1935).

9. *Fa inna Allaha khalaq ādam ʿalā ṣūratihi*. See Ṣaḥīḥ al-Bukhārī: Istidh'ān 1; Ṣaḥīḥ Muslim, Birr 115, Janna 28; *Musnad* Ibn Ḥanbal 2: 244, 251, 315, 323, 434, 463, 519. Cf. Ibn ʿArabi, *Al-Futūḥāt*, ed. Yaḥya 3 (1974): 249. See Chittick, *The Sufi Path of Knowledge* (pp. 399–400), for Ibn ʿArabi's interpretation of the "his" as refering to Adam's image in the sense of being created instantaneously in human form rather than passing through various stages of development. Such an interpretation, Ibn ʿArabi suggests, is suitable for an Islamic philosopher (*faylasūf islāmī*). For examples of various Islamic approaches to this issue, see Muḥammad Ibn Khuzaymah, *Kitāb al-Tawḥīd wa Ithbāt Ṣifāt al-Rabb* (The Book of the Affirmation of Divine Unity [*Tawḥīd*] and the Affirmation of the Attributes [*Ṣifāt*] of the Lord) (Cairo, 1968); *Zād al-Musnad*, vol. 1, no. 427 (Beirut, 1970); Raḍī al-Dīn al-Ṭā'ūsī, *Saʿd as-Suʿūd* (Najaf, 1950), pp. 33–35; Ibn Qutayba, Jalāl al-Dīn al-Suyūṭī, *Jam ʿal-Jawāmi'* (Cairo: Al-Azhar, 1979), pp. 3511–3894. Cf. M. J. Kister, "Legends in *tafsīr* and *ḥadīth* Literature: The Creation of Adam and Related Stories," in A. Rippin, ed., *Approaches to the History of the Interpretation of the Qurʾān* (Oxford: Oxford University Press), pp. 81–114.

10. A reference to the famous *ḥadīth qudsī* (ex-Qur'anic divine pronouncement): "I was a hidden treasure and loved to be known. So I created the

creatures that I might be known." The hadith is not included in the canonical hadith collections.

11. One of the fuller accounts of the myth occurs in Ibn ʿArabi, *Inshā' al-Dawā'ir* (Construction of the Circles), in *Kleinere Schriften des Ibn Al-ʿArabī*, ed. H. S. Nyberg (Leiden: E. J. Brill, 1919), pp. 36–38. Allah orders the name *ar-raḥmān* to "breathe" into existence a cosmos in which the names (including *ar-raḥmān*) will be realized and existent. Cf. Izutsu, *Sufism and Taoism*, pp. 131–33. For a translation of an account from the *Futūḥāt*, see Chittick, *The Sufi Path of Knowledge*, pp. 131–32. For the divine names as nonexistent relationships, see Izutsu, *Sufism and Taoism*, pp. 160–61 and Chittick, *The Sufi Path of Knowledge*, pp. 35–36.

12. For a general discussion of this doctrine, see William Chittick, "The Perfect Man as the Prototype of the Self in the Sufism of Jami," *Studia Islamica* 49: 135–58.

13. When your lord said to the angels:

> I am going to place a regent [*khalīfa*] on the earth,
> they said: Will you place one there
> who will corrupt it and spill blood,
> while we recite your praises and exalt you?
> He said: I know what you do not know.
>   Then he taught Adam all the names
> and showed everything to the angels, saying:
> tell me their names, if you are sincere.
>   They said: praise be to you,
> we know only what you have taught us,
> you are the all-knowing, the most wise.
>   He said: O Adam, tell them their names,
> and when he had told them their names,
> he said: did I not tell you that I know
> what is hidden in the heavens and earth,
> and know what you disclose and know what you hide?
>   Then we told the angels
> to bow before Adam
> and they did, except for Iblis,
> who was scornful and acted proud,
> and became a disbeliever.

The "your" in the first line of this passage can be interpreted specifically as addressed to Muhammad, or more generally, any hearer of the divine revelation. The passage begins with a grammatical peculiarity common in the Qur'an, a temporal clause that is never completed. Although the complete human reflects all the names of the divine, nevertheless Ibn ʿArabi insists that only the deity can properly take another life, and thus his position on Adam as a polished mirror is in no way an exoneration of human spilling of blood. For Ibn ʿArabi's radical position on this issue, see the chapter on Jonah from *Fuṣūṣ*.

14. See *Ṭabarī's Commentary on the Qur'ān* on verse 2:31 where other possibilities are given: "man, animal, earth, plateau . . . the nations [of creatures]

and so forth" (Ibn ʿAbbās); "the name of every thing" (Mujāhid); "the names of the angels" (Al-Rabīʿ); "the names of all his offspring" (Ibn Zayd). W. Madelung and A. Jones, eds., *The Commentary on the Quran* by Abu Jafar Muhammad b. Jarir al-Tabari (London, New York : Oxford University Press, 1987–), 1:229–30.

15. The account also begins with a temporal clause (When your lord . . .) that is never completed (see n. 13, above). In translating the Qur'an I avoid using quotation marks to indicate interior dialogue. A distinctive aspect of Qur'anic discourse is the frequent difficulty of deciding where one is within a series of embedded conversations. The effect of this provocative ambiguity is lost when quotations marks are used to parse the text. The command, "fall bowing before it" uses a form of the verb *sajada* (to bow or prostrate oneself in prayer), a term that refers to the distinctive positions in Islamic prayer. "Prostration" can carry a sense of abjectness inappropriate to the Islamic concept, whereas "bowing" does not fully describe the physical motion which includes touching the head to the ground. I have used "fall bowing" as an attempt to negotiate this difficult translation crux, with further instances translated simply as "bow."

A third Qur'anic passage specificies the material out of which Adam was constructed, while repeating many of the other elements of the story (15: 28–31):

> When your lord said to the angels
> I am going to create a person from hard-dried clay.
> When I have shaped him
> and have blown into him of my spirit
> fall bowing before him.
> All the angels fell bowing together
> Except Iblis who disdained to bow.

Allah is pictured as molding the clay from which Adam was formed in several Qur'anic passages (Q 85:38, 87:2, 18:38, 82:8, 32:9). It is the last of these which is the immediate reference for our text: *thumma sawwāhu wa nafakha fīhi min rūḥihi* (then he molded him and breathed into him of his spirit).

16. For a treatment of this symbolic cosmos and its possible religious and philosophical permutations, see M. Sells, "Bewildered Tongue: The Semantics of Mystical Union in Islam," M. Idel and B. McGinn, eds., *Mystical Union and Monotheistic Faith* (New York: Macmillan, 1989), pp. 101–8.

17. He was told: "bow down!" He said, "[to] no other!" He was asked, "Even if you receive my curse?" He said "It doesn't matter. I have no way to another-than-you. I am an abject lover." My translation here is based upon the edition of L. Massignon, *Kitāb al-Ṭawāsīn* (Paris: Geuthner, 1913), and the later edition of Paul Nwyia, *Kitāb al-Ṭawāsīn* (Beirut: Imprimerie Catholique, 1972). A new translation of the Hallaj Iblis story is appearing in M. Sells, *Foundations of Islamic Mysticism* (New York: Paulist Press, forthcoming). Cf. Peter Awn: *Satan's Tragedy and Redemption: Iblis in Sufi Psychology* (Leiden: Brill, 1984).

18. Ibn ʿArabi elsewhere adopts the Iblisian distinction between the inner divine will and the explicit divine command. The tension between divine will and divine command is brought out most clearly in the *Fuṣūṣ* in the Moses chapter (where Pharoah is interpreted as involved in a complex hermeneutical guise) and in the Noah chapter (where both Noah and his idolatrist enemies are depicted as acting out in the exterior world (of command) and interior dialectic (associated, it is implied, with divine will). See chap. 4, below.

19. This erotic "loss of self," a major theme in the Arabic and Persian poetic traditions, was integrated by early Sufis into the mystical loss of self that occurs during *fanāʾ*. Indeed, from the beginnings of Sufism to the present day, many poems can be read as secular love poems to a worldly beloved or as mystical love poems to the divine beloved. Although the Sufis are commonly said to have used secular poetic themes as a vehicle for expressing their otherworldly love, the almost complete interfusion of lyrical Sufism and secular poetic themes constitutes an intertextuality in which neither side can be reduced to being the vehicle for the other. For classical Sufism, see al-Qushayri, *Principles of Sufism*, trans. B. R. Von Schlegell (Berkeley: Mizan Press, 1990), which consists of selections from the famous treatise (*al-risāla*) of al-Qushayri (d. 1072 C.E.).

20. From Bukhārī, 81:38. For a discussion of the hadith of free devotions (*ḥadīth an-nawāfil*), see William Graham, *Divine Word and Prophetic Word in Early Islam* (The Hague, 1977), 173. Note that the last phrase, "the tongue with which he speaks" occurs only in some versions of the hadith.

21. Farid ad-Din ʿAttar, *Tadhkirat al-Awliyāʾ* (London, 1905) I, pp. 157, 160. Trans. by Margaret Smith, *Readings from the Mystics of Islām* (London: Luzac, 1950), p. 27.

22. The following disussion is based on the edition of A. A. Affifi, *Fuṣūṣ al-Ḥikam*, 2 vols. (Cairo: Dar Iḥyāʾ al-Kutub al-ʿArabiyya, 1946), hereafter cited as *Fuṣūṣ*, a word translated by Ralph Austin as "Bezels of Wisdom." I use the translation "Ring Settings of Wisdom." One could make a case for translating *Fuṣūṣ* as Ring Stones, Jewels, or Gems of Wisdom. There are passages where Ibn ʿArabi seems to be referring to the seal or the stone rather than to the setting.

23. To show the continuity of the three passages, I give the Arabic of all of passage 1 (*Fuṣūṣ* 1:50–51), with a line break to indicate where I have divided the passage into three sections:

لما شاء الحق سبحانه من حيث أسماؤه الحسنى التي لا يبلغها الإحصاء أن يرى أعيانها ، وإن شئت قلت أن يرى عينه ، في كون جامع يحصر الأمر كله لكونه متصفا بالوجود ، و يظهر به سره اليه : فان رؤية الشيء نفسه بنفسه ما هي مثل رؤيته نفسه في أمر آخر يكون له كالمرآة ، فانه يظهر له نفسه في صورة يعطيها المحل المنظور فيه مما لم يكن رؤيته نفسه في من غير وجود هذا المحل و لا تجليه له. وقد كان الحق سبحانه أوجد العالم كله وجود شبح مسوى لا روح فيه، فكان كمرآة غير مجلوة. ومن شأن الحكم الإلهي أنه ما سوى محلا إلا و يقبل روحا المهيا عبّر عنه بالنفخ فيه ، و ما هو الا حصول الإستعداد من تلك الصورة المسواة لقبول الفيض التجلي الدائم الذي لم يزل و لا يزال وما بقي إلا قابل ، و القابل لا يكون إلا من فيضه الأقدس. فالأمر كله منه ، ابتداؤه و انتهاؤه ، «و اليه يرجع الأمر كله»، فاقتضى الأمر جلاء مرآة العالم فكان آدم عين جلاء تلك المرآة و روح تلك الصورة.

و كانت الملائكة من بعض قوى تلك الصورة التي هي صورة العالم المعبر عنه في اصطلاح القوم «بالإنسان الكبير» فكانت الملائكة له كالقوى الروحانية و الحسية التي في النشأة الإنسانية . فكل قوة منها محجوبة بنفسها لا ترى أفضل من ذاتها، وأن فيها، فيما تزعم ، الأهلية لكل منصب عال ومنزلة رفيعة عند الله، لما عندها من الجمعية الإلهية مما يرجع من ذلك الى الجناب الإلهي ، الى جانب حقيقة الحقائق ، و __ في النشأة الحاملة لهذه الأوصاف __ الى ما تقتضيه الطبيعة الكلية التي حضرت قوابل العالم كله أعلاه و أسفله . و هذا لايعرفه عقل بطريق نظر فكري ، بل هذا الفن من الإدراك لا يكون إلا عن كشف إلهي منه يعرف ما أصل صور العالم القابلة لأرواحه.

فسمي هذا المذكور إنسانا و خليفة، فأما إنسانيته فلعموم نشأته و حصره الحقائق كلها . و هو للحق بمنزلة إنسان العين من العين الذي يكون به النظر، و هو المعبر عنه بالبصر . فلهذا سمي إنسانا ،فأنه به ينظر الحق الى خلقه فيرحمهم فهو الإنسان الحادث الأزلي و النشئ الدائم الأبدي، و الكلمة الفاصلة الجامعة قيام العالم بوجوده فهو من العالم كنقص الخاتم من الخاتم ، و هو محل النقش و العلامة التي يختم بها الملك على خزانته . و سماه خليفة من أجل هذا ، لأنه تعالى الحافظ به خلقه كما يحفظ الختم الخزائن . فما دام ختم الملك عليها لا يجسر أحد على فتحها الا بإذنه فاستخلفه في حفظ الملك. فلا يزال العالم محفوظا ما دام فيه هذا الإنسان الكامل . ألا تراه اذا زال و فك من خزانة الدنيا لم يبق فيها ما اختزنه الحق فيها و خرج ما كان فيها و التحق بعضه ببعض ، و انتقل الأمر الى الآخرة فكان ختما على خزانة الآخرة ختما أبديا .

Much of Ibn ʿArabi's writing falls somewhere between prose and verse. It does not contain the meter and strict rhyme of the classical poetry, but it frequently contains rhymed prose, interior rhythms, lyrical digressions, and assonance, which do not fit well into a sentence-and-paragraph format. One solution to this problem was offered by T. Izutsu in *Sufism and Taoism*, the first part of which is a comprehensive study of Ibn ʿArabi's thought. In order to fit the original style into periods and paragraphs, Izutsu uses interpolations to fill in the ellipses and the logical steps missing in the original. I have used the opposite method, a free verse system which attempts to follow exactly the original syntactical and logical rhythms and to reproduce faithfully the lyrical and poetic "thought rhythms" of the original. The free verse is not an attempt to decorate the original. Rather, it attempts to reproduce it as faithfully as possible. Because I have translated both the formal verses and the "prose" of Ibn ʿArabi into English verse form, I have used italics to indicate translations of formal Arabic poetry.

For a new translation of the entire Adam chapter, see M. Sells, "Towards a Poetic Translation of *Fuṣūṣ al-Ḥikam*," in *Muhyiddin Ibn Arabi: A Commemorative Volume*. For a more detailed discussion of the challenge of translating the *Fuṣūṣ* see M. Sells, "Ibn ʿArabi's Polished Mirror," (cited above, n. 1). Other translations of *Fuṣūṣ* are T. Burckhardt's translation of selected chapters, *Sagesse des Prophètes* (Paris: A. Michel, 1955), trans., Angela Culme-Seymour as *The Wisdom of the Prophets* (Swyre Farm: Beshara Publications, 1975), and R. Austin's complete translation, *Bezels of Wisdom* (New York: Paulist Press, 1980), which includes very helpful introductions to each chapter.

24. The ambiguity can be grammatically outlined as follows:

a. the real wished to see its determination from the standpoint of its divine names, since in its identity (*dhāt*) it could not be revealed or determined in any way. The phrase modifies the predicate-object relation.

b. Insofar as we can give the real a predicate, we are speaking of it from the standpoint of its manifest aspect, the divine names. The phrase modifies the subject-predicate relation.

25. *ʿayn jalāʾ tilka mirʿāt*. Here as elsewhere Ibn ʿArabi uses the term *ʿayn* both in the common sense (as I've translated here) and in the technical sense (Adam was the instantiation of that polishing). The translator is forced to choose, and in this case I believe the informal meaning is dominant. Cf. William Chittick, *The Sufi Path of Knowledge*, pp. 84–88.

26. Alternately, the passage could be read: *wa yaẓharu bihi sirruhu ilayhi* (and its mystery would appear to it through it). This reading has the advantage of not putting the real into a subject-predicate relation. The ambiguity of the split reference of the pronoun *hu* is compounded by the ambiguity between *yaẓhara sirruhu* and *yuẓhiru sirrahu*.

27. Chap. 4, below.

28. *Inshāʾ ad-Dawāʾir*, p. xx.

29. For the two phases of emanation, see Izutsu, *Sufism and Taoism*, p. 37. These two phases of emanation correspond remarkably well to Meister Eckhart's two emanations, *bullitio* (the "bubbling forth" within the divine realm) and *ebullitio* (the "bubbling over" into creation). The problem of the *aʿyān* can only be touched upon briefly here. It was a point of such difficulty that the grand master's successors felt it necessary to write a systematic treatment of the problem. See W. Chittick, "Ṣadr al-Dīn Qunawī on the Oneness of Being," *International Philosophical Quarterly* 21 (1981): 171–84.

30. Ibn ʿArabi common uses the term *aʿyān* (instantiations) ambiguously, without specifying whether he is referring to the established instantiations (*aʿyān thābita*), that is, the intelligible archetypes in the divine mind that are formally nonexistent or the existent instantiations (*aʿyān mawjūda*), the concrete entities within the phenomenal world. This ambiguity in the phrase "to see their instantiations" can be outlined as follows:

a. To see the archetypes of the real (in its manifest aspect of divine names) in the mirror of the cosmos.

b. Insofar as these archetypes are seen, they are seen through the real/complete human being in the real/complete human being.

c. Insofar as they are seen, they are not the established archetypes but rather the phenomenal existents. The archetypes remain perpetually hidden (*bāṭin*).

31. This precise point in Ibn ʿArabi's thought is highly elusive. When one attempts to chart how the two phases of emanation fit in with the metaphor of the breath of the compassionate, and with the schema of divine names and archetypal instantiations, somehow the phases of emanation seem to reverse.

32. *Amr* is one of the more difficult terms in Ibn ʿArabi's work. At times he uses it as it is often used in the Qurʾan to mean simply the a state of being, an "affair." At other times it refers to the divine creative command, the creative imperative *kun* as the logos (*Fuṣūṣ* 1: 116). This notion of *amr* is called *amr takwīnī*. Finally, *amr* can be distinguished from *mashiʾa* as two kinds of divine will, the *amr* referring to the explicitly formulated divine will of the *shariʿa*, and the *mashiʾa* referring to the absolute divine will. In our passage

only the meaning of command or logos seems to be intended, though the first, general meaning of "affair" cannot be excluded. I have thus used the word "order," with its meanings of command and arrangement to parallel the ambiguity between *amr takwīnī* (creative logos as divine will or command) and the more general meaning of affair. See Izutsu, *Sufism and Taoism*, p. 121. Muḥyī d-Dīn's use of the logos doctrine and the terms *kalima* and *amr* recalls a similar doctrine in Ismaʿīlī theory. That doctrine has been related by S. Pines to the long recension of the *Theology of Aristotle* (an interpretive translation of the fourth, fifth, and sixth *Enneads* of Plotinus). More recently Pines has compared the Islamic logos doctrine to Porphyrian prototypes exposed in P. Hadot's remarkable study, *Porphyre et Victorinus* (Paris: Etudes Augustiniennes, 1968). See S. Pines, "La Longue Recension de la Theologie d'Aristote dans ses rapport avec la doctrine ismaelienne," *Revue des Etudes Islamiques* (1954): 8–20, and "Les Textes arabes dits plotiniens et le courant 'porphyrien' dans le néoplatonisme Grec," *Le Néoplatonisme* (Colloques internationaux du centre national de la recherche scientifique: 1971), pp. 303–17.

33. In *Inshā' ad-Dawā'ir*, p. 36 of Nyberg's text, Ibn ʿArabi seems to refer to the phrase he used below, "And the angels were certain powers [*quwā*] of that form [*ṣūra*]." In *Inshā'*, this phrase is introduced by the expression "his saying" [*qawluhu*], often used to introduce a prophetic hadith. The saying of the prophet, "the angels were among the faculties or powers of that form," means that the angels are the spirit of the powers which inhere in sensible or perceptual forms or in psychic or rational powers. For an English translation of *Inshā'*, see Paul Fenton and Maurice Gloton, translators, "The Book of the Description of the Encompassing Circles," in S. Hirtenstein and M. Tiernan, eds., *Muhyiddin Ibn ʿArabi: A Commemorative Volume*, pp. 12–43.

34. Ibn ʿArabi, *Fuṣūṣ*, 1: 50–51. This linguistic implosion is often signalled in Ibn ʿArabi by the terms *subḥānahu*, *taʿālā*, and *ʿazza wa jalla*. These terms are not primarily marks of piety, as is implied by standard translations ("praised be [or is] he" or "exalted be he"). Rather, they evoke the entire apophatic dialectic, and might be translated as follows: "May he (or it) be praised through the attribute being attributed to him here, but also exalted beyond this attribute." In my translation I have used the sign ( ) to indicate these extra-discursive markers. (Though *taʿālā* might be taken to represent the apophatic exaltation beyond all attributes, and *subḥānahu* the praise through attributes, Muḥyī al-Dīn sometimes seems to use them interchangeably to mark the apophatic dialectic.)

35. This transformation of the religious ideal from "perfection," to "completion," carried out through a recontextualizing of the Arabic word *kāmil*, bears strong resemblance to Carl Jung's critique of perfection as a religious ideal, and his advocation of completion as an ideal that incorporates acceptance of all aspects of one's psychic being. C. G. Jung, *Psychology and Alchemy*, trans. R. Hull (Princeton: Bollingen), 1953, 1968; and *Aion: Researches into the Phenomenology of the Self* (Princeton: Bollingen, 1959).

Ibn ʿArabi develops his notion of completion in his treatment of the prophets Idrīs (Enoch) and Ilyās (perhaps Elijah) in *Fuṣūṣ*. Idrīs rises through the spheres, through successive realms of purification and spirituality. Ilyās descends into animal, vegetable, and mineral reality, and finally into pure elementality. The complete human being consists of movement in both directions as opposed to other systems that stress only the upward movement and focus upon perfection. The question of the role of the dark side in Ibn ʿArabi is complex, however, and further investigation might well reveal differences between Ibn ʿArabi and Jung's notion of the shadow.

36. *Inshāʾ ad-Dawāʾir* (The Construction of the Circles; cited above, n. 11), p. 22.

37. For a discussion of the "reality of realities," see Masataka Takeshita, "An Analysis of Ibn ʿArabi's *Inshāʾ al-Dawāʾir* with Particular Reference to the Doctrine of the 'Third Entity'," *Journal of Near Eastern Studies* 41, no. 4 (1982): 243–60.

38. *Inshāʾ ad-Dawāʾir*, p. 25.

39. *Fuṣūṣ*, 1:53:

لما كان الأمر على ما قلناه من ظهوره بصورته ، أحالنا تعالى في العلم به على النظر في الحادث و ذكر أنه أرانا آياته فيه فاستدلالنا بنا عليه . فما وصفناه بوصف الا كنا نحن ذلك الوصف الا الوجوب الخالص الذاتي . فلما علمناه بنا و منا نسبناه اليه كل ما نسبناه الينا . و بذلك وردت الإخبارات الإلهية على ألسنة التراجم الينا . فوصف نفسه لنا بنا : فاذا شهدناه شهدنا نفوسنا ، و اذا شهدنا شهد نفسه .

40. See *Futūḥāt* II 3.28, translated by W. Chittick, *The Sufi Path of Knowledge*, pp. 277–78: "Hands cannot be taken to mean 'power' [*qudra*], because of the dual. Nor can it be taken to mean that one hand is blessing and the other hand is power, since that is true of every existent thing, so there would be no eminence for Adam according to that interpretation [*taʾwīl*], and this would contradict the fact that His words point out Adam's eminence." For the earlier history of interpretation of the "two hands," see Kister, "Legends," pp. 103–5.

41. *Fuṣūṣ*, 1:54 . The passages from *Futūḥāt* on the names and stations, selected and translated by Chittick in *The Sufi Path of Knowledge*, pp. 264–88, serve as a sustained philosophical parallel to the more cryptic and lyrical expression of the Adam chapter of *Fuṣūṣ*.

42. *Fuṣūṣ*, 1:55:

و لهذا قال لإبليس : ما منعك أن تسجد لما خلقت بيدي ؟ وما هو الا عين جمعه بين الصورتين : صورة العالم و صورة الحق ، و هما يدا الحق.

43. *Fuṣūṣ*, 1:55:

فأنشأ صورته الظاهرة من حقائق العالم و صوره و أنشأ صورته الباطنة على صورته تعالى ، و لذلك قال فيه «كنت سمعه و بصره».

44. *Corpus Hermeticum*, ed. and trans. Walter Scott (Oxford: Clarendon Press, 1924), Libellus I, p. 122.

Chapter Four

1. Muḥyī ad-Dīn Ibn (al)-ʿArabī (born 560/1165, Andalusia; died 638/1240, Damascus). *Tarjumān al-Ashwāq* (Beirut: Dār Ṣādir, 1966), pp. 43–44. A textual variant in the last verse would alter the translation slightly: "My religion is love—wherever its camels turn / that religion is my religion, my faith" (reading *ad-dīn* for *al-ḥubb*). See Ibn ʿArabi, *Dhakhā'ir al-Aʿlāq*, ed. Muḥammad al-Kurdī (Cairo, 1968), p. 50. For the Arabic, see below, n. 33.

2. The verses were cited and made popular by Reynold Nicholson on the first page of his edition and translation of *Tarjumān*, with the comment that "they express the Sufi doctrine that all ways lead to the One God": Ibn ʿArabi, *The Tarjumān al-Ashwāq: A Collection of Mystical Odes*, trans. and ed. Reynold Nicholson (London: Royal Asiatic Society, 1911), p. iii. Nicholson cites the same verses in *The Mystics of Islam* (1914; reprint, London: Routledge & Kegan Paul, 1963, 1979, p. 105), with the comment that "love is the essence of all creeds: the true mystic finds it whatever guise it may assume." Henry Corbin cites them as a conclusion to his treatment of the Sufis as "fedeli d'amore" seeking union with Sophia, "the figure of wisdom": Henry Corbin, *Creative Imagination in the Sufism of Ibn ʿArabi*, trans. Ralph Manheim (Princeton: Princeton University Press, 1969), p. 135. They are also cited, with brief remarks similar to those of Nicholson, in the following works: Ignaz Goldziher, *An Introduction to Islamic Theology and Law*, trans. Andras Hamori (Princeton: Princeton University Press, 1981), p. 152; Reynold Nicholson, *Translations of Eastern Poetry and Prose* (Cambridge University Press, 1922), p. 148; Idries Shah, *The Sufis* (New York: Doubleday, 1964), p. 145; Seyyed Hussein Nasr, *Three Muslim Sages: Avicenna, Suhrawardi, and Ibn ʿArabi* (Cambridge: Harvard University Press, 1964), p. 118; Margaret Smith, *Readings from the Mystics of Islam* (London: Luzac, 1972), p. 97; Nasrallah, Faramarz, and Fariborz Fatemi, *Sufism* (New York: A.S. Barnes, 1976) p. 60. With the exception of Nasr, none of these writers discusses the verses within the wider context of Ibn ʿArabi's thought, and I have found no treatment of them which links them to a full discussion of the theory of the heart that is receptive of every form.

3. An earlier version of this chapter appeared as "Ibn ʿArabi's Garden among the Flames," in *History of Religions* 23.4 (1984) 287–315.

4. Ibn ʿArabi admired Islamic philosophy for its brilliance and criticized it for what he believed were its limitations and pretensions. This complex attitude is vividly displayed in the Sufi master's accounts of his meetings with Ibn Rushd (Averroës). The two failed to come to a meeting of the minds because they had different notions of "where" and what mind (as seat and faculty of true understanding) might be. The anecdotes appear in Ibn ʿArabi, *Al-Futūḥāt al-Makkiyya* 2:372–73, and in the older edition, 1:153. The stories are recounted in Corbin and in Ralph Austin's introduction to Ibn ʿArabi, *Bezels of Wisdom*, trans. Ralph Austin (New York: Paulist Press, 1980), pp. 2–3.

5. See chap. 3 above for the general problem of how attributes split into controversies over the unity of the deity, the problem of anthropomorphism,

and the question of the createdness of the Qur'an, among the various schools of *mutakallimūn*.

6. Though the passages translated below are not poetry (*shi'r*) according to Arabic technical criteria, they do not correspond well to English sentences and paragraphs. I have found that a free-verse translation allows their syntactical rhythms and their flow of thought to come through more naturally. Translations of verse proper are in italics.

7. Ibn 'Arabi, *Fuṣūṣ*, 1:119–21. For a discussion of the meaning of Allāh's compassion, see Ronald Nettler, "Ibn 'Arabi's Notion of Allah's Mercy," *Israel Oriental Studies* 8 (1978): 219–39.

8. Ibn 'Arabi, *Fuṣūṣ*, 1:119:

وصف نفسه بالنفس و هو من التنفيس : و أن الأسماء الإلهية عين المسمى و ليس إله إلا هو ، و أنها طالبة ما تعطيه من الحقائق و ليست الحقائق التي تطلبها الأسماء إلا العالم . فالألوهية تطلب المألوه، و الربوبية تطلب المربوب، و إلا فلا عين لها إلا به وجودا أو تقديرا . و الحق من حيث ذاته غني عن العالمين . و الربوبية ما لها هذا الحكم . فبقي الأمر بين ما تطلبه الربوبية و بين ما تستحقه الذات من الغنى عن العالم . و ليست الربوبية على الحقيقة و الاتصاف الا عين هذه الذات . فلما تعارض الأمر بحكم النسب ورد في الخبر ما وصف الحق به نفسه من الشفقة على عباده . فأول ما نفس عن الربوبية بنفسه المنسوب الى الرحمن بايجاده العالم الذي تطلبه الربوبية بحقيقتها و جميع الأسماء الإلهية . فيثبت من هذا الوجه أن رحمته وسعت كل شئ فوسعت الحق ، فهي أوسع من القلب أو مساوية له في السعة.

I have translated the word *'ayn* as "the same" in two places in the above passage. It is clear from the context that this is its primary meaning, and Ibn 'Arabi emphasizes it by placing the words *lā illā hu* ("nothing but he") after it. However, the term is polyvalent in Ibn 'Arabi's thought and can also mean "eye," "source," "essence," or "entification." The latter meaning is most common, and by playing on the equivocation between "same as" and "entification of," the dialectic is invoked internally. The names are the determinations of the real, and of the undetermined identity (*dhāt*), but they are also "nothing but it." "Though when the situation [of unity] is contradicted by its relations, He described Himself as having compassion on his servants" (*Fuṣūṣ*, 1:119). This "contradiction" functions rhetorically in two ways. It refers to the "tension" in the myth of the names in their nonexistent state, a tension eventually relieved by the "breath" or "sigh." Dialectically, it refers to the tension between the one and its attributes which is then shifted to a new axis of dialectic, that between the real and its creation.

9. For the use of empty parentheses to stand for the word *ta'ālā*, see chap. 3, above, n. 34.

10. Ibn 'Arabi, *Fuṣūṣ*, 1:119–20:

ثم لتعلم أن الحق تعالى كما ثبت في الصحيح يتحول في الصورة عند التجلي، و أن الحق تعالى وسعه القلب لا يسع معه غيره من المخلوقات فكأنه يملؤه . ومعنى هذا أنه اذا نظر الى الحق عند تجليه له لا يمكن أن ينظر معه الى غيره. وقلب العارف من السعة كما قال أبو يزيد البسطامي «لو أن العرش وما حواه مائة ألف ألف مرة في زاوية من زوايا قلب العارف ما أحس به» و قال الجنيد في هذا المعنى : إن المحدث إذا قرن بالقديم لم يبق له أثر ، و قلب يسع القديم كيف يحس بالمحدث موجودا.

11. Ibn ʿArabi, *Fuṣūṣ*, 1:120. This is clearly one of the passages on which the title *Fuṣūṣ al-Ḥikam* (Ring settings of Wisdom) is based. However, the use of the term is complex, and one is not always sure whether it means the setting or the stone, an ambiguity that seems deliberate. At times it seems to mean "facets"; note the relation of the English terms "bevels" and "bezels." See also chap. 3 above, n. 22.

12. Ibn ʿArabi, *Fuṣūṣ*, 1:121:

فالحق الذي في المعتقد هو الذي وسع القلب صورته ، وهو الذي يتجلى له فيعرفه . فلا ترى العين الا الحق الاعتقادي. و لا خفاء بتنوع الاعتقادات : فمن قيده أنكره في غير ما قيده به، وأقر به فيما قيده به إذا تجلى. ومن اطلقه عن التقييد لم ينكره و أقر به في كل صورة يتحول فيها و يعطيه من نفسه قدر صورة ما تجلى له اليه ما لا يتناهى، فأن صور التجلي ما لها نهاية تقف عندها . و كذلك العلم بالله ما له غاية في العارف يقف عندها ، بل هو العارف في كل زمان يطلب الزيادة من العلم به. " رب زدني علما" "رب زدني علما" "رب زدني علما" . فالأمر لا يتناهى من الطرفين.

13. I use this example to illustrate the *dhikr* in a very general manner for those not familiar with Sufi practices. We are still in need of a detailed study of *dhikr* in Sufism. For a recent study of some related issues, see Jean During, *Musique et extase: L'audition mystique dans la tradition soufie* (Paris: Albin Michel, 1988).

14. *Fuṣūṣ*, 1:122:

" ان في ذلك لذكرى لمن كان له قلب" لتقبله في أنواع الصور و الصفات و لم يقل لمن كان له عقل ، فأن العقل قيد فيحصر الأمر في نعت واحد و الحقيقة تأبى الحصر في نفس الأمر. فما هو ذكرى لمن كان له عقل وهم أصحاب الاعتقادات الذين يكفر بعضهم ببعض ويلعن بعضهم بعضا وما لهم من ناصرين. فأن إله المعتقد ما له حكم في إله المعتقد الاخر .

"They have no saviors" (*mā lahum min nāṣirīn*): in addition to the six places where these exact words occur, there are numerous other references in the Qurʾān to the same, very common theme, with slightly different phrasing.

15. Ibid., 1:70:

فان قلت بالتنزيه كنت مقيدا   وإن قلت بالتشبيه كنت محددا
وإن قلت بالأمرين كنت مسددا   و كنت إماما في المعارف سيدا

As mentioned above, I have used italics to indicate that this is a formal poem according to classical Arabic prosody, in meter and rhyme. I have translated the "prose" passages from *Ring Settings* into free verse. Whenever Ibn ʿArabi shifts into formal poetry, I signal the shift with italics, in addition to attempting to bring across, through interior poetic means, the more formal prosodic quality of the text.

16. Ibid.:

فما أنت هو : بل أنت هو وتراه في   عين الأمور مسرحا و مقيدا

17. Ibid., 1:71–72.

18. I use the word "Muhammadian" as a translation of the Arabic *Muḥammadī* in order to distinguish it from "Muhammadan," the incorrect translation of *muslim* used in earlier scholarship.

19. Ibid., 1:73.

إلا حيرة المحمدي . « زدني فيك تحيراً»
«كلما أضاء لهم مشوا فيه و اذا أظلم عليهم قاموا» . فالحائر له الدور و الحركة الدورية حول القطب فلا يبرح منه، و صاحب الطريق المستطيل مائل خارج المقصود طالب ما هو فيه صاحب خيال اليه غايته: فله من و الى و ما بينهما. و صاحب الحركة الدورية لا بدء له فيلزمه « من » و لا غاية فتحكم عليه «الى» ، فله الوجود الأتم و هو المؤتى جوامع الكلم و الحكم.

This last statement on the "totality of words and wisdoms" is an allusion to the hadith, "I was sent with [*buʿthtu*]" or "I was given [*uʿṭītu*] the totality of the words [*awāmi ʿal-kalim*]." See Chodkiewicz et al., *Les Illuminations de la Mecque*, p. 631, n. 327. Bukhari, *Saḥīḥ*, Taʿbīr 11, 22, Jihād 122, Iʿtisām 1; Muslim, Masājid, 5–8, Ashriba, 82; Ibn Hanbal, *Musnad* 2:172, 212, 250, 264, 268, 313, 412, 442, 455, 501. Cf. Chittick, *The Sufi Path of Knowledge*, p. 396.

20. See al-Farābī, in his *Philosophy of Plato and Aristotle*, trans. Muhsin Mahdi (Ithaca: Cornell University Press, 1962); and Maimonides, in *The Guide of the Perplexed* [*Dalālat al-ḥā'irīn*], trans. Shlomo Pines (Chicago: University of Chicago Press, 1963), to name only two examples from Islamicate philosophy. Ibn ʿArabi inverts the philosophical methods. Instead of rationally distinguishing among various manners of argumentation, a distinction al-Farābī believes will dispel perplexity (al-Farābī, p. 14), he deliberately mixes and fuses them. Unlike Maimonides, who claims that the allegorical interpretation of scripture will dispel the perplexity caused by literal readings (Maimonides, p. 6), Ibn ʿArabi affirms an esoteric hermeneutic which guarantees perplexity by seeing dreams within dreams and by refusing rationalist allegory. Instead of resolving contradictions, the Sufi master inverts the principle of contradiction by appealing to an ultimate *coincidentia oppositorum*. Izutsu, *Sufism and Taoism* (p. 85), states that Ibn ʿArabi affirmed a station beyond *ḥayra*: "In the mind of a sage who has experienced the Unity of Being in its real depth there is no longer any place for a 'perplexity.'" Izutsu bases this opinion on a single passage (Ibn ʿArabi, *Fuṣūṣ*, 1:78–79): "But one who understands what I have said is not perplexed." The context of this statement is a discussion of the perplexity engendered in the Sufi by the simultaneous unity and diversity of nature, a unity and diversity Ibn ʿArabī compares to a single form reflected in a plurality of mirrors, or a plurality of forms reflected in a single mirror. Izutsu's interpretation of this one statement takes it out of its particular context and makes it into a global claim bolstered by the claim of Ibn ʿArabi's commentator al-Qāshānī that perplexity is confined to those of a low spiritual station. Qāshānī, like many commentators, attempts to systematize the discourse of his master. Ibn ʿArabi might affirm a state beyond *ḥayra*, but such a state would be in dialectical relationship with the *ḥayra*. The individual that breaks free from binding will be in a state of *ḥayra*, qua indi-

vidual, though on the primordial level (the complete human being) the state of certainty (*yaqīn*) is achieved. The greater the *ḥayra* on the level of individual consciousness, the greater the certainty on the level of universal consciousness. The highest understanding is the deepest awareness of mystery.

21. Ibn ʿArabi, *Fuṣūṣ*, 1:73.

فلم يجدوا لهم من دون الله أنصارا، فكان الله عين أنصارهم فهلكوا فيه الى الأبد . فلو أخرجهم الى السيف، سيف الطبيعة لنزل بهم عن هذه الدرجة الرفيعة، و ان كان الكل لله و بالله بل هو الله.

22. *Man ʿarafa nafsahu faqad ʿarafa rabbahu*. This ḥadith rests upon an *isnād* or chain of transmission that is considered by some to be weak. A book on weak ḥadith relates that the authenticity of this hadith was put in doubt by Ibn Taymiyya, and that Ibn ʿArabi stated that even if its *isnād* is not strong, it can be validated through divinely supported intuition (*kashf*). See Ismail al-Ajluni, *Kashf al-Khifā'*, 2 vols. (Cairo, n.d.; the author died in 1162 H.), 2:361. (I am indebted to Alan Godlas for guiding me to this volume.) Cf. A. Altmann, "The Delphic Maxim in Medieval Islam and Judaism," in A. Altmann, *Studies in Religious Philosophy and Mysticism* (Ithaca: Cornell University Press, 1969), pp. 1–40. Ibn ʿArabi also uses *kashf* rather than *naql* to validate the hidden-treasure hadith (chap. 3, n. 10).

23. Ibn ʿArabi's critique of the Qur'anic prophet Noah may seem surprising, given the common stereotype concerning the conservative and restrained nature of Islamic tradition. In fact, the interpretive horizons on the Qur'an are of an extraordinary diversity and freedom within the Islamic tradition. Ibn ʿArabi's position on Noah contrasts and compares in an intriguing way with that of the *Zohar*. In the *Zohar*, Noah is harshly criticized for not defending creation against the divine wrath, for obeying without objection the order to build an ark and save himself. The explicit occasion of criticism is different in each case (Noah's linear logic and binding of the transcendent vs. his unwillingness to defend his fellow creatures against divine wrath), and the Qur'anic Noah and the biblical Noah are portrayed with very different emphases. Yet Noah's eagerness for divine wrath constitutes his essential flaw in Jewish and Islamic masterworks of medieval apophasis. See *Zohar: The book of Enlightenment*, trans. Daniel Matt (New York: Paulist Press), pp. 57–59.

24. The Arabic terms are: *tawba, warʿ, zuhd, faqr, ṣabr, tawakkul*, and *riḍā*. See al-Sarrāj, *Kitāb al-Lumaʿ fi t-Taṣawwuf* (Book of the Flashes on Sufism), ed. R. A. Nicholson, Gibb Memorial Series, no. 22 (Leiden and London, 1914), pp. 43–54. For translations, see the forthcoming M. Sells, *Foundations of Islamic Mysticism*, and Richard Grammlich, *Schlaglichter Über Das Sufitum: Abū Nasr as-Sarrājs Kitāb al-lumaʿ*, eingeleitet, übersetzt und kommentiert von Richard Gramlich (Stuttgart: Steiner, 1990), pp. 87–101. Cf. the brilliant essay on the stations and conditions by Al-Qushayrī (d. 1072 c.e.): Abū l-Qāsim ʿabd al-Karīm al-Qushayrī, *Al-Risāla al-Qushayriyya fī ʿilm at-Tasawwuf* [The Qushayrian Treatise on Sufism] (Cairo: Dār al-Kutub al-Jadīd, 1988), vol. 1, 191–96. For translations, see Sells, *Foundations of Islamic Mysticism*,

and R. Gramlich, *Das Sendschreiben al-Qushayrīs* (Wiesbaden: Steiner, 1989), pp. 146 ff.

25. As mentioned above, the open parenthesis indicates the transcendence markers, *taʿālā* or *subḥānahu*.

26. Ibn ʿArabi, *Futūḥāt* (1911) (n. 5 above), 4:76–77. The Yaḥya edition has not yet reached this point in the text.

وليس أعم في الإختصاص من عدم التقيد بمقام يتميز فيه. فما يتميز المحمدي الا بأنه لا مقام له يتعين فمقامه أن لا مقام و معنى ذلك ما نبينه و هو أن الإنسان قد تغلب عليه حالته فلا يعرف إلا بما فينتسب اليها و يتعين بها و المحمدي نسبة المقامات اليه نسبة الاسماء الى الله فلا يتعين في مقام ينسب اليه بل هو في كل نفس و في كل زمان و في كل حال بصورة ما يقتضيه ذلك النفس أو الزمان أو الحال فلا يستمر تقيده فان الأحكام الإلهية تختلف في كل زمان فيختلف باختلافها فانه عز و جل كل يوم هو في شأن فكذلك المحمدي و هو قوله تعالى ان في ذلك لذكرى لمن كان له قلب و لم يقل عقل فيقيده و القلب ما سمي الا بتقلبه في الأحوال و الأمور دائما مع الأنفاس فمن عباد الله من يعلم ما يتقلب فيه في كل نفس و منهم من يغفل عن ذلك فالقطب المحمدي أو المفرد هو الذي يتقلب مع الانفاس علما كما يتقلب معها حالا كل و احد من خلق الله فما زاد هذا الرجل الا بالعلم بما يتقلب فيه و عليه لا بالتقليب فان التقلب أمر يسري في العالم كله و فيه.

27. For the strikingly similar formulation in Eckhart, that that which is most distinct is distinct by virtue of its utter lack of any distinction, see chapter 6, n. 5 below.

28. See the sophisticated essay on *waqt* by Qushayri, (d. 1072 C.E.), *al-Risāla*, vol. 1, pp. 188–90, trans. R. Gramlich, *Das Sendschreiben al-Qushayrīs*, pp. 106–9 (cited above, n. 24), and M. Sells, "Intimacy, Awe, and Heart-Secret in Formative Sufism," in E. Waugh and F. Denny, eds., *Fazlur Rahman Legacy*, in preparation.

29. One of the clearer accounts of these atomistic theories is to be found in Maimonides, bk. 1, chap. 73, where they are discussed under the rubric of the ten premises of the *mutakallimūn*. The third premise treats the temporal aspect of the atomic theory (Maimonides, *Guide*, pp. 196–200). Cf. T. Izutsu, "The Concept of Perpetual Creation in Islamic Mysticism and Zen Buddhism," in S. H. Nasr, ed., *Mélanges offerts à Henry Corbin* (Tehran: Institute of Islamic Studies, McGill University, Tehran Branch, 1977), pp. 115–48; Joseph van Ess, *Das Kitāb an-Naqt des Naẓẓām* (Gottingen: Vaudenhoeck and Ruprecht, 1972); S. Pines, *Beiträge zure islamischen Atomenlehre* (London: Garland, 1987); and the passages translated by Chittick, *The Sufi Path of Knowledge*, pp. 96–112.

30. Ibn ʿArabi, *Fuṣūṣ*, 1:125:

و هؤلاء هم في لبس من خلق جديد . . و أما أهل الكشف فانهم يرون أن الله يتجلى في كل نفس و لا يكرر التجلي، و يرون أيضا شهودا أن كل تجل يعطي خلقا جديدا و يذهب بخلق. فذهابه هو عين الفناء عند التجلي و البقاء لما يعطيه التجلي الآخر فانهم.

31. The spirit (*rūḥ*) is mentioned in the Qur'an in connection with three moments: the creation of Adam (into whom the creator breathes the divine spirit); the inspiration of prophets; and the day of judgment. For an argument

that Qur'anic usage places spirit at the boundary between the eternal and the temporal, and that in the spirit these three Qur'anic moments are somehow one, see M. Sells "Sound, Spirit, and Gender in *Sūrat al-Qadr*," *Journal of the American Oriental Society* 111.2 (1992): 239–59.

32. Ibn ʿArabi, "*Risālat al-Anwār*" (Treatise on the lights), in *Rasā'il Ibn ʿArabī* (1948; reprint, Cairo: Dār Iḥyāʾ al-Turāth al-ʿArabī, 1968), pp. 17–18:

و لا يزال يقول في كل نفس و قل رب زدني علما ما دام الفلك يجري بنفسه و ليتجتهد أن يكون وقته نفسه ....

و يطول الوقت و يقصر بحسب حضور صاحبه فمنهم من وقته ساعة و يوم و جمعة و شهر و مرة واحدة في عمره

This treatise has been translated by Rabia Terri Harris under the title *Journey to the Lord of Power* (New York: Inner Traditions, 1981). The second part of this quote occurs in a different version utilized by Harris in her translation, pp. 62–63. In the second part of the quotation (beginning with "For one who is heedful") I have used the Harris translation with some modifications to fit into the style and conventions used throughout this chapter.

33. The Arabic text as it occurs in Nicholson, Ibn ʿArabi, *The Tarjumān al-Ashwāq: A Collection of Mystical Odes* (cited above, n. 2), p. 19:

و كم عهدت أن لا تحول و أقسمت * و ليس لمخضوب وفاء بأيمان
ومن أعجب الأشياء ظبي مبرقع * يشير بعناب و يؤمى بأجفان
ومرعاه مابين الترايب و الحشى * ويا عجبا من روضه وسط نيران
لقد صار قلبي قابلا كل صورة * فمرعى لغزلان و دير لرهبان
و بيت لأوثان وكعبة طايف * و ألواح تورات و مصحف قران
أدين بدين الحب أنى توجهت * ركايبه فالدين ديني و ايماني
لنا أسود في بشر هند و أختها * و قيس و ليلى ثم مي و غيلان

34. In fact, despite the notoriety of the "heart-that-can-take-on-every-form" verses, Ibn ʿArabi's poem as a whole has received relatively little attention. For a translation of the full poem, and an introduction to its four major themes, see Michael Sells, "Ibn ʿArabī's 'Gentle Now Doves of the Thornberry and Moringa Thicket'" (*alā yā ḥamāmāti l-arākati wa l-bāni*), *Journal of the Muhyiddin Ibn ʿArabi Society* 10 (1991): 1–11. The four major themes are: (1) the lover's loss of the beloved and the stations (*maqāmāt, manāzil*) of the beloved's journey away from the poet; (2) the death of the lover depicted in the language of mystical passing away (*fanāʾ*); (3) the stations of the pre-Islamic and Islamic pilgrim in his journey toward the Kaʿba (as parallel to the stations of the beloved away from the poet); and (4) the heart of the Sufi as the true Kaʿba, a heart that that can take on every form, around which the various stations (in a reversal of the fixed-moving paradigm) are shown to circumambulate.

35. The parallel had been established by Ibn ʿArabi earlier in the same poem (with a pun on the Arabic root of *fanāʾ* [passing away]), a pun that cannot be reduplicated in English but which I try to indicate through an unusual transitive employment of the English verb pass away:

> In the *ghadā* grove
> spirits wrestled,
> bending the limbs down over me,
> passing me away.

The *ghadā* is a species of tamarisk that was particularly associated with the love topography of early Arabic poetry. For an important discussion of such topics in Arabic poetry, see Jaroslav Stetkevych, *The Zephyrs of Najd* (Chicago: University of Chicago Press, 1993).

36. See *Dīwān Majnūn Laylā*, ed. ʿAbd as-Sattār al-Farrāj (Cairo: Dār Miṣr, n.d.). For some of the precise elegiac topography underlying Ibn ʿArabi's poem, see poem no. 251 in the *Dīwān*.

Ghaylān and Mayya, mentioned at the end of Ibn ʿArabi's poem, form another lover-beloved pair. Ghaylān (better known as Dhū ar-Rumma, d. ca 735 C.E.), was considered the last of the great poets of the the classical, bedouin style. His poetry is prized both for the beauty of his remembrances of his beloved, *Mayya*, and the exquisite desert imagery of his journey or quest themes. In earlier verses of the poem Ibn ʿArabi draws specifically on the early Arabic vocabulary of Dhū ar-Rumma. For examples of these allusions, see Sells, "Gentle Now, Doves," (above. n. 35) and M. Sells, *Desert Tracings: Six Classic Arabian Odes* (Middletown: Wesleyan University Press, 1989), pp. 67–76.

37. Ibn ʿArabi, *Dhakhāʾir al-Aʿlāq* (n. 1, above), p. 49:

لقد صار قلبي قابلا كل صورة كما قال الاخر ما سمى القلب الآ من تقلبه فهو يتنوع بتنوع الواردات عليه و
تنوع الواردات بتنوع أحواله و تنوع أحواله لتنوع التجليات الإلهية لسره و هو الذي كنى عنه الشرع بالتحول
و التبدل في الصور.

38. This hadith and its place in Ibn ʿArabi is discussed by James Morris in his translation from the *Futūḥāt al-Makkiyya* (Meccan Openings): Chodkiewicz et al., *Les Illuminations de la Mecque*, pp. 177–81, and p. 543, n. 86. The references to the hadith can be found in William Graham, *Divine Word and Prophetic Word in Early Islam* (The Hague, 1977), pp. 133–34.

For Ibn ʿArabī, the afterlife is a moment of inversion: what is hidden (*bāṭin*) in the world becomes what is apparent (*ẓāhir*) in the afterlife. The "afterlife" is defined not so much by time and futurity as by the relationship of the hidden aspects of the real to the apparent aspects. See William Chittick, "Eschatology," in Seyyed Hossein Nasr, ed., *Islamic Spirituality: Foundations* (New York: Crossroad, 1987), pp. 378–409.

39. Ibn ʿArabi, *Dhakhāʾir al-Aʿlāq*, p. 50:

حين ذهب الحب بعقولهم و أفناهم عنهم لمشاهدات شواهد محبوبهم في خيالهم.

40. See Charles Adams, "The Islamic Religious Tradition," in *Religion and Man*, ed. W. Richard Comstock (New York: Harper & Row, 1971), p. 597, who states that Ibn ʿArabi and his followers "teach outright pantheism, that there is only one reality, God, who is the *sum of all things* [emphasis mine]"

41. Louis Massignon, *Essai sur les origines du lexique technique de la mystique musulmane* (Paris: Librairie orientaliste Paul Geunther, 1922), p. 285: "Ibn ʿArabi, épris de logique formelle, élimine, en fait, toute intervention transcendante de la divinité, du domaine de la mystique."

For Ibn ʿArabi's critique of non-dialectical affirmations of transformations, see the discussion of Noah, above. Cf. *Ismail Hakki Bursevi's translation of and commentary on Fusus al-Hikam by Muhyiddin Ibn ʿArabi*, rendered into English by Bulent Rauf (Oxford: Muhyiddin Ibn ʿArabi Society, 1985), 2:265. The commentary attributed to Bursevi emphasizes that to affirm the transcendence of something entails placing into a relationship with what it is supposed to transcend, "whereas God is transcendent from both the conditions of relativity and the absoluteness, and is not conditioned either by absoluteness or by relativization or conditioning."

In regard to Ibn ʿArabi's expression "He sent Himself with Himself to Himself," Annemarie Schimmel remarks that "This does not sound like a transcendent God." See A. Schimmel, *Mystical Dimensions of Islam* (Chapel Hill: University of North Carolina Press, 1975), p. 268. The statement "He sent Himself with Himself to Himself" is an exact parallel to "it reveals to it(self) through it(self) its mystery," shown above to be controlled by split reference and perspective shift. In fact, mystical dialectic is led to such a split reference through a critique of normal affirmations of transcendence and through a commitment to a more genuine affirmation. For an apophatic thinker like Ibn ʿArabī, to say that the real is beyond the world, or transcends it, is to delimit, to imply a space, the world, from which the real is excluded. The terms "beyond" and "transcend" imply a spatial relation (even if we are speaking of a conceptual space) that lead inevitably to a reification of the real. (This point is made consistently in Ibn ʿArabi's writings, but with special clarity at the beginning of the Noah chapter of *Ring Settings*.) For the apophatic mystic, terms like "beyond space" or "transcending space" are misleading since "beyond" and "transcend" reflect the inherently spatial structures of their primary meanings and the co-relationality of predications. The simple, non-dialectical statement that the real is transcendent is doubly dangerous because it seems to be affirming transcendence, even as it objectifies and delimits the real. It leads to the error of binding.

42. For a study of the Sufi hierarchy of saints and prophets and the role of Ibn ʿArabi within it, see Chodkiewicz, *Le Sceau* (cited above, chap. 3, n. 1). For the literary background of the Sufi "boast" and its role in early Sufi cul-

ture, see Carl Ernst, *Words of Ecstasy in Sufism* (Albany: State University of New York Press, 1985). Schimmel reads the poem as "the highest self-praise" and comments that "this seemingly tolerant statement contains, rather, a statement about the author's own lofty spiritual rank." Schimmel, *Mystical Dimensions*, pp. 271–72. In *As through a Veil: Mystical Poetry in Islam* (New York: Columbia University Press, 1982), pp. 38–39, Schimmel suggests that the verses do not affirm tolerance but rather "a glowing tribute to Islam." The "tribute to Islam" interpretation implies that the term "Muḥammadī," used in Ibn ʿArabi's commentary to indicate the heart receptive of every form, means "Muslim" (*muslim*). "Muḥammadī" was mistakenly translated as "Muslim" by Nicholson (*The Tarjumān al-Ashwāq: A Collection of Mystical Odes* [n. 2 above], p. 69). As shown above, the term denotes those who model themselves upon the personal prophetic model of Muhammad, rather than on one of the other prophets mentioned in *Ring Settings*. Not all Muslims were Muhammadians. See Ibn ʿArabi, *Dhakhāʾir al-Aʿlāq* (n. 1 above), p. 50.

Ibn ʿArabi was not a political revolutionary. He supported the *shariʿa* system whereby Christians, Jews, and other "peoples of the book" were offered self-rule and protection within the larger Islamic community but not full political rights. Ibn ʿArabi's heart that is receptive of every form was less a call for sociopolitical tolerance than it was a vision of reality that neither idolizes the God of its belief nor pre-emptorily denies the God of the other's belief.

43. See the classic diatribe by Massignon, *Essai* (p. 62): "C'est elle [the school of Ibn ʿArabi], également, qui a consommé le schisme entre les vocations mystiques musulmanes et leur rayonnement social—substituant au devoir de correction fraternelle le discipline qarmate de l'arcane,—réservant l'apanage de la mystique, science ésotérique qui ne doit pas être divulguée,—a des cercles initiatiques fermés, corporations intellectuelles fossiles, 'Gobineau-Verein' ou 'Stendhal-Club' de l'extase, fumeries d'opium surnaturel." Cf. Massignon, p. 30, n. 1, and Abdurrahman Badawi, "Les Points de rencontre de la mystique Musulmane et de l'existentialisme," *Studia Islamica* 27 (1967): 75; and Schimmel, *Mystical Dimensions*, 263–74. For more detailed discussion of these views, see Sells, "Ibn ʿArabi's Garden among the Flames," pp. 308–15.

44. A. A. Affifi, *The Mystical Philosophy of Muhyid Dīn-Ibnul ʿArabī* (Cambridge University Press, 1939), p. 18: "Such is the manner [a series of metaphors] in which Ibnul ʿArabi explains this vital point of his Philosophy, but no metaphor whatever can be adequate to serve as a medium for expressing a philosophical theory." Affifi filled out his general criticism of metaphor in Ibn ʿArabi with specific examples of misleading metaphors: "'mirrors' reflecting the One Light, or lights emanating from one source, or circles developing from one center." These criticisms (typical for their time and place—see the comments of A. H. Armstrong on Plotinus, above, chap. 1, n. 33) are much less in evidence in his superb Arabic commentary accompanying his edition of *Fuṣūṣ*.

45. Ibn ʿArabi, *Dhakhāʾir al-Aʿlāq* (n. 1 above), pp. 9–10.

46. In his use of a subtle and sustained harmonics of gender within his writings, Ibn ʿArabi is following the tradition of the Qur'an which itself is constructed upon the most intense harmonies of natural and grammatical gender. For a discussion of gender in the Arabic Qur'an and the way that it is systematically neutered or masculinized in translation, see M. Sells, "Sound, Spirit, and Gender" (cited above n. 31); and "Sound and Meaning in *Sūrat al-Qāriʿa*," *Arabica* 40.3 (1993). Ibn ʿArabi offers a specific discussion of gender in his chapter on Muhammad in the *Ring Settings*.

47. See Ibn ʿArabi, *Journey*, where the Sufi master describes a series of mystical experiences with the constant exhortation not to stop at any of them. The final experience is the *fanā'* and *baqā'* which turns out to be a continually repeated transformation in each moment and each breath.

48. See chap 3 above, for Ibn ʿArabi's interpretation as a lack of *adab* the claim of the angels to "high rank and exalted station before Allah" (*mansab ʿāl wa manzila rafī ʿa ʿind allāh*), *Fuṣūṣ*, 1:49). The angels lacked *adab*.

Chapter Five

1. As Robert Lerner, *The Heresy of the Free Spirit in the Later Middle Ages* (Berkeley: University of California Press, 1972), points out (pp. 71–72) the charge of "relapse" was based upon "the questionable assumption that she had already abjured her errors at Valenciennes."

2. See Revelation 3:7.

3. The habit was similar to that worn by the lay contemplatives, the beghards and beguines. See Robert Lerner, "An 'Angel of Philadelphia' in the Reign of Philip the Fair: The Case of Guiard of Cressonessart," in *Order and Innovation in the Middle Ages: Essays in Honor of Joseph R. Strayer*, ed. W. Jordan, B. McNab, and T. Ruiz (Princeton: Princeton University Press, 1976), pp. 343–64. Cf. Paul Verdeyen, "Le procès d'inquisition contre Marguerite Porete et Guiard de Cressonessart (1309–1310)," *Revue d'histoire ecclésiastique* 81 (1986).

4. The texts relating to both Porete and Guiard's inquisition are published in Verdeyen, "Le procès." Guiard gave Marguerite's ideas a millenarian interpretation that is not to be found in *The Mirror*.

5. Verdeyen, "Le procès," p. 89. This monk's inquisitorial enthusiasm shows as well in his reference to the Jew who was burned alongside Marguerite as having returned to Judaism as a dog returns to eat its own vomit (*sicut canis ad vomitum reversus*).

6. Ibid., p. 88: Circa festum Pentecostes accidit Parisiis quod quaedam pseudo-mulier de Hannonia, nomine Margaretha, dicta Porrette, quemdam librum ediderat, in quo, omnium theologorum iudicio qui ipsum diligenter examinaverunt, multi continebantur errores et haereses, et inter ceteras, quod anima annihilata in amore conditoris sine reprehensione conscientiae vel remorsu potest et debet naturae quidquid appetit et desiderat (concedere) quod manifeste sonat in heresim.

7. Archives Nationales, layette J.428, 15a, in Verdeyen, "Le procès," p. 51:

Quorum articulorum primus talis est: "Quod anima adnichilata dat licentiam virtutibus nec est amplius in earum servitute, quia non habet eas quoad usum, sed virtutes obediunt ad nutum."

8. *Ibid.*: Item decimus quintus articulus est: "Quod talis anima non curat de consolationibus Dei nec de donis eius, nec debet curare nec potest, quia tota intenta est circa Deum, et sic impediretur eius intentio circa Deum."

9. Announced in *Osservatore Romano*, June 16, 1946. The French text was published by Guarnieri in a major study of the heresy of the free spirit. See Guarnieri, *Archivio Italiano per la storia della pietà* 4 (1965): 351–708. For a discussion of the various manuscripts, the likely date of the composition of the surviving French manuscript, the mysterious possibilities that other versions of the French text may still exist in hiding, and the three Latin manuscripts that pre-date the surviving French and probably date from the late fourteenth century, see pp. 502–12. The French manuscript was published again, alongside the Latin text, in 1986. See Marguerite Porete, *Le Mirouer des simples ames (Speculum simplicium animarum)*, Old French version, ed. Romana Guarnieri, Latin version, ed. Paul Verdeyen, S.J. (Turnholt, Corpus Christianorum 69 [1986]). All subsequent citations will be to *Mirouer*, with chapter, line number, and page number. One of the first serious studies of Porete in English can be found in Peter Dronke, *Women Writers of the Middle Ages: A Critical Study of Texts from Perpetua to Marguerite Porete* (Cambridge University Press, 1984), pp. 202–78.

10. The point is made by Kurt Ruh, "'Le Miroir des simples âmes' de Marguerite Porete," in *Verbum et Signum*, essays presented to Friedrich Ohly, vol. 2 (Munich, 1975), pp. 365–87. For the middle English version, see M. Doiron, *Archivio Italiano per la storia della pietà* (1968): 244–355.

11. *The Mirror of Simple Souls, by an unknown French mystic of the thirteenth century, translated in English by M.N, now first edited from the MSS. by Clare Kirchberger* (London: Burns Oates and Washbourne, Publishers to the Holy See, 1927); *Nihil Obstat*: Georgius D. Smith S.T.d., Censor deputatus; *Imprimatur*: Edm. Can. Surmont, Vicarius generalis.

12. This kind of courtly dialogue had been in use among beguines at least since Mechthild of Magdeburg (ca. 1207–ca. 1294), who also made Lady Love the central figure. See Emilie Zum Brunn and Georgette Epiney-Burgard, *Women Mystics in Medieval Europe* (New York: Paragon House, 1989), pp. 54–57. Ellen Babinsky has explored the relationship of *The Mirror* to the courtly-love tradition and has demonstrated how the courtly rules were adopted into the practical rules governing the beguine houses or beguinages. See E. Babinsky, "A Beguine in the Court of the King: The Relation of Love and Knowledge in *The Mirror of the Simple Souls* by Marguerite Porete" (University of Chicago, Ph.D. diss., 1991), chap. 2. The focus of the discussion here will be upon the concept of the annihilated soul and the mystical language that results from Porete's attempt to speak of such a state of annihilation in love. A sensitive treatment of the relationship of *The Mirror* to the courtly tradition can also be found in the introduction and notes to Max Huot de Longchamp's translation, Marguerite Porete, *Le Miroir des âmes simples et anéanties* (Paris:

Albin Michel, 1984). Song of Songs exegesis is less of a force in Marguerite's Mirror. Marguerite seldom places the erotic dialogue between the soul and the deity into a bridal framework and seldom offers any specific allusions to the Song. For Song of Songs tradition, see E. Ann Matter, *The Voice of My Beloved: The Song of Songs in Western Medieval Christianity* (Philadelphia: University of Pennsylvania Press), 1990.

13. For the names of the theologians, see Verdeyen, "Le procès," pp. 53–54.

14. *Mirouer* 8:3, pp. 28–29: Raison qui n'entend que le gros et laisse la subtilité.

15. The divine lover in Porete is referred to as FarNear (*Loingprés*). In some commentaries on the Middle English translation and in the 1911 English translation, the character has changed to FarNight, a change evidently caused by a mistake in copying the term FarNigh. FarNight naturally led to glosses comparing union with FarNight to the Dark Night of the Soul of John of the Cross. In Hadewijch, Love is described in similar terms: "sometimes far and sometimes near." See Zum Brunn and Epiney-Burgard, *Women Mystics*, p. 114 and n. 7, who also find it in the *mengeldichten* (mixed poems) sometimes attributed to an anonymous figure known as Hadewijch II, MD XVII.

In the Sufi dialogue between the divine and human parties, mystical union is surrounded by extremes of psychological and semantic tension. There are oscillations between states of peace and ecstasy on the one hand and states of terror and dissolution on the other. The oscillation is related to the paradox that, at the moment before union, the nearest is the most far. One also thinks of Hallaj and ʿAyn al-Qudat, Sufi writers who emphasized the coming together of the opposites nearness and farness in experience of divine love, and Niffari, in whom nearness is often suddenly inverted to farness.

16. See the discussion in Longchamp, *Le Miroir*, p. 15.

17. In response to those who have criticized the literary quality of the work as confused, Amy Hollywood has defended its unity and coherence. Hollywood sees the dynamic tension of the work as that between those characters that retain their allegorical role and resist character transformation (Lady Love, Reason), and the Annihilated Soul, which is transformed within the work, a transformation that pulls against the static nature of the allegorical personifications. See Amy Hollywood, "The Soul as Virgin Wife: Meister Eckhart and the Beguine Mystics, Mechthild of Magdeburg and Marguerite Porete" (University of Chicago, Ph.D. diss., 1991), chap. 2.

18. As will be shown below, Porete's discourse is imbued with the apophatic perspective. Too little is known about Marguerite's early life and education to specify the textual sources of her grounding in Dionysian spirituality, although *The Mirror* reflects the apophatic perspective as strongly, though in its own distinctive fashion, as the near contemporary *The Cloud of Unknowing*. Two key differences between the two great apophatic works are genre and purpose. *The Cloud* is concerned with a pedagogy of contemplation, while *The Mirror* uses the its highly literary frame to develop an original mystical theology. Cf. Robert K. Forman, "Mystical Experience in the *Cloud-*

Literature, in Marion Glasscoe, ed., *The Medieval Mystical Tradition in England*, Exeter Symposium IV (Cambridge: Brewer, 1987), pp. 177–95.

19. Parallels can be found in the Sufi *mi'raj* and the Jewish Hekhalot texts. The seven stations of spiritual attainment were a part of most Sufi schools, while the Persian mystic Farid ad-Din 'Attar writes of seven valleys. 'Attar's valleys in their general outline and in some of their specific depictions offer some tantalizing similarities to Porete's seven stages. 'Attar's valleys are the quest, love, knowledge, independence, unity, amazement, and annihilation. See Farid ad-Din 'Attar, *The Conference of the Birds*, trans. Afkham Darbandi and Dick Davis (London: Penguin, 1984). The beguine Beatrice of Nazareth speaks of seven manners of love, while her sister-beguine, Hadewijch, writes of seven names of love. See Zum Brunn and Epiney-Burgard, *Women Mystics in Medieval Europe*, pp. 70–94, and *Hadewijch: The Complete Works*, trans. Mother Columba Hart, O.S.B. (New York: Paulist Press, 1980), p. 254. On Hadewijch, see S. M. Murk-Jansen, "The Mystic Theology of the Thirteenth-Century Mystic, Hadewijch, and its Literary Expression," *The Medieval Mystical Tradition in England* 5 (1992): 117–28.

20. The stages are outlined in chap. 118, pp. 316–33.

21. Guiard, the Angel of Philadelphia, who impulsively came to Porete's defense and thus, in his own words, "exposed himself" to the Inquisition, saw the seven stages as seven periods of the Church leading toward the seventh or apocalyptic stage, and saw himself as heralding the sixth stage. At the sixth station, we have a conjunction of a spatial metaphor, with Porete's annihilated and clarified soul representing the sixth stage of ascent, and a temporal or historical metaphor, with Guiard as the Angel of Philadelphia heralding the sixth stage of Church. See Lerner, "An 'Angel of Philadelphia'," cited above, n. 3.

22. *Mirouer* 13: 21–30, pp. 54–55: Qui dit—c'est assavoir ou septiesme chaptire—que ceste Ame n'a compte, n'a honte ne a honneur, n'a pouvreté ne a richisse, ne a aise ne a mesaise, ne a amour ne a hayne, ne a enfer ne a paradis.

Reason goes on immediately to say:

Et avec ce dit que ceste Ame a tout et n'a nient, elle scet tout et ne scet nient, elle veult tout et ne veult nient, comme it dit devant ou neufviesme chapitre. Et si ne desire, dit Raison, ne despit ne pouvreté, ne martire ne tribulacions, ne mesme ne sermons, ne jeunes ne oraisons, et si donne a nature tout ce qu'elle luy demande sans remors de conscience.

"In addition to that, it says that this Soul has all and has nothing, knows all and knows nothing, wishes all and wishes nothing, as it says above in chapter nine, so that she is concerned neither with scorn nor poverty, martyrdom nor tribulations, masses nor sermons, fasts nor prayers. She gives to nature whatever it demands of her without remorse of conscience."

There are a number of important cognate passages concerning the state of the soul that has given up its will entirely, including the two mentioned above by Reason (chaps. 7 and 9).

Mirouer 7: 3–5, pp. 24–25: Ceste Ame, dit Amour, ne fit compte ne de honte ne de honneur, de pouvreté ne de richesse, d'aise ne de mesaise, d'amour ne hayne, d'enfer ne de paradis.

"This Soul, says Love, is concerned neither with shame nor honor, poverty nor wealth, comfort nor discomfort, love nor hate, hell nor paradise."

Miroüer 9:19–25, pp. 32–33: laquelle Ame ne desire ne ne desprise pourvreté ne tribulation, ne messe ne sermon, ne jeune ne oraison, et donne a Nature ce qu'il luy fault, sans remors de conscience; mais telle nature est si bien ordonnee par transformacion de unité d'Amour, a laquelle la voulenté de ceste Ame est conjoincte, que la nature ne demande chose qui soit deffendue.

"This Soul neither desires nor despises poverty or tribulation, mass or sermon, fast or prayer. She gives to nature what it needs, without remorse of conscience. However, such a nature is so ordered through the transformation of the unity of Love, to which the will of this Soul is joined, that the nature does not ask anything that is forbidden."

Cf. Mirouer 16:20–24, pp. 66–67. After a long disquisition by Amour on the abolition of the will, Amour declares:

Ceste fille de Syon ne desire ne messes ne sermons, ne jeunes ne oraisons.

"This daughter of Zion desires neither mass nor sermons, fasts nor prayers."

23. Mirouer 5: 9–10, pp. 18–21: qui ne face rien pour Dieu; qui ne laisse rien a faire pour Dieu.

24. Mirouer 41:3–10, pp. 128–29: Pource n'a telle Ame nulle mesaise de peché que elle fist oncques.

"Such a soul has no worry about any sin she might have committed before."

25. Mirouer 48:1–2, pp. 144–45: Comment l'Ame n'est mie franche, qui desire que la voulenté de Dieu soit faicte en elle a son honnour.

26. Mirouer 81: 1–5, pp. 230–31.

27. Mirouer 13: 33–43, pp. 56–57: Car mon entendement et mon sens et tout mon conseil est pour le mieulx que je sçay conseiller, que on desire despiz, pouvreté, et toutes manieres de tribulacions, et messes, et sermons, et jeunes, et oraisons, et que on ait paour de toutes manieres d'amour, quelles qu'elles soient, pour les perilz qui y pevent estre, et que on desire souverainement paradis, et que on ait paour d'enfer, et que on refuse toutes manieres de honneurs, et les choses temporelles, et toutes aises, en ostant a nature ce que elle demande, fors sans plus ce sans quoy elle ne pouroit vivre, a l'exemple de la souffrance et passion de nostre seigneur Jhesuchrist.

28. Mirouer 90: 28–30.

29. Mirouer 55: 1–30, pp. 158–61.

30. Mirouer 21:3–8, pp. 78–79. Ores, Amours, dit Raison, encore vous fais je une demande, car ce livre dit que ceste Ame prent congé aux Vertuz en tous faiz, et vous dictes que les Vertuz son tousjours avec telle Ames plus parfaictement que avec nul aultre. Ce sont deux paroles contraires, ce me semble, dit Raison; je ne les sçay entendre.

The Latin uses the expression *accepit licentiam* for the French *prent congé aux*

Vertuz: O Amor, ait Ratio, adhuc rogo vos de una petitione. Quia este liber dicit quod ista anima accepit licentiam a virtutibus omnino, et vos dicitis quod omnes virtutes sunt continue cum talibus animabus perfectius quam cum aliis quibuscumque. Ista sunt duo contraria, ut mihi videtur, ait Ratio, nescio bene intelligere.

The language of "taking leave of virtues" appears in almost identical form in books 6 and 8.

31. *Mirouer* 21: 9–12, pp. 78–81: Je t'en appaiseray, dit Amour. C'est vérité que ceste Ame a prins congé aux Vertuz, quant a l'usage d'elles et quant au desir de ce que elles demandent, mais les vertuz n'ont mie prins congié a elles, car elles sont tousjours avec elles.

See also 6:3–11, pp. 24–25, where the soul announces that she had long been a slave to the virtues, but is now liberated. Addressing herself directly to the virtues, she declares: but now "I take leave of of you forever [*je prens congé de vous a tousjours*]. My heart will be more free [*plus franc*] and more gay [*plus gay*]."

32. At this point of annihilation, the soul wills nothing and seeks nothing. The soul's disencumbering of itself of all will and all works reaches an extreme in the repeated assertions that the annihilated soul does not will to do anything for God and does not will to refrain from anything for God. For a critique of those who accuse Porete of quietism, see below, chap. 7.

33. The annihilated soul no longer wills the works of spiritual poverty or religious consolations in this life or in the afterlife. She takes leave of the virtues (finding no further "use" for them). She gives to nature all that nature desires without remorse of conscience. These claims make up the basic content of the surviving articles condemned at Porete's inquisition. The precise location within *The Mirror* of the articles that were condemned has been the object of controversy. The more controversial statements are repeated several times throughout *The Mirror*. After decades of persecution going back to Robert le Bougre, the Beguines had incorporated the persecution process itself into their mystical path and viewed the various procedures as stages along that path. Could it be that some sections of *The Mirror* were composed during the inquisitorial process and in reference to it? In chapters 13–21, mentioned above, Reason cites chapter and verse of what she calls "this book" (*iste liber*), along with the exact points found in the extant articles of condemnation. Reason's character and literary role require her to repeat the same questions; she must tire herself out by repetitive questioning before the soul is freed of her. Even so, one cannot help but wonder if this particular section, beyond such literary rationale and beyond the patience with repetition common in medieval texts, might reflect a response-in-progress to repeated inquisitorial objections and the inability of the "reason" of the inquisitors to understand the "double words" of Lady Love—or even if some passages may have been added by Porete's followers after her death as a direct response to the articles of inquisition.

Article 15 of the condemnation suggests that of all the aspects of the soul's abandonment of the will, it was the nonwilling of the sacraments that seems to have touched off the strongest reaction from the Inquisition. While Colledge finds in chapter 15 of *The Mirror* (a dense discussion of the Eucharist) the text that prompted article 15, Verdeyen, "Le procès," p. 52, argues that it was the more explicit statement in chapter 16:20: *Ceste fille de Syon ne desire ne messes ne sermons, ne jeunes ne oraisons* ("This daughter of Zion desires neither masses nor sermons, fasts nor prayers"). As cited above (n. 22), the formula in 16:20 is echoed in almost identical terms in chapters 9 and 13.

34. *Mirouer* 84:44–47, pp. 240–41: A Dieu en est de ceste oeuvre, qui fait en moy ses oeuvres. Je ne luy doy point de oeuvre, puisque luy mesmes oeuvre en moy; et se je y mectoye le mien, je defferoye son oeuvre.

See also *Mirouer* 41: 11–16, pp. 128–29: "This soul, says Love, is not with herself, and she is therefore excused by everyone. And he in whom she is, performs his work through her, for which she is well acquitted, with the witness of God himself, says Love, who is the worker of this work on behalf of this soul, a soul who has no work whatsoever within her."

Ceste Ame, dit Amour, n'est mie avec elle, par quoi elle doit estre de tous excusee; et celluy en qui elle est fait son oeuvre par elle, pour laquelle chose elle en est bien acquictee, a tesmoing de Dieu mesmes, dit Amour, qui est ouvrier de ceste oeuvre ou prouffit de ceste Ame, laquelle n'a en elle point de oeuvre.

35. *Mirouer* 61: 27–31, pp. 178–79: Le Loingprés est la Trinité mesmes, et luy monstre sa demonstrance, que nous nommons "mouvement," non mye pource que l'Ame se meuve ne la Trinité, mais la Trinité oeuvre a ceste Ame la monstre de sa gloire. De ce ne scet nul parler, sinon la Deité mesmes.

36. *Mirouer* 89: 3–4, pp. 252–53: Cest Ame a tout donné par franchise de noblesse de l'ouevre de la Trinité.

37. *Mirouer* 7:11–25, pp. 26–27: Ainsoys est ce don donné du Treshault, en qui ceste creature est ravie par planté de congnoissance, et demeure rien en son entendement. Et telle ame, qui est devenue rien, a donc tout et si n'a nyent, elle vieult tout et ne vieult nient, elle sçait tout et ne sçait nient.

Et que peut ce estre, dame Amour, dit Raison, que ceste Ame peut vouloir ce que ce livre dit, qui desja a dit devant qu'elle n'a point de voulenté?

Raison, dit Amour, ce n'est mie sa voulenté qui le vieult, mais ainçoys est la voulenté de Dieu, qui le vieult en elle; car ceste Ame ne demoure mie en Amour qui ce luy face vouloir par nul desirer. Ainçoys demoure Amour en elle, qui a prinse sa voulenté, et pource fait Amour sa voulenté d'elle, et adonc oeuvre Amour en elle sans elle.

38. *Mirouer* 39:26–29, pp. 124–25: Car Amour demoure en elle, qui l'muee en luy. Si que ceste ame mesme est Amour, et Amour n'a en luy point de discrecion; mais en toutes choses convient avoir discrecion, excepté en amour.

Quia amor in ea manet qui eam in se mutavit. Ita quod talis anima adnichilata est amor, et amor not habet in se aliquam discrecionem, licet in omnibus sit necessaria discretio praeterquam in amore.

39. *Mirouer* 52: 6–21, pp. 152–55.

40. *Mirouer* 25:10–19, pp. 90–93.

41. *Mirouer* 95: 14–18, pp. 266–67: Ses dons son aussi grans, comme est luy mesme qui a donné cecy, lequel don le meut de luy en luy mesmes. C'est mesmes Amour, et Amour peut quanqu'elle veult; a pource ne peut Crainte, ne Discrecion, ne Raison contre Amour rien dire.

42. This theme in Eckhart is discussed in detail in chap. 6, below.

43. *Mirouer* 94:13–15.

44. *Mirouer* 50:3–6, pp. 148–149: Ceste Ame est emprainte en Dieu, et a sa vraye emprainture detenue par l'union d'amour; et a la maniere que la cire prent la forme du seel, en telle maniere a ceste Ame prinse l'empreinte de cest vray exemplaire.

45. See D. R. Sutherland, "The Love Meditation in Courtly Literature," in *Studies in Medieval French Presented to Alfred Ewert* (Oxford: Clarendon Press, 1961, pp.165–93, especially p. 165.

46. *Mirouer* 88: 53–58, pp. 250–53.

47. See Zum Brunn and Epiney-Burgard, *Women Mystics*, p. 60.

48. *Hadewijch: The Complete Works*, p. 254.

49. Ibid, p. 255. I have changed the capitalization convention of the translation to be coherent with the conventions used throughout this study.

50. Ibid, p. 136, from poem XIX. For a recent examination of the literary character and controversial authorship of the *mengeldichten*, from which the Hadewijch passages in this study are taken, see S. M. Murk-Jansen, *The Measure of Mystic Thought: A Study of Hadewijch's Mengeldichten* (Göppingen: Kümmerle Verlag, 1991).

51. From Zum Brunn and Epiney-Burgard, *Women Mystics*, pp. 138–39, from Poem XXVI. See also Hadewijch d'Anvers *Poèmes des béguines traduits du moyen-neérlandais*, ed. J. B. Porion (Paris: Editions du Seuil, 1954).

52. *Mirouer* 58: 8–11, pp. 168–69: Mais pou ce luy dure. Ca c'est une ouverture a maniere de esclar et de hastive closure, ou l'en ne peut longuement demourer, ne elle n'eust oncques mere, qui de ce sceust parler.

53. *Mirouer* 58:12–23, pp. 168–69: L'ouverture ravissable de l'espandement de celle ouverture fait l'Ame, après sa closure, de la paix de son oeuvre si franche et si noble et si descombree de toutes choses (tant comme la paix dure, que est donnee en ceste ouverture), que qui se garderoit aprés telle avanture franchement, ou cinquiesme estat, san cheoir ou quart, se trouveroit, car ou quart a voulonté et ou cinquiesme n'en a point. Et pource que ou cinquiesme estat, dont ce livre parle, n'a point de voulenté—ou l'Ame demoure après l'oeuvre de Loingprés Ravissable que nous appellons esclar a maniere de ouverture et de hastive closure,—nul ne pouroit croire, dit Amour, la paix sur paix de paix que telle Ame reçoit, se ce n'estoit il mesmes.

54. *Mirouer* 80:35–37, pp. 228–29: Le sourhaulcement ravissable qui me sourprent et joinct au millieu de la mouelle de Divine Amour en quoy je suis fondue, dit ceste Ame.

The Soul answers Reason's question as to who is her closest neighbor. She goes on to say that one should remain silent about this being, since it is impossible to say anything of it.

55. *Mirouer* 90: 28–30, pp. 256–57: Telles gens font le contraire de la sen-

sualiuté, ou aultrement ilz rencherroiennt en perdicion de telle vie, se ilz ne vivoient au contraire de leur plaisance.

56. *Mirouer* 90: 31–37, pp. 256–57: Et ceulx qui sont frans, font tout le contraire. Car, tout ainsi comme il leur convient faire en vie d'esperit tout le contraire de leur voulenté, se ilz ne veulent perdre paix, ainsi, par le contraire, font les frans tout ce qu'il leur plaist, se ilz ne veulent perdre paix, puisque ilz sont venuz en l'estat de franchise, c'est a dire, qu'ilz soient cheuz des Vertuz en Amour, et d'Amour en nient.

57. See Edmund Colledge and Romana Guarnieri, "The Glosses by 'M.N'. and Richard Methley to *The Mirror of Simple Souls*," *Archivio italiano per la storia della pietá* 5 (1968): 357–81.

58. This argument entails an intricate set of apophatic transformations difficult to explain during an inquistorial process bent on judging articles as single propositions taken out of context. Cf. the last section of chap. 6 below.

59. In *The Greater Hekhalot*; see G. Scholem, *Major Trends in Jewish Mysticism* (New York: Schocken, 1941), pp. 46–47.

60. See the examples from Hallaj and Niffari, M. Sells, "Bewildered Tongue: The Semantics of Mystical Union in Islam," in M. Idel and B. McGinn, eds., *Mystical Union and Monotheistic Faith* (New York: Macmillan, 1989), pp. 101–15.

61. See R. Ruether, "Misogyny and Virginal Feminism in the Fathers of the Church," in idem, ed., *Images of Women in the Jewish and Christian Traditions* (New York: Simon and Schuster, 1974), pp. 150–83. The following passages cited by Ruether are particularly germane to Porete's view of nature, love, and the "fall of love": the first, on p. 161, from Jerome to the virgin Demetrias, *Ep.*, 130.10: "You must act against nature or rather above nature if you are to forswear your natural functions, to cut off your own root, to cull no fruit but that of virginity, to abjure the marriage bed, to shun intercourse with men and, while in the body, to live as though out of it"; and the second, on p. 176, from Augustine's *De Sermone Dom. in Monte*, 41: "A good Christian is one who in the same woman loves the creature of God whom he desires to be transformed and renewed, but hates in her the corruptible and mortal conjugal connection, sexual intercourse and all that pertains to her as a wife" (translation reworded to clarify grammar). For such views as they were reflected in twelfth-century Christianity, see Marie-Thérèse d'Alverny, "Comment les théologiens et les philosophes voient la femme," *Cahiers de civilisations médiévale* 20 (1977): 105–26. Cf. Augustine, *Ad Imperfectum Contra Julianum* 6,25: "Nature, which the first human being harmed, is miserable. . . . What passed to women was not the burden of Eve's fertility, but of her transgression. Now fertility operates under this burden, having fallen away from God's blessing." Trans. Elaine Pagels in *Adam, Eve, and the Serpent* (New York: Random House, 1988), p. 133. For a comparison of Porete and Eckhart on the specific issue of fertility, see chap. 7 below.

62. Colledge has suggested that Marguerite was confused in the way the stages were presented and that the seven-stage schema contradicts another schema in *The Mirror*: that of the three deaths. Hollywood shows, however,

that the three deaths and seven stages fit together well. The first two stages correspond to the life of grace born of the death of sin. The second two stages correspond to the life of the spirit born of the death of nature. The final stages correspond to the death of the spirit and the death of the life of works. Stages one and three are stages of contentment with one's position. Stages two and four are stages of struggle to move beyond it. A. Hollywood, "The Soul as Virgin Wife," chap. 2 (cited above, n. 17).

63. *Mirouer* 81: 3–11, pp. 230–31: Or a ceste Ame, dit Amour, son droit non du nient en quoy elle demoure. Et puisque elle est nient, il ne luy chault de nient, ne d'elle ne de se proesmes ne de Dieu mesmes. Car elle est si petite, que elle ne se peut trouver; et toute chose creee luy est si loing, qu'elle ne le peut sentire; et Dieu est si grant, que elle n'en peut rien comprendre; et pour tel nient est elle cheue en certaineté de nient savoir et en certaineté de nient vouloir. Et ce nient, dont nous parlons, dit Amour, luy donne le tout.

64. *Mirouer* 51:28 (Latin, 51:24). The full passage, 51:17–30, pp. 150–53, reads: This is the end of my work, says this soul, to will nothing always. For just as I will nothing, says this soul, I am alone in him without myself, and completely freed, and when I will anything, she says, I am with myself and I lose my freedom. But when I wish nothing and have lost everything out of my will, then I lack nothing. Free being maintains me. I will nothing in anything.

O very precious Hester, says Love, who has lost all your usages, and through this loss have the usage of doing nothing, you are truly precious. For in truth this usage and this loss is made in the nothingness of your love, and in this nothingness, says Love, you are passed out and remain dead. But you live, beloved, says Love, in his will in all. That is his chamber and it pleases him for you to stay there.

65. *Mirouer* 41:7–10, pp. 128–29.

66. *Mirouer* 87:3–4, pp. 246–47.

67. *Mirouer* 87: 11–13, pp. 246–47: Hay, Dieux, dit Raison, comment ose l'en ce dire? Je ne l'ose escouter. Je deffaulx vrayement, dame Ame, en vous oïr: le cueur m'est failly. Je n'ay point de vie.

68. *Mirouer* 87: 14–25: pp. 248–49: Helas! pourquoy n'est pieça, dit ceste Ame, ceste morte! Car tant comme je vous ay eue, dame Raison, je n'ay peu tenir franchement mon heritage, et ce qui estoit et est mien; mais maintenant je le puis tenir franchement, puisque je vous ay d'amour a mort navree.

Or est morte Raison, dit ceste Ame.

Donc diray je, dit Amour, ce que Raison diroit, se elle estoit en vous en vie. Elle demanderoit a vous, amye de nous, dit Amour a ceste Ame qui est mesmes Amour et nulle aultre chose que Amour, depuis que Amour eut /de/ sa divine bonté Raison et les oeuvres des Vertuz dessoubz ses piez gictee et a mort menee, sans nul retour.

69. For one of several references, see *Mirouer* 9:29–39, pp. 34–35, where Dame Amour places this *entendement* beyond the reach of *maistres de sens de nature*, *maistres d'escripture*, and *ceulx qui demourent en amour de l'obedience des vertuz*. In the prelude, even the beguines are included in the list (122: 96–101, p. 344):

Beguines dient que je erre,
   prestres clers et prescheurs,
Augustin et carmes,
   et les freres mineurs.

70. See chap. 12 of *The Mirror* where the important concept of the "understanding of love" is figured as a character in the court of love, as *La Haultesse d'Entendement d'Amour*, pp. 49–52.

71. The literature in this area is large. For one important study, see Kathryn Gravdal, *Ravishing Maidens: Writing Rape in Medieval French Literature and Law* (Philadelphia: University of Pennsylvania Press, 1991. Of particular interest (pp. 1–12) is Gravdal's excursus on the semantic field and legal definitions of *raptus*.

72. This expression occurs earlier in Beatrice of Nazareth, where love for deity is spoken of as "without a why," *sonder enich waeromme*: *Seven manieren*, II, p. 7, ll. 4–6. See Zum Brunn and Epiney-Burgard, *Women Mystics*, p. 81, and n. 24, p. 198.

73. *Mirouer* 100:22–25, pp. 276–77: Il n'a nient plus a faire de luy ne d'aultruy ne de Dieu mesmes, nient plus que se il ne fust mie; si que il est.

74. *Mirouer* 111: 10–21, pp. 302–3:
Love: But he who has peace, stays willing nothing there where he was before he had a will. Divine has nothing "for which" it might reprehend him.
O God, how well said! says the freed soul. But it is appropriate for him to do this without me, just as he created me without me of his divine *bonté*. Now I am, says this soul, a soul created of him without me, to work between him and me many works of virtue, him for me and me for him, as long as I flow back into him. I cannot be in him until he places me with him without me, just as he placed me without me of himself. It is the uncreated *bonté* that loves the *bonté* which she has created. Now the uncreated *bonté* has her own free will. She gives us our own free will of her *bonté*, outside of her power, without a why, except for ourselves and the very being of *bonté*.
Hee, Dieux, comme c'est bien dit! Dit l'Ame Enfranchie; mais il convient qu'il face ce sans moy, ainsi comme il me creat sans moy de sa bonté divine. Or suis je, dit ceste Ame, ame cree /e/ de luy sans moy, pour o/e/uvrer entre luy et moy fortes oeuvres de vertuz, luy pour moy et moy pour luy, tant que je reflusse en luy; et si ne puis estre en luy, se il ne m'y mect sans moy de luy, aisi comme it me fist san moy de lui mesme. C'est la Bonté increee qui ayme la bonté qu'elle a creee. Or a Bonté increee, de son propre, franche voulenté; que nous donne de sa bonté aussi franche voulenté, hors de sa puissance, sans nul pourquoy, sinon que pour nous mesmes, et pour estre de sa bonté.

75. *Mirouer* 89:1–11, pp. 252–53. See below, chap. 7 for the French text and more detailed discussion.

76. See below, chap. 7, for further discussion of this "exchange of wills" in Porete and in consonant texts from Meister Eckhart.

77. *Mirouer* 91: 7–23, pp. 256–59: C'est droit, dit Amour, sa voulenté est nostre: elle a passé la Rouge Mer, ses ennemis son dedans demourez. Son plaisir est nostre voulenté, par la purté de l'unité du vouloir de la Deité, ou

nous l'avons enclose. Sa voulenté est nostre, car elle est cheue de grace en parfection de l'oeuvre des Vertuz, et des Vertuz en Amour, de d'Amour en Nient, et de Nient en Clarifiement de Dieu, qui se voit des yeulx de sa majesté, que en ce point l'a de luy clarifiee. Et si est se remise en luy, que elle ne voit ne elle ne luy; et pource il se voit tout seul, de sa bonté divine. Il sera de luy en telle bonté ce qu'il savoit de luy ains que elle ne fust mie, quant il luy donna sa bonté, dont il la fist dame. Ce fut Franche Voulenté, qu'il ne peut de luy ravoir sans le plaisir de l'Ame. Or l'a maintenant, sans nul pourquoy, en tel point comme il l'avoit, ains que telle en fust dame. Ce n'est nul fors qu'il; nul n'ayme fors qu'il, car nul n'est fors que luy, et pource ayme tout seul, et se voit tout seul, et loe tout seul de son estre mesme.

The Latin offers an interesting and clearer alternative to the difficult passage (91: 13–17) beginning with *Et si est si remise* ("And she is so returned)":

Et est ita in ipsum resoluta quod non videt nec se nec ipsum. Et ideo ipse Deus videt se solum sua divina bonitate. Ipse ita se rehabet de ipsa in tali bonitate, sicut se habebat de se, antequam esset, quando dedit ei suam bonitatem de qua fecit eam dominam.

78. *Mirouer* 89:1–11, pp. 252–53. This text and the issues of exchange of will and living without a why are examined in more detail below, chap. 7.

79. The Latin gives *intermedium* for *entredeux*. The French *entredeux* provides a more personal play—"go-between" or "interloper"—upon the giving up of all mediums (*moyens, intermedium*). *Mirouer* 93: 23–24, pp. 262–63: Et pource eut elle, sans nul entredeux en l'ame d'elle, en ung corps mortel de la Trinité glorieuse vie.

80. *An yakūn kamā kāna idh kāna qabla an yakūna*. See Abdel Kader, *The Life, Personality and Writings of Al-Junayd* (London: Luzac, 1962), Arabic text, pp. 56–57.

81. Sahl ibn ʿAbdallah at-Tustarī, *Tafsīr al-Qurʾān al-ʿAẓīm* (Cairo: Dār al-Kutub al-Gharbiyya al-Kubrā, 1329/1911). pp. 40–41. For a translation of the relevant passages and a discussion of this important theory in Tustari, see Gerhard Böwering, *The Mystical Vision of Existence in Classical Islam: The Qurʾānic Hermeneutics of the Ṣūfī Sahl at-Tustarī, d. 283/896* (Berlin: Walter de Gruyter, 1980), pp. 153–57.

82. See M. K. Pope, *From Latin to Modern French with Especial Consideration of Anglo-Norman* (New York: Barnes and Noble, 1934, 1961), pp. 322–24, especially on the confusion of *lui* with *li* (#840:1), p. 324.

83. *Mirouer* 100: 27–32, pp. 276–77: Pource l'appelle je clere, que elle surmonte l'aveugle vie adnientie; l'aveugle soustient a ceste cy ses piez; la clere est la plus noble et la plus gentile. Elle ne scet qui soit, ne Dieu ne homme; car elle n'est mie; mais Dieu le scet de luy, en luy, pour elle, d'elle mesmes [Latin: Sed Deus scit hoc de se in ipsa, pro seipsa de seipso]. Telle dame ne quiert mais Dieu; elle n'a de quoy, elle n'a de luy que faire. Il ne lui fault mie; pourquoy le querroit elle donc?

See *Mirouer* 81: 21–22, pp. 230–31: If God works his work in her, it is of him in her without her for him/her: Se Dieu fait son oeuvre en elle, c'est de luy en elle, sans elle, pour elle. // Si Deus facit in ea opus suum, hoc est de se in ipsa propter se sine ipsa.

The ambiguity recurs in verses 24–27 of the same passage. A similar ambiguity occurs in *Mirouer* 95: 14–16: (translated and discussed above, 124: Ses dons son aussi grans comme est luy mesmes qui a donné cecy, lequel don le meut de luy en luy mesmes // Ista enim dona sunt ita magna, sicut est ipsemet, cuius sunt quae donat isti animae. Quae etiam dona mutant eam in illummet propter ipsam.

84. The historical point was made by Denis de Rougement, *Love in the Western World*, trans. Montgomery Belgion (New York, 1956), though Rougement's theoretical points are flawed by a substantive understanding of deity and of union. For a recent discussion of the issue, see Maria Rosa Menocal, *The Arabic Role in Medieval Literary History: A Forgotten Heritage* (Philadelphia: University of Pennsylvania Press, 1987).

85. *Mirouer* 93:13–20, pp. 260–63: especially 16–17: Elle ne savoit mie, quant elle le queroit, que Dieu fust partout.

86. *Mirouer* 93: 8–13, pp. 260–61: Mais quant elle fut ou desert, Amour l'emprint, qui l'adnientit, et pource oeuvra adonc Amour en elle pour elle sans elle, et vesquit adonc de divine vie, qui luy fist avoir glorieuse vie. Adonc trouva elle Dieu en elle, sans le querir, et aussi elle n'ot de quoy, puisque Amour l'ot emprinse.

87. See Ioan Culianu's discussion of the medieval understanding of life as *maesta*, in *Eros and Magic in the Renaissance*, trans. M. Cook (Chicago: University of Chicago Press, 1987), originally published as *Eros et magie à la Renaissance*, 1984.

88. Chap. 7, below, will take up in detail the remarkable consonances and contrasts between the writings of Porete and Eckhart. Special attention will be given to Eckhart's inversion of the standard Martha and Mary hierarchy, his equation of courtly nobility with the common and equal, and his account of the "work" that takes place within the soul, and to how these Eckhartian positions play upon Porete's treatment of the same issues.

89. See chap. 15 of *The Mirror*, for example, where memory, understanding, and love in the annihilated soul are associated with the father, the son, and the spirit. De Longchamp (*Le Miroir*, p. 242, n. to 9:1) sees in this trilogy the reflection of Augustinian trinitarian anthropology. De Longchamp points to chapters 9, 10, 57, 80, 92, 95 in particular as reflecting the "Augustinian climate" that permeates *The Mirror*.

90. *Mirouer* 21:44–47, pp. 82–83: Je suis Dieu, dit Amour, car amour est Dieu, et Dieu est amour, et ceste Ame est Dieu par condicion d'amour, et je suis Dieu par nature divine, et ceste Ame l'est par droicture d'amour. Si que ceste precieuse amye de moy est aprinse et menee de moy sans elle, car elle est muee en moy.

91. Hadewijch, *The Complete Works*, p. 354.

92. Ibid, pp. 354–55. Also implicated in fire is the name of Hell, the seventh name, p. 356:

> Of this Love wherein I suffer.
> For there is nothing Love does not engulf and damn,
> And no one who falls into her

And whom she seizes comes out again,
Because no grace exists there.
As Hell turns everything to ruin,
In Love nothing else is acquired
But disquiet and torture without pity;
Forever to be in unrest,
Forever assault and new persecution;
To be wholly devoured and engulfed
In her unfathomable essence,
To founder unceasingly in heat and cold,
In the deep, insurmountable darkness of Love.
This outdoes the torments of love.

93. *Mirouer* 25:10–19, pp. 90–93: Celluy qui art n'a mie froit, et celluy qui se noye n'a mie soif. Or est telle Ame, dit Amour, si arse en la fournaise du feu d'amour, qu'elle est devenue proprement feu, par quoy elle ne sent point de feu, car en elle mesmes elle est feu, par la vertu d'Amour qui l'a muee ou feu d'amour. Ce feu art de luy en tous lieux et en tous momens de heure sans prendre nulle matere, ne povoir vouloir prendre, fors que de luy mesmes. Car quiconques sent de Dieu par matere qu'il voye ou oye dehors luy, ne pour labour qu'il face de luy, cil n'est mie tout feu, ainçoys y a matere avec tel feu.

Dame Amour goes on then to speak of joy, using the complementary metaphor of water, saying that the freed soul swims in the sea of joy (*Mirouer* 28: 2–7, pp. 96–97): "This soul swims in the sea of joy, that is in the sea of delights flowing forth from the divinity. She feels no joy. She is joy itself and swims and flows in joy without feeling any joy. She remains in joy and in her and is herself joy by virtue of joy who has transformed her into itself."

Telle Ame, dit Amour, nage en la mer de joye, c'est en la mer de delices fluans et decourans de la Divinité, et si ne sent nulle joye, car elle mesmes est joye, et si nage et flue en joye, sans sentir nulle joye, car elle demoure en Joye, et Joye demoure en elle; c'est elle mesme joye par la vertuz de Joye, qui l'a muee en lui.

94. *Mirouer* 64: 12–13, pp. 186–87: Ceste amour, dont nous parlons, c'est l'unions d'amans, et feu embrasé qui art sans souffler [L: qui ardet absque sufflante].

95. Thomas Aquinas, *Summa Theologiae*, 2a2ae, 11, 3, responsio (Blackfriars edition, New York, 1989: 32:88–89).

96. Verdeyen, "Le procès , p.82.

97. Some have argued that the inquisitorial authorities really intended some kind of mercy here. That argument falls apart in the face of consistent evidence that the Church authorities made clear to the secular arm in no uncertain terms exactly what it was expected to do, i.e., carry out the death penalty. See A. S. Tuberville, *Medieval Heresy and the Inquisition* (London: Crosby Lockwood and Son, 1920), p. 222, citing Vacandard, Lea, and Langlois. Tuberville goes on (p. 222, n. 2) to cite Vacandard: "We regret to state, however, that the civil judges were not supposed to take these words literally. If they were at all inclined to do so, they would have been quickly called to a sense

of their duty by being excommunicated." Equally compelling is the negative evidence: No case has been cited of an inquisitorial authority rushing to the secular authority before or after an execution and explaining that *citra mortem* means "short of death." Cf. A. C. Shannon, *The Popes and Heresy in the Thirteenth Century* (Villanova: Augustinian Press, 1949), pp. 102–16.

98. See the account by Guibert of Nogent in Walter Wakefield and Austin Evans, *Heresies of the High Middle Ages: Selected Sources* (New York: Columbia University Press, 1969), p. 104: "Meanwhile, we proceeded to the Council of Beauvais to consult the bishops about what should be done in this case. But during that time, the faithful people, fearing clerical leniency, rushed to the prison, seized the men, and having laid a fire under them, burnt them all together outside the city. The people of God were righteously wrathful against them, lest their cancer be spread." Cf. Edward Peters, ed., *Heresy and Authority in Medieval Europe: Documents in Translation* (Philadelphia: University of Pennsylvania Press, 1980), p. 74.

99. Aquinas, *Summa Theologiae,* supplementum tertiae partis, q. 97, art. 5. The denial that inquisitorial fire and hellfire are the same is made in the objection to the corporeality of hellfire, but Aquinas lets it stand. For the connection between hellfire and burning of heretics in popular accounts, see Peter the Venerable's account of Peter of Bruys in Wakefield and Evans, *Heresies*, p. 121: "After this impious man had assuredly made the transit from fire to fire, from brief passing flame to eternal flame." Cf. ibid., p. 244, for Caesarius of Heisterbach's account of an incident in Cologne in 1163. After the alleged heretics are burned in the cemetery of the Jews, a young girl throws herself upon the body of her master, "with him descending into hell to burn forever."

100. A good example is given in Wakefield and Evans, *Heresies*, p. 249, translated from Hugh of Poitiers, *Historia Vizeliacensis monasterii*, republished in *Recueil des historiens des Gaules et de la France*, ed. Gouqet et al., 24 vols (Paris 1738–1904) 12: 317–44; also in Migne, *P.L.* 194: 1561–1682. Hugh recounts that heretics arrested at Vézelay agreed to undergo ordeal by water. On hearing of the ordeal, the congregation shouts "thanks be to God!" and when the abbot asks what should be done "with those who remain obdurate," the congregation shouts "Let them be burned! Let them be burned!" One of the heretics was almost unanimously judged to have failed his first ordeal by water, and was given a second ordeal at his request. Hugh's account continues: "But the water scarcely received him at all. Thus twice condemned, he was sentenced by all to the fire. But the abbot came to his assistance and ordered instead that he be banished after a public flogging. Others of the accused, however, to the number of seven, were given to the flames and were burned in the vale of Ecouan."

Another famous account concerns heretics arrested near Soissons. See Wakefield and Evans, *Heresies*, pp. 101–4, translated from Guibert of Nogent. Cf. Peters, *Heresy and Authority*, 72–74; J. Russell, *Dissent and Reform in the Early Middle Ages* (Berkeley: University of California Press, 1965), pp. 46–47; Moore, *Birth of Popular Heresy*, pp. 67–69. For Guibert, see John F. Benton, ed. and trans., *Self and Society in Medieval France: The Memoirs of Abbot Guibert of Nogent* (New York: Harper and Row, 1970), and Georges Bourgin, ed., *Guibert de Nogent: Historie de sa vie (1053–1124)* (Editions A. and J Picard: Paris, 1907). Wakefield's translation is from Bourgin's text, pp. 212–15. The events of 1114 are in summary: (a) The alleged heretics are given communion at mass, (b) the Bishop chants litany and performs exorcism; (c) the accused take oath not to have taught contrary to the faith; (d) One of them, Clement, "when cast into the vat, floated on the top like a stick, at which sight the whole church was carried away with boundless joy [p. 104]. (e) The people, fearing clerical leniency, seize the heretics and burn them together outside the city, "Lest their cancer be spread."

101. See the end of Guibert's account, p. 104, cited in the previous note: "lest their cancer spread." Cf. R. I. Moore, "Heresy as Disease," in W. Lourdaux and D. Verhelst, eds., *The Concept of Heresy in the Middle Ages* (Leuven: University Press, 1976), pp. 1–12. Chilean dictator Augusto Pinochet defended the atrocities that took place after the 1973 coup against the Allende presidency with the metaphor of a surgeon who must cut out cancer from the patient, the surgery causing necessary but ultimately beneficial pain.

102. Aquinas, *Summa Theologiae*, 2a2ae, 11, 3, responsum (Blackfriars edition, 32: 88–89). Thomas cites Jerome's comment as it appeared in the *Decretum* of Gratian, an influential canonical collection of the early twelfth century. It is not clear from this passage by itself whether Jerome intended expulsion or a more drastic penalty. What Aquinas thinks the metaphors mean, however, is clear both from the immediate argument (on behalf of death for heretics) and from the historical context of the time, where the cutting off of the dead flesh was being carried out in an organized fashion by the Inquisition. In an earlier argument on behalf of compulsion in religion, Aquinas cites Augustine's refutation of those who cry that "one is free to believe or not to believe." Augustine argued that Christ set the example for compulsion by compelling Paul to believe. *Summa Theologiae*, 2a2ae,10,8 (Blackfriars edition, 32: 62–63); Augustine, *Ad Bonifacium Comitem. Ep.* CLXXXV, 6. *P.L.* 33, 803. In the same passage, Aquinas cites Augustine's argument (in *Cointra Epistolam Permeniani* III, 2. *P.L.* 43, 92) that the "tares and wheat" parable shouldn't be used to allow the judgment of heretics to be put off. When a heretic has no defenders and there is no danger of a schism, then "the severity of the discipline should not sleep." In conclusion, he cites Augustine yet again, from the same text (*Ad Bonifacium*): "No one wishes a heretic to perish. But the house of David did not deserve to have peace unless his son Absalom had been killed in the war he raised against his faith."

103. Recounted by the archdeacon of Oxford, courtier to Henry II, and exuberant storyteller Walter Map (d. ca. 1209), *De Nugis Curialium* (Courtiers' Trifles), ed. and trans. M. R. James (Oxford: Clarendon Press, 1983), pp. 118–25, and retold in Wakefield and Evans, *Heresies*, pp. 255–56.

See Wakefield and Evans, pp. 148–50, for an account of the heresy of "a certain Arnold" from Brescia who urged revolt against Church authority in Rome. He was burned and his ashes were scattered on the Tiber, "lest his body be held in veneration by the mad populace." This passage is cited by Wakefield and Evans from Charles Mierow, trans., *The Deeds of Frederick Barbarossa by Otto of Freising and His Continuator, Rahwin* (New York, 1953), pp. 61, 142–44.

For a cleric who saves heretics from a crowd who wishes to burn them, see Wakefield and Evans, *Heresies*, pp. 140–41.

On the heretics condemned in 1022 near Soisson: "Unconcerned, they showed no fear of the fire, predicted that they would emerge unscathed from the flames, and laughed as they were bound on the pyre. They were promptly reduced to ashes, so completely that not a trace of their bones was found." Wakefield and Evans, *Heresies*, pp. 75–76, translated from Adémar of Chabannes, *Chronique*, ed. Jules Chavanon (Paris, 1897), pp. 184–85.

104. Wakefield and Evans, *Heresies*, p. 120. There is an interesting continuity between the martyrdom of early Christians at Vienne and the inquisitorial practices at Vienne several centuries later. In both cases those accused of theological impropriety were also subject to wild accusations of sexual orgies. The attitude of the accused toward their imminent death is similar. But one essential difference remains. The Romans applied a variety of death penalties to the Christians. From the mid-thirteenth century on, burning became the primary sentence for relapsed heretics in Europe. See W. H. C. Frend, *Martyrdom and Persecution in the Early Church* (Grand Rapids: Baker House, 1965, 1981), pp. 1–30.

105. Verdeyen, "Le procès," p. 89.

106. See Tuberville, *Medieval Hersey*, p. 219.

107. See Verdeyen, "Le procès," p. 61: "Unless either before or after the sentence she should repent, returning directly and willingly to the unity of the catholic faith and abjuring her error in public acquiescence to the judgement of her inquisitor" (nisi confestim ante sententiam vel post penituerit recurrens sponte ad fidei catholice unitatem et errorem suum ad arbitrium ipsius inquisitoris publice consentiens abiurare). "In which case, in order to obtain satisfaction for her great excess and, lest she infect others with her pestilent doctrines, she should be placed in perpetual imprisonment."

108. Penelope Johnson, "Fire in the Middle Ages," a talk given at the Delaware Valley Medieval Association, University of Pennsylvania, November 3, 1990.

109. See the account by Guibert of Nogent concerning the heretics arrested near Soissons: "They hold meetings in cellars and secret places, *the sexes mingling freely.* When candles have been lighted, in the sight of all, light women with bare buttocks (it is said) offer themselves to a certain one lying behind them. Directly the candles are extinguished, they all cry out together "Chaos" and each one lies with her who first comes to hand" (emphasis added). Wakefield and Evans, *Heresies*, p. 103. Also recounted in Peters, *Heresy*, p. 73: "They have their meetings in underground vaults or unfrequented cellars, *without distinction of sex.* After they have lighted candles, some loose woman lies down for all to watch, and, so it is said, uncovers her buttocks, and they present their candles at her from behind; and as soon as

the candles are put out, they shout 'Chaos' from all sides, and everyone fornicates with whatever woman comes first to hand" (emphasis added). The same account in Wakefield and Evans, *Heresies*, p. 104, states that the report that one of the heretics had failed the trial by water, "brought together a *great throng of both sexes*, such as none of those present recalled having seen" (emphasis added).

Walter Map (cited above, n. 106) also recounts the typical tales of bestiality and orgy in presenting his heretics. In this case, after kissing various parts of the anatomy of a black cat, each heretic "seizes the man or woman next to him and they commingle as long as each is able to prolong the wantonness."

See also the story of the ten canons of the Church of the Holy Cross at Orléans who were accused of being Manicheans in 1022. Upon the apparition of a demon in the likeness of a beast, the heretics were said to have sex with "mother, sister, or nun," as an act of piety (Wakefield and Evans, *Heresies*, p. 79). Wakefield and Evans translate the account from *Vetus Aganon* vi.iii, ed. Benjamin-Edmé-Charles Guérard, in *Cartulaire de l'abbaye de Saint-Père de Chartres* (Collection des cartulaires de France, vol. 1; in *Collection de documents inédits sur l'histoire de France* (Paris, 1840), 1:109-15.

110. Wakefield and Evans, *Heresies*, p. 103 (and Peters, *Heresy*, p. 73): Any offspring from this union results in the following practice: the child is passed through fire, thrown continually through it from hand to hand until dead and reduced to ashes. Ashes are used to make bread, "of which a morsel is given to each as a sacrament. Once that has been eaten, it is very rarely that one is brought back to his senses from that heresy." See also Wakefield and Evans, *Heresies*, p. 76-81. According to this account (1022 C.E.), when a child was born, heretics at Orléans cremated it, then preserved its ashes for veneration like that given the body of Christ and as a gift to the sick at the moment of death—as a "viaticum." Queen Constance struck out the eye of one of the heretics, Stephen, her confessor. The heretics were then burned along with the evil ashes taken from incinerated infants.

111. This comparison is argued by Lerner, *The Heresy of the Free Spirit*, pp. 10–34, and passim.

112. Ernest W. McDonnell, *The Beguines and Beghards in Medieval Culture* (New York: Octagon Books, 1969), p. 367 (emphasis added). The same list of characteristics is repeated by McDonnell verbatim (p. 492) in referring to those uncloistered beguines not bound to a "well ordered" existence, what he elsewhere calls the "libertine type" (p. 496). To my knowledge there is no evidence whatsoever to indicate the character of Porete's private life; at any rate McDonnell cites none and feels no need to cite any. Cf. Katharina M. Wilson, ed., *Medieval Women Writers* (Athens: University of Georgia Press, 1984), pp. 1–30, and Gwendolyn Bryant, "The French Heretic Beguine: Marguerite Porete," in the same volume, pp. 204–26.

113. Thus in the canon lawyer's advice to the inquisitor (Verdeyen, "Le procès," p. 61), Porete "must be held as a heretic and definitively condemned as a heretic and relinquished to the secular authority to receive the penalty owed for the quality of her crime": pro heretica est habenda et diffinitive

tamquam heretica condempnanda reliquendaque curie seculari, debitam ultionem pro qualitate criminis receptura.

114. For the characterization of Porete as a "high priestess" of the free-spirit heresy, see Colledge, Historical Introduction, E. Colledge and B. McGinn, ed. and trans., *Meister Eckhart: The Essential Sermons, Commentaries, Treatises and Defense* (New York: Paulist Press, 1981), p. 8; for "heresiarch," see Ernest W. McDonnell, *The Beguines and Beghards*, p. 490 (see also p. 492). For the depiction of *The Mirror* as a "work of heresy written by a teacher of false doctrine skilled in concealing her unorthodoxy," see E. Colledge and R. Guarnieri, "The Glosses by 'M.N.' and Richard Melthey to *The Mirror of Simple Souls*," *Archivio Italiano per al storia della pietà* 5 (1968): 381–82. The charge of concealment is a commonplace. See also McDonnell, *The Beguines and Beghards*, p. 366, who says of "nonregular" beguines: "Far from revealing the true consequences of their doctrine, it was their practice to win appeal by employing symbolical language and allegorical interpretation of scripture." For a critique of Guarnieri's views on the alleged involvement of Beatrice and Hadewijch in the heresy of the free spirit, see Bernard Spaapen, "Le Mouvement des 'frères du libre esprit' et les mystique flamandes du XIIIème siècle," *Revue d'ascétique et de mystique* (1966): 423–37. Spaapen argues that Guarnieri takes references to the free spirit out of context and thus misrepresents the intent of the writers. Spaapen makes no analysis of Guarnieri's treatment of Porete, though the basic flaw in methodology he demonstrates could well apply to her treatment of Porete as well. Cf. R. Guarnieri, "Fréres du libre esprit," *Dictionnaire de spiritualité ascétique et mystique*, 5 (1964): 1241–68.

115. Lerner, *The Heresy of the Free Spirit*, passim. Lerner notes that trials of alleged free-spirit heretics are devoid of any clear information concerning an organized ideological trend. De Longchamp accepts the existence of a free-spirit heresy, but argues that Porete had no part in it. See his introduction to Porete, *Le Miroir des âmes simples et anéanties*.

116. McDonnell, *The Beguines and Beghards*, p. 491, writes of her "audacity" in presenting her prohibited book to Bishop John of Châlons and in extending her "propaganda" to Paris, and in "obstinately" refusing to take the preliminary oath. Colledge states that "Despite all the Soul's protestations of her wretched [sic] nothingness, the entire book is characterized by a stubborn, willful determination to persist in its opinions, by a spiritual arrogance which could surely find no place in a truly 'Simple Soul'." E. Colledge, "Liberty of Spirit: The Mirror of Simple Souls" in *Theology of Renewal*, 2, ed. L. K. Shook (Montreal, n.p. 1968), p. 114. See Lerner, *The Heresy of the Free Spirit*, p. 201, n.3, for a strong argument against the view that Porete concealed her heretical doctrines in obscure language.

117. See Zum Brunn and Epiney-Burgard, *Women Mystics*, p. 97, who note that in her "List of the Perfect," Hadewijch of Antwerp refers to a Beguine condemned to death by le Bougre "for her just love [*Minne*]." Le Bougre conducted persecutions in Flanders from 1235 to 1238. See also C. H. Haskins, "Robert le Bougre and the Beginnings of the Inquisition in Northern France," in idem, *Studies in Medieval Culture* (Oxford: Clarendon, 1929), and

Jean Guiraud, *Histoire de L'Inquisition au Moyen Age* (Paris: Editions Auguste Picard, 1938) 2:185–218.

118. *Mirouer* 39:27–29, pp. 124–25.

119. See Longchamps (above. n. 12) and Hollywood (above, n. 17).

120. 1 Cor. 13:12. See, for example, Longchamps, *Le Miroir*, introduction, pp. 16–19.

121. *Mirouer* 96–97, pp. 267–72.

122. *Mirouer* 88: 53–58, pp. 250–53: Mais ceulx qui tousjours loyaulx luy sont, sont tousjours sourprins d'Amour, et adnientiz par Amour, et tous desrobez d'Amour, et si n'ont cure fors d'Amour, pour souffrir et endurer a tousjourmés les tourmens, pose qu'ilz fussent aussi grans, comme Dieu est grant en bonté. Ne oncques n'ama finement l'Ame que de ce doubte, que ce ne soit verité.

123. *Mirouer* 65:6–9, pp. 186–87.

Chapter Six

1. Except where noted, all citations from Eckhart are from Josef Quint and Josef Koch, eds., *Meister Eckhart: Die deutschen und lateinischen Werke* (Stuttgart and Berlin: Kohlhammer, 1936–). The German works, edited by Quint, will be cited by the number of the particular sermon or treatise, followed by DW, volume number and page. The Latin works, edited by Koch, will be cited by the name of the treatise or sermon and the section number, followed by LW, volume number and page. The translations, unless otherwise noted, are my own. In making them I have consulted the translations of Bernard McGinn (Latin) and Edmund Colledge (German), and the translations from the German sermons by M. O'C. Walshe. See Edmund Colledge and Bernard McGinn, *Meister Eckhart: The Essential Sermons, Commentaries, Treatises, and Defense* (New York: Paulist Press, 1981); and M. O'C. Walshe, *Meister Eckhart: Sermons and Treatises*, vol. 1 (London: Watkins, 1979). For a representative selection of Eckhart's works in translation, see Colledge and McGinn (which includes an excellent theological introduction); Walshe; and Bernard McGinn and Frank Tobin, *Meister Eckhart: Teacher and Preacher* (New York: Paulist Press, 1986). For a short introduction to Eckhart, see John Caputo, "Fundamental Themes in Meister Eckhart's Mysticism," *The Thomist* 42 (1978): 197–225.

2. Eckhart's contributions to the German language are discussed throughout Frank Tobin's *Meister Eckhart: Thought and Language* (Philadelphia: University of Pennsylvania Press, 1986). See in particular pp. 147–79.

3. Eckhart's terminology for being and existence is complex. See Vladimir Lossky, *Théologie négative et connaisance de Dieu chez Maître Eckhart* (Paris: Vrin, 1960); Emilie Zum Brunn and Alain de Libera, *Maître Eckhart: Métaphysique du verbe et théologie négative* (Paris: Beauchesne, 1984); and Emilie Zum Brunn et al., *Maître Eckhart à Paris: Une critique médiévale de l'ontothéologie* (Paris: Presses Universitaires de France, 1984).

4. *In Sap.* 154; 2:490: Omne quod indistinctione distinguitur, quanto est indistinctius, tanto est distinctius; distinguitur enim ipsa indistinctione. Et e

converso, quanto distinctius, tanto indistinctius, quia distinctione sua dinstiguitur ab indistincto. Igitur quanto distinctius, tanto indisctinctius; et quanto indistinctius, tanto distinctius, ut prius.

"Everything which is distinguished by indistinction, is more distinct insofar as it is indistinct, because it is distinguished by its own indistinction. Conversely, the more distinct it is, the more indistinct it is, because it is distinguished in indistinction by its own distinction. Thus it will be the more indistinct insofar as it is distinct or vice versa."

Cf. *In Sap.* 144: 2:482: 5–7; *Comm. Jn.* 99; LW 3:85; 562; LW 3:489; *In Exodum* 114; 2:112; and Bernard McGinn, "Theological Introduction," in Colledge and McGinn, *Eckhart*, pp. 30–39.

5. For a detailed treatment of essence and existence in Eckhart, see Lossky, *Théologie négative* (cited above, n. 3). For the distinction between essence and existence in Avicenna, see F. Rahman, "Essence and Existence in Avicenna," *Medieval and Renaissance Studies* (Warburg Institute) 4 (1958): 1–16; A.-M. Goichon, *La Distinction de l'essence et de l'existence d'àpres Ibn Sina* (Paris: Brouwer, 1937); and L. E. Goodman, *Avicenna* (New York: Routledge, 1993), pp. 67–83.

6. *Comm.Ex.* 15-16; LW 2:21–22: . . . idem scilicet essentiam et esse, quod soli deo convenit, cuius quiditas est sua anitas, ut ait Avicenna [Met. 8 c. 4], nec habet quiditatem praeter solam anitatem, quam esse significat. Tertio notandum quod repetitio, quod bis ait: "sum qui sum," puritatem affirmationis excluso omni negativo ab ipso deo indicat; rursus ipsius esse quandam in se ipsum et super se ipsum reflexivam conversionem et in se ipso mansionem sive fixionem; adhuc autem quandam bullitionem sive parturitionem sui—in se fervens et in se ipso et in se ipsum liquescens et bulliens, lux in luce et in lucem se toto se totum penetrans, et se toto super se totum conversum et reflexum undique, secundum illud sapientis: "monas monadem gignit—vel genuit—et in se ipsum reflexit amorem—sive ardorem" [Prop. 1, *Liber XXIV Philosophorum*].

Propter hoc *Ioh. 1* dicitur: "in ipso vita erat." Vita enim quandam dicit exseritionem, qua res in se ipsa intumescens se profundit primo in se toto, quodlibet sui in quodlibet sui, antequam effundat et ebulliat extra. Hinc est quod emanatio personarum in divinis ratio est et praevia creationis. Sic enim *Ioh. 1:* "in principio erat verbum"; et post demum: "omnia per ipsum facta sunt."

7. Cf. Eriugena's preference for the Greek terms which he translated as "being with" and "having with" (above, chap. 2) over the Latin *participatio*, which derives from *pars* (part) and *capere* (take). "To take part" in the apophatic sense demands an unsaying or speaking away of the metaphor of part and whole, or a conception of a whole that is more than the sum of its parts and of "parts" that are more than divisions of the whole.

8. *Latin Sermon* XLIX, 3; LW 3:425–26: "Strictly speaking, an image is a simple, formal emanation, transfusive of essence in its entirety, pure and naked. As such it falls under the consideration of the metaphysician. Efficient and final causality, through which the physicist considers natural bodies, are excluded. Image is, therefore, an emanation from the deepest interior, in si-

lence, with everything exterior excluded, a certain life—as if you were to imagine something swelling up out of itself and within itself and boiling within itself, without any conception of boiling over."

Note quod imago proprie est emanatio simplex, formalis transfusiva totius essentiae purae nudae, qualem considerat metaphysicus circumscripto efficiente et fine, sub quibus causis cadunt naturae in consideratione physici. Est ergo imago emanatio ab intimis in silentio et exclusione omnis forinseci, vita quaedam, ac si imagineris rem ex se ipsa et in se ipsa intumescere et bullire in se ipsa necdum cointellecta ebullitione.

9. John 1: 1–6: In principio erat verbum, et verbum erat apud deum, et deus erat verbum. Hoc erat in principio apud deum. Omnia per ipsum facta sunt, et sine ipso factum est nihil, quod factum est; in ipso vita erat, et vita erat lux hominum; et lux in tenebris lucet, et tenebrae eam non comprehenderunt.

10. *Comm. Jn.* 2; LW 3:6: Procedens est in producente, item quod est in ipso ut semen in principio, ut verbum in dicente, item quod est in ipso ut ratio, in qua et per quam procedit quod producitur a producente.

11. *Comm. Jn.* 5; LW 3:7: In analogicis semper productum est inferius, minus, imperfectius et inaequale producenti; in univocis autem semper est aequale, eandem naturam non participans, sed totam simpliciter, integraliter et ex aequo a suo principio accipiens.

12. *Comm. Jn.* 6; LW 3:7.

13. *Summa Theologiae*, 1a, 31, 3, no. 4 (Blackfriars edition, p 60): Et ideo quia in divinis distinctio est secundum personas non autem secundum essentiam, dicimus quod pater est alius a filio, sed non aliud; et e converso dicimus quod sunt unum, sed non unus.

It might be asked how such a distinction could fit in with the Johannine phrase *deus erat verbum* (the word was God), with *deus* being masculine yet the locus of unity rather than distinction. For Thomas, *deus*—although grammatically masculine—is not a proper name, but rather indicates the nature or essence of the divine, its neuter "whatness" (*Summa Theologiae*, 1a, 13, 8–9).

In addition, Thomas makes almost precisely the same distinction that Eckhart makes between the interior processions that remain one with their source, and the procession outward, and cites an almost identical example (the house—cf. Eckhart's chest—in the mind of the craftsman). *Summa Theologiae*, 1a, 27, 2 (Blackfriars edition, 6:6). See especially: "What proceeds according to a procession that is outward [*ad extra*] must be different from that from which it proceeded. But that which proceeds within an intelligible procession need not be different; the more perfectly it proceeds, the more it is one with that from which it proceeded."

Id quod procedit secundum processionem quae est ad extra oportet esse diversum ab eo a quo procedit. Se id quod procedit intra processu intelligibili non oportet esse diversum; immo quantum perfectius procedit tanto magis est unum cum eo a quo procedit.

14. *Comm. Jn.* 6; LW 3:7–8: Licet in analogicis productum sit descendens a producente, est tamen sub principio, not apud ipsum. Item fit aliud in na-

tura, et sic non ipsum principium. Nihilominus tamen, ut est in illo, non est aliud in natura, sed nec aliud in supposito. Arca enim in mente artificis non est arca, sed est vita et intelligere artificis, ipsius conceptio actualis.

15. Following Eriugena, Eckhart gives three meanings to the "was" of "in the beginning was the word": substantial (the word as the substance of the principle); imperfect (the word as being born); and perfect (the word as having been born). Because of the condemnation of Eriugena by Honorious III, Eckhart may not have had access to the original texts of Eriugena. He probably consulted at least the *Clavis physicae*, a paraphrase of the *Periphyseon* that circulated widely after Eriugena's death. See Cappuyns, *Jean Scot Erigène* (Brussels: Louvain, 1933), pp. 232–51.

16. *Comm. Jn.* 7–8; LW 3: 8–9.

17. *Comm. Jn.* 10; LW 3:10: Arca in mente et in arte ipsa nec arca est nec facta est, sed est ars ipsa, vita est, conceptus vitalis artificis est. Et hoc est quod sequitur: "quod factum est in ipso vita erat."

18. *Comm. Jn.* 10; LW 3:11. This light symbolism recalls Eriugena's theophany (above, chap. 2).

19. To avoid the distracting gender-specific semantic field of man (manhood, manliness, be-a-man, he-man), I have translated the Latin *iustus* throughout as either "just person," or, when the context makes it possible, "the just." I have not attempted to change the masculine pronouns. Eckhart's attempt at a balanced gender-dynamic works, not as it does in Porete, through a revolutionary use of feminine figures and feminine grammatical constructions based upon them, but through an inversion and radicalization of certain aspects of trinitarian mythology (see chap. 7, below). When writing in my own voice, as opposed to translation, I shift between masculine and feminine pronouns.

20. *Comm. Jn.* 14–15; LW 3:13–14: Rursus tertio: iustus verbum est iustitiae, quo iustitia se ipsam dicit et manifestat. Nisi enim iustitia iustificaret, nemo ipsam cognosceret, sed sibi soli esset cognita, secundum illud: "deum nemo vidit unquam: unigenitus, qui est in sinu patris, ipse enarravit," infra *Ioh. 1*; "neque patrem quis novit nisi filius," *Matth. 11*; et "*nemo scit, nisi qui accipit*," *Apoc. 2*. Universaliter enim perfectionem divinam nemo novit, "nisi qui accipit," puta iustitia sibi soli nota est et iusto assumpto ab ipsa iustitia. Et hoc est quod dicit auctoritas quod trinitas, deus, sibi soli nota est et homini assumpto. Unde in Psalmo: "beatus, quem elegisti et assumpsisti."

Eckhart goes on to say: Rursus quarto constat quod iustitia habet in se ipsa exemplar, quod est similitudo sive ratio, in qua et ad quam format et informat sive vestit omnem et omne iustum.

21. *Comm. Jn.* 16; LW 14: Ex quo patet sexto quod iustus est proles et filius iustitiae. Filius enim est et dicitur eo quod fit alius in persona, non aliud in natura, *Ioh. 10*: "ego et pater unum sumus": "sumus" distincti in persona, quia nihil se ipsum gignit; "unum" in natura, quia aliter iustitia non gigneret iustum, nec pater filium, qui fieret alius, nec esset generatio univoca. Et hoc est quod hic dicitur: "deus erat verbum."

22. *Comm. Jn.* 17; LW 3:15: Quod si id ipsum unum in natura: pater et

filius, iustitia et iustus, septimo sequitur quod iustus sit aequalis, non minor quam iustitia, nec filius quam pater. Et hoc est: "verbum erat apud deum." Li "apud" enim aequalitatem significat, ut dictum est prius.

The words "was with God" could also be used to indicate subordination, and Eckhart elsewhere seems to follow the more traditional approach, using "with" to signify likeness but not equality. Yet here he wishes to draw his apophatic dialectic to an extreme.

23. *Comm. Jn.* 17–18; LW 3:15: Rursus octavo: iustitia pariendo iustum sive iustificando non desinit esse iustitia, nec desinit esse principium et ratio iusti. Et hoc est quod dicitur: "verbum hoc erat in principio apud deum."

Adhuc nono constat quod iustitia, sed nec iustus ut sic non cadunt sub motu et tempore sicut nec vita nec lux. Et propter hoc iustus sic semper nascitur ab ipsa iustitia, sicut a principio, quo iustus, natus est, sicut est de generatione luminis in medio et eius conservatione: eo ipso continue, quia non continue. (*Comm. Jn.* 17—18; LW 3:15)

24. *Comm. Jn.* 19–20; LW 16: Points eleven and twelve:

Iterum autem undecimo constat quod iustitia omne opus suum operatur mediante iustitia genita. Sicut enim non posset quidpiam iustum gigni sine iustitia, sic nec esse iustum genitum sine iustitia genita. Iustitia vero genita ipsa est verbum iustitiae in principio suo, parente iustitia. Hoc est ergo quod hic dicitur: "omnia per ipsum facta sunt, et sine ipso factum est nihil."

Rursus duodecimo: iustus in ipsa iustitia iam non est genitus nec genita iustitia, sed est ipsa iustitia ingenita. Et hoc est quod dicitur: "quod factum est" sive productum quocumque modo productionis "in ipso vita erat," id est "principium sine principio." Hoc enim proprie vivit quod est sine principio. Nam omne habens principium operationis suae ab alio, ut aliud, non proprie vivit.

25. See n. 13, above, for Thomas on the trinitarian processions and the oneness of essence. Eckhart's language of "nature" in his trinitarian discussions parallels Thomas's oneness of essence, but his language of nothingness in relationship to the ground of the divine has no counterpart in Thomas.

26. Colledge and McGinn, *Eckhart*, pp. 34–39.

27. As mentioned earlier (chap. 1, n. 4) the defense of Eckhart that relies upon contrasting his vital language with the static henology of the Neoplatonic one is based on a misunderstanding of the dynamic nature of the Plotinian apophasis and metaphors of emanation.

28. *Predigt* 21; DW 1:363: Er ist ein vater aller gotheit. Ich spriche dar umbe ein gotheit, dâ noch niht ûzvliezende enist.

29. See Bernard McGinn, "The God beyond God," *Journal of Religion* 61.1 (1981): 11–12.

30. *Predigt* 15; DW 1:252: Begin der gothait.

31. *Predigt* 26; DW 2:31: Si enwil ouch niht got, als er got ist. . . . Waz wil si denne? Si enweiz: si wil in, als er vater ist.

32. *Predigt* 13; DW 1:217: I have taken the term "primal brightness" from the fine translation of Walshe, *Eckhart*, 1:189.

33. *Predigt* 53; DW 2: 533: "To say 'father' is to understand 'son'. One can-

not be a father without a son, nor a son without a father. One entails the other in an eternal be-ing beyond time."

Swâ man "vater" nennet, dâ verstât man "sun." Vater enmac niht gesîn er enhabe einen sun, noch sun, er enhabe einem vater; sie tragent doch in in über zît êwic wesen.

34. *Predigt* 2; DW 1:43: Mit guoter wârheit und alsô waerlîche, als daz got lebet! Got selber luoget dâ niemer în einen ougenblik und geluogete noch nie dar în, als verre als er sich habende ist nâch wîse und ûf eigenschaft sîner persônen. Diz ist guot ze merkenne, wan diz einic ein ist sunder wîse und sunder eigenschaft.

35. *Predigt* 42; DW 2:420.

36. As noted above, the later Greek Neoplatonists tended to emphasize one or the other of these paradigms. An almost identical dynamic can be found in Kabbalistic controversies over the relation between ʿ*ayn sof*, the "without limit" beyond the sefirot, and Keter, the first of the sefirot that is something referred to as "nothing" (*ayin*).

37. The two perspectives, along with the perspective of *ebullitio* (creation), are combined in a passage from the German sermon 49. Below I translate the passage and interpolate into it a commentary marking out the various perspectives (*Predigt* 49; DW 2:434):

> In this same word the father hears and causes to be recognized and gives birth to himself [*self-causality, perspective of sameness*] and also the same word [*father-son causality, perspective of distinction*] and all things [*perspective of outer emanation in its interior pre-movement*] and his godhead—all from the perspective of the ground [*al ze grunde*], [giving birth to] himself according to nature [*i.e., the sameness of nature in trinitarian doctrine*], and this word with the same nature in another person [*i.e., the distinction of begetting between persons*].

In disem selben worte hoeret der vater und bekennet der vater und gebirt der vater sich silben und ouch diz selbe wort und alliu dinc und sîne gotheit al ze grunde, sich selben nâch der natûre und diz wort mit der selben natûre in einer andern persône.

38. *Predigt* 16b; DW 1:264: Allez, daz dar in enpfangen wirt, daz ist in dem vazze and daz vaz in im und ist daz vaz selbe.

39. *Predigt* 16a; DW 1:258. Translated by Walshe, *Eckhart*, 1:121. This sermon is written in a different dialect, but it has been shown to parallel strongly the inquisitional *rotuli*.

40. *Predigt* 16b (*Quasi vas auri solidum*); DW 1:264. Translated by Walshe, ibid., 1:123. Ein ieglich vaz hât zwei dinc an im: ez enpfaehet und entheltet. Geistlîchiu vaz und lîplîchiu vaz hânt underscheit. Der wîn ist in dem vazze; daz vaz enist niht in dem wîne, noch der wîn enist niht in dem vazze als in den breten; wan waere er in dem vazze als in den breten, sô enmöhte man in niht getrinken. Anders ist ez umbe daz geistlîche vaz. Allez, daz dar în enpfangen wirt, daz ist in dem vazze and daz vaz in im und ist daz vaz selbe.

41. *Comm. Jn.* 27; LW 3:21. See also Eckhart's discussion of image and purely formal casuality in n. 8, above.

42. *Predigt* 16a; DW 1:258–59. Translated by Walshe, *Eckhart* 1:121.

43. *Predigt* 16a; DW 1:259, Walshe 1:121–22. I have changed Walshe's translation of the last clause, *hi enbecummere hē niet*, to read "led him not encumber himself with it" rather than "let him not worry," in order to bring across the parallel to Porete's language of encumberment (see chap. 7, below).

The association of will and intellect with medium is made even more explicit in a parallel passage from 16b, trans. Walshe, *Eckhart*, 1:125: "You should know that this simple divine image [the son] which is impressed on the soul's inmost nature is received without means [*mittel*]. It is the inmost and noblest part of the [divine] nature that is most truly patterned in the image of the soul, and here neither will nor wisdom is a means; as I have said, if wisdom is a means, it is the image itself."

*Predigt*16b; DW 1:268: Ir sult wizzen, daz daz einvaltic götlîche bilde, daz in die sêle gedrücket ist in dem innigesten der natûre, âne mittel sich nemende ist; und daz innigeste und daz edelste, daz in der natûre ist, daz erbildet sich aller eigenlîchest in daz bilde der sêle, und hie enist niht ein mittel weder wille noch wîsheit, als ich ê sprach: ist hie wîsheit ein mittel, daz ist daz bilde selber.

44. Aristotle, *De Anima* 424a, in Richard McKeon, ed., *Introduction to Aristotle* (Chicago: University of Chicago Press, 1973), p. 146.

45. Porete, *Mirror* 501–6, pp. 148–49, uses the very same wax analogy to speak of the union of the annihilated soul with its divine lover, though without elaborating it or attributing it directly to the *De Anima*: "This Soul is imprinted in God, and has taken its true imprint through the union of love. Just as the way that wax takes the form of the seal, so has this Soul taken the imprint of its true exemplar." See chap. 5, n. 44, above.

46. In *Comm. Jn.* 25; LW 3:20, Eckhart cites a commentary to Aristotle's *De Anima* as maintaining that "the birth of the visible species in the faculty of sight does not need an external light. . . . It is only because of the transmitting medium that it needs an extrinsic light."

Rursus septimo: talis expressio sive gignitio imaginis est quaedam formalis emanatio. Propter quod commentator vult in *II De anima* quod parturitio speciei visibilis in visu non requirit lumen extrinsecum . . . sed tantum propter medium deferens lumen extrinsecum requirit.

Cf. Aristotle, *De Anima* 419a, translated in McKeon, *Introduction*, p. 200: "The following experiment makes the necessity of a medium clear. If what has colour is placed in immediate contact with the eye, it cannot be seen. Colour sets in movement not the sense organ but what is transparent, e.g., the air, and that, extending continuously from the object of the organ, sets the latter in movement."

47. Aristotle, *De Anima* 425b–26a (emphasis added). From the translation in McKeon, *Introduction*, 219–20, with slight alterations.

48. For detailed comparison between Porete and Eckhart on this issue, see chap. 7, below.

49. *Predigt* 39; DW 2:253–55: Der gerehte ensuochet niht in sînen werken; wan die iht suochent in irn werken, die sint knehte und mietlinge, oder die umbe einic warumbe würkent. Dar umbe, wilt dû în- und übergebildet werden in die gerehticheit, sô enmeine niht in dînen werken und enbilde kein warumbe in dich, noch in zît noch in êwicheit, noch lôn noch saelicheit, noch diz nocht daz; wan disiu werk sind alliu waerlîche tôt. Jâ, und bildest dû got in dich, swaz dû werke dar umbe würkest, diu sint alliu tôt, und dû verderbest guotiu werk; und niht aleine verderbest dû guotiu werk, mêr: dû tuost ouch sünde.

Again, compare with Porete's language of the soul's taking the imprint (*l'emprainte*) of the divine lover at the moment of mystical union (chap. 5, n. 44) Cf. *Predigt* 5b; DW 1:91–92: war umbe lebest dû . . . ich lebe dar umbe daz ich lebe.

50. See above, n. 42.

51. *Predigt* 16b; DW 1:266: Swenne daz antlite geworfen wirt vür den spiegel, sô muoz daz antlite dar inne erbildet werden, ez welle oder enwelle.

52. *Predigt* 25; DW 2:11: Swenne der wille alsô vereinet wirt, daz ez wirt ein einic ein, sô gebirt der vater von himelrîche sînen eingebornen sun in sich in mich. War umbe in sich in mich? Dâ bin ich ein mit im, er enmac mich ûzgesliezen niht, und in dem werke dâ enpfaehet der heilige geist sîn wesen und sîn werden von mir als von gote. War umbe? Dâ bin ich in gote. Ennimet er ez von mir niht, sô ennimet er ez ouch von goete niht; er enmac mich ûzgesliezen niht, in keiner wîse niht.

53. *Predigt* 12; DW 1:194: Got würket alliu sîniu werk dar umbe, daz wir der eingeborne sun sîn. Swenne got sihet, daz wir sîn der eingeborne sun, sô ist gote sô gâch nâch uns und îlet sô sêre und tuot rehte, als ob im sîn götlich wesen welle zerbrechen und ze nihte werden an im selben, daz er uns offenbâre allen den abgrunt sîner gotheit und die vüllede sînes wesens und sîner natûre.

54. *Predigt* 6; DW 1:100: Die niht ensehent under sich noch über sich noch neben sich noch an sich, die niht enmeinent noch guot noch êre noch gemach noch lust noch nuz noch innicheit noch heilicheit noch lôn noch himelrîche.

55. Ibid., 1:101: [R]ehte als ob ez sîn saelicheit sî, un sîn wesen swebet dar an und sîn genüegede und sîn wollust.

56. Ibid., 1:102: [D]ie alliu dinc glîch enpfâhent von gote, swaz ez joch sî, ez sî grôz oder klein, liep oder leit, und al glîch, noch minner noch mêr, einz als daz ander. Wigest dû daz ein iht mêr dan daz ander, sô is im unreht. Dû solt dînes eigenen willen alzemâle ûzgân.

57. Ibid., 1:103–4.

58. Ibid., 1:104.

59. Ibid., 1:105.

60. Ibid., 1:106: Waz ist leben? Gotes wesen ist mîn leben. Ist mîn leben gotes wesen, sô muoz daz gotes sîn mîn sîn und gotes isticheit mîn isticheit, noch minner noch mêr.

61. Ibid., 1:107. See Colledge and McGinn, *Eckhart*, p. 187. Wer sint die alsô glîch sint? Die niht glîch sint, die sint aleine gote glîch. Götlich wesen

enist niht glîch, in im enist noch bilde noch forme. Die sêlen, die alsô glîch sint, den gibet der vater glîch und entheltet in nihtes niht vor. Swaz der vater geleisten mac, daz gibet er dirre sêle glîch, jâ ob si glîch stât ir selber niht mêr dan einem andern, und si sol ir selber niht naeher sîn dan einem andern. Ir eigen êre, ir nuz und swaz ir ist, des ensol si niht mêr begern noch ahten dan eines vremden. Swaz iemannes ist, daz sol ir weder sîn vremde noch verre, ez sî boese oder guot.

62. Ibid., 1:109–10: Der vater gebirt sînen sun in der êwicheit im selber glîch. 'Daz wort was bî gote, und got was daz wort': ez was daz selbe in der selben natûre. Noch spriche ich mêr: er hât in geborn in mîner sêle. Niht aleine ist si bî im noch er bî ir glîch, sunder er ist in ir, und gebirt der vater sînen sun in der sêle in der selben wîse, als er in in der êwicheit gebirt, und niht anders. Er muoz ez tuon, ez sî im liep oder leit. Der vater gebirt sînen sun âne underlâz, und ich spriche mêr: er gebirt mich sînen sun und den selben sun. Ich spriche mêr: er gebirt mich niht aleine sînen sun, mêr: er gebirt mich sich und sich mich und mich sîn wesen und sîn natûre. In dem innersten quelle dâ quille ich ûz in dem heiligen geiste, dâ ist éin leben und éin wesen und éin werk. Allez, waz got würket, daz ist ein; dar umbe gebirt er mich sînen sun âne allen underscheit.

63. *Predigt* 38 (*Ave gratia plena*); DW 2:243–44.

64. *Predigt* 38; DW 2:244.

65. *Predigt* 43; DW 2:326: Gnâde ist ein înwonen und ein mitewonen der sêle in gote. In both of these sermons Eckhart makes a point of saying that grace does not "work."

66. In this case, grace and the procession of the son would be two sides of one coin, like gradual and sudden enlightenment in some Buddhist discussions. I have taken here a somewhat stronger view than Frank Tobin of the closeness of grace to the birth of the son. Cf. Frank Tobin, *Meister Eckhart*, 105–15.

67. *Predigt* 13a; DW 1:225.

68. *Predigt* 53; DW 2:530: Gotes ûzgang ist sîn îngang.

69. Théry, "Edition Critique des pièces relative au procès d'Eckhart," p. 247, no. 42: Quadragesimus secundus articulus dicit sic: homo debet diligere proximum sicut se ipsum, non quod homo diligat proximos suos ad idem bonum vel in ordine ad eundem deum, ad quem deum homo se ipsum diligit, sed debet eos ita intense diligere sicut se ipsum per omnem modum.

70. Walshe, *Eckhart*, 1: 283, with slight alteration in the translation.

71. Translated in Colledge and McGinn, pp. 234–35 (with the capitals removed).

Meister Eckharts Buch Der Göttlichen Tröstung und Von Dem Edlen Menschen (Liber "Benedictus"), ed. Josef Quint (Berlin: Walter de Gruyter, 1952), p. 54: Noch is daz sibende in dem worte, daz got mit uns ist in lîdenne und mitlîdet mit uns: daz uns krefticlîche sol troesten gotes eigenschaft dâ von, daz er daz lûter ein ist sunder alle zuovallende menge underscheides, joch in gedanken; daz allez, daz in im ist, got selbe ist. Und, wan daz wâr is, sô spriche ich: allez, daz der guote mensche lîdet durch got, daz lîdet er in gote, und gote ist mit im lîdende in sînem lîdenne. Ist mîn lîden in gote, und mitlîdet got, wie mac mir danne lîden leit gesîn, so lîden leit verliuset un mîn leit in gote ist und mîn leit got ist. Waerlîche, also got wârheit ist und swâ ich wârheit vinde, dâ vinde ich mînen got, die wârheit: alsô ouch, noch minner noch mê, sô ich vinde lûter lîden durch got und in gote, dâ vinde ich got mîn lîden.

72. See Donald Duclow, "My Suffering Is God: Meister Eckhart's *Book of Divine Consolation,*" *Theological Studies* 44 (1983): 570–86.

73. Eckhart's stress upon the birth of the son, in the trinity and in the soul, as operating through purely formal causality and as salvific in itself is at least in apparent contrast with Aquinas's assertion that redemption involves efficient causality. For Eckhart, the birth of the son entails the liberation of the soul from the realm of efficient causality and its assumption into the realm of formal causality and univocal relations. See above, n. 8. See also Richard Woods, O.P., "I am the Son of God," *Eckhart Review* (June 1992): 27–45.

74. On this point, see the detailed analysis of Bernard McGinn, "Eckhart's Condemnation Reconsidered," *The Thomist* 44.3 (1980): 390–414, esp. p. 409.

Chapter Seven

1. See Kurt Ruh, "Meister Eckhart und die Spiritualität der Beginen," in *Kleine Schriften* (Berlin, 1984) 2:327–36; Alois Haas, "Meister Eckhart im Spiegel der marxistischen Ideologie," in *Sermo mysticus: Studien zu Theologie und Sprache der deutschen Mystik* (Fribourg, 1979), pp. 246–49; Edmund Colledge, O.S.A., and J. C. Marler, "'Poverty of the Will': Ruusbroec, Eckhart and The Mirror of the Simple Souls," in *Jan Van Ruusbroec: The Sources, Content, and Sequels of His Mysticism,* ed. P. Mommaers and N. de Paepe (Louvain: Louvain University Press, 1984) p. 15. Cf. Herbert Grundmann, "Ketzerverhöre des Spätmittelalters als quellenkritisches Problem," *Deutsches Archiv für Erforschung des Mittelalters,* 21 (1965), 519–75.

2. Colledge and Marler, "'Poverty of the Will'."

3. Multiple examples are given in ibid., pp. 28–30. See *Mirror* 7:11–26, pp. 26–27: Ainsoys est ce don donné du Treshault, en qui ceste creature est ravie par planté de congnoissance, et demeure rien en son entendement. Et telle Ame, qui est devenue rien, a adonc tout et si n'a nyent, elle vieult tout et ne vieult nient, elle sçait tout et ne sçait nient.

Et que peut ce estre, dame Amour, dit Raison, que ceste Ame peut vouloir ce que ce livre dit, qui desja a dit devant qu'elle n'a point de voulenté?

Raison, dit Amour, ce n'est mie voulenté qui le vieult, mais ainçoys est la voulenté de Dieu, qui le vieult en elle; car ceste Ame ne demoure mie en Amour qui ce luy face vouloir par nul desirer. Ainçoys demoure Amour en elle, qui a prinse sa voulenté, et pource fait Amour sa voulenté d'elle, et adonc oeuvre Amour en elle sans elle, par quoy il n'est mesaise qui en elle puisse demourer.

4. See above, chap. 5, n. 22; chap. 6, n. 54.

5. *Mirouer* 97: 19–22, pp. 270–71: Glosez ces motz, se vous le voulez entendre, ou vous les mal entendrez, car ilz ont aucune semblance de contrar-

ieté, qui n'entend le noyau de la glose, mais semblance n'est mie verité, mais verité est, et nulle aultre chose.

6. *Mirouer* 111: 37–41, pp. 304–05: Glosez, se vous voulez, mais se vous povez; se vous ne povez, *vous ne l'estes mie*; se vous l'estiez il vous ouvreroit. Ja ne seriez si parfont adnientie, se vous aviez de quoy vous le peussez oïr, car aultrement ne le des je mie. Se sa bonté vous a toullu le oïr, je ne le desveil mie (emphasis added).

7. *Predigt* 52; DW 2:487: Nû bite ich iuch, *daz ir alsô sît*, daz ir verstât dise rede; wan ich sage iu in der êwigen wârheit: ir ensît denne glîch dirre wârheit, von der wir nû sprechen wellen, sô enmuget ir mich niht verstân (emphasis added).

Colledge and Marler render the first part of this statement as "Now I beg you to be disposed to understand what I say to you." However, the force of *daz ir alsô sît* is stronger than "be disposed." Eckhart implies here what he makes explicit in the next clause, that the hearer must be "equal to," i.e. must "be" that which he or she would understand.

8. *Predigt* 52; DW 2:488–89: und enverstât ir sie niht, so enbekûmbert iuch dâ mite niht, wan ich wil sprechen von sô getâner wârheit, die lützel guoter liute suln verstân.

9. *Predigt* 52; DW 2:506, 1–3: Wer dise rede niht enverstât, der enbekümber sîn herze niht dâ mite. Wan als lange der mensche niht glîch enist dirre wârheit, als lange ensol er dise rede niht verstân; wan diz ist ein unbedahtiu wârheit, diu dâ komen is ûz dem herzen gotes âne mittel.

10. *Predigt* 16a; DW 1:259: Dict nict en verstaet, hi enbecummere he niet.

11. See above, chap. 5, n. 53.

12. *Mirouer* 68:13, pp. 192–93: si bestes et si asnes. Cf. Porete, *Mirror*, 84:30–34, pp. 238–41.

13. *Predigt* 52; DW 2: 490:8: Aber ich spriche, daz sie sint esel.

14. *Mittel* also meant "currency" or "money." For the relationship of religious poverty and commercial economy, see Lester K. Little, *Religious Poverty and the Profit Economy in Medieval Europe* (Ithaca: Cornell University Press, 1978).

15. Colledge and Marler, "'Poverty of the Will,'" p. 31; *Predigt* 52; DW 2: 500; *Mirouer* 136:7–8, p. 399: ipsa non habet fundam, ergo non habet locum; si non habet locum, ergo non habet amorem.

The French manuscript has a lacuna at this point.

16. *Mirouer* 48:1–7, pp. 144–45: Comment l'Ame n'est mie franche, qui desire que la voulenté de Dieu soit faicte en elle a son honnour.—xlviije chappitre. Adoncques ne veult l'Ame nient, dit Amour, puisqu'elle est franche; car cil n'est mie franc, qui veult aucune chose de la voulenté de son dedans, quelque chose qu'il vieulle. Car de tant est il serf a luy mesmes, puisqu'il a voulenté que Dieu face sa voulenté a son honnour mesme.

Dame Amour goes on to say (7–10) that God will refuse his kingdom to such people, a statement Colledge and Marler suggest is an allusion to Christ's temptation in Matthew 4, where Jesus is offered all the kingdoms in return for his submission, which "was asked under colour of God's will being fulfilled—that stones should be made into bread, so that God's Son might not go hungry." Colledge and Marler, "'Poverty of the Will,'" p. 27.

17. *Predigt* 52; DW 2: 491–92: Der mich nû vrâgete, waz denne ein arm mensche sî, der niht enwil, dar zuo antwürte ich und spriche alsô: als lange als der mensche daz hât, daz daz sîn wille ist, daz er wîl ervüllen den allerliebesten willen gotes, der mensche enhât niht armuot, von der wir sprechen wellen; wan dirre mensche hât einen willen, mit dem er genuoc wil sîn dem willen gotes, und daz enist niht rehtiu armuot. Wan, sol der mensche armuot haben gewaerlîche, sô sol er sînes geschaffenen willen alsô ledic stân, als er tete, dô er niht enwas. Wan ich sage iu bî der êwigen wârheit: als lange als ir willen hât, ze ervüllenne den willen gotes, und begerunge hât der êwicheit und gotes, als lange ensît ir niht arm; wan daz ist ein arm mensche, der niht envil und niht enbegert.

18. The argument is made by Colledge and Marler, "'Poverty of the Will.'"

19. The parallel between Porete and Eckhart's language of reversion to a pre-creative state has been noted by Bernard McGinn, "Mystical Union and the Christian Mystical Tradition," in M. Idel and B. McGinn, eds., *Mystical Union and Monotheistic Faith* (New York: Macmillan, 1989), pp. 73–74.

20. This passage in cited in full in the following note. The conception of the soul or self's reversion to a pre-creative state is sometimes called "exemplarism," but that term can be misleading if the reversion implies, as it does in Porete and Eckhart, a reversion not to an ideal form but to a state of pure nothingness or formlessness.

21. Predigt 52; DW 2: 492–93: Dô ich stuont in mîner êrsten sache, dô enhâte ich keinen got, und dô was ich sache mîn selbes; dô enwolte ich niht, noch enbegerte ich niht, wan ich was ein ledic sîn und ein bekenner mîn selbes nâch gebrûchlîcher wârheit. Dô wolte ich mich selben und enwolte kein ander dinc; daz ich wolte, daz was ich, und daz ich was, daz wolte ich, und hie stuont ich ledic gotes und aller dinge. Aber dô ich ûzgienc von mînem vrîen willen und ich enpfienc mîn geschaffen wesen, dô hâte ich einen got; wan ê die crêatûren wâren, dô enwas got niht 'got' [sic], mêr: er was, daz er was. Aber dô die crêatûren gewurden und sie enpfiengen ir geschaffen wesen, dô enwas got niht 'got' [sic] in im selben, mêr: er was 'got' [sic] in den crêatûren.

22. *Mirouer* 89:1–11, pp. 252–53: Ceste Ame a tout donné par franchise de noblesse de l'oeuvre de la Trinité; en laquelle Trinité ceste Ame plante si nuement sa voulenté, que elle ne peut pecher, se elle ne se desplante. Elle n'a de quoy pecher, car sans voulenté nul ne peut pecher. Or elle n'a garde de pecher, se elle lesse sa voulenté la ou elle est plantee, c'est en celluy qui la luy avoit donnee de sa bonté franchement; et pource la vouloit ravoir, par son preu, de s'amye nuement et franchement, sans nul pourquoy pour elle.

23. *Mirouer* 111: 31–41, pp. 304–5: Or ne puis je estre, dit Forfaicte Voulenté, ce que je doy estre, jusques ad ce que je ressoie la ou je fus, en ce point que je fus, ains que je yssisse de luy aussi nue comme Il est, qui est; aussi nue comme j'estoie, quant j'estoie qui n'estoie mie. Et ce me convient avoir, se je vueil le mien ravoir, aultrement ne l'auroie je mie.

Glosez, se vous voulez, mais se vous povez; se vous ne povez, vous ne l'estes mie; se vous l'estiez il vous ouvreroit. Ja ne seriez si parfont adnientie, se vous aviez de quoy vous le peussez oïr, car aultrement ne le dis je mie. Se sa bonté vous a toullu le oïr, je ne le desveil mie. Cf. chap. 5, above, 73, 84.

24. For the French text, see chap. 5, n. 77.

25. *Predigt* 2; *Predigt* 4; the ending of *Predigt* 45, and passim throughout the German sermons.

26. *Predigt* 4 and passim throughout the German sermons.

27. For citations and analyses of the key texts in Porete,

28. *Meister Eckhart: Sermons and Treatises*, vol. 2, trans. and ed. M. O'C. Walshe (Great Britain: Element Books, 1979), pp. 270–72.

29. E. Colledge, trans., in Colledge and McGinn, *Meister Eckhart*, pp. 199–203.

30. Meister Eckhart, *Meister Eckhart: A Modern Translation*, trans. R. B. Blakney (New York: Harper, 1941), p. 23.

31. Colledge and Marler, "'Poverty of the Will,'" p. 19. Reiner Schürmann is one translator who refuses to rewrite Eckhart's text, rendering Eckhart's prayer/unpraying as "I pray to God to rid me of God." R. Schürmann, *Meister Eckhart* (Bloomington: Indiana University Press, 1978), p. 219.

32. *Predigt* 52; DW 2:493–94. This passage follows the two passages from *Beati pauperes spiritu* discussed and cited above. I have placed a [sic] next to the German terms Quint has changed:

Nû sprechen wir, daz got nâch dem, als er 'got' [sic] ist, sô enist er niht ein volmachet ende der crêatûre; alsô grôze rîcheit hât diu minste crêatûre in gote. Und waere daz sache, daz ein vliege vernunft haete und möhte vernünfticlîche suochen den êwigen abgrunt götlîches wesens, ûz dem si komen ist, sô spraechen wir, daz got mit allem dem, daz er 'got' [sic] ist, sô enmöhte er niht ervüllen noch genuoc tuon der vliegen. Her umbe sô biten wir got, daz wir gotes ledic werden und daz wir nemen die wârheit und gebrûchen der êwiclîche, dâ die obersten engel und diu vliege und diu sêle glîch sint in dem, dâ ich stuont und wolte, daz ich was, und was, daz ich wolte. Alsô sprechen wir: sol der mensche arm sîn von willen, sô muoz er als lützel wellen und begern, als er wolte und begerte, dô er niht enwas. Und in dirre wîse ist der mensche arm, der niht enwil.

33. "I pray God—that is, He Who is everything and none of the things which this signifier names, *nomen omninominabile et nomen innominabile*—to rid me of 'God,' that is to say, of all those nominal effects which try to cow us into submission, all of those historico-cultural-linguisic effects which are collected together by the word 'God'." John Caputo, "Mysticism and Transgression: Derrida and Meister Eckhart," in *Continental Philosophy II: Derrida and Deconstruction*, ed. Hugh Silverman (New York: Routledge, 1989), p. 34. Caputo's response to Derrida—rich in other areas—reinforces the vocabulary of distinction between God and "God" that allows an easy purchase upon the alleged referent of Eckhart's mystical language.

34. Eckhart's apophatic "Here I may truly say," echoes the Sermon on the Mount (Matt. 5:17–43), where a series of positions marked by "You have

heard it said" are then followed by new positions introduced by "But I say to you." The most powerful occurrence of Eckhart's statement is in the sermon entitled *Beati pauperes spiritu*, a phrase from the Sermon on the Mount, which also contains a number of locutions such as "You have heard it say," and "But I say."

35. *Predigt* 48; DW 2:418–21. See Colledge and McGinn, *Meister Eckhart*, p. 198.

36. *Predigt* 2; DW 1:39.

37. It may be true that "Eckhart makes use of equivocation by reference to show that God in himself finally transcends every possible referent" (Colledge and Marler, "'Poverty of the Will,'" p. 2). However such a statement does not illuminate the nature of Eckhart's discourse. For an apophatic writer like Eckhart, the statement "God in himself finally transcends every possible referent," leads ineluctably to its own unsaying.

A second problem in Colledge and Marler's rewriting of Eckhart *ad meliorem* is that such a procedure contradicts their own estimations of Porete and Eckhart, according to which Eckhart gives "brilliant" formulations to ideas Porete was incapable of expressing properly. Ironically, it is not the supposedly confused Porete, whose text Colledge and Marler (following Quint) rewrite *ad meliorem*, but the allegedly brilliant Eckhart who evidently was unable to express clearly the commonplace scholastic distinction between God in himself and God in creatures. See ibid., p. 38, for the assertions (repeated almost verbatim from p. 25) that Porete was "confused," showed an "inability to order her material or to deal clearly with the themes which she announces," and was "incapable of expressing herself economically, and able only occasionally to rise to the clarity found in Eckhart."

38. "How to Avoid Speaking: Denials," transl. Ken Frieden, in S. Budick and W. Iser, eds. , *Languages of the Unsayable: The Play of Negativity in Literature and Literary Theory* (New York: Columbia University Press, 1989), pp. 3–70, esp. p. 8; reprinted again in H. Coward and T. Foshay, eds., *Derrida and Negative Theology* (Albany: SUNY Press, 1992), pp. 79–142. For the original French version, see "Comment ne pas parler: Dénégations," in Jacques Derrida, *Psyché: Invention de l'autre* (Paris: Galilée, 1987), pp. 535–95. In his original French version, p. 541, Derrida uses the French translation of Jeanne Ancelet-Hustache, *Sermons* (Paris: Le Seuil), p. 101. That translation reads as follows: Avant même qu'il y eût de l'être, Dieu opéra. Des maîtres a l'esprit fruste disent que Dieu est un être pur; il est aussi élevé au-dessus de l'être que le plus élevé des anges l'est au-dessus d'un moucheron. Je parlerais aussi fausement si je nommais Dieu un être que si je disais du soleil qu'il est blême ou noir. On page 7, Derrida states: "Until now, confronted by the question or by the objection, my response has always been brief, elliptical, and dilatory."

39. For the German text, see n. 32, above.

40. See *Mirouer* chaps. 55, 57 and 96, and Eckhart, *Predigt* 2, below, and *Predigt* 39.

41. For the German, see above, chap. 6, n. 62.

42. E. Colledge accused Porete of teaching "a false quietism of an extreme form." (If quietism is a heresy, is false quietism heretical as well?) Colledge goes on to say: "She seems to go out of her way to assert, as crudely as possible, that the proper state of an illumined and liberated soul is a total passivity." See E. Colledge, "Liberty of Spirit: The Mirror of Simple Souls" in *Theology of Renewal*, 2, ed. L. K. Shook (Montreal, n.p. 1968), pp. 102–3. Colledge links this charge to his claim that Porete's *Mirror* is based upon a Manichean dualism. The only evidence for this claim is Porete's use of the terms "holy church the lesser" and "holy church the greater" which for Colledge indicates (p. 111) a connection to the gnostic dualism "Man-Church": "It is difficult to doubt that Margaret's 'Holy Church the Greater' is the Gnostics' *Ecclesia*." Colledge concludes (p. 117) that Marguerite founded her "liberty of the spirit" upon "loathing and hatred for that human nature which God 'wonderfully formed and yet more wonderfully reformed'." Porete's book is in fact a sustained critique of those in the fourth station who must act contrary to their own will and nature and become enslaved to their own desires for ascetic holiness.

This dilemma is present in the *Bhagavad Gita*. See *The Bhagavadgītā in the Mahōbhōrata*, trans. and ed. J. A. B. van Buitenen (Chicago, University of Chicago Press, 1981), chap. 3, pp. 81–85. The *Gita* is explicit on the difference between disinterested action (acting without attachment to the fruits of the action) and mere lack of activity: "A person does not avoid acquiring *karman* just by not performing acts nor does he achieve success by giving up acts. For no one lives for a moment without doing *some* act." The *Gita* then goes into an excursus on the delusion that we are carrying out our own acts; rather it is the *gunas* that act through us. Just as the goal of yoga within the *Bhagavad Gita* involves the central notion of nonattachment to the fruits of one's actions, so Porete's annihilated soul is no longer attached to the rewards of her actions or their reputation. In the *Gita* this nonattachment can be achieved through three kinds of yoga, the last of which, *bhakti*, involves a loss of self-regard through the transferral of all regard to one's divine lover. Porete's use of sexual allusion, the centrality of eros to the mystical path, is in the spirit of *bhakti*, the debauched lover of the Krishna-Radha tradition, for example. Will is transcended not through the abandonment of desire but through the intensification of desire and the focusing of desire until the lover loses herself.

As in the *Gita*, the question is not whether one acts or does not act (for as Krishna points out, to refrain from acts is an act), but whether one realizes that the acts are being carried out within one without his or her will. The distinction between disinterested action and indifference will be taken up further in the epilogue, below.

43. Numerous examples of this point have been given in the previous chapter. Perhaps one of the most explicit occurs in the *Mirror*: 41: 11–16, pp. 128–29: "This soul, says Love, is not with herself, and she is therefore excused by everyone. And he in whom she is, performs his work through her, for which she is well acquitted, with the witness of God himself, says

Love, who is the worker of this work on behalf of this soul, a soul who has no work whatsoever within her." For the French text, see chap. 5, above, n. 34.

44. *Mirouer* 94:13–16, pp. 262–63.

45. *Mirouer* 95: 14–18, pp. 266–67: Ses dons sont aussi grans, comme est luy mesmes qui a donné cecy, lequel don le meut de luy en luy mesmes. C'est mesmes Amour, et Amour peut quanqu'elle veult; et pource ne peut Crainte, ne Discrecion, ne Raison contre Amour rien dire.

The Latin of the same passage uses the more transitive verb *mutare* (transform), and offers a different set of pronouns: "which gift transforms her [the soul] into him on account of her" (*Quae etiam dona mutant eam in illummet propter ipsam*). In the earlier chapter on Porete, this passage was cited as an example of the reference breakdown, where the Latin and French, normally in accord, choose different antecedents and genders. Here the question revolves on the Latin *mutare* (to change, transform). The French seems to indicate a kind of interior motion, while the Latin indicates the transformation of the soul into that interior motion. Both senses—motion and transformation—are found in Eckhart, and both center, as in Porete, on the divine gift that is nothing less than the giver itself.

46. The theme pervades Eckhart's German works especially. See, for example, *Predigt* 15b (pp. 189–92 in Colledge and McGinn, *Eckhart*), where the person who has achieved freedom and nakedness is given everything that God has, and that gift is then figured in terms of the birth of the son in the soul.

47. Through these three understandings of the "gift" and the "work" Eckhart builds upon and transforms a long tradition in Christianity of speaking of the birth of the son or the word in the soul. For that earlier tradition, see Hugo Rahner, "Die Gottesbeburt. Die Lehre der Krichenväter von der Geburt Christi aus dem Herzen der Kirche und der Gläubigen," *Zeistchrift für katholische Theologie* 59 (1933): 333–418, reprinted in Rahner, *Symbole der Kirche* (Salzburg: Müller, 1964), pp. 13–87.

48. Both authors associate the means with the will and reason (*raison* in Porete, *intellectus, sapientia* in Eckhart). Both use the Aristotelean metaphor of the birth of the son or the word in the soul. For that earlier tradition, see Hugo Rahner, "Die Gottesbeburt. Die Lehre der Kirchenväter von der Geburt Christi aus dem Herzen der Kirche und der Gläubigen," *Zeitschrift für katholische Theologie* 59 (1933): 333–418, reprinted in Rahner, *Symbole der Kirche* (Salzburg: Müller, 1964), pp. 13–87.

49. It has been argued that the language of courtly love placed women in an idealized position, but that this pedestal may have been the counterpart of the stake: the idealized lady and the condemned heretic of the Inquisition were opposite faces of the same coin. See E. William Monter, "The Pedestal and the Stake," in R. Bridenthall and C. Koonz, eds., *Becoming Visible: Women in European History* (Boston: Houghton Mifflin, 1977). There were, however, women troubadours as well. See Meg Cogin, *The Women Troubadours* (New York: Norton, 1980); and *The Voice of the Trobairitz: Perspectives on the Women*

Troubadours, ed. W. Paden (Philadelphia: University of Pennsylvania Press, 1989).

50. *Predigt* 6; DW I: 99. Cf. Tobin, *Meister Eckhart*, pp. 172–73, who discusses the same use of *gemeine* in *Predigt* 9 and *Predigt* 29. Tobin's emphasis is on Eckhart's wish to "startle" and gain "the attention of his listeners" when he called deity *daz aller gemeineste*. Tobin states that "the preacher actually wishes to say that all universal or transcendental qualities come from God." The apophatic perspective here might read the language according to Eckhart's principle that that which is most distinct is distinct by virtue of its lack of any distinction. Tobin does go on to discuss the dialectical relationship of the lowly or common and the noble. Although the expression does and should "startle," I would stress that the startling quality is not only a rhetorical or decorative device but a logical outcome of a dialectic that ties together Eckhart's entire mystical theology. The commonality is meant to be taken with full seriousness, even and especially in the informal language Tobin has illuminated.

51. No attempt is made here to link this apophatic nothingness to twentieth-century phenomenology or existentialism. "Nothingness" is used here in the precise apophatic sense developed through the seven readings in this study. For a comparison and contrast between Eckhart and Heidegger, see J. Caputo, *The Mystical Element in Heidegger's Thought* (Athens: Ohio University Press, 1978). For a philosophical treatment of Eckhart with close comparisons to aspects of Heidegger's thought, see R. Schürmann, *Meister Eckhart* (cited above, n. 31).

The dialectic of nothingness and everything, and its relation to freedom, is of course a perennial theme. As the songwriter puts it: "Freedom's just another word for nothing left to lose, and nothing: it ain't nothing, but it's free." Kris Kristofferson, "The Ballad of Bobby McGee."

52. Mary Daly, *Gyn/Ecology: The Metaethics of Radical Feminism* (Boston: Beacon Press, 1978), p. 38. This naming of "the three Divine Persons" is the paradigmatic model for the pseudogeneric term *person*, excluding all female mythic presence and denying female reality in the cosmos. For Daly, these male processions are an active principle for patriarchal "possessing" of women. The theological is reflected in the social. As a prologue to her discussion of trinitarian processions, Daly cites the following passage from Virginia Woolf's *Three Guineas*: "There it is, then, before our eyes, the procession of the sons of educated men, ascending those pulpits, mounting those steps, passing in and out of those doors, preaching, teaching, administering justice, practicing medicine, making money." To those who would respond that the holy spirit is feminine, Daly counters that "the drag queen belongs in the male parade." As with apophasis, Daly's language is as notable for how it works as it is for what it says, and this paraphrase cannot possibly do justice to the manner in which Daly turns words against the embedded mythopoetic meanings she considers to be controlled by patriarchal myth makers and myth stealers.

Daly relates processional theology to what she sees as the central episode in the feminist account of Christianity: the witch burnings that took place from the mid-fifteenth century until the seventeenth. These burnings are viewed as a foundational event for modern language, institutions, and cultures, a hidden atrocity still silencing women through its inscription within the fabric of culture, and through its covering over of its own traces. The covering over of the intensity, extent, and true horror of the witch burnings is one more aspect of the witch burnings themselves.

53. Mary Daly *Gyn/Ecology*, p. 82, gives a compelling analysis of this subject. She begins by stating that "It should not be imagined that Mary had any real role in this conception and birth." Daly then goes on to discuss the critiques of Helen Diner and Anne Dellenbaugh which focus on the the Virgin Mary's passivity. For Diner, the virgin birth is the opposite of parthenogenesis, because "Mary does nothing, whereas in parthenogenesis the female accomplishes everything herself." Dellenbaugh discusses the myth as stripping women of their integrity, portraying the female as a mere "hollow eggshell." For Daly, the Virgin Mary is a symbol of the tamed goddess whose creativity and power have been appropriated and taken over by the patriarchal domination of Christian myth.

54. Elizabeth Schüssler Fiorenza, "A Feminist Critical Interpretation for Liberation: Martha and Mary: Luke 10: 38–42," *Religion and Intellectual Life* 3 (1986): 21–35. Fiorenza's constructive hermeneutics reads Luke's story as a reaction against the role of women's service (*diakoinia*) within pre-Lukan "housechurches"—a role that combined service and proclamation within the eucharistic setting.

55. Eckhart was capable of statements that reflected the very associations inverted by Porete in her "fall of love." At the end of *Predigt* 20b, Eckhart compares the soul to a man when it is gazing upward toward the deity, and to a woman when it turns down to the world. This statement contrasts of course with the equality between male and female asserted by Eckhart in *Predigt* 6 (chap. 6, above), as well as in *Predigt* 27.

56. *Predigt* 2; DW 1:31–32. Cf. below, n. 68.

57. See the detailed discussion of Eckhart's transformation of the meaning of "in" and the apophatic significance of that transformation: chap.6, above.

58. The term "catatonic" is used by Daly, *Gyn/Ecology*.

59. *Predigt* 2; DW 1:24: Unser herre Jêsus Kristus der gienc ûf in ein bürgelîn und wart enpfangen *von einer juncvrouwen, diu ein wîp was* (emphasis added). Another sermon attributed to Eckhart is even more explicit in its unconventional interpretation of Martha above Mary: *Predigt* 86, which begins from the same passage, *Intravit Jesus in quoddam castellum*, trans. Frank Tobin, in B. McGinn, ed., *Meister Eckhart: Teacher and Preacher* (New York: Paulist Press, 1986), pp. 338–45. As the translator remarks, the language and style of the sermon differs from the body of Eckhart's known sermons. In my view, Sermon 2 challenges the standard Mary/Martha and Contemplation/Acts hierarchies in a manner more deeply grounded in Eckhart's apophatic writing, and for that reason I choose to discuss it here.

60. The play on *enpfangen* was noted in Colledge and McGinn, *Meister Eckhart*, nn. 2, 3, and 4, p. 335.

61. *Predigt* 2; DW 1:24–25: Eyâ, nû merket mit vlîze diz wort: ez muoz von

nôt sîn, daz si ein juncvrouwe was, der mensche, von der Jêsus wart enpfangen. Juncvrouwe ist alsô vil gesprochen als ein mensche, der von allen vremden bilden ledic ist, alsô ledic, als er was, dô er niht enwas.

62. *Predigt* 2; DW 1:26. Als ich was, dô ich niht enwas.

63. *Predigt* 2; DW 1:43: Got selber luoget dâ niemer în einen ougenblik und geluogete noch nie dar în, als verre als er sich habende ist nâch wîse und ûf eigenschaft sîner persônen.

64. *Predigt* 2; DW 1:28–29: Ein ieglîchiu eigenschaft eines ieglîchen werkes, daz die vrîheit benimet, in disem gegenwertigen nû gote ze wartenne und dem aleine ze volgenne in dem liehte, mit dem er dich anwîsende waere ze tuonne und ze lâzenne in einem ieglîchen nû vrî und niuwe, als ob dû anders niht enhabest noch enwellest noch enkünnest, ein ieglîchiu eigenschaft oder vürgesetzet werk, daz dir dise vrîheit benimet alle zît niuwe, daz heize ich nû ein jâr.

65. See above, chap. 4, n. 32, on those who lose the years, the months, the weeks, the days and those who pass away and are reconstituted in every moment, *waqt*.

66. *Predigt* 2; DW 1:29: Wan dîn sêle bringet dekeine vruht, si enhabe daz werk getân, daz dû mit eigenschaft besezzen hâst, noch dû engetriuwest gote noch dir selber, dû enhabest dîn werk volbrâht, daz dû mit eigenschaft begriffen hâst; anders sô enhâst dû dekeinen vride. Dar umbe sô enbringest dû ouch dekeine vruht, dû enhabest dîn werk getân. Daz setze ich vür ein jâr, und diu vruht ist nochdenne kleine, wan si ûz eigenschaft gegangen ist nâch dem werke und niht von vrîheit. Dise heize ich êlîche liute, wan sie an eigenschaft gebunden stânt. Dise bringent lützel vrüte, und diu selbe ist nochdenne kleine, als ich gesprochen hân.

67. Aquinas, *Summa Theologiae*, 2a, 2ae. 152, 5 (Blackfriars edition, p. 186), translation mine.

68. *Predigt* 2; DW 1:30–31: Ein juncvrouwe, diu ein wîp ist, diu ist vrî und ungebunden âne eigenschaft, diu ist gote und ir selber alle zît glîch nâhe. Diu bringet vil vrühte und und die sint grôz, minner noch mêr dan got selber ist. Dise vruht und dise geburt machet disiu juncvrouwe, diu ein wîp ist, geborn und bringet alle tage hundert mâl oder tûsent mâl vruht joch âne zal gebernde und vruhtbaere werdende ûz dem aller edelsten grunde; noch baz gesprochen: jâ, ûz dem selben grunde, dâ der vater ûz gebernde ist sîn êwic wort, dar ûz wirt si vruhtbaere mitgebernde. Immediately after this extraordinary passage the sermon, almost as a reflex, turns to a continual repetition of the words "father" and "fatherly heart."

69. See *Predigt* 2; DW 1:42.

70. Margaret Miles has said the following about the "naked soul" metaphor: "Similarly, in the fourteenth-century mystical tradition founded by Meister Eckhart and carried to Martin Luther by Tauler and Suso, nudity received the less literal interpretation of the soul's divestment of cares, attachments, and ideas in order to expose the 'core of the soul' where God is to be found. Ironically, the soul, departing from the body at death, was painted as a tiny, colorless naked body, carried to heaven in a napkin by angels." See

M. Miles, *Carnal Knowing: Female Nakedness and Religious Meaning in the Christian West* (Boston: Beacon Press, 1989), pp. xiii–xiv. This statement attributes to Eckhart the metaphor of the naked soul, without mentioning the beguine tradition (from Mechtild to Hadewijch, Hadewijch II, and Porete) in which that metaphor was developed, and without mentioning who portrayed the naked soul as carried to heaven in a napkin. It should be clear from the readings in chapters 5–7 in this book that the "nakedness of the soul" theme is more central to Porete than it is to Eckhart. Eckhart uses the metaphor, but his notion of mystical union is based more on virginity and virgin birth than upon the erotic and sexual imagery in which the "nakedness of the soul" metaphor was used by the beguines. In the beguine writings, the nakedness of the soul is at the center of a wide range of related motifs: self-abandon, loss of discretion, ravishment. The image in Porete and Eckhart has little to do with being carried to heaven on a napkin. With both writers, the naked-soul image entails an abandonment of attaining heaven and avoiding hell as a religious goal. With Porete, the image entails a reappropriation and valorization of what had been negatively associated with women, the fall, nature, and sexuality. With Eckhart, it is partially subservient to his reinterpretation of virginity and virgin birth and his placement of the birth metaphor within the trinity.

71. See Carolyn Walker Bynum, ". . . And Woman His Humanity: Female Imagery in the Religious Writing of the Later Middle Ages," in Bynum, S. Harrel, and P. Richman, eds., *Religion: On the Complexity of Symbols* (Boston: Beacon Press, 1986), 257–288. Cf. Bynum, *Holy Feast and Holy Fast* (Berkeley: University of California Press, 1986); and idem, *Jesus as Mother: Studies in the Spirituality of the High Middle Ages* (Berkeley: University of California Press, 1982). Bynum acknowledges, in *Religion: On the Complexity of Symbols*, p. 262, the exclusion of Eckhart from her consideration—on the grounds that comparing a university-trained theologian "with a virtually illiterate Italian nun or tertiary would reveal differences in educational background and philosophical sources so vast that differences owing to gender or social experience could never be determined." Yet other educated males who fit her categories are not excluded. In a later work, Bynum acknowledges that Marguerite Porete does not fit her gender categories either: "With the predictable and fascinating exception of the 'heretic' Marguerite Porete, all thirteenth century women who wrote at length on spiritual matters emphasize the eucharist." See Bynum, *Fragmentation and Redemption: Essays on Gender and the Human Body in Medieval Religion* (New York: Zone Books, 1992), p. 24. Neither Eckhart nor Porete lived in a vacuum; both had many followers and a powerful influence on vernacular piety. Eckhart wrote numerous works in the vernacular, which were directly accessible to the "virtually illiterate" nuns and tertiaries; indeed it was these nuns and tertiaries who helped preserve Eckhart's sermons through oral tradition. Porete's *Mirror* was circulated in several vernaculars (French, Italian, and English) and became a centerpiece of vernacular contemplative piety.

72. Tobin, in *Meister Eckhart*, n. 33, p. 195, criticizes the use of the term

feminist in connection with Eckhart and points out that Matthew Fox did not provide an argument to demonstrate his claim that Eckhart was influenced by the beguines. Cf. Matthew Fox: *Breakthrough: Meister Eckhart's Creation Spirituality in New Translation* (New York: Image Books, 1980), pp. 35–40. Without calling them feminists, my analysis demonstrates how radically Porete and Eckhart broke with prescribed gender roles and how vitally they addressed gender concerns that are very much with us today. Cf. the volume being edited by Bernard McGinn, *Meister Eckhart and Women Mystics*, based upon revised versions of six papers (by S. Murk-Jansen, Paul Dietrich, F. Tobin, Maria Lichtmann, A. Hollywood, and M. Sells) given at the 26th International Medieval Conference, Kalamazoo, Michigan, in May 1993.

Epilogue

1. See chaps 4 and 6 above. Similarly, Plotinian emphasis upon an ideal of free, dispassionate, overflowing creativity outside of the world of suffering contrasts with Eckhart's ideal of a com-passionate deity, i.e., a deity that suffers with the suffering of the virgin soul, and is one with the soul in that suffering.

2. Reiner Schürmann, *Meister Eckhart: Mystic and Philosopher* (Bloomington: Indiana University Press, 1978) uses the term "anarchic" to describe Eckhart's thought, within a context informed by Heideggerian existentialism. I use the term here more narrowly to depict the specific moment of apophatic turning back (*epistrophē*).

3. A joke involving stereotypes can function cathartically by helping to release and expose aggressive sentiments or it can reinforce the communal roots of that aggression. Some of the humor of Lenny Bruce consisted of the exaggeration, performance, and parody of ethnic stereotypes within a sexually explicit language ruled by the courts as obscene. Defenders of Bruce see his humor as one of exposure and critique of repressed prejudices. Removed from context, his parodies of ethnic stereotypes are offensive in the extreme.

4. Porete's attempt to live in self-abandon brought her neither to a quiet life nor a life of pleasure. It led instead to a series of calmly courageous acts on behalf of her right to author and circulate the *Mirror*, acts in the face of intimidation, ending in her burning at the stake. Porete was convinced that the soul that has achieved the fourth station, and then abandoned its own self, will not be abandoned by its divine lover.

5. Wayne Proudfoot, *Religious Experience* (Berkeley: University of California Press, 1985), p. 192. Cf. Franz Brentano, *Psychologie vom empirischen Standpunkt* (Leipzig, 1874). For a short discussion of the three modes of intentionality of consciousness according to Brentano, see R. Chisholm, "Brentano," *Encyclopedia of Philosophy* (New York: Macmillan, 1967) 1:365–66. The three modes are: (1) thinking of A, having A "before the mind"; (2) taking an intellectual stand with respect to A; and (3) taking an emotional stand with respect to A.

6. In the recent debate over the "core" mystical experience, both positions can be seen as essentializing. Those advocating a common "core" of mys-

tical experience have been attacked for their attempts to describe such a core and have been accused of reducing the distinctiveness and variety of traditions to a homogenized "essence." Yet, the pluralists can fall into an immediate essentializing, as in the statement (Introduction, n. 26) referring to the experience of "nothingness" as an experience of "something." Thus the grammatical object, which the entire effort of apophasis is directed toward displacing, is immediately reinserted at the begining of the secondary discussion.

7. See the work of Forman et al., and Barnard, cited above in the Introduction, n. 22.

8. Our five apophatic authors wrote within a historical and social context that presupposed a guide for any individual following the mystical path. Plotinus refused for years to circulate his writings outside his own philosophical school, because of the importance of such personal guidance. Eckhart spoke as a "meister" who was in fact appointed as a spiritual guardian and director for many in his audiences. Ibn ʿArabi's Sufi world is based upon a hierarchical chain of masters, "shaykhs," who guide the Sufi through the various stations in the mystical ascent, taking special care that no station is skipped or inadequately realized. To move to a higher station before mastering the lower can lead to moral, psychological, and social disaster. The Jewish tradition of Kabbalah contemporary with Ibn ʿArabi was even more emphatic about the dangers of mystical practice and thought, and the need for careful preparation. Again, when Ibn ʿArabi speaks of "the station of no-station," a station in which the linear movement of "from" and "to" is transcended, he does so within the context of that linear movement. When the Sufis speak of the station of poverty, and then of a poverty so total that one gives up one's own poverty, the living of the station of poverty is the essential contextual precondition for a meaningful abandonment of poverty.

9. There are a number of contemporary languages of the unsayable that have developed in the past several decades. How does the "Autrement qu'être ou au-delà de l'essence" of Levinas compare to the "beyond being" of Plotinus? Similar questions might be raised about apophasis as it takes place within the Greek and Abrahamic theistic traditions (the subject of this study) and its counterparts in Eastern thought. See Robert Scharlemann, ed., *Negation and Theology*, and Howard Coward and Toby Foshay, *Derrida and Negative Theology*, cited in the Introduction. Clearly the urge to say the unsayable is one that is both historically and geographically pervasive. To enter into such comparisons now would require another volume. However, the exposition of apophatic language offered here may challenge preconceptions about Western vs. Eastern thought, and medieval vs. modern thought. Medieval apophasis in the Abrahamic traditions exposes the common portrayal of medieval absolutist faith "in God" as an imposition of a stereotyped generic name of deity upon a culture that developed a critique of generic God-language as radical as any.

SELECTED BIBLIOGRAPHY

• • •

I mention here some of the books and, in rare cases, articles of particular importance to this study; a full bibliography on each of the five writers covered in this book would be enormous. At the beginning of each chapter are mentioned books, cited below, that give fuller bibliographies.

PLOTINUS
(Recent bibliography in Kenney, 1989)

TEXTS AND TRANSLATIONS

Armstrong, A. H. *Plotinus with an English Translation*. Text and English Translation, *Enneads* 1–6. 7 vols. London: Loeb, 1966–88.
Badawi, A. *Neoplatonici apud Arabes*. Medieval Arabic text. *Islamica*, 19. Cairo: Maktabat al-Nahḍa al-Arabiyya, 1955.
Bréhier, E. *Enneades*. French translation. 6 vols. Paris: Les Belles Lettres, 1924–38.
Cilento, V. *Plotino, Enneadi*. Italian translation. 3 vols. Bari: Laterza, 1947–49.
Dodds, E. R. *Select Passages Illustrative of Neoplatonism*. London: Society for Promoting Christian Knowledge, 1923.
Harder, Richard. *Plotins Schriften*. Text and German translation. 7 vols. Hamburg: Meiner, 1956–62.
Henry, P., and H. R. Schwyzer. *Plotini Opera. Editio Maior*. With translation of the Arabic Plotinus by G. Lewis. 3 vols. Paris: Desclée de Brouwer, 1951–71.
———. *Plotini Opera. Editio Minor*. Text. 3 vols. Oxford: Oxford University Press, 1964–83.
MacKenna, Stephen. *Plotinus*. English translation. 5 vols. London: The Medici Society, 1921–30. London: Faber and Faber, 1956, 1962, 1969.
———. *Plotinus*. Abridged with an introduction and notes by John Dillon. London: Penguin, 1991.
———. *Plotinus*. A new edition, with comparisons to other translations. Burdett, N.Y.: Larson Publications, 1992.
O'Brien, E. *The Essential Plotinus*. English translation of selected passages. Indianapolis: Hackett, 1975.

Studies

Accademia Nazionale dei Lincei: *Atti del Convegno sul Tema: "Plotino e il Neoplatonismo in Oriente e in Occidente."* 1974.

Armstrong, A. H. *The Architecture of the Intelligible Universe in the Philosophy of Plotinus.* Cambridge University Press, 1940.

———. *Plotinian and Christian Studies.* London: Variorum, 1979.

———, ed. *Classical Mediterranean Spirituality.* New York: Crossroad, 1986.

Arnou, R. *Le Désir de Dieu dans la philosophie de Plotin.* Paris: Alcan, 1921.

Atkinson, M. *Plotinus: Ennead V:1.* Text, translation and commentary. New York: Oxford University Press, 1983.

Beierwaltes, W. *Plotin über Ewigkeit und Zeit.* Frankfurt, 1967. Commentary on Enn. III 7.

Blumenthal, H. J. *Plotinus' Psychology: His Doctrine of the Embodied Soul.* The Hague: M. Nijhoff, 1971.

Blumenthal, H. J., and R. A. Markus. *Neoplatonism and Christian Thought.* London, 1981.

Bréhier, E. *La philosophie de Plotin.* Paris: Boivin, 1928. Translated by J. Thomas, *The Philosophy of Plotinus.* Chicago: University of Chicago Press, 1958.

Bussanich, J. *The One and Its Relation to Intellect in Plotinus.* Leiden: Brill, 1988.

Deck, John N. *Nature, Contemplation, and the One: A Study in the Philosophy of Plotinus.* Toronto: University of Toronto Press, 1967.

Dionysius. Journal published by the Department of Classics, Dalhousie University. Edited by A. H. Armstrong, R. D. Crouse, and J. A. Doull.

Dodds, E. R. "The Parmenides of Plato and the Origin of the Neoplatonic One." *Classical Quarterly* 22 (1928): 129–43.

Dörrie, H. *Platonica Minora.* Collected essays. Munich: W. Fink, 1976.

Entretiens Hardt. Entretiens sur l'antiquité classique V. "Les Sources de Plotin." Geneva: Fondation Hardt, 1960.

Ferwerda, R. *La Signification des images et des métaphores dans la pensée de Plotin.* Groningen: Wolters, 1965.

Fuller, B. A. G. *The Problem of Evil in Plotinus.* Cambridge: University Press, 1912.

Gandillac, Maurice. *La Sagesse de Plotin.* Paris: Vrin, 1966.

Graeser, Andreas. *Plotinus and the Stoics.* Leiden: Brill, 1972.

Guitton, Jean. *Le Temps et l'éternité chez Plotin et Saint Augustin.* Paris: Vrin, 1959.

Hadot, P. *Plotin ou la simplicité du regard.* Paris: Plon, 1963.

———. *Porphyre et Victorinus.* 2 vols. Paris: Etudes Augustiniennes, 1968.

Harris, R. B., ed. *The Significance of Neoplatonism.* Norfolk: International Society for Neoplatonic Studies, 1976.

———. *The Structure of Being.* Albany: International Society for Neoplatonic Studies, 1982.

———. *Neoplatonism and Indian Thought*. Norfolk: International Society for Neoplatonic Studies, 1982.
Henry, P. "Le problème de la liberté chez Plotin." *Revue néoscolastique de philosophie* 33 (1931): 50–79; 180–215; 318–39.
———. *Plotin et l'occident*. Louvain: Spicilegium Sacrum Louvaniese, 1934.
———. *Etudes plotiniennes*. Paris: Desclée de Brouwer, 1948.
Inge, W. R. *The Philosophy of Plotinus*. London: Longmans, Green, 1918.
Journal of Neoplatonic Studies. Binghamton, N.Y.: The Institute of Global Cultural Studies.
Katz, J. *Plotinus' Search for the Good*. New York: King's Crown Press, 1950.
Kenney, John Peter. *Mystical Monotheism: A Study in Ancient Platonic Theology*. Providence: Brown University Press, 1991.
McGinn, Bernard, *The Foundations of Mysticism*. New York: Crossroad, 1991.
Merlan, P. *From Platonism to Neoplatonism*. The Hague: M. Nijhoff, 1950.
———. *Monopsychism, Mysticism, Metaconsciousness*. The Hague: M. Nijhoff, 1963.
Meijer, P. A. *Plotinus on the Good or the One* (Enneads VI.9). Amsterdam: Gieben, 1992.
Moreau, J. *Plotin: ou la gloire de la philosophie antique*. Paris: Vrin, 1970.
Morwedge, P., ed. *Neoplatonism and Islamic Thought*. Albany: SUNY Press, 1992.
Mortley, Raoul, and D. Dockrill, eds. *The Via Negativa*, supplementary number of *Prudentia*. 1981.
———. *From Word to Silence: The Rise and Fall of Logos*. Bonn: Hanstein, 1986.
O'Daly, G. P. *Plotinus' Philosophy of the Self*. New York: Barnes & Noble, 1973.
O'Meara, D. *Structures hiérarchiques dans la pensée de Plotin*. Leiden: Brill, 1975.
O'Meara, D., ed. *Neoplatonism and Christian Thought*. Albany: International Society for Neoplatonic Studies, 1982.
Le Néoplatonisme. Colloque International du Centre National de la Recherche Scientifique, Royaumont, 1969. Paris: CNRS, 1971.
Phillips, John. "Plotinus and the 'Eye' of Intellect." *Dionysius* 14 (1990): 79–104.
Pistorius, P. V. *Plotinus and Neoplatonism*. Cambridge: Bowes & Bowes, 1952.
Rist, J. M. *Plotinus: The Road to Reality*. Cambridge University Press, 1967.
———. "*Theos* and the One in Some Texts of Plotinus." *Medieval Studies* 24 (1962): 169–80.
Sells, Michael A. "Apophasis in Plotinus: A Critical Approach." *Harvard Theological Review* 78.3–4 (1985): 47–65.
Schroeder, F. *Form and Transformation: A Study in the Philosophy of Plotinus*. Montreal: McGill-Queen's University Press, 1992.
Theiler, W. *Forschungen zum Neuplatonismus*. Berlin: de Gruyter, 1966.
Trouillard, J. *La Purification plotinienne*. Paris: Presses Universitaires de France, 1955.
———. *La Procession plotinienne*. Paris: Presses Universitaires de France, 1955.
Trouillard, J., et al. *Etudes néoplatoniciennes*. Neuchâtel: Baconnière, 1973.

Wallis, R. T. *Neoplatonism*. London: Duckworth, 1972.
———. "NOUS as Experience." In R. B. Harris, ed. *The Significance of Neoplatonism*.
Wallis, R.T., and J. Bregman, eds. *Neoplatonism and Gnosticism*. Albany: SUNY Press, 1992.
Westra, Laura. *Plotinus and Freedom: A Meditation on Enneads 6:8*. Lewiston, N.Y.: Mellen, 1990.
Wolters, A. M. *Plotinus 'On Eros': A Detailed Exegetical Study of III 5*. Toronto: Wedge, 1984.

ERIUGENA
(Recent bibliographies in Otten, 1991, and Moran, 1989).

Text and Translations

Commentaire sur l'évangile de Jean. Edited and translated by Edouard Jeaneau. Paris: Editions du Cerf, 1972.
L'Homélie sur le Prologue de Jean. Edited and translated by Edouard Jeaneau. Paris: Editions du Cerf, 1969.
De Divina Praedestinatione. Edited by G. Madec. Turnhout: Brepols, 1978.
Corpus Dionysiacum, I and II. Edited by Beate R. Suchla, G. Heil, and A. M. Ritter. Patristische Texte und Studien, 33 and 36. Berlin: de Gruyter, 1990 and 1991.
Dionysiaca. Edited by Ph. Chevallier, 2 vols. Paris: Desclée de Brouwer, 1937–49.
Opera Omnia. Edited by H.-J. Floss. *Patrologiae Cursus Completus*. Series Latina. Paris: J. P. Migne. 1872.
Periphyseon (De Divisione Naturae) liber primus. Edited and translated by I. P. Sheldon-Williams and L. Bieler. Dublin: Dublin Institute for Advanced Studies, 1968.
Periphyseon (De Divisione Naturae) liber secundus. Edited and translated by I. P. Sheldon-Williams and L. Bieler. Dublin: Dublin Institute for Advanced Studies, 1972.
Periphyseon (De Divisione Naturae) liber tertius. Edited and translated by I. P. Sheldon-Williams and L. Bieler. Dublin: Dublin Institute for Advanced Studies, 1981.
Periphyseon. The Division of Nature. Translated by I. P. Sheldon-Williams and J. J. O'Meara. Montreal: Bellarmin, 1987.
Periphyseon: On the Division of Nature. Edited and translated by Myra Uhlfelder. Summaries by Jean Potter. Indianapolis: Bobbs-Merrill, 1976.

Studies

Allard, G. -H. *Johannis Scotti Eriugenae Periphyseon: Indices generales*. Montreal: Institut d'études médiévales, 1983.
Allard, G. -H., ed. *Jean Scot écrivain*. Montreal: Bellarmin, 1983.
Allegro, C. *Giovanni Scoto Eriugena. Fede e ragione*. Rome: Citta Nuova, 1975.

Beierwaltes, E. "Negatio Affirmation." In Roques, 1977.
———. "Sprache und Sache. Reflexionem zu Eriugenas Einschätzung von Leistung und Funktion der Sprache." *Zeitschrift für Philosophische Forschung* 38 (1984): 523–43.
Beierwaltes, E., ed. *Eriugena: Studien zu seinen Quellen*. Heidelberg: Carl Winter Universitätsverlag, 1980.
———. *Eriugena Redivivus*. Heidelberg: Carl Winter Universitätsverlag, 1987.
Bett, Henry. *Johannes Scotus Erigena: A Study in Mediaeval Philosophy*. Cambridge University Press, 1925.
Bieler, L., and J. J. O'Meara, eds. *The Mind of Eriugena*. Dublin. Papers of the Dublin Colloquium, 14–18 July, 1970.
Bonafede, G. *Scoto Eriugena*. Palermo: CELUP, 1969.
Cappuyns, Maieul. *Jean Scot Erigène: sa vie, son oeuvre, sa pensée*. Paris: Desclée de Brouwer, 1964.
Dal Pra, Mario. *Scoto Eriugena ed il neoplatonismo medievale*. Milan: Fratelli Bocca, 1941.
Duclow, Donald. "Divine Nothingness and Self-Creation in John Scottus Eriugena." *Journal of Religion* 57 (1977): 109–23.
Foussard, J. -C. "Apparence et apparition: la notion de 'phantasia' chez Jean Scot." In Roques, 1977: 337–48.
Gersh, Stephen. *From Iamblichus to Eriugena*. Leiden: Brill, 1978.
Gregory, Tullio. *Giovanni Scoto Eriugena: Tre Studi*. Florence: Le Monnier, 1963.
Jeaneau, Edouard. *Etudes érigéniennes*. Paris: Etudes augustiniennes, 1987.
Lees, Rosemary Ann. *The Negative Language of the Dionysian School of Mystical Theology: Approach to the Cloud of Unknowing*. Salzburg: Analecta Carthusiana, 1983.
Marenbon, J. *From the Circle of Alcuin to the School of Auxerre: Logic, Theology and Philosophy in the Early Middle Ages*. Cambridge University Press, 1981.
McGinn, B. "Negative Theology in John the Scot." *Studia Patristica* 13: 232–238.
McGinn, B., and J. Meyendorff, eds. *Christian Spirituality. Origins to the Twelfth Century*. New York: Crossroad, 1985.
Moran, Dermot. *The Philosophy of John Scottus Eriugena: A Study of Idealism in the Middle Ages*. New York: Cambridge University Press, 1989.
O'Meara, J. J. *Eriugena*. Oxford: Clarendon Press, 1988.
Otten, Willemien. *The Anthropology of Johannes Scottus Eriugena*. Leiden: Brill, 1991.
———. "The Dialectic of the Return in Eriugena's *Periphyseon*." *Harvard Theological Review* 84:4 (1991): 399–421.
Riccati, C. *Processio et Explicatio: La Doctrine de la création chez Jean Scot et Nicolas de Cues*. Naples: Bibliopolis, 1983.
Roques, R. *Libres sentiers ver l'érigénisme*. Rome: Editioni dell' Ateneo, 1975.
Roques, R., ed. *Jean Scot Erigène et l'histoire de la philosophie*. Paris: C.N.R.S., 1977.

Schrimpf, G. *Das Werk des Johannes Scottus Eriugena im Rahmen des Wissenschaftverständisses seiner Zeit.* Münster: Aschendorff, 1982.

IBN ʿARABI
(Bibliography in Yahya, 1964, and Chittick, 1989).

TEXTS AND TRANSLATIONS

Dhakhāʾir al-Aʿlāq: Sharḥ Tarjumān al-Ashwāq. Edited by Muḥammad al-Kurdī. Cairo: n.p., 1968.
Diwān Ibn ʿArabī. Bulāq, 1855; Baghdad: Maktabat al-Muthanna, 1963.
al-Fanāʾ fīʾl-Mushāhada. Translated by Michel Vâlsan. *Le livre de l'extinction dans la contemplation.* Paris: Editions de l'Oeuvre, 1984.
Fihrist al-Muʾallafāt. "The Works of Ibn ʿArabī." Edited by A. A. Affifi. *Revue de la faculté de lettres de l'Université d'Alexandrie* 8 (1954): 109–17, 193–207.
Fuṣūṣ al-Ḥikam. Edited with commentary by A. A. Affifi. Cairo: Dār Ihyāʾ al-Kutub al-ʿArabiyya, 1946.
Fuṣūṣ al-Ḥikam. Translated by T. Burckhart. *Sagesse des prophetes.* Paris: A. Michel, 1955.
Fuṣūṣ al-Ḥikam. Translated by R. W. J. Austin. *Bezels of Wisdom.* New York: Paulist Press, 1980.
Al-Futūḥāt al-Makkiyya. Edited by Othman Yahya. Cairo: al-Hayʾa al-Misriyya al-ʿAma li al-Kitab, 1972–. 13 vols. have appeared.
Al-Futūḥāt al-Makkiyya. 4 vols. Bulāq: Dar al-Kutub al-ʿArabiyya al-Kubra, 1911.
Al-Ittiḥād al-Kawnī. Translated by D. Gril. *Le Livre de l'arbre et des quatre oiseaux.* Paris: Deux Océans, 1984.
Kleinere Schriften des Ibn al-Arabī. Edited by H.S. Nyberg. Leiden: E. J. Brill, 1919.
Les Illuminations de la Mecque (Al-Futūḥāt al-Makkiyya): Textes choisis/Selected Texts. Translated by M. Chodkiewicz, W. C. Chittick, Ch. Chodkiewicz, D. Gril, and J. Morris. Paris: Sindbad, 1989.
Mishkāt al-Anwār. Translated by Muhammad Vâlsan. *La Niche des Lumières.* Paris: Les Editions de l'Oeuvre, 1983.
Rasāʾil Ibnuʾl-ʿArabī. Hyderbad: Jamaʿiyya Daʾirat al-Maʿarif al-ʿUthmaniyya, 1948; Cairo: Dar Ihya al-Turath al-ʿArabi, 1968. One of the treatises (*risālat al-anwār*, "the treatise on the lights") has been translated by Rabia T. Harris. *Journey to the Lord of Power.* New York: Inner Traditions, 1981.
Shajarat al-Kawn. Translated by A. Jeffrey. Lahore, Pakistan: Aziz Publishers, 1980.
Sufis of Andalusia. Translated by R. W. J. Austin. London: Allen & Unwin, 1971. From *Ruḥ al-quds* and *Durrat al-Fakhirah.*
The Sufi Path of Knowledge. Selections with commentary from the *Futuhat.* Translated by William Chittick. Albany: SUNY Press, 1989.
Tarjumān al-Ashwāq. Beirut: Dar Sadir al-Tibaʿa wa al-Nashr, 1961.
Tarjumān al-Ashwāq. Translated by R. Nicholson. London: Royal Asiatic Society, 1911; reprint, London: Theosophical Publishing House, 1978.

STUDIES

Addas, Claude. *Ibn ʿArabī ou la quête du Soufre rouge.* Paris: Gallimard, 1989.
Affifi, A. A. *The Mystical Philosophy of Muhyid Dīn Ibnul ʿArabi.* Cambridge University Press, 1939.
———. Commentary on *Fuṣūṣal-Ḥikam.* Cairo: Dar Ihya' al-Kutub al-ʿArabiyya, 1946.
Asin Palacios, Miguel. *Abenmassara y su escuela. Origines de al filosofia hispanomusulmana.* Madrid: E. Maestre, 1914. *The Mystical Philososphy of Ibn Masarra and His Followers.* Translated by Elmer H. Douglas and Howard W. Yoder. Leiden: Brill, 1978.
———. *La escatologia musulmana en la Divina Comedia.* Madrid: E. Maestre, 1919.
———. *El mistico murciano Abenarabi.* Madrid: Rivista de archivos, 1926–27.
———. *Islam and the Divine Comedy.* Translated and abridged by Harold Sunderland. London: J. Murray, 1926.
———. *Islam Christianizado.* Madrid: Editorial Pluturco, 1931.
Balyani, Awhad al-Din. *Epître sur l'unicité absolue.* Translated by M. Chodkiewicz. Paris: Les Deux Océans, 1982.
Chittick, William: *The Sufi Path of Knowledge: Ibn al-ʿArabi's Metaphysics of Imagination.* Albany: SUNY Press, 1989.
———. "Sadr ad-Din Qunawi on the Oneness of Being." *International Philosophical Quarterly* 21 (1981): 171–84.
———. "Death and the World of the Imagination." *Muslim World* 78 (1988): 51–82.
Chodkiewicz, M. "Ibn ʿArabi, La lettre et la loi." *Mystique, culture et société.* Edited by M. Meslin. Paris: Université de Paris-Sorbonne, 1983: 27–40.
———. *Le Sceau des saints prophétie et sainteté dans la doctrine d'Ibn ʿArabi.* Paris: Gallimard, 1986.
———. *An Ocean without Shore: Ibn Arabi, The Book, and the Law.* Albany: SUNY Press, 1993.
Corbin, H. *Creative Imagination in the Sufism of Ibn ʿArabī.* Translated by Ralph Manheim. Princeton: Princeton University Press, 1974.
Hirtenstein, S., and M. Tiernan. *Muhyiddin Ibn ʿArabi: A Commemorative Volume.* Shaftsbury, Dorset: Element Books, for the Muhyiddin Ibn ʿArabi Society, 1993. Includes five new translations and twelve studies.
Homerin, Th. E. "Ibn ʿArabi in the People's Assembly: Religion, Press, and Politics in Sadat's Egypt." *Middle East Journal* (1986): 462–77.
Izutsu, T. *Sufism and Taoism.* Berkeley: University of California Press, 1984.
Journal of the Muhyiddin Ibn ʿArabi Society. Oxford.
Kashani, ʿAbd al-Razzaq. *Sharḥ Fuṣūṣ al-Ḥikam.* Cairo: Mustafa al-Babi al-Halabi, 1966.
Al-Kitāb al-Tadhkārī. Addresses, lectures, essays. Cairo: 1969.
Knysh, Alexander. "*Irfan* Revisited: Khomeini and the Legacy of Islamic Mystical Philosophy." *Middle East Journal* 46.4 (1992): 631–53.
Landau, Rom. *The Philosophy of Ibn ʿArabī.* New York: Macmillan, 1959.

Morris, J. "Ibn ʿArabi and His Interpreters." *Journal of the American Oriental Society* 106 (1986) and 107 (1987).

———. "The Spiritual Ascension: Ibn ʿArabi and the Miʿrâj." *Journal of the American Oriental Society* 108 (1988).

Nasr, Seyyed Hussein. *Three Muslim Sages*. Cambridge: Harvard University Press, 1964.

Nicholson, R. A. *Studies in Islamic Mysticism*. Cambridge University Press, 1921.

Sells, Michael A. "Ibn ʿArabi's Garden Among the Flames: A Reevaluation." *History of Religions* 23.4 (1984): 287–315.

———. "Ibn ʿArabi's Polished Mirror: Perspective Shift and Meaning Event." *Studia Islamica* 67 (1988): 121–49.

———. "Bewildered Tongue: The Semantics of Mystical Union in Islam." In M. Idel and B. McGinn, editors. *Mystical Union and Monotheistic Faith: An Ecumenical Dialogue*. New York: Macmillan, 1989. Pp. 87–124, 163–74.

———. "Ibn ʿArabi's 'Gentle Now, Doves of the Thornberry and Moringa Thicket'." *Journal of the Muhyiddin Ibn ʿArabi Society* 10 (1991): 1–8.

———. "Towards a Translation of the *Fusus al-Hikam*." In S. Hirtenstein and M. Tiernan, 1993.

Takeshita, Masataka. *Ibn ʿArabi's Theory of the Perfect Man and Its Place in the History of Islamic Thought*. Tokyo: Institute for the Study of Languages and Cultures of Asia and Africa, 1987.

Yahya, O. *Histoire et classification de l'oeuvre d'Ibn ʿArabī*. Damascus: Institute français de Damas, 1964.

PORETE
(Recent bibliography in Babinsky, 1993)

TEXTS AND TRANSLATIONS

Dronke, P. *Women Writers in the Middle Ages: A Critical Study of Texts from Perpetua (203) to Marguerite Porete (1310)*. Cambridge University Press, 1984.

The Mirror of the Simple Souls. Translated by Ellen Babinsky. New York: Paulist Press, 1993.

Le Miroir des simples âmes. Edited by R. Guarnieri, in *Il Movimento del Librero Spirito. Archivio italiano per la storia della pietà*, vol. 4. Rome: Edizioni di Storia e Letteratura, 1965: 501–636, 637–708.

Marguerite Porete. *"The Mirror of Simple Souls": A Middle English Translation*. Edited by M. Doiron. *Archivio italiano per la storia della pietà*, vol. 5. Rome: Edizioni di Storia e Letteratura, 1968.

Speculum simplicium animarum. Edited by P. Verdeyen. *Le mirouer des simples âmes*. Edited by R. Guarnieri. Latin and French on facing pages. Turnhout: Brepols, 1986.

The Mirror of Simple Souls. Translated by C. Kirchberger. London: Orchard Books, 1927.

Le Miroir des âmes simples et anéanties. Introduction, translation, and notes by M. Huot de Longchamp. Paris: Albin Michel, 1984.

"The French Heretic Beguine: Marguerite Porete." Translation by Gwendolyn Bryant, in Katharina M. Wilson, ed., *Medieval Women Writers*. Athens: University of Georgia Press, 1984.

Women Mystics in Medieval Europe. Edited and translated by Emilie Zum Brunn and Georgette Epiney-Burgard. Translated from the French by Sheila Hughes. New York: Paragon House, 1989.

STUDIES

Colledge, E., and R. Guarnieri. "The Glosses by 'M.N.' and Richard Methley to *The Mirror of Simple Souls*." An Appendix to Margaret Porete, *The Mirror of Simple Souls: A Middle English Translation*, edited by M. Doiron, *Archivio italiano per la storia della pietà*, vol. 5. Rome: Edizioni di Storia e Letteratura, 1968, 357–82.

Colledge, E., and J. C. Marler. "'Poverty of the Will': Ruusbroec, Eckhart and the Mirror of Simple Souls." In *Jan van Ruusbroec, The Sources, Content and Sequels of His Mysticism*. Edited by. P. Mommaers, N. de Paepe. Louvain: Louvain University Press, 1984: 14–47.

Dinzelbacher, P. *Mittelalterliche Frauenmystik*. Paderborn: Shöningh, 1993.

Grundmann, H. *Religiöse Bewegungen im Mittelalter*. Darmstadt: Wissenschaftliche Bushgesellschaft, 1961.

Hadewijch. *The Complete Works*. Translation and introduction by C. Hart. New York: Paulist Press, 1980.

Hadewijch. *Mengeldichten*. Edited by J. van Mierlo. Antwerp: Staandard, 1952.

———. *Hadewijch d'Anvers: Poèmes des Béguines traduits du moyen néerlandais*. Edited by J. B. Porion. Paris: Seuil, 1954; reprint, 1985.

———. *Hadewijch d'Anvers: Visions*. Edited by J. B. Porion. Paris: O.E.I.L., 1987.

Hollywood, Amy. "The Soul as Virgin Wife: Meister Eckhart and the Beguine Mystics, Mechthild of Magdeburg and Marguerite Porete." Ph.D. diss., University of Chicago, 1991.

Langlois, C. -V. "Marguerite Porete." *Revue historique* 54 (1894).

Lerner, R. E. *The Heresy of the Free Spirit in the Later Middle Ages*. Berkeley: University of California Press, 1972.

———. "An Angel of Philadelphia in the Reign of Philip the Fair." In *The Middle Ages: Essays in Honor of Joseph R. Strayer*. Edited by W. C. Jordan et al. Princeton: Princeton University Press, 1976: 343–64, 529–40.

McDonnell, E. W. *The Beguines and Beghards in Medieval Culture*. New York: Octagon Books, 1969.

Murk-Jansen, S. M. *The Measure of Mystic Thought: A Study of Hadewijch's Mengeldichten*. Göppingen: Kümmerle, 1991.

———. "The Mystic Theology of the Thireenth-Century Mystic, Hadewijch, and Its Literary Expression." *The Medieval Mystical Tradition in England* 5 (1992): 117–28.

Orcibal, J. "Le Miroir des simples âmes et la secte du Libre Esprit." *Revue d'histoire des religions* 88 (1969): 35–60.

Petroff, E. *Medieval Women's Visionary Literature*. New York: C. Bynum, 1986.
Ruh, Kurt. "Le Miroir des Simples Ames de Marguerite Porete ." In *Verbum et Signum*, vol. 2. Munich: Wilhelm Funk, 1975: 365–87.
———."Beginnenmystik: Hadewijch, Mechthild von Magdeburg, Marguerite Porete." *Zeitschrift für deutsches Altertum und deutsche Literatur* 106 (1977): 265–77.
Ruh, Kurt, ed. *Abendländische Mystik im Mittelalter*. Stuttgart: J. B. Metzlersche, 1986.
Spaapen, Bernard. "Le Mouvement des 'Frères du libre esprit' et les mystique flamandes du XIIIème siècle." *Revue d'ascétique et de mystique* (1966): 423–67.
Verdeyen, P. "Le procès d'inquisition contre Marguerite Porete et Guiard de Cressonessart (1309–1310)." *Revue d'histoire ecclésiastique* 81 (1986): 47–94.

ECKHART
(Recent bibliography in Tobin, 1986)

Texts and Translations

Blakney, Raymond B. *Meister Eckhart. A Modern Translation*. New York and London: Harper & Row, 1941. Includes sermons of dubious authenticity.
Clark, James M. *Meister Eckhart. An Introduction to the Study of His Works with an Anthology of His Sermons*. Edinburgh: Nelson, 1957.
Clark, James, and John Skinner. *Treatises and Sermons of Meister Eckhart*. New York: Harper, 1958.
Colledge, Edmund, and Bernard McGinn. *Meister Eckhart: The Essential Sermons, Commentaries, Treatises and Defense*. New York: Paulist Press, 1981.
Die deutschen und lateinischen Werke. Herausgegeben im Auftrage der deutschen Forschungsgemeinschaft. Stuttgart and Berlin: W. Kohlhammer, 1936–.
Fox, Matthew. *Breakthrough: Meister Eckhart's Creation Spirituality in New Translation*. New York: Image Press, 1980.
Maurer, Armand. *Master Eckhart. Parisian Questions and Prologues*. Toronto: Pontifical Institute of Mediaeval Studies, 1974.
McGinn, Bernard, editor, with the collaboration of Frank Tobin and Elvira Borgstadt. *Meister Eckhart: Teacher and Preacher*. New York: Paulist Press, 1986.
Schürmann, Reiner. *Meister Eckhart. Mystic and Philosopher*. Bloomington: Indiana University Press, 1978.
Walshe, M. O'C. *Meister Eckhart: Sermons and Treatises*. 3 vols. London: Watkins, 1979; reprint, Longmead: Element Books, 1987.

Studies

Albert, Karl. *Meister Eckharts These vom Sein. Untersuchungen zur Metaphysik des Opus Tripartitum*. Saarbrücken: Universitäts-und Schulbuchverlag, 1976.
Brunner. F. *Maître Eckhart*. Paris: Seghers, 1969.
Caputo, John. "The Nothingness of the Intellect in Meister Eckhart's 'Parisian Questions'." *The Thomist* 39 (1975): 85–115.

———. *The Mystical Element in Heidegger's Thought*. Athens, Ohio: Ohio University Press, 1978.
———. "Fundamental Themes in Meister Eckhart's Mysticism." *The Thomist* 42 (1978): 197–225.
Davies, Oliver. *Meister Eckhart: Mystical Theologian*. London: SPCK, 1991.
Degenhardt, Ingeborg. *Studien zum Wandel des Eckhartbildes*. Leiden: Brill, 1967.
Denifle, Heinrich. "Meister Eckharts lateinische Schriften und die Grundanschaung seiner Lehre." *Archiv für Literatur-und Kirchengeschichte des Mittelalters* 2 (1886): 417–615.
Dourely, John. *The Goddess, Mother of the Trinity: A Jungian Implication*. Lewiston, N.Y.: Mellen, 1990.
Duclow, Donald. "My Suffering Is God: Meister Eckhart's *Book of Divine Consolation*." *Theological Studies* 44 (1983): 570–86.
Eckhart Review. Published by the Eckhart Society. Oxford.
Flasch, Kurt, ed. *Von Meister Dietrich zu Meister Eckhart*. Hamburg: Felix Meiner, 1984.
Forman, Robert. *Meister Eckhart: Mystic as Theologian*. Longmead: Element Press, 1991.
Fues, W. *Mystik als Erkenntnis?* Bonn: Bouvier, 1981.
Gandillac, M. de. "La 'dialectique' de Maître Eckhart." *La mystique rhénane*. Paris: Presses Universitaires de France, 1963.
Haas, Alois M. *Sermo mysticus. Studien zu Theologie und Sprache der deutschen Mystik*. Fribourg: Universitätsverlag, 1979.
Hof, Hans. *Scintilla animae. Eine Studie zu einem Grundbegriff in Meister Eckharts Philosophie*. Lund: Gleerup, 1952.
Kelley, C. F. *Meister Eckhart on Divine Knowledge*. New Haven and London: Yale University Press, 1977.
Kieckhefer, R. *Repression of Heresy in Medieval Germany*. Philadelphia: University of Pennsylvania Press, 1979.
Klein, Alessandro. *Meister Eckhart: La dottrina mistica della giustificazione*. Milan: Mursià, 1978.
Langer, Otto. *Mystische Erfahrung und spirituelle Theologie*. Munich: Artemis, 1987.
Laurent, M. -H. "Autour du procès de Maître Eckhart. Les Documents des Archives Vaticanes." *Divus Thomas* (Piacenza). Series III 13 (1936): 331–48, 430–47.
Lossky, Vladimir. *Théologie négative et connaissance de Dieu chez Maître Eckhart*. Paris: Vrin, 1960.
McGinn. Bernard. "Meister Eckhart's Condemnation Reconsidered." *The Thomist* 44 (1980): 390–414.
———. "The God beyond God: Theology and Mysticism in the Thought of Meister Eckhart." *Journal of Religion* 61 (1981): 1–19.
———. "Meister Eckhart: An Introduction." In *Introduction to the Medieval Mystics of Europe*, edited by Paul Szarmach. Binghamton: SUNY Press, 1984, pp. 237–58.

———. "Love, Knowledge and *Unio mystica* in the Western Christian Tradition." In M. Idel and B. McGinn, editors. *Mystical Union and Monotheistic Faith: An Ecumenical Dialogue.* New York: Macmillan, 1989: 59–86, 185–94.

Mieth, D. *Die Einheit von vita activa und vita contemplativa in den deutschen Predigten und Traktaten Meister Eckharts und bei Johannes Tauler.* Regensburg, 1969.

Mojsisch, B. *Meister Eckhart, Analogie, Unovozität und Einheit.* Hamburg: Meiner, 1983.

Otto, Rudolf. *Mysticism East and West. A Comparative Analysis of the Nature of Mysticism.* New York: Macmillan, 1932.

Pelster, Franz. "Ein Gutachten aus dem Eckhart-Prozess in Avignon." *Aus der Geisteswelt des Mittelalters. Festgabe Martin Grabmann* (Beiträge Supplement III). Münster, 1935: 1099–1124.

Rahner, H. "Die Gottesgeburt. Die Lehre der Kirchenväter von der Geburt Christi im Herzen der Gläubigen." *Zeitschrift für katholische Theologie* 59 (1933): 333–418. Reprinted in H. Rahner, *Symbole der Kirche.* Salzburg, 1964.

Ruh, Kurt, ed. *Altdeutsche und altniederländische Mystik.* Darmstadt: Wissenschaftliche Buchgesellschaft, 1964.

———. *Meister Eckhart. Theologe, Prediger, Mystiker.* Munich: Beck Verlag, 1985.

Schmoldt, Benno. *Die deutsche Begriffssprache Meister Eckharts.* Heidelberg: Quelle and Meyer, 1954.

Soudek, E. *Meister Eckhart.* Stuttgart: Metzler, 1973.

Théry, Gabriel. "Edition critique des pièces relatives au procès d'Eckhart contenues dans le manuscrit 33 de la bibliothèque de Soest." *Archives d'histoire littéraire et doctrinal du moyen âge* 1 (1926): 129–268.

The Thomist. 42, no. 2. Special Issue. *Meister Eckhart of Hochheim 1227/28.* 1978.

Tobin, Frank. *Meister Eckhart: Thought and Language.* Philadelphia: University of Pennsylvania Press, 1986.

Ueda, Shizuteru. *Die Gottesburt in der Durchbruch zur Gottheit. Die mystische Anthropologie Meister Eckharts und ihre Konfrontation mit der Mystik des Zen-Buddhismus.* Gütersloh: Mohn, 1965.

Weeks, Andrew. *German Mysticism.* Albany: SUNY Press, 1993.

Welte, Bernard. *Meister Eckhart. Gedanken zu seinen Gedanken.* Freiburg: Herder, 1979.

Winkler, Eberhard. *Exegetische Methoden bei Meister Eckhart.* Tübingen: Mohr, 1965.

Zapf, J. *Die Funktion der Paradoxie im Denken und sprachlichen Ausdruck bei Meister Eckhart.* Cologne, 1966.

Zum Brunn, Emilie and Alain de Libera. *Maître Eckhart: Métaphysique du verbe et théologie négative.* Paris: Beauchesne, 1984.

Zum Brunn, Emilie, et al. *Maître Eckhart à Paris. Une critique médiévale de l'ontothéologie.* Paris: Presses Universitaires de France, 1984.